In Memory Of

*The
Wiman
Family*

Parents at Risk

Ramona Thieme Mercer, R.N., Ph.D., F.A.A.N., has studied early parenting in low- and high-risk situations, and transition to the maternal role for past 25 years. She retired as Professor Emeritus from the Department of Family Health Care Nursing, the University of California, San Francisco, where she taught from 1973 to 1988. Her career has included positions as head nurse in pediatrics and staff nurse in intrapartum, postpartum, and newborn nursery units. Her current activities include lecturer, consultant, writer, and visiting professor. She was selected as the 1990 recipient of the American Nurses Foundation's Distinguished Contribution to Nursing Science Award.

PARENTS AT RISK

Ramona T. Mercer,
R.N., Ph.D., F.A.A.N.

Springer Publishing Company
New York

Copyright © 1990 by Springer Publishing Company, Inc.

Springer Publishing Company, Inc.
536 Broadway
New York, NY 10012

90 91 92 93 94 / 5 4 3 2 1

Library of Congress Cataloging-in-Publication Data

Mercer, Ramona Thieme.
    Parents at risk / Ramona T. Mercer.
       p. cm.
    Includes bibliographical references.
    ISBN 0-8261-7240-7
      1. Pregnancy—Psychological aspects. 2. Pregnancy, Complications
of—Psychological aspects. 3. Parents—Mental health.
4. Parenting— Psychological aspects. 5. Family—Mental health.
I. Title.
RG560.M48   1990
155.9′16—dc20   90-35580
                                                                CIP

Printed in the United States of America

Contents

PART III: INFANTS WITH A SPECIAL CHALLENGE

PART IV: SPECIAL CHALLENGES IN THE ENVIRONMENT

Preface

Even under the very best of circumstances, parenting consumes one's physical and mental energies and time, probably to a greater extent than any other task. Whether it is the first, second, or fifth birth of a child for the parent, unknown challenges emerge in the establishment of a new and unique relationship. When things don't go as expected and disappointment or illness occurs, the additional strains, grief, and encompassing problems place the parents in a state of increased vulnerability in being able to nurture their infants.

The focus of this book is parental role achievement in unusual circumstances, beginning during pregnancy and progressing through the first year following birth (parental role identity is usually achieved during the period of infancy). The unusual circumstances can be either within the individual parent, the infant, or a social and physical environment that poses particular challenges and stressors for parents. The underlying themes of the book are "How do parents respond and adapt to the situation?" and "How can persons who are privileged to work with families at this crucial time be most helpful?"

An encounter with a mother whose 11-month-old son had just had corrective surgery for bilateral clubfeet illustrates an unusual circumstance in the birth of an infant with a congential handicap, and the need for expert supportive care during the perinatal period and infancy. As this mother lovingly held her son against her breast and rocked him, she reviewed with great emotional feeling her initial reaction to her beautiful blue-eyed baby:

> I was drowsy from the delivery, but they brought him in and unwrapped him, and I saw those feet. I'll never forget that moment. I cried and cried. They gave me a sedative, and I went to sleep, but all night I dreamed about those feet. That was all I could see—the feet. Then I thought the next day that I had dreamed it. It was not true. He didn't really have feet like that. I

unwrapped them, and *there they were.* I started crying again. I couldn't even hold him. I had to get them to take him back to the nursery.

At this moment, it was easy to see the love and concern that this mother had for her son. What had occurred in the process of this mother's moving from "I couldn't even hold him" to her ability to lovingly care for him? I recalled my years of experience as a staff nurse on maternity units. I remembered the uncomfortable feelings that I had experienced in the delivery room and afterward when I helped mothers who faced sorrow and disappointment in an infant who was born prematurely, who was ill, or who had an impairment. This motivated me to continue to question adaptation to the parental role in a variety of circumstances. What we have learned through research programs and clinical practice has provided insight into the ways in which parents and families adapt to the unexpected events that occur during childbearing and early childrearing. The emergence of new groups of vulnerable parents and increased technology implores us to continue to search for better ways to care for vulnerable parents and families.

Whether the baby has arrived too early or has a physical handicap, or the parents have become parents prematurely, have a problem with substance abuse, have family structures departing from the majority, have a health problem, have role conflicts, or face other stressful life events there is a common thread. In each of these situations, the parent is at special risk in negotiating the parent role in which attachment to and enjoyment of the infant are central and he or she can feel competent in one of the greatest roles of a lifetime. Parents in at-risk situations often must make far-reaching decisions, establish priorities, and deal with profound loss and disappointment at a time when they should be receiving warm and happy support from family and friends. Under circumstances that are unusual, family and friends often do not know how to respond appropriately and are apt not to respond at all.

Circumstances that place the parent with a newly born infant in jeopardy also increase the anxiety and tension in those who are providing immediate and long-range care for the parents and the infant. The effects are similar whether the anxiety and tension result from feelings of inadequacy in talking with a mother about her acutely ill child, or in implementing emergency life-saving procedures. The health practitioner may respond defensively or in a manner that is not warm and caring, and spend less time assessing and meeting the parents' psychosocial needs. The parents' psychosocial resources, when functioning at an optimal level, augment the parents' potential for parenting. Consequently, parents with special problems who are shunned by family and friends who don't know quite what to say or how to respond, may receive less opportunity than other parents to talk about their gravest concerns.

This seeming lack of support for vulnerable parents is not intentional. Friends and family don't respond for fear of worsening the circumstances by "saying the wrong thing." Clinicians caring for these vulnerable parents may unconsciously respond to parents' healthy reactions to loss with avoidance behaviors because they are also uncomfortable and afraid of saying the wrong thing.

Health professionals, especially nurses, are faced with a unique opportunity and challenge to help parents during the initial crucial weeks following birth and during early months of parenthood. The nurse's practice involves extended contact and more time with the family during pregnancy and infancy than other professionals. Recent research found that planned home visits by nurses during pregnancy and early parenthood contributed to healthier babies at birth, better outcome for parents' education and careers, and healthier infants and toddlers (Olds et al., 1988). There is optimism that as science and technology continue to provide resources for more sophisticated medical and physical care that saves more lives, nurses and other health professionals will be able to increase the quality of life of parents and infants. Months of work and thousands of dollars of life-saving, critical care mean little if the parents become emotionally withdrawn from each other and their child.

Part I of this book addresses the philosophical and theoretical basis of the book and research describing the impact of parenting in general. In addition, individual and family adaptation to threat or loss is discussed. This forms a basis for understanding vulnerable parents' behavioral responses to threatening events occurring during the childbearing and early childrearing period. Those who are knowledgeable in these topics may prefer to read Parts II, III, and IV first, and use Part I as a reference if needed. The major theme in the book is the belief in the interactive effects of parent, child, and the social and physical environment in adaptation to the parenting role. A problem or perceived problem in any one of the three areas can contribute to dysfunctional parenting, and assets in each of these areas can buffer the effects of unusual circumstances and contribute to optimal adaptation.

Part II deals with special problem areas of parents that challenge the parenting role—when parents are premature or is high-risk, and when mothers have a chemical dependency problem (little research is available on how chemical dependency affects fathers during pregnancy and infancy). Part III focuses on special problem areas arising from the infant—when the infant is born prematurely or when the infant has a birth defect or handicap. Part IV focuses on selected physical and social environment situations that are particularly challenging for parents, those in a different family structure, and parenting in acutely socially deprived and stigmatized situations. Possible health professional interventions and responses in these unique situations are discussed in each chapter.

The book is based on research and theories from the disciplines of anthropology, medicine, nursing, psychology, social work, and sociology. The aim is to suggest approaches to providing health care for vulnerable parents and to raise questions for further exploration.

Acknowledgments

Many people contributed directly and indirectly to the philosophical and knowledge base for this book. During the writing of the book, two persons who contributed in quite different ways died. My mother, Nell, as a teenage mother allowed me the freedom to expand my horizons and dream the impossible dream and provided the resources necessary for me to achieve my goals. Because of her sacrifices from my birth, just a few weeks before the stock market crash in 1929, I was privileged to travel to other parts of the world, expand my education, and pursue a career that she was not able to pursue. I am extremely grateful to her and my father, William, for their superb parenting.

Deanna Sollid, a master nurse clinician, childbirth educator, businesswoman, and project director for my grant, Antepartum Stress: Effect on Family Health and Functioning, met an untimely accidental death. Her contributions to perinatal nursing and to helping mothers adapt to early breast-feeding and mothering were outstanding. Her dynamic creativity and dedication to the profession were evident as she shared her skills and wisdom with others through consultation, lectures, and writing. I was most fortunate to have her expertise in the recruitment of 600 expectant parents who were studied over five test periods (from the 24th to 34th weeks of pregnancy through 8 months postpartum). Her enthusiasm, calm, foresight, and knowledge were important factors contributing to my synthesis of this gigantic project.

My research career has focused on factors impacting on early parenting in a variety of situations and a comparison of mothers' and non-mothers' development over the life course, as I have continued work on the theory of maternal role attainment. *Parents At Risk* reflects the learning derived from all of these projects.

Appreciation is expressed to the funding agencies for two large projects that provided much of the data base for Chapters 4, 5, 7, and the section on single mothers in Chapter 9. The project, Factors Having an Impact on Maternal Role Attainment the First Year of Motherhood, was supported by Maternal and Child Health (Social Security Act, Title V) Grant MC-R-060435. Close to 300 mothers were studied over the first year of motherhood (teenagers, women in their 20s, and women 30 and older). Kathryn Hackley was the masterful project director of this work.

The project, Antepartum Stress: Effect on Family Health and Functioning, was funded by the National Center for Nursing Research, National Institutes of Health, under Grant R01 NR 01064. This study compared stress among mothers and fathers who experienced an obstetrical risk situation requiring antenatal hospitalization and mothers and fathers who experienced a normal pregnancy. As principal investigator, I was fortunate to have as co-investigators Sandra Ferketich, Katharyn May, and Jeanne DeJoseph.

Michelle Bushong, Mary Margaret Gottesman, and Saralie Bisnovich Pennington generously contributed their valuable insights from their experiences with parents in at-risk situations. Their chapters have added vital information for clinicians.

I am indebted to all parents who participated in the research projects to teach us something about the art of parenting and to all parents with whom I have had the opportunity to work. Their strengths, their ability to adapt, to love, and to work in the most difficult of circumstances have left me with the deepest respect and awe for their abilities.

Ruth Chasek, Karen O'Brien, and Philip Rappaport, editors at Springer, were very helpful in their suggestions and astute editing. Their contributions were valuable throughout the process of getting the book published.

Special appreciation is expressed to Dr. Kathryn Barnard for allowing me to use her copyrighted material. Her child health assessment interactional model is used as an organizing framework for the book to illustrate the interactional challenges facing parents at risk.

Ramona Thieme Mercer

Contributors

Michelle Bushong, R.N., M.S., C.N.M., is a certified nurse-midwife. She received her master's degree from the University of Utah in Salt Lake City. She has spent several years practicing as a nurse-midwife in a tertiary care setting where she gave full scope midwifery care to high risk populations. Ms. Bushong has had extensive experience in caring for substance abusing women throughout pregnancy. She is currently the program coordinator for the Santa Clara County Perinatal Substance Abuse Treatment Program in San Jose, California.

Mary Margaret Gottesman, R.N., Ph.D., is an Assistant Professor in Maternal-Child Health at the University of California, Los Angeles. She teaches the graduate specialty programs in pediatric and neonatal nursing. Dr. Gottesman is the Principal Investigator for DHHS, Division of Nursing grant, "Increasing Access to Nursing Services for the Homeless." Funds from the grant support the operation of a nurse-managed pediatric clinic for homeless and indigent children. The majority of the children are from minority groups at high risk for AIDS. In addition, Dr. Gottesman is the Principal Investigator for the DHHS, Division of Nursing grant, "Specialization in Neonatal Critical Care." Her research focuses on the description of the high-risk maternal-child populations and interventions to decrease their risk status. Dr. Gottesman received her B.A. in nursing from the College of Saint Catherine in St. Paul, Minnesota, her M.S. in nursing from the University of Minnesota, and her Ph.D. in nursing from the University of Rochester, Rochester, New York.

Saralie Bisnovich Pennington, M.S.W., L.C.S.W., is the director of Family Services at Operation Concern, a gay and lesbian outpatient psychotherapy clinic in San Francisco, California. She is also in private practice and is a member of the Community Advisory Board of the Department of Social Work at California State University in San Francisco. A founder and chairperson of the organization, Straights for Gay Rights, Ms. Pennington is the mother of a college student.

PART I

THEORETICAL BASIS FOR ASSESSMENT OF PARENTING

1

Introduction

Parenting, one of the most challenging and fulfilling roles of a lifetime, is a blend of observable behaviors of nurturing and guiding a child's development into adulthood within a specific social system. The parenting role evolves as a process that changes with developmental stages of the child. Parenting behaviors include an emotional tie to the child that permeates the socially and culturally defined patterns of physical and social child-rearing tasks. The emotional quality of parenting enables the child to grow and to develop into a physically and emotionally healthy individual. The parents' emotional tie to the infant/child and ability to love, provide, and care for the infant/child are recognizable through their overt pleasure of interaction with, and expressed concern and need for, continuing relationships with the infant/child.

The transition to parenthood in the best of circumstances is challenging and demanding as adaptations are made in assuming the new role and assimilating the baby into the family unit. Transitions as major modes of development are turning points in a person's life in which a new direction is taken that requires a change in role behaviors, responsibilities, goals, identity, and feelings about one's self in general (Mercer, Nichols, & Doyle, 1989). When something goes awry around the time of childbirth or when the social circumstances in which the transition occurs departs from the social norms, parents' challenges are profoundly increased, and the personal change and adaptation needed for pursuing the new direction in life (as parent, or parent of a second, third, or fifth child), are more difficult to achieve. In such situations, parents often lack the resources, objectivity in appraising the situation, and ability to deal with the many impinging forces demanding their time, attention, and reserves without help from both their family and the community.

The birth of an infant who is handicapped, born prematurely and/or seriously ill, the parent whose health is threatened or who is seriously ill, the child-parent, the parent who is chemically dependent, or who is from a different family structure or social group than the majority, all place the parent at risk for making the most optimal adaptation to parenthood. These situations with vulnerable parents also arouse many ambivalent feelings in the health professional. Although there are strong wishes to be helpful through emotional support and guidance, the health professional finds it difficult to deal with parents' behavioral responses of anger or withdrawal in grief responses, or of parents' refusal to follow a prescribed regimen important to their and/or their infant's health. Such behavioral responses by clients suggest to health professionals that they have failed in their counseling roles. In addition, the health professional's identification with the parents may be strong, and this strong empathic response adds to their difficulty in health counseling. Overcoming this ambivalence and difficulty in responding is important, however, as parents need and benefit greatly from help at these critical transitions.

A small amount of help during the time of transition or crisis can have far reaching positive consequences. Persons experiencing transitions, especially the transition to parenthood, are more accessible to help from health professionals. Importantly, persons experiencing transitions need to be linked with information and resources available from those who are knowledgeable about their particular type of experience in an often crisis situation (Silverman, 1982).

Advanced technology that makes it possible to save smaller infants who are sicker, along with many stressful environmental and family variables, add to the unpredictability of childbearing crises. These crises all place parents at risk in making the transition to parenting roles. An examination of the parent at risk, the extent of the problem, of anticipated and unanticipated transitions or events, and the theoretical framework from which parents at risk are viewed, are the focus of this chapter. The theoretical framework includes theory about variables affecting the transition to the parenting role. This framework is used for the assessment and intervention of special at risk situations.

PARENTS AT RISK

The concept "high risk" or "at risk" evolved along with perinatal medicine's technical sophistication that increasingly enabled the identification of groups of patients who needed special or additional care. The specialized, additional care has a preventive focus; with timely interventions, many future problems can be prevented and a healthy outcome may be achieved. Multiple screening measures utilized during pregnancy and the perinatal period alert the health professional about the extent of risk or potential risk factors. The high-risk maternity patient is identified by one or more of many medical, social, and physical characteristics, such as the presence of diabetes or hypertension, carrying twins, and being under- or over-age. The high-risk neonate is similarly identified by a large number of characteristics, diagnoses, and prognoses.

The status "high risk" or "at risk" alerts everyone that in the presence of the identified symptomatology and situation, special attention and care are imperative to prevent any or increased pathology, disability, or death. In order to *prevent* diabetic coma in the pregnant woman or the death of her fetus, careful monitoring of all facets of her and her fetus's physical status are vital components of her high-risk care. Care for high-risk patients has an aura of urgency, caution, alertness, expertise, and diagnostic specialization, all of which are geared to save life and prevent future problems or deterioration.

Parents at risk are those parents who are more vulnerable because of a stressful incident or other personal stressor experienced prior to or during the pregnancy, birth experience, or the first year following birth. They experience emotional and/or physical interruptions that demand energy and attention over and beyond that usually required for transition to and attainment of parenting roles. These emotional and/or physical demands leave parents exhausted and/or in profound grief and often with few resources, such that there is little energy left for the psychological, social, and physical work of achieving the parenting role. Timely, sensitive, and nurturing intervention during these early months of parenting can provide parents with the reassurance, and physical and emotional help needed to bolster their self-images and to move into their new role/s.

When any event interrupts the usual patterns of pleasurable parent-infant interactions during the perinatal period and early postpartal months, it also places undue stress on parents. This stress can lead to role strain, feelings of guilt, conflict, increased anxiety, depression, and fatigue. The same sort of special intensive and extensive care that other at-risk or high-risk clients receive are indicated for helping these vulnerable parents with their early parenting. This book focuses on the health professional's role during the perinatal period and the first year following the infant's birth, during which time most parents realize their maternal and paternal roles.

SCOPE OF THE PROBLEM

Child abuse, the most glaring example of dysfunctional parenting, has been slowly but steadily showing an increase over the last decade. Although the argument is made that greater awareness of child abuse has contributed to part of the increase in reports of abuse, the National Committee for Prevention of Child Abuse (1989) has linked the increase with the increase in drug abuse. In 1980, 1.1 million cases of child abuse were reported; in 1988 over 2.2 million were reported. The number of deaths from child abuse were reported as 899 in 1985; by 1988 they had increased to 1,125 (National Committee for Prevention of Child Abuse, 1989).

A study of physically abusive and nonabusive families who were matched on social class and demographic characteristics found distinct differences between the two groups in child-rearing practices and beliefs (Trickett & Susman, 1988). Abusive parents saw child rearing as more difficult, less enjoyable, and were less satisfied with their children than were nonabusive parents. The abusive family context for child rearing was characterized by suppression of affection and expressions of satisfaction, while conflict, anger, and anxiety were quite evident (Trickett & Susman, 1988). In addition, abusive families did not rely on reasoning as an effective discipline technique, did not encourage independence and autonomy in children, and in general tended to isolate their families from the outside world.

There were 3,809,394 babies born in the United States during 1987, and the projections are that increases will continue to be around 1% annually through 1990 (National Center for Health Statistics, 1988; 1989). Teenage births have been just under 500,000 annually the past few years. The major problem of teenage pregnancy is its impact on the teen's future; teenage pregnancy leads to truncated education, eroded earnings, single parenthood, and costs society through loss of young productive workers (Adams, Adams-Taylor, & Pittman, 1989).

More than half of teenage births are to unmarried teenagers, with disadvantaged young women three to four times more likely to become unwed mothers than advantaged teenagers (Wetzel, 1987). Among 20- to 24-year-olds, about one-fourth are unmarried; the combination of being single and a young mother impedes efforts to achieve goals and independence (Wetzel, 1987).

From 1980 to 1986 the increase in the number of births for unmarried women was nearly double the increase in the rate (National Center for Health Statistics, 1988). The almost one-third increase in the number of unwed births since 1980 is in part a reflection of the 13% increase in the number of unmarried women in the child-bearing ages; birth rates have tended to increase more for unmarried women in their late twenties and thirties than for younger women (National Center for Health Statistics, 1988). Being married was associated with handling irritating child behaviors more positively at 1, 8, and 12 months following birth (Mercer, 1986a). Single mothers in their twenties and thirties found that although there has been a gradual acceptance of single motherhood by society, married mothers do not accept single mothers as friends and colleagues (Mercer, 1986a). Thus a departure from the traditional family structure of a married couple continues to carry with it a degree of stigma.

From one-third to one-half of the pregnant populations fall into perinatal high-risk categories (Sokol et al., 1977). This seems to be a high figure; however, researchers have reported that complications and problems during the perinatal period, although not all high risk, lead to parental discomfort and disappointment. Entwisle and Doering (1981) reported that 17% of the 120 women studied from pregnancy had serious complications at birth; another 16% experienced an unanticipated cesarean birth. Others reported that 55% of 87 women experienced some complication during childbirth (Grossman et al., 1980). Mercer (1986a) reported that 50% of 276 women experienced some complication during childbirth. The most common complication during the third trimester of pregnancy is preterm labor, affecting from 7% to 8% of all pregnancies; high neonatal morbidity and mortality rates are associated with premature birth (Gonik & Creasy, 1986). High-risk factors leading to antenatal hospitalization included preterm labor (72%), preeclampsia (8%), bleeding (4%), diabetes control (3%), intrauterine transfusions (3%), asthma (2%), renal disease (1%), thyroid disease (1%), and less than 1% each of other conditions (6%) (Mercer & Ferketich, 1988).

There are at least 225,000 homeless children in the United States, with some agencies estimating that the figure may be as high as 2,000,000 (MacNamara & Goodavage, 1988); one-third of the homeless families in the United States have children. One child in four under the age of 6 lives in poverty in America; one in every three poor children is not covered by health insurance (MacNamara & Goodavage, 1988). Premature birth, teenage birth, and increased perinatal morbidity and mortality are associated with poverty.

Statistical reports of at-risk populations vary somewhat, but the high number of parents who are at risk for parenting speaks to the challenge, especially to nurses and social workers. Medical expertise and diagnoses play a greater role in screening and prescribing for high-risk perinatal patients; however, the nurse's and social worker's expertise plays a greater role in the screening and monitoring of environmental and psychosocial factors for parents.

ANTICIPATED AND UNANTICIPATED
OR CATASTROPHIC TRANSITIONS

Anticipated Transitions to Parenthood

Parenthood as an anticipated transition carries with it some stress due to change of lifestyle, family relationships, self-identity, and the day-by-day vigilance required to care for an infant. Parenthood may be thought of as a normative transition, except when it occurs at a non-normative age for the society, such as during adolescence in the United States. In many situations, the pregnancy is planned, and even if un-planned there is an unconscious wish to have a child at some time, and the gestational period allows mental and physical preparation for the transition from nonparent to parent.

The period of pregnancy provides much lead time for parents to anticipate and begin work toward their parental roles. Parenting behaviors reflect societal norms, which are the common beliefs about what parents should and should not do. These are learned indirectly as the woman or man is parented as a child. In reality there are six persons parenting an infant in the typical beginning family with a first child: the mother and father, and, indirectly, their parents. The new father and mother consciously or unconsciously use their own parents as either positive or negative role models (Mercer, 1986a; Mercer et al., 1989). In addition, intergenerational influences are evident in parental attach-ment to the infant. A woman's positive relationship with her mother as a child had a positive effect on maternal attachment during the first week and 8 months following birth; her partner's current positive rela-tionship with his father had a positive effect on paternal attachment the first week (Mercer & Ferketich, 1990a). Gladieux (1978) also observed that a woman's positive relationship with her father was associated with a satisfying pregnancy from beginning to end, while the relation-ship with her mother was associated with third-trimester satisfaction with the pregnancy. Others observed that childhood relationships with the same-sex parent influenced maternal and paternal adaptation to the parenting role in the form of pleasure and emotional investment in the child, sensitivity to, and acceptance of the child (Cox et al., 1985). The mother's relationship with both of her parents was important in her adaptation to the parenting role.

Anticipated events leave parents with ability to have some control in planning how the event takes shape and how the course of the event may be expected to develop. Having a higher sense of mastery, or feeling in control of one's life, was a consistent predictor of parental competence among both men and women during the first 8 months following birth (Mercer et al., 1987).

Unanticipated Transitions

Unanticipated transitions or nonnormative transitions represent more of a catastrophe for parents. Unanticipated transitions may come in the form of birthing a handicapped or premature infant or as a parent developing ill health. Coping with catastrophe strains resources; when one family member is affected, other family members who would usually be a major resource of support for the affected member need help themselves to deal with the catastrophic event.

Several characteristics of catastrophic events differentiate them from normative or expected stressors: the sudden onset, a type of loss that is experienced by only a few persons, lack of existing guidelines for dealing with such events, the unknown time frames, and the uncontrollable, disruptive, and/or destructive nature of the event to the family all pose a serious threat, have great emotional impact, and may precipitate illness (Figley, 1983). A pregnancy has a predictable course and a predictable end and outcome; however, a premature labor that leads to a critically ill infant is an example of a catastrophic event. There is little or no time for the family to prepare for dealing with the early labor; parents feel a loss of a normal pregnancy, opportunity to attend childbirth classes, and a healthy, full-term infant. There are fewer peers in the same situation, and although there are numerous guidelines and classes for parenting a normal infant, less information is available about parenting a premature infant. Parents have no control in making choices about the type of labor and delivery desired; the cost of caring for a premature infant takes away from family resources. There is a real threat that their infant may die or have a life-long chronic illness because of immaturity, thus affecting the parents emotionally such that they may become depressed or ill themselves. Another example of a catastrophic event is the middle-class family accustomed to middle-class comforts who is plunged into poverty when jobs are lost or when ill health forces a wage-earner to give up a job; all of the characteristics of a catastrophic event are applicable in this situation also.

THEORETICAL FRAMEWORK EXPLAINING PARENTING

The current state of knowledge about the variables affecting parenting and the transition to the parental role presented in Chapter 2 provide the basis for the theoretical approach to at-risk situations in this book. The overall proposition is that the early months following birth are a time of parental adaptation and adjustment to the parenting role, during which early parent-infant meshing of cues and personality traits have an impact on the development of the parenting role, including the attachment process, and on the infant's development. The parenting role does not evolve automatically or intuitively for the vast majority of humans; many adults have never held a newly born infant prior to holding their own. Several variables impact on the parenting role as it evolves over a lifetime, ending only at the death of either the parent or of the child.

Three clusters of variables have been consistently linked with parenting (Belsky, 1984; Millor, 1981), achievement of the parental role (Mercer, 1981a; Walker, Crain, & Thompson, 1986a), and child development and health status (Barnard & Eyres, 1979): characteristics of the parent, the child, and the environment. Helfer (1973) first articulated the interactive force of these three clusters of variables by specifying the conditions under which an extreme form of dysfunctional parenting, child abuse and neglect, occurs: a parent with special characteristics, a child who is imagined to be or is actually different, and one or more events perceived as stressful by the parents. Millor (1981) included in her interactional model both community and family tolerance for physical punishment as having effects on parenting in the form of parental nurturance and discipline behaviors indicating either parental role sufficiency or parental role insufficiency.

A model depicting the dynamic ongoing interaction between mother, infant, and the environment and allowing observations and assessments at any point in time was reported by Barnard and Eyres (1979) (see Figure 1). In this book, special characteristics of parents (those who are teenagers, have a high-risk obstetrical problem, or a chemical dependency problem), infants who are different (those born prematurely or with handicaps), and stressful environmental situations (families with an alternate family structure and acutely socially deprived and stimatized) are presented. However, there is never only the one problem that exists; there are always the interactive and transactive forces of the parent, infant, and environment that determine ultimate parenting outcome. The mother's characteristics and her adaptation to the infant's demands and needs, the infant's characteristics, and the animate and inanimate environment are constantly interacting. At any point in time the areas of overlap in Figure 1 represent the interaction between parent, environment, and child; the interaction that the health professional sees at a particular time is affected by all of these components.

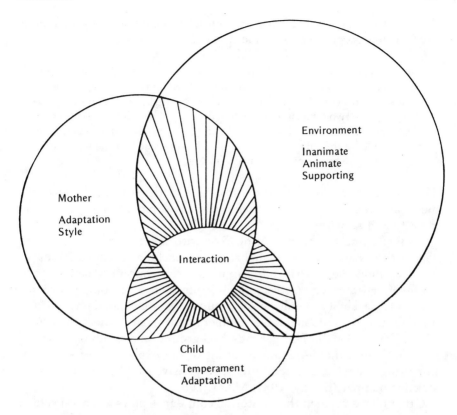

Figure 1. Interactive model of three clusters of variables explaining parenting. From *Child Health Assessment Part 2: The First Year of Life*, p. 132, by Kathryn E. Barnard and Sandra J. Eyres, DHEW Publication No. HRA 79-25, Hyattsville, MD: U.S. Department of Health, Education, and Welfare. Copyright 1979 by Kathryn E. Barnard. Reprinted with permission of Kathryn E. Barnard.

Influence of Parental Characteristics and Resources

Parents' emotional capacities for parenting begin developing with their own birth, become focused during pregancy as the unborn baby develops, and fully materialize after the baby's birth. Competent parenting reflects in part successful parental role attainment; in addition to achieving competence in the role, the parent must integrate the parenting role with other roles that are a part of the established core self so that there is satisfaction and pleasure with the new identity and responsibilities that it entails. Parent-infant attachment is a process that is a part of both competent parenting and parental role attainment;

Rubin (1977) used the term "binding-in" to describe the attachment process that occurs over a period of 12 to 15 months:

> The origin and end-point of the process are in the maternal identity itself. Maternal identity and binding-in to the child are two major developmental changes, each dependent on the other, in the three trimesters of pregnancy and the two trimesters following delivery of the child. Developmental progress in maternal identity and binding-in is promoted or retarded on the one side by the infant itself and on the other side by society, particularly closely related family members. (p. 67)

Thus Rubin also addressed the interaction of the parent, the environment, and the infant as influencing the development of the maternal identity and attachment.

Parents come to the parenting role with a range of personal and coping resources; these personal resources include psychosocial maturity that allows self-sacrifice for an infant, self-concept or self-esteem, sense of mastery or control of one's life, sense of competence for parental role, ability to enlist a social support system, good physical and mental health, and adaptable temperament traits (Mercer, 1981a; Mercer et al., 1987). The parent's background and childhood experiences influence the development of his or her expression of affection, nurturing behavior, and ability to be responsive to children in a nonrestrictive manner (Belsky, 1984; Millor, 1981).

Others have verified that maternal confidence plays a central role in adaptation to motherhood during the first 2 years; if the first-time mother has had experience with infants and feels confident in her ability to care for her baby and read the baby's signals, then maternal attachment is facilitated (Williams et al., 1987). Although self-esteem and parenting confidence were strongly correlated ($r = 0.64$), parenting confidence was related more strongly to several aspects of adaptation to motherhood than was self-esteem (Williams et al., 1987), indicating that parenting confidence encompassed more than self-esteem.

Greater psychosocial maturity affords parents the flexibility they need to achieve the parental role; the older the first-time mother, the greater is her personality integration, self-concept, and flexibility of child-rearing attitudes (Mercer, 1986a; 1986b). This explains in part why teenage parents have greater difficulty in parenting. Self-esteem and sense of mastery were consistent predictors of parental competence among mothers and fathers during the first 8 months following birth (Mercer et al., 1987).

The mother with greater psychosocial maturity is able to meet the more difficult child's needs with greater sensitivity. When first-time mothers had higher empathy, greater flexibility, higher self-concept, and a lower level of the maternal temperament trait of intensity (reaction to stimuli), their maternal role attainment was not affected by their infant's temperament (Mercer et al., 1982). Infants had been assigned to the temperament clusters of easy, slow to warm up, and difficult (Carey & McDevitt, 1978).

Sense of mastery, sometimes used synonomously with coping, is the extent a person feels in control of his or her life experiences, in contrast to being directed by fate (Pearlin & Schooler, 1978). Mastery is the ability to reduce responses to stress to a tolerable level, to mobilize resources to reduce the source of threat, and to find alternate sources of satisfaction to replace any losses (Caplan, 1981). Personal control over an impending threat may be behavioral (through direct action on the environment), cognitive (through the interpretation of events), or decisional (through choice of alternative actions) (Averill, 1973). The relationship between stress from negative life events and anxiety is greater for those who do not feel an internal sense of control over their lives (Sandler & Lakey, 1982).

Stressor responses such as anxiety and depression affect parent and parent-infant relationships within the family, the family unit as a whole, and individual family members (Mercer et al., 1986). Several studies have demonstrated the interaction of the parent, infant, and situation as indicated by Figure 1 at different points in time. Mothers with higher anxiety during pregnancy were more hostile and interacted less positively with their child at 8 months postpartum than did mothers with low anxiety (Davids, Holden, & Gray, 1963). Increased maternal anxiety has also been associated with greater neonatal risk, more delivery complications, greater depression, and less confidence in coping and parenting capacities (Barnett & Parker, 1986; Blumberg, 1980; Lederman, 1984b).

Maternal depression was associated with less affectionate maternal-infant interactions and fewer vocalizations to the infant at 1 and 3 months postpartum (Fleming et al., 1988). Depressed mothers also failed to modify their behavior in synchrony with their infants' changing behavior and responded more slowly to their infants' vocalizations (Bettes, 1988). Fathers who were depressed 8 or more days during the early postpartal period maintained less contact with their infants (Zaslow et al., 1985).

Infants in turn are affected negatively by high parental anxiety or depression. Female infants of highly anxious mothers were less alert and active; their mothers interacted less skillfully and communicated less with them at 3 and 6 months after birth (Farber, Vaughn, & Egeland, 1981). In laboratory situations, infants were more playful when their mothers expressed joy; they showed greater sadness, anger, and gaze aversion when their mothers expressed sadness (Termine & Izard, 1988). Others also observed negative effects of mothers' simulated depression on 3-month-old infants; infants produced greater protest and wary behavior, tending to continue these responses briefly after mothers switched from depressed to normal interaction (Cohn & Tronick, 1983).

Influence of Infant Characteristics

The newborn infant has many interactive competencies that may be illustrated to parents to add pleasure to their interactions with the infant. Als et al. (1979) grouped the interactive behaviors on the Brazelton Neonatal Behavioral Assessment Scale (Brazelton, 1973) into four behavioral dimensions: interactive capacities, motoric capacities, state control organizational capacities, and organizational capacities in physiologic responses to stress. The newborn's interactive capacities include the ability to alert to and turn the head toward a human voice (Brazelton, 1979). During the first hours and days following birth, infants are able to imitate adult facial gestures of mouth opening and closing (Meltzoff & Moore, 1983). The infant's earliest motor capacities include the ability to bring the hands to the mouth and to suck a finger or thumb (Als et al., 1979). The infant's organization capacities includes the ability to come to an alert state and to calm him- or herself. Infants are able to maintain caregiving behaviors and to exert control over parents through their motoric capacities indicating their conditions, sensory and fatigue limits, and protest behaviors (Bell, 1974).

More difficult infants have been associated with parental anxiety and depression (Ventura, 1982). Difficult infants also pose major concerns for the family, requiring large family adjustments (Kronstadt, et al., 1979).

Effects of difficult infants have been observed on short- and long-term mothering behaviors. Early negative perceptions of infant behavior continue to affect the maternal-child relationship even though perceptions of infant behavior change in a more positive direction (Campbell, 1979). Mothers of preschool children who were difficult or slow to warm up tended to use negative behaviors such as controlling the child through guilt and temper and detachment behaviors (Simonds & Simonds, 1981).

Zahr (1987) found among Lebanese mothers and their infants that it was their combined temperaments that affected maternal and dyadic behaviors, especially when both mothers and infants were rated as having an easy temperament. Others found that social status, anxiety level, and the mother's mental health status were related to the 4-month-old infants' temperament ratings, suggesting that early ratings of temperment may reflect individual differences in mothers rather than differences in infants. (Sameroff, Seifer, & Elias, 1982).

Significant correlations were observed at 4 months between five of the nine temperament categories (adaptability, rhythmicity, persistence, quality of mood, and distractibility) between 20- to 29-year-old mothers and their infants, but only for rhythmicity, persistence, and threshold to stimulus among mothers 30 and older, and only for adaptability among teenage mothers (Mercer, 1986a). There were no significant differences at 8 months in maternal gratification in the role, observed maternal behavior, or self-reported ways of handling irritating child behavior according to whether the infant was easy, intermediate low, slow to warm up, intermediate high, or difficult (Mercer, 1986a). However, mothers who had difficult or slow-to-warm-up infants scored significantly lower on their attachment scores. A personality factor made up of the mother's self-concept, empathy, flexibility, and the temperament trait of intensity predicted maternal role behaviors at 1 year, whereas infant temperament did not (Mercer, 1986c).

Influence of Situational Context and Environmental Factors

Life events and other environmental variables that occur and exist prior to the pregnancy and childbirth provide the social backdrop in which parents must adapt to their role along with the sequence of events occurring during the process of parents' transition to the role. These events or variables may or may not be stressors that lead to a distress response such as anxiety and depression. Some life events are viewed as having positive effects and as such appear to provide a supportive environment for the parenting role (Mercer et al., 1982).

Being a high-risk maternity patient or having a high-risk infant is associated with a level of stress such that it may be considered a crisis situation. Yet a situation that is a crisis for one parent may not be considered a crisis by another; therefore, while some factors are obvious in screening for more vulnerable parents or parents at risk, other stressors are more subtle.

Stress has been linked with less positive maternal attitudes and maternal behavior (Crnic et al., 1983). Stress has been associated with abusive behaviors, and abusive mothers demonstrated a pattern of attachment disorders in contrast to a control group of mothers (DeLozier, 1982). Abusive parents reported greater stress from life changes than did nonabusive parents (Conger, Burgess, & Barrett, 1979).

Social support in the environment has consistently been indicated as a moderator of stress. Just as stress from life events is not all bad, social support is not always good, appropriate, or supportive (Hobfoll, 1985).

Social support may be viewed as the social embeddedness of the person (the social network), perceived social support, and actual received support (Barrera, 1986). Membership in a support network is associated with the person's perceptions and expectations of the network; there is less perceived reciprocity among friends, and family support is expected and often not appreciated as much as help from others (Antonucci, 1985). When there is a lack of reciprocity in the network, the network is more often thought of as inadequate, and the support has a less positive outcome (Antonucci, 1985). Dysfunctional families also have asymmetrical reciprocity with their social networks as well as more stressful home environments; they report giving more help than they receive, particularly from family members (Lindblad-Goldberg & Dukes, 1985).

Perceived support is the belief that help or empathy is readily available if needed (Sarason & Sarason, 1985). Perceived support has been a greater buffer in stressful situations than received support (Cohen et al., 1985; Mercer et al., 1987) The efficacy of formal support on maternal adaptation when the infant was premature was dependent on the mothers' need for support; mothers needing more support also found that it was more difficult to get the desired support from family and friends (Affleck et al., 1989).

Perceived support may be more a characteristic of the person than of the environment. Perceptions of support may be related to childhood losses of support or feelings of inadequate relationships during childhood (Sarason & Sarason, 1985). College students' adult social support systems were linked with their perceptions of early affective relationships with their parents (Flaherty & Richman, 1986). Other variables influencing individual differences in seeking and obtaining support include age, race, and locus of control (feeling in control of one's life as opposed to feeling ruled by fate) (Wilcox & Vernberg, 1985).

Received support, the help a person gets in time of crisis, is thought by some to be an indication of the stress experienced rather than a mediator of outcome (Barrera, 1981; Hobfoll, 1985). Enacted or received support may be classified as emotional, informational, appraisal, or tangible assistance (physical help) (House, 1981). Mothers' received support declines significantly over the first year of motherhood; less change is observed among men, who report significantly less received support than women overall (Mercer et al., 1987).

SUMMARY

Research concerning parent characteristics, infant characteristics, and characteristics of the environment that affect parenting provides a knowledge base to assist in screening for parents who are at risk. Parents at risk are parents who are more vulnerable because they experience situations or problems around the time of their infant's birth and early parenthood that tax their resources such that energy and emotion for getting acquainted with and attached to their child are hampered. Parents at risk need special help to avoid disability or pathology in their parenting patterns through a supportive environment that helps them learn self-confidence and to enjoy and develop love for their child. Just as a high-risk patient is not always predictable in other situations, the practitioner cannot always predict the parent at risk.

Single acts do not disallow a parent's emotional tie nor indicate the parent is at risk, although a single act may alert the health professional that further observation and communication with colleagues who are working with the parent are warranted to validate whether the observed act was part of a beginning pattern, or a "bad moment" on a "bad day."

Timely intervention for parents at risk can provide the resources they need to establish positive, enjoyable parent-child relationships. The fewer the resources a parent has, the greater the professional and social intervention that is needed.

In each of the chapters in parts II–IV, strategies for facilitating early parent-infant interactions and promoting parental competence and mastery will be discussed in relation to a specific risk situation. In some circumstances the infant cannot respond to the parents or the environment; in other situations the parent is handicapped in interactions. These constraints will be considered in fostering positive parental perceptions and positive parent-infant interactions.

2

Transition to Parenthood: The Process of Parental Role Attainment

Becoming a parent leads to change in both previous lifestyle and in future life goals for the individuals and for the family unit. Reviewing some of these changes under normal circumstances highlights the impact of unexpected or handicapping circumstances that require even greater change and adaptation by family members.

The transition to parenthood has consistently been associated with family stress and, in particular, stress in the couple relationship. In contrast to the idea that, with attainment of the parental role, family function including the couple relationship becomes stronger or more positive, we see a decline in both at 4 and 8 months following birth when compared to pregnancy and shortly after birth (Mercer et al., 1987). Evidence was found that over the first 2 years, the mother-child and marital relationship develop independently of each other (Williams et al., 1987). How the parenting role and the child develop depends on the ongoing interactive transactional process among the parents, the child, and the social context or environment in which the family lives. One environmental influence is the historical time; historical factors contribute to shaping how children born in a particular era are reared and how they view the world. Each historical event influences the larger social system within which the family is lodged, and the child in turn is reared for functioning in that particular social system.

In examining the forces interacting in early parenting, the infant's physical and innate characteristics and competencies are interacting with parents and siblings in the family system; the infant influences these family members, who are also influencing the child's development. The family system is interacting with the larger social context—

employment places, schools, community facilities—and influences this social context that also influences the family (Bronfenbrenner, 1977). This concept may be visualized by viewing the infant as an individual embedded within a family system represented by a smaller circle within a series of larger circles. The family system is nested within the community or cultural context, and the local community is nested within the national context. Forces from the larger national context influence the family such as the national income tax system, national registration of males at age 18, and the social security system. The family influence on these matters is reflected in adult votes and other participation in the political system. The smaller community also has laws and regulations specific to the state and/or county; in addition, cultural influences are evident, particularly in neighborhoods. The family maintains boundaries between the family system and other social systems, exerting control over the extent of interchange between the family and these other systems (Kantor & Lehr, 1975) such that the family may be viewed as a semi-closed system as opposed to an entirely open system (Rodgers, 1964).

This chapter first focuses on the impact of childbearing on the family and, in particular, on the couple relationship. An appreciation of the impact of parenting on the family is important in order to be especially sensitive in counseling parents at risk. Attachment is defined according to its use in this book, with the process of parental role acquisition or attainment presented next as a trajectory of evolving behaviors during the first year following birth. The process of parental role acquisition provides a guide for the assessment of the interactions of parents, infant, and the environment over time as depicted in the model shown in Figure 1 in the preceding chapter. At any point in the process of the parental role transition, it is the interaction of the parent's ongoing personal characteristics or traits, response style, and adaptation to the infant at that time interacting with the infant's characteristics within an animate and inanimate environment (Barnard & Eyres, 1979) that provide the information health professionals need for counseling and supportive care.

IMPACT OF BIRTH ON THE FAMILY UNIT

Having a child alters the established relationships between family members and affects both short-term and long-term goals. The family's responsibility in nurturing and socializing a child increases the number and complexity of roles for individual family members and the kinds of adaptive changes that must occur within the family unit. Parents' long-range planning extends to the child's education and achievement of independence from the family of birth. Short-range planning to meet the family's basic needs and recreation is also extensive with the infant's new demands imposed on the family system. Planning a short trip, for example, involves organizing and packing numerous small items just to feed and diaper the infant.

In early studies of first-time parents, the transition to the parenting role was viewed as a crisis because of the disruption that necessitated a decisive change in parents' ususal patterns of action (Dyer, 1965; LeMasters, 1965). The impact of parenthood is highly variable and is viewed as more stressful to some than to other couples (Hobbs & Cole, 1976). Whether or not a couple views the experience of parenthood as a time of major stress, the experience is one of major change. Change occurs in the family routine and decision making, as well as in the parents' self-concepts (Shereshefsky & Yarrow, 1973).

Factors of greatest concern to new mothers cluster around their emotional and physical fatigue, interrupted sleep, worry about personal appearance, and feelings of edginess or emotional upset (Mercer, 1986a; Russell, 1974). Fathers' greatest concerns go beyond the physical or emotional self, although the majority (61%) saw interrupted sleep and rest as a concern, 53% to 54% saw suggestions from in-laws, increased money problems, change in plans, and the additional work that came with fatherhood as troublesome (Russell, 1974).

The addition of a new family member requires a reassignment of roles, status position, and values. First-time fathers who are able to develop a coherent role that meets their wives' and their infants' needs adjust better than men who are unsure of how much they wish to be involved with their infants (Fein, 1976). The baby's health, negotiating processes between husband and wife in deciding the divisions of labor, and family and work support were also important to men's adjustment. Colicky, though healthy, babies caused depression and feelings of rage, guilt, desperation, and exhaustion. It is not difficult to imagine the greater impact of an infant who is ill or who has a serious handicap.

Adding to the difficulty with parenting roles in the United States is the fact that the role is ill defined, insufficiently delimited, and surrounded by a romanticized myth, and the incumbents are ill prepared (Grossman et al., 1980; LeMasters, 1965). Toffler (1970) spoke of the paradox around the role of parenthood; although the role continues to increase in complexity, it continues to be filled largely by amateurs. The mobility of new families also contributes to difficulty in parenting; although new parents meet peers in their new locations who are supportive in many ways, the peers are also searching for similar resources (e.g., information and baby-sitters). The availability or nearness of an older generation can help young parents avoid feeling overwhelmed by the immediate present.

Poorer family functioning has been associated with increased maternal medical complications (Smilkstein et al., 1984) and lower infant birth weight (Ramsey, Abell, & Baker, 1986). Parenthood is associated with decreased psychological well-being and self-satisfaction when no complications are present (McLanahan & Adams, 1987).

The transition to parenthood for the first time highlights couple differences, introduces new areas of difference, and leads to increased opportunity for conflict in the couple relationship (Cowan & Cowan, 1988). Cowan and Cowan (1988) maintain that five domains influence marital and family adaptation:

> Characteristics of individuals in the family, particularly their self-concept and self-esteem
> Couple relationship, division of labor, and communication patterns
> Parent-child relationships
> Connection between the new family's patterns and each parent's family of origin
> Balance between each parent's source of stress such as employment roles and social support network

Each domain refers to a different system level moving from individual, dyad, and triad to the third generation and other social systems; the interactions across each system level influence individual, couple, and family adaptation to and satisfaction with the new infant (Cowan & Cowan, 1988).

Adaptive families are notable for their flexibility and reciprocity (Fedele, et al., 1988). In flexible families, roles are not rigidly fixed, so that it is not important who fulfills the role; what is important is the ability of a parent to step in if the usually designated parent cannot fulfill a role for any reason. Such flexibility enables healthy growth and development of children in situations of impairment of one parent.

In order to plan more relevant family support programs during the transition to parenthood, Kagan and Seitz (1988) categorized families into three groups: mainstream, nontraditional, and high-risk. Mainstream families were defined as families headed by a husband and wife who did not have any extraneous conditions to drain their energies for parenting, although they were not stress free. Nontraditional families were defined by their unique family structure—remarriage, adoptive, foster children, and twins. High-risk families included families with premature infants, below the poverty level, headed by a single teenager, with an adult or infant who is biologically handicapped or mentally retarded, and with mentally ill or severely depressed parents. Mainstream families are best served by information and referral and parenting education services (Kagan & Seitz, 1988). Nontraditional families desire the same services as mainstream families, but their services need to be directed to the specific group needs (e.g., parenting twins or step-parenting). In both nontraditional and high-risk families, home visits and crisis intervention programs are needed. As Kagan and Seitz noted, situations for high-risk families pose unique long-term threats to family stability, and many programs have evolved in response to the needs of new parents in these high-risk circumstances. Vulnerable parents at risk are those in high-risk and nontraditional (different family structure) family situations also identified by Kagan and Seitz.

IMPACT OF PARENTHOOD ON THE COUPLE RELATIONSHIP

Although a decline in marital satisfaction occurs following childbirth (Belsky, Lang, & Huston, 1986; Mercer et al., 1987, Miller & Sollie, 1980), the marital adjustment seems to be related to the extent of change occurring within the family (Harriman, 1986). The greater the division of labor toward traditionalism, the greater the decline in wives' evaluation of positive areas of marriage (Belsky et al., 1986).

Mothers perceive greater overall change in their lives with parenthood (Harriman, 1983) but are less likely to know what their mate's major concerns are during this transition than their mates are to know theirs' (Broom, 1984). The mother's perception of marital satisfaction during early parenthood is more complex than the father's, but a relationship that is perceived as equitable is more salient for men than for women (Tomlinson, 1987a).

Different factors contribute to mothers' and fathers' perceptions of their couple relationship shortly following birth (during postpartal hospitalization) and at 8 months after birth. Shortly following their infants' births, 33% of the variance in low-risk mothers' mate relationship was explained; lower state and trait anxiety, being married, more positive feelings about their pregnancies, and being younger were associated with a more optimal mate relationship (Mercer et al., 1987). For low-risk fathers, 34% of their perceived mate relationship was explained; higher perceived support, higher attachment to the infant, less stress from negative life events the past year, and being married were associated with a more positive mate relationship. Eight months after birth, 31% of the mothers' mate relationship was explained; a higher sense of mastery, greater perceived and received support, poorer health status, less stress from negative life events the year prior to birth, and a lower pregnancy risk score were associated with a more positive mate relationship. Fifty percent of the variance in fathers' mate relationship was predicted; higher self-esteem, greater stability of self-esteem at 1 month, greater received social support during pregnancy, less frequent contact with their mothers, and a more positive relationship with their fathers as children were associated with a more positive mate relationship (Mercer et al., 1987). Although social support is important to both mothers and fathers at 8 months, different variables are associated with satisfaction with the mate relationship for fathers and mothers.

Different factors are also associated with satisfactory marital adjustment for mothers and fathers 5 months following birth (Rankin, Campbell, & Soeken, 1985). Social support for child care and household tasks were related to a more positive marital adjustment for mothers only. During pregnancy mothers had overestimated the husband's involvement with household chores following the birth as well as support from other family members with both child care and household chores. Men were more realistic in their expectations, however (Rankin et al., 1985).

Mothers and fathers also differed in the type of support that was important to their adjustment to parenthood (Wandersman, Wandersman, & Kahn, 1980). Fathers' well-being, marital interaction, and parental competence were associated with emotional marital support and parenting group support; mothers' well-being and marital interaction were associated with emotional marital and network support. Participation in parenting groups did not play a major role in postpartal adjustment for either mothers or fathers 5 to 6 months after birth; marital cohesion, the difficulty of the baby, parents' resources and coping skills, and their previous adaptations contributed to adaptation to parenthood (Wandersman et al., 1980). In contrast to Wandersman and associates' findings that the social network was important to mothers' adjustment during the transition to parenthood, Stemp, Turner, and Noh (1986) found that the extent of the mother's social network had no impact on changes in their psychological distress over the first year after birth; however, they did find that the perception of social support and extent of marital intimacy each contributed to change in reported psychological distress. A reason for differences in support from the social network may be explained by conflict in the network; Crawford (1985) cautioned that although help may be well intentioned, it may lead to conflict between the mothers and others in their social network. Abernethy (1973) found that a tight network in which all network members were closely associated led to greater maternal competence; the common experiences of close network members contributes to greater consensus on both advice and physical help given.

ATTACHMENT DEFINED

Despite the challenges and conflicts they face, parents generally move into parenting roles with good intentions. Existing options make it possible to avoid parenting; thus some thought and decision have usually preceded the decision to become a parent. While the statistics that indicate that more than 2.2. million reports of child abuse were filed in 1988 (a 3% increase over 1987) (National Center on Child Abuse Prevention Research, 1989), there were more than 60 million children for whom there were no reports of abuse. The numbers of children who are abused can be greatly reduced if the social and health care systems can coordinate their efforts to provide support for parents and facilitate parents' potential to develop their caring (attachment to the child) and nurturing abilities.

Historically, the mother-infant relationship has been respected for its profound impact on the developing child. Early works discussed attachment from the infant's perspective, fear of losing the mother as the primary attachment figure (Freud, 1959), and the absence of the infant's tie to a primary mothering person as was observed in early institutions for infant care (Freud & Burlingham, 1944; Provence & Lipton, 1962). It wasn't until Kempe and his associates coined the term, "battered child syndrome," in 1962 that the upsurge of research in the attachment process as it evolves for parents began.

Attachment, a component of the parental role and parental identity, is viewed in this book largely from the parents' perspective. Attachment is viewed as a process in which an enduring affectional and emotional commitment to an individual is formed; it is facilitated by positive feedback between partners through mutually satisfying experiences. The reciprocal interactions between partners are a central component of the process. As a dyadic relationship, each partner acts on and responds to cues from the other. As a process, a progression or development involving emotional and cognitive change occurs in both partners over time (Mercer, 1977a). Attachment, a bidirectional process, is differentiated from bonding, a unidirectional process from parent to infant shortly following birth (Campbell & Taylor, 1979).

Three concepts in this definition of attachment merit emphasis. First, attachment as a process follows a progressive or developmental course involving change over time. It is rarely instantaneous, but the changes, both affective or emotional and cognitive, occur gradually within each partner of the attaching dyad. In a process involving humans, no single event causes irrevocable negative consequences. Some events may add to the difficulty by which the process proceeds, but the numerous factors interacting in an attachment process make it possible for attachment to occur despite some negative feedback from a partner or a negative occurrence.

A second important concept is that attachment is facilitated by positive feedback in the interchange between attaching partners. Positive feedback includes social, verbal, and nonverbal responses, either real or perceived, that indicate acceptance by the attaching partner. An infant's grasp reflex around a parent's finger means, "I love you," to the parent. The infant's eye contact and tracking of the parents' faces and voices also communicates interest in and acceptance of the parent.

A third concept to emphasize is that attachment occurs through mutually satisfying experiences. The pleasurable experiences outweigh the displeasureable interactions in satisfying parent-infant interactions. If a newly delivered mother is in severe pain or is physically exhausted, pain relief and/or assistance are needed for her to enjoy her early interactional experiences with her infant. The unique differences of individuals and the pressing demands of daily living are such that many dyadic interactions are not satisfying. However, the new mother who is attaching to her infant reflects, "Mothering is bitter-sweet, but the sweet by far outweighs the bitter."

The attachment process is also a discriminatory process in that each member of the attaching dyad prefers the partner over others. The child's attachment is characterized by affection for and discrimination through specificity to a particular person (Ainsworth, 1964). Components of maternal attachment identified by Robson and Moss (1970) included the mother's feelings that her infant occupied an essential position in her life, a sense of warmth or love, possession, devotion, protectiveness, concern for the infant's well-being, anticipation of prolonged contact, and a need for and pleasure in ongoing transactions with the infant. Once the emotional tie is established, the attached individual experiences emotional distress, including anxiety, anger, and depression, when unwillingly separated from the partner (Bowlby, 1977).

There has been disagreement as to how attachment is defined. Rosenthal (1973) argued that mother-infant interaction should be viewed as attachment, since attachment is a characteristic of the patterns of interaction between the two, rather than a thing resulting from the interactions. Lamb (1974) countered that the emphasis must be on the specific, enduring, and affectional bond, rather than on the specific behaviors, since behaviors will differ when comparisons are made between two or more mother-infant dyads. Attachment behaviors, however, do not remain constant across all situations, but are influenced by the social context (Sroufe & Waters, 1977).

THE PROCESS OF PARENTAL ROLE ATTAINMENT/ACQUISITION

The usual transition to the maternal or paternal role follows four stages of role acquisition: anticipatory, formal, informal, and personal (Thornton & Nardi, 1975). The anticipatory stage of maternal or paternal role attainment begins in earnest during the pregnancy; prior to that time, some random fantasy of parenting may occur, but with the thought of "someday." The formal stage of parental role-taking begins with assumption of the role at birth; during this stage, role behaviors dictated by society and health professionals are rigidly adhered to. Some time around the second month, parents move into the informal stage characterized by progression from rigidly following others' rules and directions to adapting and developing unique role behaviors that are appropriate for their particular infant. The achievement of a sense of harmony, confidence, and competence in role performance is the end point of maternal role attainment when the maternal identity is fully integrated into her self-system (Rubin, 1967) and occurs around the sixth to ninth month after birth; although men's paternal role acquisition has not been similarly traced, similar behaviors should indicate role achievement. This definition is congruent with Thornton and Nardi's end point of role achievement, the personal stage.

Three levels of adaptation are required as the process of role acquisition proceeds: adaptation at the physical or biological level, the psychological or emotional and cognitive level, and at the social level (Mercer, 1986a). At each stage of role acquisition, all three levels of adaptation are evident, but one or more level may be predominant.

Anticipatory Stage

During the anticipatory phase, couples choose a physician, hospital or other location for the infant's birth, and many attend childbirth classes in order to be prepared and participate in the birth to the fullest. Attendance at childbirth classes has been associated with desire/ability to be in control of events (Entwisle & Doering, 1981; Felton & Segelman, 1978; Mercer, 1986a), higher education, age, and socioeconomic status (Whitley, 1979). An obstetrical risk situation often requires a different type of birth experience and takes away some extent of parental control.

The Expectant Mother

The hormonal changes of pregnancy, the increasingly active fetus, and the partner's response to the pregnancy contribute to the woman's early anticipatory work toward attaining the maternal role. During the anticipatory phase of maternal role development, the woman accepts the pregnancy (Bibring et al., 1961; Lederman, 1984a), then later when she feels fetal movement, accepts the unborn child and begins a relationship with her coming infant (Caplan, 1959; Cranley, 1981a, 1981b; Leifer, 1977, 1980; Stainton, 1985a, 1985b). She attempts to resolve any conflicts in her relationship with her mother and moves the relationship to a different level—that of becoming a peer with her mother (Ballou, 1978; Bibring, 1965; Lederman, 1984). Her relationship with her husband is reassessed as she studies his involvement in the pregnancy and balances her dependence-independence needs (Ballou, 1978; Lederman, 1984a). This psychological work has commonly been referred to as the tasks of pregnancy.

The expectant mother's identification with a motherhood role proceeds through much fantasy and role-play (Lederman, 1984a; Rubin, 1967, 1984; Sherwen, 1987). Rubin (1967) described an early step in the role attainment process as mimicry; mimicry is characterized by a somewhat magical faith that certain rites or activities help to prepare one to be a mother. Expectant mothers seek role models for learning how to go about assuming the role of mother and the expectations of what to do through mimicry. Rubin (1967) described role-play as a second step in taking on the maternal role. In role-play the expectant mother offers to baby-sit for a friend and tests herself in the role of giving to an infant. Rubin (1967) saw fantasy as a move from taking on the role to "taking-in," a beginning internalization of the role. The expectant mother's wishes, fears, and daydreams reflect her emotional commitment to the unborn baby as she fantasizes about what mothering will be like for her.

Accomplishment of the identified tasks of pregnancy has been associated with successful adaptation to parenting. Josten (1982) used a Prenatal Assessment of Parenting Guide (Josten, 1981) based on Rubin's (1975, 1984) four tasks of pregnancy (perception of the complexities of mothering, developing attachment for the baby, acceptance of the coming child by significant others, and ensuring physical well-being) to see whether there were differences in achievement of these tasks by their early parenting. Mothers who proved to be inadequate mothers had not accomplished the tasks of realizing the complexities of the mothering role, acceptance of the child by significant others, and ensuring physical well-being. This Assessment of Parenting Guide enabled public health nurses to predict with 87% accuracy those mothers who would be competent and those who would have problems in the parenting role (Josten, 1981). The two groups of mothers had not differed significantly in their attachment to the unborn baby.

Maternal fetal attachment was a predictor of maternal-infant attachment at early postpartum hospitalization and at 1 month among low-risk women, but not at 4 and 8 months after birth, suggesting that the relationship established following birth becomes independent of attachment to the unborn infant (Mercer & Ferketich, 1990a). Maternal fetal attachment was significantly higher than paternal fetal attachment (Mercer et al., 1988), perhaps reflecting the more intimate relationship women experience with the unborn infant. Stainton (1985a), however, found that men also established relationships with their unborn infants and had identified infant characteristics and behaviors related to appearance, communication, gender, sleep/wake cycle, and temperament.

Two major psychological tasks have been suggested for both expectant fathers and mothers during early pregnancy: to distinguish between illness and pregnancy, and to shift patterns of dependence and nurturance (Deutscher, 1970; Grossman et al., 1980). Because of the less intimate involvement with the unborn baby and social and cultural directives, men could be expected to have different experiences during the anticipatory phase. However, the process that has been described by several researchers suggests that the process is similar, but the timing of the progression differs for men.

The Expectant Father

Deutscher (1981) observed that the man's personality boundaries are fluid during the 9 months of pregnancy. This more permeable boundary permits his experimentation with the future roles of the family with triangular relationships following birth by playing, both in his fantasy and his relationship with his wife, the parts of baby, mother, father, and competing sibling. Following childbirth, with the father's movement into the formal role as father, he establishes a relationship with his infant, and the infantile and narcissistic elements of pregnancy are transformed into a healthy paternal love (Deutscher, 1981).

May (1982) described three phases of men's increasing emotional and behavioral involvement during the pregnancy. The announcement phase, the period of suspecting and confirming pregnancy, brings either joy or conflict, depending on the man's readiness for the pregnancy. However, his involvement in the pregnancy is minimal at this point. The moratorium phase is the time of the man's adjustment to the reality of the pregnancy, and the length is influenced by his desire for the pregnancy. Typically men maintained emotional distance from the pregnancy that allowed them to work through their ambivalence about the pregnancy until about the 25th week of pregnancy. The focusing phase ends the "not real—not mine" quality of the moratorium. At this point the expectant father seems to enter into the role-play, fantasy, and introjection-projection-rejection stages described by Rubin (1967) for women as he begins to redefine himself and his world in terms of the father role. May described men's use of their own fathers as role models; many changed their friends to include those who either had or were expecting children. May's proposed trajectory for fathers is not too different from the phases that Gloger-Tippelt (1983) projected for mothers during the course of pregnancy:

1. A disruption phase, which begins at conception and extends to about 12 weeks, in which the woman faces radical change on all levels. This seems to correspond with the May's announcement phase. Randell (1988) also observed the announcement phase among first-time expectant mothers who were 30 and older, in which great lengths were gone to for verifying and making known the pregnancy.
2. An adaptation phase, from 12 to 20 weeks; this seems to parallel May's moratorium phase for men but proceeds much more rapidly for women.
3. A centering phase, from 20 to 32 weeks, which seems to encompass May's focusing period after the 25th week of pregnancy.
4. The anticipation and preparation phase, in which active preparation for the birth occurs from 32 weeks to birth; the men's focusing period seems to fit into this phase also.

A wide range of detachment-involvement during pregnancy was reported by May (1980) and included men who had observer, instrumental, and expressive styles. Observer styles were noted among 45% of the men, who remained somewhat aloof from the happenings of the pregnancy, although they were invested in the couple relationship. Observer-style fathers included both those who were unhappy about the pregnancy and needed some detachment to adapt and those who were happy but preferred a more passive involvement. Thirty-five percent of the men were expressive styles, caught up in the emotional impact of the pregnancy and viewing the emotional experience as reflecting their readiness to become fathers. Expressive-style fathers attempted to experience as much of the pregnancy as possible. Only 20% of the fathers were instrumental styles who assumed the role as caretaker or manager and took great pride in carrying out the traditional role as husband and father. All of the instrumental-style fathers were of an ethnic minority and represented a midpoint in the detachment-involvement continuum (May, 1980). The tremendous impact of culture on parenting roles must always be kept in mind when assessing parental role attainment.

Formal/Initial Adaptation Stage of Parental Role Attainment

The formal stage of parental role attainment begins with birth of the infant and continues for approximately 6 to 8 weeks. During this stage role behaviors are largely guided by others in the parents' social system—close family, health professionals, and social custom. The major task of this stage for parents is getting acquainted with their infants so that they can mesh their parenting activities with cues from the infant; Sander (1962) called this stage a period of initial adaptation.

Early parent-infant interactions lay a vital foundation for future relationships. The newborn infant's helpless appearance attracts adults, and the infant's emotional expressions, especially of contentment, satisfy an important need of parents (Emde, 1980). The months of expectation during pregnancy culminate in an "emotional high" following birth as parents inspect and claim their infant. Greenberg and Morris (1974) chose the term, "engrossment," to describe fathers' early feelings toward their infants that were associated with increased self-esteem. Most parents, especially those who have been actively interacting with the unborn infant, are emotionally and cognitively ready at birth to begin active identification of their infant as a unique individual. In claiming their infant as part of the family, the infants' features that are like and unlike other family members are noted.

This critical period of parents meshing their parenting to their infants' cues and needs includes the *physical recovery phase* of maternal adaptation, observed by Mercer (1986a). Although much parental adaptation is at the psychological and social levels during the formal stage of parental role attainment, the physical or biological level plays a large role during the first month of adaptation, when sleep deprivation and fatigue are prevalent in both parents and the mother recuperates from childbirth. The social support network recognizes the need for extra help during the early physical recovery phase, and family members or hired help are often enlisted. However, by the end of the first month, mothers' received support has decreased significantly (Mercer et al.,

1987). Fathers did not report the decrease in received help that mothers reported; however, they reported less received support initially. Men tend to rely largely on their mates for support (Antonucci, 1985). It is vital that early acquaintance and initial adaptation to the infant begin as soon after birth as possible, while the parents have the safe environment of the hospital and some physical help.

Sensitive Period

Early research suggested that the first few hours following birth were a sensitive period for the formation of parent-to-infant attachment (commonly called bonding) that had significant long-term effects; however, later work did not find this to be true (Campbell & Taylor, 1979; Curry, 1979; Lamb, 1982, 1983; Mercer, Hackley, & Bostrom, 1982; Mercer & Ferketich, 1990a; Williams et al., 1987).

First-time mothers who had interactional contact with their infants within the first 2 hours following birth ($n = 165$) did not differ significantly in their maternal role attainment index at 1 year following birth from mothers who did not have this contact ($n = 32$) (Mercer et al., 1982). The maternal role index was a factor weighted by observed maternal behavior, self-reported ways of handling irritating child behavior, gratification in the maternal role, infant growth, and maternal infant attachment. Williams and associates (1987) found that the amount of early mother-infant contact in the hospital was unrelated to other facets of parenthood at 2 years after birth, supporting their contention that while such experiences are relevant, they are but "a small fraction of the much longer span of the developing attachment relationship" (p. 253).

In another study of low-risk women, later contact with their infants following birth was associated with higher maternal attachment at 8 months following birth (Mercer & Ferketich, 1990a). Later contact following birth is usually associated with the need for medical examination and/or treatment of the infant, cesarean birth with the mother anesthetized, or some complication. This finding suggests a tendency for mothers to form a somewhat stronger tie when events around the birth raise a sense of vulnerability of the infant that precludes early interaction.

Research on father-infant interactions and attachment shows that there are more similarities than differences between fathers and mothers (Jones, 1985), although early research on father participation focused on quite different aspects of behavior, ranging from play activities only to taking sole responsibility for child care for a period of time (Cronenwett, 1982). Fathers are also anxious and have concerns as new

fathers. Fishbein (1984) found that when there was congruence between mother's and father's attitudes regarding the projected role of
the newborn, fathers experienced less stress.

Palkovitz (1985) reviewed research concerning fathers' birth attendance, early contact, and extended contact with newborn infants and
could not find any conclusive evidence regarding the effect of these
experiences on father involvement in infancy. Although lay persons
have strong beliefs about father-infant bonding (the development of
father-to-infant attachment early following birth), their beliefs are not
founded on reading scientific journals but from general knowledge
(Palkovitz, 1988). Thus many parents still attribute magical qualities to
the first few hours following birth for forming attachment, although
there is no scientific documentation to this effect.

Caldwell (1962) cautioned that it was dangerous to emphasize a
critical period for infant attachment because of individual differences;
her caution is also appropriate to apply to adult attachment. Dunn's
(1975) proposal that the postpartal period is a time of adjustment,
rather than a sensitive period, for the mother and infant when they are
buffered against difficulties inherent in the process is the philosophy
assumed here. Adults' cognitive and emotional capacity and resiliency
to respond positively under very trying circumstances make it impossible to delimit a specific period as a sensitive period for the formation
of attachment to their infants.

Whenever possible, it is important to provide the privacy and environment for parents to have special time with their infants following
birth. It is equally important to assure parents who are concerned about
having missed this special time that there is no evidence to support any
effect of this early separation on parent-infant attachment. Parental
love and interactions with their infant when they have the opportunity
lead to the same outcome experienced by those who have early interactions.

Parent-infant interactions during the first 6 to 8 weeks allow the
parent to assimilate expected parental role behaviors in relationship to
the unique infant, including the evolving attachment for the infant, and
to accommodate to a changing role. Events or circumstances may delay
the initiation of the attachment process, make the process more difficult, or prolong the process. Perhaps most importantly, supportive
persons in the parents' social network can provide positive sanctions to
new parents' early parenting attempts and facilitate parent-infant interactions by timely intervention. Supportive persons can provide a
safe environment to help parents and infants experience each other to
the optimal potential of each during the period of adaptation; in times
of crises health professionals have a major role in providing this sup-

port. In situations of a parent at risk, a lack of supportive help leaves a frightened person, who is often inexperienced in the role, to deal with much anxiety, depression, and exhaustion alone. Thus the pleasures of the early interactions are missed.

Early Parenting Tasks Following Birth

Early maternal postpartal tasks have been identified as including the mother's integrating her labor and delivery experience, resolving any loss of expectations about her pregnancy, childbirth or her infant, ascertaining the normalcy of her infant, developing caretaking skills, and redefining her roles (Mercer, 1981b). Rubin (1984) emphasized that the mother's identification of the child establishes her identity in relation to the child.

The mother's cognitive behavior in conceptualizing her newborn varies in focus by culture. Chao (1979) identified three distinct yet complementary cognitive operations among mothers who were identifying their infants in the United States: orienting, evaluating, and delineating. Orienting behaviors were the mother's attempts to verify thoughts or expectations about her newborn infant. Evaluating behaviors were the mothers' value judgments after searching for the accuracy of her expectations for the infant. Delineating behaviors were the mother's comparisons of the actual infant with her mental ideal of the infant. When Chao (1983) replicated that study among Chinese mothers, she found no differences between cultures in women's orientation behaviors, but American mothers used evaluating and delineating behavior more frequently. Chinese and American mothers were similar in their focus on the infant's appearance and social characteristics; however, both focused more on the infant's body function than other aspects, with American mothers focusing on body function and physical state more frequently than Chinese mothers. Chinese mothers also made fewer comments in their encounters with their infants, suggesting another cultural difference. Orienting behaviors were at a peak on the first day following birth among both groups of women, evaluating behaviors peaked on the third day, and delineating behaviors peaked on the fourth day after birth.

A study of attachment behavior among Egyptian mothers also found some cultural similarities to and differences from that reported for American mothers (Govaerts & Patino, 1983). Govaerts and Patino observed that in contrast to Klaus and associates' (1970) observations of a progression from fingertip to palmar touch within 10 minutes, Egyptian mothers used largely fingertip touch with very little palmar contact. This is congruent with Rubin's (1963) observations of the progression of maternal touch from exploratory fingertip touch initially, to the third day or so when she uses her palms comfortably in holding the infant. Other explanations may account for differences in touch; in 1963 women were more heavily medicated during labor and more drowsy following birth. Klaus and associate's subjects viewed their naked infants under a heat lamp, while Govaerts and Patino reported that the hospital temperature was cool, and the infants were dressed. Egyptian mothers' most frequent comments were concerns about the baby and feeding; comments centered second on physical characteristics, and third on assimilation of the baby into the family. Govaerts and Patino attributed the emphasis on the family to the centrality of the Egyptian family as the origin of the mother's value system, social acceptance, personal honor, and dignity.

Competence in feeding the infant is a consistent concern in the studies of early mother-infant interaction. Walker, Crain, and Thompson (1986a) found that for primiparas, self-confidence in mothering was associated with maternal feeding behavior, but for multiparas only their feelings about themselves were associated with maternal behavior. These researchers also found that mothers' attitudes about themselves became more positive at 4 to 6 weeks after birth (Walker, Crain, & Thompson, 1986b). Mercer (1986a) found that maternal infant attachment was predicted at 1 month largely by child-rearing attitudes (12.6%), infant-related stress (8.7%), positive life events (3.6%), and self-concept (1.6%) among first-time mothers. Observed maternal behavior was predicted by race, education, and marital status (6.9%), perception of the birth experience (6.6%), easy infant temperament (3.6%), infant health (3.3%), child-rearing attitudes (2.9%), self-concept (2.1%) and physical help from mate (1.8%).

Most mothers (85%) reported from a moderate amount to a great deal of father involvement in the care of their infants during the first month (Mercer, 1986a). Fathers performed the full range of care activities, with 83% playing with their infants, 78% feeding, 42% bathing, and 37% soothing or comforting.

Grossman et al. (1980) identified fathers' tasks during the first year of fatherhood: to view self as a father and feel competent and comfortable with that view (paternal role attainment); to balance family needs with personal needs; to be involved in, yet maintain perspective on, the intense, anxiety-arousing period of his child's infancy; to help his wife minimize her anxieties and prevent her from becoming excessively consumed by the early mother-infant bond; and to develop a relationship with the new infant. Deutscher (1970) saw a major task of the father as the *rescue function*, in which the father uses his separateness from the experience to help his wife gain distance and reduce her anxieties about mothering.

Informal Stage of Parental Role Acquisition

The informal stage of role acquisition begins after the parents have successfully learned appropriate responses to their infant's cues, and they begin to respond according to the uniqueness of their transactions and family system as opposed to following textbooks' or health professionals' directives. Sander (1962) calls the time from 2½ to 5 months one of the most pleasureable of the parenting stages; this is the period of reciprocal exchange with much interactional emotion and play with the child. This period was called the achievement phase of maternal role attainment (Mercer, 1986a), extending to 4 or 5 months after birth. The achievement phase was characterized by the mother's sense of accomplishment; she feels highly competent in caring for her infant during this period. On the biological level, she has recuperated from childbirth. The infant has usually settled into a predictable schedule, and the infant's spontaneous laughs and vocalizations offer valued and pleasureable feedback.

Maternal infant attachment was predicted at 4 months among first-time mothers by infant-related stress (13.4%), child-rearing attitudes (4.8%), infant persistence (3.6%), empathy (2.7%), early mother-infant separation (1.3%), self-concept (1.2%), and informational support (1%) (Mercer, 1986a). Observed maternal behavior was predicted by race, education, and marital status (13.9%), child-rearing attitudes (8%), self-concept (4.9%) infant-related stress (1.5%), infant rhythmicity (1.1%), maternal health (0.8%), and maternal adaptability (0.8%).

The Personal Level of Parental Role Acquisition: Maternal or Paternal Role Attainment

The parental role is achieved when the parent feels a sense of harmony in the role, enjoys the infant, sees the infant as a central person in his or her life, and has internalized the parental role. The range of time for achieving the parental role is highly variable. Among 294 first-time mothers, 4% felt they had achieved the role during pregnancy. At the end of the first 2 weeks, one-third felt they had achieved the maternal role; by 2 months, 50% had achieved the role; by 4 months, 64%; by 9 months, 85%, with 4% saying they had not achieved the role at 1 year (Mercer, 1986a).

Sander (1962) described two periods of mother-child adaptation that may overlap the personal stage of parental role attainment or internalization of the role: the period of early directed activity by the infant from 5 to 9 months, and the period of infant concentration on the mother from 9 to 15 months. The mother's keenness in reading cues is important as the infant becomes more active in initiating mother-infant interactions. In the period of concentration on the mother, the child's initiative is extended to be able to manipulate the mother to some extent. Sander suggested that this latter period "separates the women from the girls," (i.e., mothers whose identity as a mother is secure from those who are only partially committed). Fear of strangers is strong during this time, and although the infant may cling, the mother must be secure enough and have confidence in the ultimate separateness of her child to be able to enjoy and yield to this possession.

Mercer (1986a) observed a disruption phase in maternal role behavior that had peaked around 8 months after birth that apparently is associated with the physical level of adaptation of the changing infant-mother interactions described by Sander. Many changes at the social level of adaptation were also observed as role strain in balancing career, wife, and mother roles occurred. At the psychological level, a discontinuity in the level of caretaking skills required challenged the woman's feelings of competence as a mother. A process that was termed "maternal individuation" was also observed at 8 months as mothers needed to limit the demands of their infants and focus on regaining their identities apart from the mother role. By 1 year, a reorganization phase was observed. For some, maternal individuation was not complete at this time, but the process was well under way. Rubin (1984) described the same process:

> The maternal identity is achieved and stabilized in some mangificent programmatic ordering even before self as a person and a woman, her own full identity of self in the world, is achieved. That sense of identity, when she feels like herself again, is achieved when her body image in action in the world is contiguous and consistent with her self-concept, about eight or nine months after childbirth (p. 127).

Integrating the parent role with other roles is not always easy and may lead to role conflict and role strain. Higher levels of role strain have been associated with poor health, lack of emotional support from family, lower levels of marital satisfaction, lack of husband agreement with wife's choice of roles other than mother, and dissatisfaction with child care if employed (Van Meter & Agronow, 1982). Role conflict did not differ between mothers who were employed and those who were unemployed, but mothers with careers (long term commitment to) reported more conflict than mothers with jobs (short-term employment); mothers with greater role conflict, irrespective of their employment status, experienced greater difficulty in making the transition to the maternal role (Majewski, 1986).

SUMMARY

The period during and following birth is an important screening period with great potential impact for parents and their children. The health professional's contact with parents during the postpartal period is usually more intensive and extensive than it was during pregnancy or will be again until the birth of another child. Identifying parents at risk during this early period and providing additional supportive help with intensive follow-up can help parents adjust to a new role in a healthy manner as individuals and as a family unit. For improved quality and length of life of all children, it is important that supportive care and diligent follow-up for all parents at risk be provided.

Acquisition of the parental role can be expected to proceed over the course of the first year in a predictable order. While the adaptation required by parents at the physical, social, and psychological levels may appear overwhelming, their resiliency and motivation for parenting can overcome great handicaps.

The health professional works with parents who have had quite different life experiences and cultural shaping that affect their adaptation to crisis situations and their relationships with their child. Parenting practices, such as the amount and kind of parent-infant contact and who cares for the infant at various stages, differ by culture. Parents-to-be learn these practices as a child in their original nuclear family unit. Although parents may alter the cultural prescription somewhat on assuming the parental role, their parenting largely follows that practiced in the particular culture of which they are a part. Each parent's personal resources in relation to her or his child must be assessed in relationship to unique life experiences and environmental circumstances in order to plan meaningful intervention.

3

Individual and Family Adaptation to Threat or Loss

All parents at risk experience greater stress than that that usually accompanies the birth of a child. Varying degrees of loss are experienced, whether the loss is the expected child, an expected outcome for the childbearing experience, or an expected experience in early parenting. The physical or environmental context in which these crises occur may exacerbate or diminish their effect on the individual and the family. However, individual and family adaptation to threat, loss, or crisis situations usually follows a predictable pattern.

Concepts relative to levels of stress and individual defenses that are commonly used are discussed in this chapter to provide a basis for understanding parental response to threat and loss. A discussion of the person's cognitive mastery of a stressful situation, the social environment, and the grief process are included to increase awareness of the constraints and contributions of the cultural and social environment in adaptation to stressful events. A discussion of family adaptation to loss or crisis concludes the chapter.

DEFINITION OF TERMS COMMONLY USED

Several terms are often used interchangeably in referring to concepts of loss, crisis, stress, and how the individual deals with these situations in achieving personal equilibrium and adaptation. For clarification, the terms most commonly used in the discussion that follows are defined.

Crisis refers to an unsettling or threatening event that creates disequilibrium. The unsettling or threatening event is different from previous life experiences and calls for adaptive responses that require the person to examine new ways of dealing with change. Crises are either situational or maturational. Situational crises include a premature birth, birth of an infant with a handicap, or a threat to the infant's or mother's health. Maturational crises include the usual adaptation and work in attaining a parental role; in situations of becoming a parent prematurely or opting for parenthood within a nontraditional family structure, unique stressors arise.

Adaptation to a crisis can lead to increased ability to cope and adapt through psychological and environmental readjustment. Caplan and Grunebaum (1967) caution that the resolution of crises may be postponed, maladaptive, or lead to ill health. Intervention at times of crisis is aimed at helping the individual and family cope and at modifying environmental factors when possible.

Loss is defined as the deprivation of a valued person, object, or wished-for outcome. A valued person, object, or wish that is lost is relinquished emotionally through a grief process. No one gives up someone or something of value willingly, and a healthy adaptation to such loss requires personal protest through grief work, followed by a reorganization of one's life with new goals.

Threat is defined as any event or series of events that places a desired or valued person or outcome in jeopardy, thus creating disequilibrium for the individual. For example, premature labor poses a very real threat for the unborn baby.

Stress is the person's response to a stressor—loss, threat, or other crisis—that pervades the person's total being. Stress refers to the total psychological and physiological self-response to parental loss or threat inherent in the crises of childbearing and early child rearing. This definition is based on Selye's (1982) definition of stress as the body's nonspecific response to demands.

Anxiety and depression are common emotional states or distress responses to a stressor. Spielberger and associates (1983) distinguished between trait and state anxiety; *trait anxiety* is the person's proneness to perceive stress situations as dangerous or threatening. *State anxiety* is a response to a specific situation, and as such is more transitory but relates to the person's trait response. Anxiety is characterized by feelings of apprehension, nervousness, and uneasiness; along with these feelings, the person may feel a sense of helplessness, a sense of isolation or alienation, a sense of insecurity, or a threat to identity. The level of anxiety reflects tension created by reduced cognitive ability to organize, structure, or assign meaning to an event (Lazarus & Folkman, 1984). *Depression* is the affective component of depressed mood or lowered spirits from within the person characterized by a group of depressive symptoms clustered around affect (feeling sad or lonely), altered somatic and other activity (difficulty sleeping, eating), and altered interpersonal relationships (Radloff, 1977).

Coping and defenses are commonly used interchangeably, although they are quite different. *Coping* is used here in the sense that Murphy (1962) spoke of coping. Coping involves active cognitive work in choosing among alternatives for resolving and adapting to a crisis event. The person's choice includes use of all previous learnings that are necessary to master a particular problem (Murphy, 1962). *Defense mechanisms* are usually a part of the person's overall coping; however, defenses are not consciously chosen. Defense mechanisms are unconscious responses developed early in life that the ego utilizes to defend itself. Defenses are derived from the past and are rigid and inflexible. Conversely, the choice inherent in coping allows the person much flexibility and openness in planning for the future. The greater the threat to an individual, the more strongly the ego must defend against the conflict.

The *ego* is the mental construct that coordinates the unconscious drives and defenses that demand immediate gratification, the individual's conscience or ideal that represents a goal to be reached, and the constraints and demands of the social and environmental forces. This coordination within the self must be done at the least cost to self to provide the greater satisfaction for self and yet be acceptable to society.

CRISIS THEORY AND CLINICAL PRACTICE

The state of crisis has certain characteristics that form a theoretical basis for health professionals' clinical practice. A crisis is self-limited in that it does not continue indefinitely, with some solution usually found within 6 weeks (Caplan, quoted by Rapoport, 1965). A crisis state has characteristic phases—a beginning, middle, and end. The grief process is an example of phases of a crisis. The onset of crisis is characterized by a period of disorganization, then a recovery phase, followed by reorganization (Hill, 1965). A person's level of reorganization may be lower, the same, or higher than it was before the crisis; thus there is an opportunity for personal growth with a crisis, just as there is opportunity for setback.

A Parent's Receptiveness to Intervention

The major goal of crisis intervention for vulnerable parents is to help the parent regain at least the same level of functioning that was evident before the crisis. The health professional's goal is not aimed at major personality change but at using the crisis situation for potential growth and helping the parent achieve a comfortable adaptation to the crisis.

Three principles of crisis theory speak to the parent's openness to the health professional's intervention at the time of crisis. First the outcome is not determined by earlier factors, although earlier factors do have their impact. It is the combination of external factors in the situation (supportive intervention) and internal factors (established defenses and previous coping, ego strength) that play a larger role in the outcome (Baldwin, 1978). Well-timed intervention based on the parent's special needs has the potential to lend ego strength and influence the outcome positively.

A second principle of crisis theory is that persons experiencing a crisis are more open to receiving help; they are motivated to seek help and/or health care. The third principle is that outside help does not have to be extensive. Focused help at the time of receptivity during a crisis may be much more effective than much more extensive help given at a time when the person is less open (Rapoport, 1965).

The health professional directs assessment for crisis intervention toward the stressful situation and the environmental circumstances, the parent's response to the situation, and the level of coping. In crises due to traumatic stress, the refractory period (time from impact of the stressor to mobilization of coping behaviors) is maximized such that the person experiences a period of shock and immobilization (Baldwin, 1978). Maladaptive coping processes may be learned during this refractory period (e.g., the parent may indulge in alcohol as a means of escape). The health professional may use a generic approach to crisis intervention, considering that predictable patterns of response to crisis have been identified; however, the uniqueness of the parent's characteristics and differences in the supporting environment and the infant require special attention.

ASSESSING RESPONSES TO THREAT OR LOSS

Understanding a person's responses to stress serves a twofold purpose. Awareness of the process in adaptation to crises fosters self-awareness in dealing with threat or loss, in addition to understanding the parents' methods. By understanding and recognizing the level of stress a parent is experiencing, the health professional can accept parents' aggressive, threatening behavior as a healthy reaction rather than as a personal attack.

LEVELS OF STRESS

The greater the threat, the greater the stress under which a person is operating. The point at which the health professional can respond to parents' cues is dependent on the professional's level of stress in dealing with the parents' crisis situation. At greater levels of stress, the ego reverts to lower levels of development in a desperate effort to reach stability.

Some of the normal tension-relieving regulatory devices utilized by the ego in minor stresses of everyday life include touch, rhythm, soft voice, effort to gain approval or love through human contact, proud self-discipline, laughing it off or crying it out, falling asleep, talking it out, thinking, muscular activity, fantasizing, dreaming, swearing, slips of the tongue, reaction formation, and somatic responses such as frequent urination, defecation, eating, smoking, or drinking (Menninger, 1954a). Depending on the parents' or the health professional's usual tension-relieving behavior, the reaction to threat or stress may include any of the above means. The health professional often uses proud self-discipline, talking it out, and increased activity. The mother under stress may cry, fantasize, or need to urinate every 30 minutes. The regulating interactive process between mother and health professional may result in increased stress for both. Increased activity on the part of health professional (usually the nurse in the in-hospital situation) unconsciously takes the nurse away from the mother who may need touch or a soft voice as a tension-reducing mechanism.

When usual normal tension-relieving behaviors fail to relieve stress and achieve personal stability, the ego resorts to more radical means of gaining equilibrium. As the stress increases, so does the pain experienced by the person and the energy spent by the ego in efforts to regain control.

The description and discussion of the five levels of ego response to increasingly demanding stress are derived from Menniger (1954b). The *first level of ego responses* are hyperfunctions or exaggerations of usual ego functioning, yet they are uncomfortable and unpleasant for the person. Thus first level ego responses reduce a person's efficiency, pleasure, and energy. When the stressful situation disappears, the ego's defenses are no longer needed or used. If the stress persists or becomes intensified, a *second level of ego defense* may become evident; this includes some detachment from reality. There is a partial withdrawal or partial distortion of reality. The parent may faint, have amnesia about a particular event, or may distort the health professional's explanation of the event.

The *third level of ego defense* is characterized by disorganized explosive outbursts of aggression; there is a brief loss of control of the ego. We see such brief loss of control in laboring women, who when experiencing the severe pain of transition, may strike out at anyone standing nearby. The loss of control is always humiliating for an adult to deal with, but the ego may stabilize quickly, with or without ill effects. If, however, the ego has been exhausted or severely damaged, a further retreat or detachment from reality may occur. When a total loss of reality or reality testing occurs, disorganization of a high degree is obvious. The threat, pain, fear, guilt, and frustrations facing the ego can be dealt with only by denial and fantasized destruction of parts or all of the real world at the *fourth level of ego response*. Although equilibrium is restored at an extremely low functional level by such devices, the ego can still recover to normal functioning. The *fifth order of ego response* to stress is irreparable. Disorganization is such that it leads to self-destruction.

The ego constantly strives to recover former optimal functioning after handling emergencies. Minor stresses are usually handled by minor healthy devices. The greater and more prolonged the stress, the more extreme and less healthy are the ego's regulatory devices that require an escape, if only temporarily, from reality.

The person's response to stress indicates the level of hurt or pain and threat as well as the temporal dimension of the stress. Through the parent's behavioral responses, we can observe something of the magnitude of the stress and the lengths to which the ego must go to defend self to maintain equilibrium. Assessing coping styles, resources, and methods of defense used by the ego provides a basis for further intervention.

COPING

Coping is the parents' attempt to prevent, avoid, or control their emotional distress as they resolve crisis situations. Coping resources are not what people do but what is available in their coping repertoires. Coping resources include social and psychological resources. Social resources include the family's interpersonal network—extended family, friends, fellow employees, neighbors, voluntary and governmental associations, and health professionals. Psychological resources include the personality characteristics that parents utilize to help ward off threats to their equilibrium. Some of the personality characteristics are self-esteem, sense of control or mastery, defenses, and temperament.

Pearlin and Schooler (1978) studied life strains and coping responses of persons aged 18 to 65 and found three major types of coping: (1) altering the stress situation (a parent cannot alter an infant's birth defect); (2) controlling the meaning of the stressful experience after the event but before the stress is experienced by either positive comparisons (my infant is not as bad off as the infant in the next isolette), by selective ignoring such as minimizing the infant's illness and maximizing a desirable quality of the infant, or by creating a strategy for making the suffering manageable (God is testing my worthiness as a parent); and (3) controlling the stress after the event has occurred, such as enlisting members from the support system.

The fewer coping responses and coping resources an individual has, the greater the probability that role strain, as in parenting, will result in emotional distress such as depression or anxiety. Pearlin and Schooler (1978) observed that women tended to use selective ignoring, which exacerbates stress. Age was not a factor in coping ability. Education and income, indicators of social status, were associated with self-esteem and mastery. Leifson (1980) reported that among parents who had infants with handicaps, the more education they had, the better they handled the crisis, but the greater difficulty they had with their social functioning. Older parents also had greater difficulty with the crisis. Overall, it seems that less educated and poorer persons who are exposed to more hardships have fewer resources to deal with stress as a result of those hardships.

DEFENSES

As discussed earlier, when a person is faced with an emotional crisis, both conscious and unconscious efforts are employed in the attempt to establish equilibrium. Defenses are unconsciously driven responses to threat that are established early in life. It is important for health professionals working with parents under great stress to realize that parents responding with defense mechanisms are neither deliberately or knowingly maintaining a defensive behavior. Rather, the person's ego is working hard to protect that person in a situation that threatens not only the parent's immediate life situation, but also life-long dreams and goals. Temporary use of defenses may be viewed as a healthy protest to a threatening situation. Overuse of defenses or prolonged use of a defense, such as denial, may misserve the person. When the health professional observes the first defense response, this is a signal that the parent is threatened and is experiencing anxiety.

Some of the defenses that are more commonly seen when parents are faced with loss or anxiety are denial, projection, reaction formation, rationalization, fantasy, displacement, sublimation, and intellectualization. Clinical examples are used to illustrate these commonly observed defensive behaviors.

In the use of *denial*, the person blocks or does not permit awareness of the situation as it is. This sometimes occurs only during the first few days following the stressful event. The inital use of denial serves the person as a delay that allows him or her to marshall resources or strength from within to handle the situation. It is as if the person knows what he or she can handle and reduces the stressful event into manageable doses. Just a little more information each day enables the person to cope and to remain in control. Adaptation often calls for delay, retreat, regrouping of forces, giving up untenable positions, seeking new information, and planning new strategies (White, 1974). We see parents who verbalize, "This can't happen to me. I can't believe it. It seems like a dream. I'll wake up and find that it isn't real." The parent may use denial by saying, "He's only a resident. What does he know about mongolism. I want an expert's advice." It seems that if the parent can deny that the diagnosis is real for a short time, he or she will have gathered enough information to organize his or her thinking and planning and to be able to accept reality. The partial denying, as it seems to be, permits a degree of hope that seems essential at the moment to serve as motivation for the parents to even try for a solution to the situation. Dreams and goals cannot be reliquished immediately without seeing an acceptable substitute. It is important at this point that the health professional does not reinforce the parents' denial by avoiding discussing the infant's condition or by focusing on the miracles of modern medicine.

Intellectualization is an attempt to avoid the disturbing impact of an event through mastery of knowledge about the stressor. The parent who uses intellectualization seems to deny emotional reaction to the event and reads, researchers, and becomes physically and mentally involved acquiring information about the particular condition or mishap. A parent may go to the library and review all of the research or publications by the attending physician to determine the physician's competency. The parent reads all relevant facts, including therapeutic recommendations. This parent often presents a threat to the health professional by asking highly technical or unanswerable questions.

Rationalization is an attempt to justify the threat or event and seems to offer a small measure of comfort. However, the parent's line of thinking may be quite illogical. For example, the parent may say, "It is because we are so strong and have such faith in God that we were chosen to rear this special child."

In the use of *projection*, the parent defends against unconscious feelings of guilt or involvement in the event by projecting the blame for the child's condition on someone else. "The nurse did not pick up the irregular heart tones soon enough," or "The doctor should have responded sooner." In the event of a severely malformed child whom the parent wishes would die, the parent may say, "You aren't doing everything you could do." Actually, the parent is unconsciously feeling he or she didn't do everything that could have been done.

In *reaction formation*, we see a parent doing the opposite of what he or she really wishes to do. The parent really longs for the severely handicapped child's death but does everything possible to protect the child from harm, even depriving other family members from providing care. Some of the parent's care responses may be noticeably rough and harsh.

Both fantasy and sublimation seem to be useful delaying tactics for parents in channeling information until they have achieved internal control of their feelings. *Fantasy* is an escape, however temporary, from reality. It usually suggests a desired flight from the stressor. Fantasies may be expressed as daydreams or as wishes. "I was thinking how wonderful it would be if I could have a special nursery with nurses to care for the baby, to protect him from visitors, and keep him away from everything." This fantasy suggests a possible solution that would also protect the parent from the social stigma of having had a malformed infant and from having to care for the baby. It is a preliminary problem-solving device. The parent is dealing with, "How am I going to care for this baby?"

Parents who use *sublimation* as a defense achieve gratification by channeling hostile feelings into an acceptable mode of expression. This defense is illustrated by the parent who begins a parents' group or a special fund drive for children with a similar handicap to that of his or her child.

Displacement may cause the greatest difficulty of all defenses within the family unit. Displacement usually is demonstrated by expressing disappointed, angry feelings about the ill baby or other stressful event to the partner. The baby's faults become the partner's faults and these are dwelt on. Thus the person who could be the major source of support is attacked.

In working with the parent at risk, a major concern is at what point do we access that defenses are no longer helpful to the parent and that psychotherapeutic intervention is needed? Persistent, affective states such as anger, guilt, or depression that do not show signs of subsiding, self-destructive acting out, or persistent denial warrant psychiatric intervention.

COGNITIVE MASTERY

An important strategy of adaptation is to secure adequate information about the threatening situation. The simultaneous management of adequate information, satisfactory internal control (of distress responses), and a degree of autonomy are major components of adaptive behavior (White, 1974). The discussion of the psychological strategies of adaptation deals with maintaining internal control as well as autonomy of choice involved in coping. All of these modalities of adaptation are intrapsychic, that is, they are occurring in the mind.

Whenever a threat occurs, the threat activates the ego to protect the status quo, depending of course on the person and on the person's social environment. But since part of the coping process involves choice about possible alternatives in dealing with the stressful situation, the person needs all of the available factual information surrounding or relevant to the threatening event. This is perhaps one of the areas of greatest omission by health professionals. Ignoring the parent's need for all factual knowledge, however painful, may be a grave error in situations in which parents must make plans for the immediate time and into the distant future. Because it is uncomfortable for anyone to discuss unpleasant situations and to experience the accompanying emotional responses, avoidance is frequently practiced.

Accurate information is crucial to parents for several reasons. Parents' defense of denial allows for their selective listening initially, and while factual information may have been given earlier, it may not have been heard. Health professionals, in an effort to dose the information, may inadvertently give misleading facts. This creates dissonance for the parents, who must then work harder at sorting out the truth.

The parent faced with a crisis situation may limit the informational input or may seek additional informational input according to his or her ability to handle the information. This must be respected. As the parent acquires information, however, the alternatives that arouse fear also seem to help arouse defenses and coping to function more effectively (Janis, 1982). The parent begins to worry about how he or she will manage. In "worry-work" the parent thinks about "what it will be like for me" after the infant's discharge from the hospital and a difficult feeding problem arises. If the parent, through "worry-work" and obtaining factual information, anticipates the process, then the situation is not entirely foreign when it occurs. The parent has mentally practiced for the exercise of managing a child who is a difficult feeder.

Planning for the future was the greatest cognitive activity of mothers who had babies with birth defects (Mercer, 1975). The parent has to continue to function as a member of the family unit and as a member of society and has to make decisions accordingly.

ENVIRONMENTAL OR SOCIAL CONTEXT OF ADAPTATION

Regardless of the parents' intrapsychic maintenance of equilibrium and choice of alternatives, their ability to adapt to the demands of life and, more specifically, to stresses occurring with parenting depends on their total life experiences in addition to innate biological capabilities. The individual is also a member of the family, which interacts with the larger social environment. The family and larger social environment define which events are disrupting or highly valued and methods for dealing with threats or crises in many cases. An infant is born as a member of an ethnic or minority group, into a family of poverty, or into a upwardly mobile middle class family. The social context of birth provides particular advantages and disadvantages, both in learning strategies for adaptation and in available support for adapting to threat or crisis.

Family Response to Crisis

Hill (1965) described the family as an interacting and transacting organization that, compared with other social organizations, is handicapped with dependents who cannot contribute equal work and decision making. Yet no other organizational system reflects such stresses and strains of life, because the family is the "bottleneck through which all troubles pass" (Hill, 1965, p. 34).

Families maintain boundaries (Kantor & Lehr, 1975) and exert control over the extent of its members' interaction with other social systems. As semi-closed systems (Rodgers, 1964), families must preserve the delicate balance of maintaining the integrity and identity of the family by not being too open to systems and influences outside the family, while permitting the necessary interaction of its members with the larger world (Leavitt, 1982). The family provides stability for its members as it adapts to change through maintaining continuity over time; part of the stability provided is through the familiarity and love of its members, such that trust, caring, and predictability of relationships within the family are evident (Leavitt, 1982).

The personal characteristics of each family member interact to influence the family system, and the family system as a whole in turn affects each person's development. Thus the family's response to crisis is affected by each family member. Leavitt (1982) described four phases of family responses to crisis: impact, disorganization, recovery, and reorganization. In the impact phase, the family may use defenses used by the individual; all family members may cooperate in maintaining a defense such as denial. During the disorganization phase, an increase in family tension, conflict, helplessness, anxiety, and depression is evident. In the recovery phase, the family has marshalled interim coping patterns and has begun to find meaning in the crisis; in the reorganization phase, the family has come to terms with and is adapting to the crisis event.

Families experience hardships in at-risk situations. For example, in the situation of having a chronically ill child, the stress leads to strained family relationships, modifications in family activities and goals, increased chores and time commitments, financial burdens, adaptation of the home environment, social isolation, medical concerns, and grieving (Patterson & McCubbin, 1983).

Several characteristics have been identified to facilitate the assessment of functional versus dysfunctional families during stress. Functional families are able to identify the stressor and to view the stressor as a family problem rather than as an individual's problem (Figley, 1983). Families who cope best with crises have better communication patterns and greater emotional support within and outside the family (Riddle, 1973). The functional family is highly cohesive and able to derive a solution to the crisis through flexibility of its members and use of resources both within and outside the family (Figley, 1983; Riddle, 1973). Turning to overt or covert abuse of one or more of its members and/or to indulgence in substance abuse characterizes a dysfunctional family.

Health professionals must gain a family's trust before intervention can be accepted or effective. Families are often afraid that the health professional's intervention will interfere with family values and practices or that the health professional's enlistment of community agency support will lead to loss of parental control.

Cultural Heritage

Culture is defined as a total way of life that is learned and passed on from generation to generation. Except for children of new immigrants, a person's cultural heritage is expressed in the particular social environment of birth. Within the family unit, rules for behavior and appropriate responses to situations are learned from birth. When working with parents at risk, knowledge of the parents' cultural and social background is important. For example, the grief process is handled differently from culture to culture. Furthermore, among different ethnic groups there are varying degrees to which individuals cling to cultural beliefs or incorporate the cultural beliefs of the health agency or from the area in which they live. Health professionals of a different ethnic group may be viewed as racists who lack understanding of the parent's ethnic group. The scope of this book does not permit discussion of the multiple cultural expressions of the many diverse ethnic groups, but the emphasis is that it is important to become acquainted with the parents' cultural and social background. If intervention is not to be viewed as interference, it must be consistent with the family's values and goals.

For example, if a mother's cultural beliefs prohibit specific foods during the postpartal period, it creates problems for the mother to be urged to eat those recommended foods. If the health professional learns which foods are culturally acceptable, counseling can be planned to see that essential nutrients are obtained from foods the family tradition approves of. The mother will appreciate the respect for her customs and will then be more closely attuned to other suggestions that may be offered in other areas.

The fit between the social structure of which the person is a part and the environmental demands placed on the parent helps determine the success of the parent's adaptation (Mechanic, 1974). This lack of fit is perhaps why many minority groups have difficulty adapting to stressors in the health care system. The cultural background in the ghetto has not provided the rules and directions for functioning in large inner city health centers. Yet the minority parent may have a large support system that another parent lacks. Motivation for solving a situational problem is learned from cultural values and incentives that are part of the person's larger social structure. The personal and family adaptation to threat or loss are dependent on the individual's and the family's ability to deal with the environmental demands, their motivation to do so, and their capability of maintaining a state of equilibirium. Support systems may be critical in determining whether an adaptive outcome occurs.

The impact of the social context was demonstrated in a study of mothers who had an infant with a birth defect (Mercer, 1975). The mothers' directed more energy toward determining social acceptance and support for themselves, as mothers who had delivered a defective child, and for their child than toward emotional or cognitive responses. A person's self-esteem and self-image are socially derived. It is through the interaction with other people that a self-image is developed. Although some cultures value facial disfigurement and have special ceremonies to scar the face, in the United States every effort is made to remove the slightest flaw, and much money is spent for orthodontic work to assure straight, beautiful teeth. These contrasts dramatize that what is valued by one culture may be rejected by another; likewise, an event that is a stressor for one culture may not be so for another. For example, the white, urban United States–reared mother who has had a stillbirth is usually quite fearful that something will go wrong with her next pregnancy and that she may have another stillbirth. The Hispanic woman who believes that her stillbirth was due to her being outside during an eclipse of the moon may be free of worry about a stillbirth with the next pregnancy, as long as she avoids going outside during a lunar eclipse.

In some cultures, when a man dies, one of his brothers cares for the bereaved wife as his own. Widows in England and the United States have reported both stigma and deprivation as a result of widowhood; persons who were warm and friendly prior to their husband's death reacted with embarrassment and discomfort to them after the husband's death, and they were deprived of financial security provided by the husband as well as social activity (Parkes, 1972). The widow in the culture that dictates that the brother-in-law take her as wife does not face such stigma.

Goffman (1963) described stigma as any situation that deprives a person of full social acceptance. Because of cultural beliefs, many of the situations that parents at risk face present social stigma for the parents in addition to the acute crisis or stress of parenting. For example, there are those who believe an infant's deformity represents a sin by the parents. If the social support system views the parent as unacceptable, any threat is even more ominous, and the parent's adaptation is much more difficult.

GRIEF PROCESS

Freud (1937) was one of the first persons to describe the grief process as a normal, adaptive process with characteristic behaviors that under other circumstances would reflect pathology. He described the grief process as a painful, reluctant withdrawal of attachment from a lost object or an abstraction of any object by which each memory and hope that binds the person to the lost object is remembered. By careful review of all interactions with the lost object, the deep emotional ties are relived in memory and consequently freed for new attachments.

Asch (1968) postulated that all new mothers experience grief and depression because of three emotionally significant losses: the pregnancy state; the feelings and fantasies associated with the image of the unborn infant; and the fantasies of old mother-child relationships in the role of the mother-that-was (infant or child) and new mother-child relationships in the role of the mother-that-is. Women who have enjoyed the pregnant state will sometimes comment that they miss the baby's movements or the extra attention that their pregnant condition commanded. The careful identification with which a woman claims her infant as a new family member reflects that the infant is quite different from her fantasy of the infant-to-be. Part of the careful, tedious identification process may be an active resolution of the mother's loss as she deals with the dissonance between her fantasy and the infant in reality. All women realize that in the transition to motherhood they have forever relinquished the state of nonmother. This is an inescapable transition; once a mother, she is a mother until she dies.

Grief is a universal phenomenon; everyone at some point in life is faced with a loss. The grief process follows a definitive pattern described by Lindemann (1944). Initial somatic distress characterized by tightness in the throat, shortness of breath, sighing, empty feelings in the abdomen, muscular weakness, tension, and mental pain occur. Insomnia and loss of appetite follow. The person is preoccupied with the loss and is angry that the loss has occurred; hostility may be directed toward others. The grieving person is disorganized and frustrated in the usual pattern of daily living.

The acute grief process was reported to resolve within a 4- to 6-week period (Lindemann, 1944). Others have proposed that the process is resolved insofar as distress symptoms are not present within a year or two (Mawson et al., 1981). However, follow-up of families 7 to 9 years after the death of a child with cancer found that they still experienced pain and loss and continued to feel an empty space left by their deceased child (McClowry et al., 1987).

Four phases of grief work are evident based on the work of Freud (1937), Bowlby (1960, 1969), and Parkes (1970, 1972): (1) numbness or shock; (2) protest and yearning; (3) disorganization; and (4) reorganization. The initial response to loss reflects a stunned reaction or disbelief that the crisis event has occurred. The protest and yearning phase is characterized by behaviors of revolt or anger against the loss and a painful longing for what is lost. The disorganization phase is portrayed by behaviors reflecting depression, chaos, and despair. Reorganization behaviors reflect a problem-solving action followed by realistic changes and plans in resolving the crisis event and formulating new goals or attachments.

Although the initial response in the grief process, numbness and shock, is time specific (occurring in 1 week or less), other phases overlap and occur simultaneously, with perhaps predominance of each phase in the order described above. Those who have worked with those in the grief process have all reported vacillation between phases.

SUMMARY

The strategies available to the parents who face threat or loss include their psychological and social resources, personality traits, cognitive mastery of the situation that enables them to make workable choices, and their capacities or skills in meeting environmental demands. The family in which the parent is a member provides both emotional and physical support as well as stability and continuity in dealing with crises. These strategies come from the parents' total life experiences in their cultural background, their innate biological capacities, and their learning from previous coping experiences.

The parents' social environment places constraints on their adaptive abilities from the view of rules that must be followed and from the resources it provides during the time of crisis. The person derives his or her total self-concept, as well as mental and physical nourishment, from interaction with others in the social system. If the crisis evokes a taint of stigma, as in situations of single or lesbian motherhood, the parent faces isolation from others at a time when she needs them most, which adds to the difficulty of dealing with the crisis.

When parents are faced with an event that poses a threat to their ego or the loss of something of value, they will respond with a repertoire of coping and defensive behaviors. However, initially the behavior will be disorganized, and the parent may experience somatic responses for a time. The level of stress that parents are experiencing is reflected in their observable behaviors. Supportive intervention during times of crisis aids the parent in achieving a healthy resolution of the problem and in possibly strengthening future coping capacities and abilities. Importantly, the increased receptivity of parents at times of crisis and their favorable response to small amounts of timely intervention, should encourage the health professional's motivation to intercede in behalf of parents at risk.

PART II
PARENTS WITH
A SPECIAL CHALLENGE

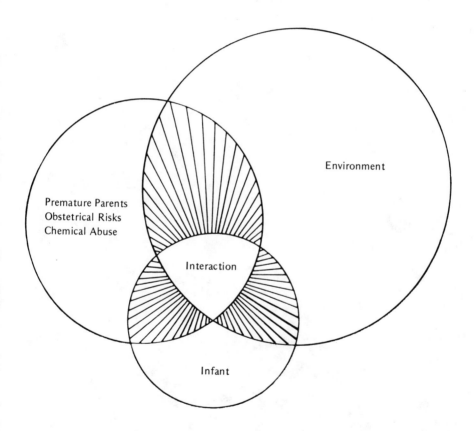

FIGURE 2.
Interactive model adapted from *Child Health Assessment Part 2: The First Year of Life*,
p. 132, by Kathryn E. Barnard and Sandra J. Eyres, DHEW Publication No.
HRA 79-25, Hyattsville, MD: U.S. Department of Health, Education, and
Welfare. Copyright 1979 by Kathryn E. Barnard. Reprinted with permission of
Kathryn E. Barnard.

4

When Parents Are Premature

Reaching the age of 20 does not automatically ensure emotional, social, psychological, and cognitive maturity. The stage of launching into adulthood ranges from ages 16 to 25 years, as young women achieve an identity and independence by breaking away from their families (Gould, 1972; Mercer et al., 1989). Adolescent development is best viewed in relationship to early adult development because of the continuity in the transition to adulthood. Although development proceeds from the simple to the more complex, from global thinking and responses to a higher level of differentiation and specificity (Werner, 1967), the progression is not linear. Rather, the person's evolving development and adaptability reflect an interaction of self with others in the environmental context that may be visualized as a spiral in which plateaus are reached before movement continues to a higher level of development (Kegan, 1982; Rubin, 1984).

Although the focus of this chapter is the teenage parent, concepts are applicable to older, yet immature persons. Becoming a mother verifies biological maturity. Cognitive maturity that is accompanied by an ability to conceptualize at an abstract level usually occurs around the time of biological maturity, but it may not. Some persons may never achieve a level of deductive reasoning and conceptualization indicative of mature thought processes. Emotional and social maturity, comfort with one's self and one's identity, come much later. Thus young parents represent a range of psychological readiness, emotional and social maturity, and cognitive abilities available for the task of parenting.

Characteristics of parents and their lifestyle, immaturity and the social handicaps that are inherent among youth that add to the difficulty of parenting, are the core of this chapter. Anticipatory guidance, support, and health care must be relevant to the person's level of

development if they are to be effective. Adolescents' responses in interaction with environmental situations and characteristics of their child
indicate the level of parenting ultimately achieved. Developmental
tasks of both adolescence and young adulthood are reviewed along with
stage differences of the early, middle, and late adolescent parent, the
impact of families on adolescent development and teenage parents, and
psychosocial handicaps of teenage parents. Guidelines for assessing the
adolescent's family, psychosocial development, and achievement of adolescent tasks are suggested; these assessments begin at first contact
with the young woman and continue over several sessions. Assessment
of the teenager's parenting over the first year following birth conclude
the chapter.

TASKS OF ADOLESCENCE AND YOUNG ADULTHOOD

The stereotype of adolescence is that it is a discrete phase of upheaval
that leads to a somewhat discontinuous, more quiescent adulthood. In
reality, there is a major carryover of the psychological work during
adolescence into adulthood of an integrated coping style and development of competencies, goals, and life choices (Newman, 1979). The
adolescent's ability and/or opportunity to experiment, encounter, and
deal with conflict forecasts the extent to which maturation occurs
through adulthood (Valliant, 1977).

Achievement Of A Stable Identity

The achievement of an identity, the development of an inner sameness
and continuity of the personality within a social network that recognizes this sameness and continuity is a major task of adolescence (Erikson, 1959). Only when adolescents can imagine themselves in a definite, reasonably attainable role that is acceptable to them and their
social environment do they feel they are unique as individuals. Achievement of a stable identity is not to be considered as an end point or
viewed as static; a stable view of self along with the flexibility to adapt
to new experiences are evidenced as a person's identity continues to
evolve and change direction over the life course (Bourne, 1978). Determinants of identity are the self concept—how a person sees self and
how the person perceives that others see and accept her- or his self.
   Marcia (1980) operationalized four identity statuses in an instrument
that includes questions about occupational choice, religious belief systems, political philosophies, and sex role preferences. When a person
has experienced a crisis and made a commitment to an occupation and

beliefs based on self evaluations, the individual is classified as *identity achievement* (e.g., the adolescent whose life's goal is motherhood decides to keep and rear her child). In the *moratorium status*, the youth is in the process of making formal commitments and values (e.g., the adolescent who is making decisions about her role as mother, student, and employee). *Foreclosure status* is characterized by the youth who did not encounter a crisis but adopted parental or other imposed commitments and values (e.g., the poor adolescent mother, trapped in a family with few options, with pregnancy viewed as an escape). In *identity diffusion* the youth has neither made a commitment nor experienced a crisis (e.g., the pregnant adolescent who refuses to discuss alternatives in her life and/or denies she has any problems).

High school or college students who are in the identity achievement status demonstrate greater ego strength than the other three status groups; they also persevere and perform better on stressful concepts (Marcia, 1980). Moratoriums are quite variable but closely resemble identity achievers. The foreclosed group have a strong commitment to obedience, strong leadership, and respect for authority; their self-esteem is the most vulnerable of all groups.

Rowe and Marcia (1980) emphasized that an identity did not have to be achieved to be functional for a person; a foreclosed identity may be the most adaptive solution in a society that rewards conferred over constructed identities. In such cases a foreclosed identity becomes dysfunctional only when a radical change occurs within a short time in the society or the person leaves that society for a different one.

Applying this concept to cultural groups in a society in which foreclosed identities are functional, what is the impact on youths who without cultural support and sanction undergo a crisis and achieve a self-chosen identity apart from their cultural group? How difficult is it for the adolescent from China, Viet Nam, or Mexico to achieve an identity in San Francisco, Detroit, or Boston?

Typical Behaviors Indicating Achievement of Identity

The ability to face and adapt to stress are good indicators of identity achievement. There is sufficient stability in the self-concept to weather ups and downs well. Exploring and seeking conflicting ideas and world views are essential components of adaptation of a coping style for adulthood. Disagreements with parents, teachers, or other authority figures are to be expected and foster development when there is an objective communication of views.

There is progress, maintenance of a status quo, and sometimes backsliding during the intensive work at sorting out and selecting goals for one's life. This is an expected ongoing process; these goals are reassessed at later developmental stages in adulthood.

Behaviors Indicating Difficulty With Identity Achievement

In dealing with frustrations of conflict and stress, the outcomes of problems with identity achievements are reflected in health problems and major illnesses. Heading the list of behaviors indicating difficulty with identity achievement are accidents, suicide, premature pregnancy and motherhood, and substance use and abuse.

A study of identity formation among a sample of pregnant and nonpregnant adolescents revealed developmental differences in Erikson's stages (Protinsky, Sporakowski, & Atkins, 1982). Pregnant adolescents scored significantly lower on the overall identity score and on three of five subscales, indicating earlier developmental deficiencies. Pregnant teenagers scored lower on the trust versus mistrust ego identity component, indicating that they had not acquired a sense of the time perspective; thus they had difficulty postponing immediate gratification in order to obtain a future goal. The subscale in which the greatest difference was found was in initiative versus guilt ego identity, first learned at preschool age, indicating that those adolescents who were not pregnant were more successful in role experimentation. Pregnant adolescents also scored lower on the industry versus inferiority ego identity, a school-age task, suggesting a sense of inadequacy about themselves and their abilities.

Adolescents experiencing identity confusion appear unable to find a direction in life or to define any goals, either educational or vocational. They may be avoiding making such long-term decisions out of fear or from psychosocial inability to explore and make decisions.

Acceptance and Achievement of Comfort With Body Image

The body image is a part of the person's total self-concept that is central to identity formation and is particularly important during both adolescence and pregnancy because of rapid changes in both instances. Acceptance and achievement of comfort with body image is accomplished through internalization of the mature body and increased physical size. Anyone who has lost 50 pounds will realize that a drastic change in body image takes time to adapt to; the tendency is to continue to look at size 16 instead of size 10 dresses or to allow extra space for navigating a larger body. The adolescent requires time to internalize added height, a curvier body, and larger breasts.

Dissatisfaction and preoccupation with body image changes are expected and normal. Good self-concepts are important for comfort with identity, however. Healey and DeBlassie (1974) observed that junior high school males had higher self-concepts than females. Spanish-American students had higher self-concepts than blacks who scored higher than Anglo whites, although differences were not significant. Others failed to find significant differences in self-concepts of Mexican Americans and non-Mexican American late adolescents (Frazier & DeBlassie, 1982).

Adolescents' general appearance reflects their feelings about themselves. Observations of the following indicate the adolescent's feelings about body image: cleanliness and grooming; clothes in good repair and coordinated according to the current style; erect posture; making eye contact as opposed to looking away; and hesitancy to undress for an examination. The health professional should query teens whether anything about their body worries them, since to be different means to be abnormal to an adolescent.

Acceptance of Sexuality and Adjustment To An Adult Sexual Role

In the acceptance of their sexuality and adjustment to an adult sexual role, adolescents must internalize stronger sexual urges and drives. In early adolescence, the adolescent is fond of and prefers same-gender peers, while toward the end of adolescence the majority become oriented toward the opposite gender. About 10% of the population is homosexual, and in late adolescence-early adulthood, some of those 10% are aware of the attraction toward same gender partners, but few have the self-comfort to accept the homosexual identity within the largely homophobic society until later in life. The oedipal conflict reemerges during adolescence (Blos, 1979). The adolescent usually resolves the accompanying feelings by identifying with the parent of the same gender, rejecting the opposite-gender parent as a love object, and seeking a safe heterosexual relationship with a peer.

Achievement of intimacy with others is central to this task. Intimacy refers to an ability to form relationships and commitments with others, along with an ethical code to stand by such commitments despite the possible need for compromises and self-sacrifices (Erikson, 1968). Depth of intimacy relates to the person's openness and closeness, respect, affection, loyalty, mutuality, capacity to accept and resolve differences, and maturity of sexual attitudes and behavior (Orlosky, 1976). Unless individuals accept and have a feeling for who they are, they cannot trust themselves to become intimate with another. Orlosky (1976) identified five intimacy statuses:

1. Intimate as reflected by the ability to form close relationships with both genders and involvement in a committed relationship with the opposite gender; the late-adolescent mother is often at this stage.
2. Preintimate status is similar to the intimate status, with the exception of the presence of an enduring heterosexual relationship.
3. Stereotyped relationships are reflected by inability to maintain more than superficial relationships with both genders and a tendency to exhibit little communication or closeness.
4. Pseudointimate persons have entered into a committed heterosexual love relationship but, as with their other relationships, it lacks closeness and depth; many adolescent mothers fall into this category.
5. Isolates withdraw from social situations and have only casual acquaintances without personal relationships. The adolescent mother who is an isolate may be a victim of sexual abuse in her home.

Although the adolescent strongly needs intimate relationships, intimacy is among the least precise of all impulses. Intimacy demands both honesty and authentic self-disclosure (Mitchell, 1976). Self-disclosure may be related to gender differences in intimacy with friends. Females in general disclose more than males when revealing general and personal information (Davidson, Balswick, & Halverson, 1980); males disclose more in revealing sexuality to parents and to peers. Females tend to score higher on intimacy, while males score higher on autonomy, initiative, and identity (Rosenthal, Gurney, & Moore, 1981).

Favorable resolution of the intimacy-isolation crisis is closely related to successful resolution of the identity crisis (Orlofsky, Marcia, & Lesser, 1973). Genuine intimacy generally occurs only after a reasonable sense of identity has been established.

Typical Behaviors Denoting Intimacy

The adolescent fears alienation from peers most of all. There is a struggle to learn to be open and honest in relationships, because the adolescent is critical of self.

The adolescent who is working successfully on intimacy is a joiner and is active in school activities, hobbies, and/or sports. By competing in sports activities, teamwork is learned along with respect for skill and sharing. Through group interactions, identification with a group member is more easily accomplished, and relationships can be established.

Behaviors Indicating Problems with Intimacy

The adolescent's confusion over sexual identity, which is strongly linked with ability for intimacy, may be quite painful. Compulsive experimentation or sexual acting out with both genders may occur.

The adolescent who is an isolate and remains withdrawn from others has not made any progress on the task of intimacy. The clinician may inquire about close friends of either gender and how committed the adolescent is to these relationships. If there are only casual conversations with school mates and no prolonged interactions with self-disclosure and personal commitment, the young person needs help in learning to like self so that fear of rejection in reaching out to others is diminished.

Does the young mother have a friend with whom she can talk about anything at all? Cavanaugh (1986) observed depression or anorexia among girls who did not have such an intimate friend.

Development of A Personal Value System

In the development of personal value system, the adolescent becomes aware and able to move from following rules to avoid punishment to considering the feelings and rights of others. Kohlberg's (1964) stages of moral development are linked with cognitive development. However, they are also controversial, because moral development differs from culture to culture and girls develop somewhat differently than boys in their emphasis on moral values (Gilligan, 1982). Briefly, Kohlberg projected three levels: premoral, or preconventional; role conformity, or conventional; and self-accepted moral principles, or postconventional.

Level I: Premoral or Preconventional

STAGE 1.   Punishment and Obedience Orientation

Action: Person obeys rules to avoid punishment.
"I'll use a condom because I don't want VD."

STAGE 2.   Naive Instrumental Hedonism

Action: Person conforms to obtain rewards, have favors returned.
"I'll use a condom, otherwise, Jane won't let me do it."

Level II: Role-Conformity or Conventional

STAGE 3.   Maintains Good Relationships for Others' Approval

Action: Conforms to avoid disapproval, to be liked.
"All the guys say that it doesn't feel good with a condom;

I won't use one because I don't want them to think I'm queer."

STAGE 4.   Authority Maintaining Morality

Action: Conforms to avoid censure by legitimate authorities, and resultant guilt.
I'll use a condom because my mom and dad would sure be upset if I got Jane pregnant."

Level III: Self-Accepted Moral Principals or Post-Conventional

STAGE 5.   Morality of Contract, Democratically Accepted Law, Individual Rights

Action: Conforms to maintain respect of impartial spectator.
"It isn't right to risk getting Jane pregnant; we'll discuss this and choose a contraceptive together."

STAGE 6.   Morality of Individual Principles of Conscience

Action: Conforms to avoid self-condemnation.
"It is unfair to exploit Jane's love for me. Since I don't feel the same about her, I won't have intercourse with her."

Discussion of teenage situations will help the health professional determine something about the level of the teenager's moral development. Examples of situations to discuss are:

John has been pressuring Jane to have intercourse. She is afraid she'll get pregnant, does not want to go on the pill, and really doesn't want to have intercourse. What should she tell John?

Judy, who is having intercourse with her boyfriend, tells Louise that it's fun, and as long as she doesn't get caught, there's nothing wrong. What would you tell Louise?

Judy got veneral warts after deciding to have intercourse. She had noticed the growths on her boyfriend but didn't know they were contagious until she went to the doctor. What should she say to her boyfriend the next time she sees him?

Janelle, a 17-year-old, decided her baby deserved a better home than what she could provide and put the baby up for adoption. What kinds of rights does a newborn baby have?

Mrs. Jones' 15-year-old daughter left some applicators of foam on her dresser. What should Mrs. Jones do about this?

Preparation For Productive Citizenship/Job/Career

Preparation for productive citizenship and career is closely related to achieving independence. Youths living in poverty have neither the encouragement or the means for lengthy preparation in this area. Several studies have indicated that the young woman trapped in a culture of poverty has motherhood as her adult goal. In their study of low-income adolescents and white, middle-class couples, Gabriel and McAnarney (1983) observed that the decision to become a parent was related to different subcultural values. Black adolescents, in contrast to white, middle-class adults, did not see marriage as a prerequisite for motherhood, nor did they view completion of schooling and economic independence as maturational phases that needed to precede mother-hood. Instead, these adolescents believed that becoming mothers would help them to achieve maturation and acceptance as adults. This finding may in part explain why teenage mothers reported higher gratification in the mothering role the first 8 months following birth (Mercer, 1985a, 1986a).

Gabriel and McAnarney stressed that the black adolescents may have conveyed this belief because they did not see other adult roles as available to them. Speraw (1987), who studied blacks, Hispanics, whites, and Pacific Asians, also reported that some adolescents (largely black and Hispanic) saw motherhood as the key to maturity and a brighter future. This would explain why health care programs are unsuccessful in promoting birth control, because the real needs of the adolescents, who see very few viable options in their lives, are not addressed. A negative identity by societal standards, such as an unmarried mother, is superior to no identity.

Areas to discuss to determine something about the young woman's goals for her life include:

Tell me about your classes at school that are really interesting to you.
Who can take care of your baby when you go back to school?
Are you able to attend school regularly?
What do you want to do as your life's work?
How did you decide about what you wanted to do?

Achievement of Independence From Parents

Adolescents, above all, seek to become competent in their social environment. As this competence is gained, the young person gradually becomes able to function independently of parental guidance. The young mother who is emancipated from family expectations and controls has selected a set of values that are meaningful for her personal goals.

The American culture's great emphasis on independence may tend to overshadow the adult's continued dependency needs, especially in times of life transitions. For example, in the transition to parenthood, the issue of dependency and intimacy and how these are handled are very relevant to the successful adaptation to parenthood. Conflict in the resolution of dependency issues with parents may make it more difficult for the young parent to permit dependency at phases of pregnancy and early parenthood when all adults also experience dependency.

It is essential that a balance in the adaptation to peer norms occurs in which the young adult is not antisocial, rebellious, or exclusively peer oriented. There is a great discrepancy in the steps involved of moving from a dependent child to an independent young adult by lower- and middle- or upper-class status, as well as from culture to culture. The adolescent who has a psychosocial moratorium for moving toward independence does not exist as a reality in most of the world. In underdeveloped countries, 13-year-olds are helping to support the family, and teenage boys die fighting in the army.

Typical Behaviors Indicating Achievement of Independence

The young woman who has achieved independence does not have to prove her arguments to her parents. Persons who are sure of their values and social and community identities are comfortable when others' views do not agree with their's; they are able to respect others' opinions with comfort.

Emancipation from family usually means both financial and psychological freedom or independence, although there may be times when help is sought from the family. Adults comfortable with this emancipation do not feel threatened when illness or other transition periods in their life course require temporary dependence on others.

The young woman who has achieved independence experiences satisfaction with who she is and with directions that she is taking for achieving goals for her life at the time. Self confidence is evidenced by a stability in her relationships and self-presentation to others.

Difficulty in Achieving Independence Behaviors

There are young people who have a fear of being on their own and of growing up. These persons are extremely egocentric, narcissistic, have high intelligence and self-expectations, remarkable resistance to regression, and lack of self-criticism and assertiveness (Blos, 1962).

Randolph and Dye (1981) developed a scale to measure this phenomenon, which they labeled as the "Peter Pan Syndrome." Items measure trust, support, guidance, identification, closeness, understanding and communication with parents, relationships with peers, adults, self-esteem, belief in the ability to succeed as an adult, and positive or negative future view orientation. Adolescents who wished to remain a child had excessive dependency needs, intense fear of their inability to assume responsibilities and demands of adulthood, intense fear of sexual impulses, low self-esteem, poor peer relations, were academic underachievers, felt that adults were unacceptable role models, and were extremely egocentric (Randolph & Dye, 1981).

Early Adulthood Tasks

Levinson and associates (1978) identified four major tasks of early adulthood that either overlap with or represent a continuation of the adolescent tasks just discussed: formulating a life's dream; establishing mentor relationships with experienced adults; establishing an occupation; and establishing love relationships and a family. Erikson (1959) identified intimacy versus isolation as the major task of young adulthood, the work toward this task during adolescence being toward solidarity versus social isolation.

The anticipated, socially defined transitions (such as graduating from high school, going to college, finishing college or vocational training, going to work, and getting married) were observed to predominate during the years 16 to 25 and reflected the major work of women on their identities, independence, and intimate relationships during this period (Mercer et al., 1989). Choices or demands of life situations during these years launching into adulthood had long-range impact on the rest of their life trajectory.

STAGES OF ADOLESCENCE

Adolescent mothers represent a wide range of developmental differences—from 12 (or younger) to 19 or 25. Within this age range are three developmental stages; early, middle, and late adolescence, each characterized by different modes of thinking and behaving and by different moral orientations and motivations for behavior. Development does not always proceed uniformly; a middle adolescent may continue with a high level of egocentrism yet may function at a high level of cognitive abstraction. Thus, although age ranges are used to describe the three stages, age range cannot be relied on as a reflection of early, middle, or late adolescent behavior.

Each adolescent's behavioral response must be assessed individually and stereotyping avoided. Recognition of the stage of cognitive development and behavioral response regardless of the young mother's age is necessary for effective teaching and health counseling. If the adolescent doesn't understand the content the clinician is attempting to explain, or if the content lacks meaning for her, the adolescent's behavior is unlikely to change.

Early Adolescent

The early adolescent experiences several abrupt discontinuities in the transition from childhood to puberty through around 14 years of age. Physically, the pubertal growth spurt and body changes are the most rapid since those during infancy. The surge of physical growth and sexual maturation are accompanied by an increase in hormones, which affect mood changes as well as sexual feelings. The early adolescent is dealing with a totally unfamiliar body that evokes very different feelings than experienced earlier. Any change in the body is usually met by strong emotional feelings. If coupled with the physical and hormonal changes of pregnancy and postpartum, the change is massive.

Socially, the early adoleslcent faces vast change characterized by the entry into junior high school. The youth is self conscious moving into the role of teenager. A new set of behaviors have to be learned—new language, different clothes, hairstyles, and teen behavior.

This is the period of the initial breaking away from the family. Hero worship of a teacher or a friends's parent adds to the adolescent's parent feeling rejected. Parents are often afraid that if they are too strict their adolescent will totally reject them. In their attempts to be a good parent, the adolescent may receive freedom that terrifies them and peer advice that is inept.

In their rigid interpretation of the world, early adolescents usually interpret everything in bipolar terms, as either black or white or right or wrong (Blos, 1979). The early adolescent is most likely at the second or conventional stage of moral development, being concerned with following rules and in conforming to maintaining and supporting the social order (Kohlberg & Gilligan, 1972).

If early adolescents have achieved a cognitive level of conceptual thinking and problem solving, they are not consistent in utilizing their newly acquired logic. They are unready for the decision making or responsibility that parenting requires. The early adolescent considers future consequences in decision making half as often as the middle adolescent and one-fourth as often as the late adolescent (Lewis, 1981). When the early adolescent's mother assumes responsibility for her infant, she usually appreciates it. She passively enjoys mothering that she may continue to receive from her mother; developmentally it is her right. She may view the infant as an intruder who takes both time and her own mother away from her, and she may react with hostility toward the infant. She has no desire to achieve the maternal task of moving to a peer status with her mother. Although she is seeking independence from her mother, she longs for closeness with her mother and is very much dependent on her.

In a highly egocentric stage, the early adolescent is at the peak of indulging in an imaginary audience and in a personal fable (Elkind, 1980). The young woman's preoccupation with herself leads her to believe others also watch her and pass judgment on her appearance and behavior (thus the imaginary audience). In her personal fable she views herself as very special and invincible since everyone is so preoccupied with her; this fallacious invincibility leads to her taking risks, such as in unprotected intercourse: "Others may get pregnant, but I won't."

The early adolescent determines her normality by comparing herself to her peers. If her breasts are not as large or she hasn't begun menstruation and her peers have, she sees herself as abnormal.

She is likely to interpret 1:1 counseling with a health professional as the equivalent of parental intrusion. However, when given the opportunity to participate in small groups of same-aged peers with a common problem, she is able to respond with mutual advice and support. The early adolescent presents the greatest challenge to the health professional.

Early adolescents 13 years and younger play with toys placed in the prenatal clinic for the older pregnant women's children. When this youthful mother delivers, she may be bored with all of the time in the hospital and may ask for a colorbook and crayons. One 14-year-old openly stated after a full year of motherhood, "No, I don't feel like a mother, and I never will. She is more like a sister." The "never will" is a typical teenage response because a future time seems far away to a young person. When a person's past perspective is short, a future that goes beyond the number of years already experienced is fathomless.

Pregnancy is far more likely to deter the development of the very young teenager than that of the older teenager. If the very young teenager does not have the help of a stable adult, she cannot provide the care that her infant needs. Experiences in a residential home that provided for growth of the child mother and her infant as equal clients indicated that it takes about 2 years of intensive, supportive help for the child mother to reach a point in her own development at which she can properly care for her child on her own (Benas, 1975).

Middle Adolescent

The middle adolescent is around 15 through 16–17 years. She is adapting to her earlier bodily changes and carefully noting her continued breast development. She was probably pleased with the enlarged breast changes accompanying her pregnancy. Her self-identity is in a state of flux.

Formal operational thought is usually acquired by middle adolescence, and future plans become more important. Middle adolescents are able to plan for the future more consistently and to show remarkable growth. They are able to identify broad areas of interest and skills and to make choices in their school program.

Middle adolescents seem to enjoy their newly acquired intellectual powers, especially in idealistic and altruistic terms. They vacillate in their ideologies from day to day; they may vow to be a vegetarian one day and eat three hamburgers the next. About one-half will seek an outside opinion in making an important decision (Lewis, 1981).

The peer group is valuable to middle adolescents for reasons other than belonging. They identify with the group, who they see as helpful critics in responding to ideas and helping to meet disappointment or other emotional stress. Role models in the peer group set their behavioral standards.

The middle adolescent female tests her attractiveness to males by flirting with her father and noting his response to her. In seeking her father's attention and approval, she competes with her mother. This causes much discomfort in the family.

In her striving for independence, she may show overt rebellion within the family or withdrawal from family activities. She would much prefer a trip to the shopping mall with her friends than a picnic with her family.

She has a rich fantasy life, falls in love, and may write love letters to herself that she would like to receive from her boyfriend. The middle adolescent begins to show a decrease in egocentrism—the imaginary audience, personal fable, and self focus—although they still predominate in her life (Enright, Shukla, & Lapsley, 1980).

When the middle adolescent becomes pregnant she often places the blame for the pregnancy on someone else. She may see the pregnancy as furthering her autonomy and power or as having something of her own (Hatcher, 1976). Although she tends to be stoic and idealistic, she may enlarge on and brag about the symptoms of pregnancy. One 16-year-old expressed disappointment in having a premature infant because she had not had opportunity to have a photograph made of her large abdomen. However, because of their being nearer completion of high school and their problem-solving advantage, 16- to 17-year olds have the potential for tremendous growth and maturation during pregnancy and early motherhood.

The Late Adolescent

The late adolescent, from 17 to 18 through 19 or 25, is approaching the achievement of independence. She no longer has to show her individuality through indiscriminate protest. She has no need to act out.

The late adolescent's cognitive functioning is fairly stable. Problems are viewed objectively and realistically, and remote possibilities are rejected. Two-thirds of the late adolescents suggest outside consultation in important decision making (Lewis, 1981). Late adolescents are beginning to define their life goals, may be working full time, and usually have identified vocational goals. Their behavior is less chaotic and more predictable (Blos, 1962).

Importantly, the body image is fairly stable. Aside from the changes during pregnancy, the late adolescent does not usually experience further physical growth. Gender role definition has firmed and is nearly secured (Blos, 1962). They usually have a unique, stable, realistic, positive self-identity.

Relationships are no longer narcissistic; late adolescents are able to give and to share. Socially centered activities have assumed importance. It is possible that the postconventional level of moral reasoning has been achieved, and the adolescent responds to protect individual rights of others and democratically derived laws. The postconventional level of moral reasoning is not assured along with cognitive development, however; about 40% of adults never reach this level (Lovenger, 1976).

The late adolescent is more likely to have a stable relationship with the father of her baby than either the middle or early adolescent. She is able to understand the responsibilities of motherhood and is capable of motherly, nurturing feelings, since her dependency needs are a less consuming issue.

This young woman has gained a new level of relationships with her family. She is able to accept her parents as human beings who do make mistakes. She is able to appreciate what her family has done and does for her. Her family in turn can accept her becoming a mother more easily than the family with a young teenage mother. Both the older teenager's more independent behavior and her mother's ability to recognize this independence reflect the older teen's greater maturity advantage. Mothering is not a passive job; mothering requires active involvement, decision making, and independent judgments.

The late adolescent mother is able to utilize 1:1 counseling well and, with help, to move on with her future plans and goals. Because of these qualities, the health professional feels more of a sense of accomplishment and less frustration when counseling them.

HANDICAPS OF ADOLESCENT PARENTING

A pregnant adolescent is faced with the adult role of mothering if she chooses to rear her child and the adult role of wife if she chooses to get married. She needs to continue her teenage role as student to prevent foreclosure of future opportunities. Her child's birth has potential to accelerate her development if the teenager has achieved a level of cognitive functioning and empathic sensitivity necessary to perceive her infant's cues. The converse is also true; the complexity of assuming adult roles without cognitive, emotional, and social maturity can be catastrophic for both the young mother and her infant when there is not an extensively supportive environment.

Economically, their earning potential is limited because of educational deficits. Fifteen years after birth, teenage mothers are more often the head of single-parent households and their children are more likely to be living in poverty (Kellam et al., 1982).

Experientially, the teenager has had fewer years to observe parenting and other adult roles. Emotionally, she is more egocentric about her own needs than the older parent, who has been sharing a marital/mate relationship for some years. Because of her immaturity, if she marries, she has a higher probability of divorce. She is more likely to have more children than women who become mothers at a later age (Pittman & Adams, 1988). If she does not have early and good prenatal care, her infant is more likely to have a lower birth weight and a higher rate of morbidity and mortality than do children of older mothers (Clewell, Brooks-Gunn, & Benasich, 1989; Adams, Adams-Taylor, & Pittman, 1989).

The majority of adolescents are frightened and sad about their pregnancies initially (Speraw, 1987). Teenagers are less ready for their pregnancies than older women and are more worried as they feel the pregnancy is neither planned nor at a good time (Mercer, 1986a).

Even though teenagers' births were more often spontaneous with fewer medical interventions, teenagers viewed their childbirth experience less positively than older women (Mercer, Hackley, & Bostrom,

1983). They reported being more scared during the childbirth experience than older women, and when comparing their experience of giving birth with their mother's, they felt that their own experience was less satisfying.

The teenage mother is often socially isolated. Peers without children do not understand the time and energy demands of children, and the teenager moves to the periphery of usual adolescent activity; adult mothers pity her as a child mother (Mercer, 1985b, 1986a). Social isolation was cited as a major life change by pregnant adolescents in Speraw's (1987) study; this included isolation from peers and, among Pacific Asians, isolation from families whom they felt they had disgraced.

Social supports from both the community and family are often inadequate. Good day-care centers for infants are lacking; teenagers often do not earn enough to pay the high costs of child care and resort to less safe caretakers. For example, in one study, a retired couple in their 60s were taking care of a teenager's infant along with several other infants (Mercer et al., 1982). Societal attitudes toward pregnant teenagers have changed since the 1960s, when the attitude was one of punitiveness, and pregnant students were dismissed from school. Federally financed demonstration programs begun in 1963 to foster support and care for teenage mothers helped to change societal attitudes and support, but unfortunately that support continues to be inadequate.

Teenage mothers more often than older women report they were separated from their parents before the age of 12; the father is the parent most often missing from the home, with divorce being the reason for the separation (Mercer, 1986a). Frommer and O'Shea (1973) observed that women separated from their parents before the age of 11 tended to respond to their infants with either overanxiety in attempts to be a perfect mother or with lack of care. Those who had been separated were also more depressed than those who had not been separated from their parents as a child.

Pregnant teenagers' relationships with their parents are often strained, and they may experience some isolation from their families. Their need for financial and other help mandates dependency at a time when they yearn for independency, and this increases the teenage mothers' conflict. They may experience identity confusion because they are still themselves children in need of nurturing care with an infant who also needs nurturing.

Teenage parents often have unrealistic expectations about both the mothering role and infant behavior and development (Becker, 1987). They have more punitive child-rearing attitudes. Although they show interest through more time in positive contact with their infants, they tend to be less verbal in their interactions with their infants and to spend less time in caretaking with their infants than older mothers (Call, Hoffman, & Oh, 1987).

Teenage parents have immature coping responses, and as research indicates, parenting is stressful for adults (McLanahan & Adams, 1987). They may be unable to separate the stress from other life events from the infant's crying or from themselves. Those with less well established ego boundaries are more likely to respond with immature or punitive measures toward the infant when some other factor is the source of their stress or unhappiness (Egeland, Breitenbucher, & Rosenberg, 1980). Teens have not learned to delay their own pleasure for another person's pleasure or for later gratification. Developmentally, they are trying hard to gain control in the state of adolescent disequilibrium, and the young infant's unpredictable, uncontrollable behavior adds more stress that the teenager cannot control. Cognitively, the teenager's decision-making process is less sophisticated than that of a more mature person, who also has the luxury of more viable options.

The Teenage Father

Health professionals often do not have opportunity to see or make little effort to access teenage fathers. Teenage fathers also need much social support, however. One of the most critical needs of young fathers is job training (Rivara et al., 1986), since a disproportionate number are from environments of poverty and lack educational preparation or job skills (Hardy & Duggan, 1988; Pittman & Adams, 1988; Wetzel, 1987). Young fathers are often unable to earn enough money to contribute to the support of their children (Smollar & Ooms, 1987).

Almost all teenage fathers indicate that they are unready for fatherhood, and this unreadiness does not tend to diminish much as the pregnancy advances (Westney, Cole, & Munford, 1986). Fathers who do not want to become fathers are not likely to be supportive of their mate's prenatal care or health or to indicate a desire to care for or interact with their expected infant. Teen fathers often have difficulty coping with the pregnancy, feel stressed, and are depressed as they experience conflict over the roles of adolescent and father. Despite these problems, one study found that many of the teen fathers were interested in what happens during childbirth as well as in learning child care (Elster & Panzarine, 1980).

However, not all adult fathers are ready for a pregnancy and react in one of three ways to their mates' pregnancies. There are observer styles who do not become actively involved, expressive styles who attend antepartal classes and become emotionally involved, and instrumental styles who paint the baby bed and the nursery and see the physical arrangements are made (May, 1982).

Teenager fathers are uninformed about sex, sexuality, and reproductive physiology, but their knowledge in these areas does not differ from that of other teenagers who are not fathers (Robinson, 1988). The implication is that for unintended pregnancy to be reduced, teenage males as well as females need to be informed in the area of reproduction knowledge.

INITIAL ASSESSMENTS FOR INTERVENTION

From the review of developmental challenges facing adolescents moving into young adulthood and of their handicaps in premature parenting, it is clear that they present a challenge to the health professional. Three behaviors demonstrated by adolescent mothers—resistance, ambivalence, and inconsistent responses (Spietz, 1986)—are frustrating to the health professional just as they are frustrating to the youth's parents. Resistance is exhibited by strong, seemingly unreasonable opinions, confrontations, or unwillingness to follow suggested guidelines. In such situations the teen interprets the clinician's information as "the only way," and this heightens the teen's defensiveness. If choices can be presented, the teen can enhance decision-making skills and may become less defensive. In making decisions, teens need relevant information on which to base a decision; must perceive, interpret, and store that information accurately; must personalize the information; and need the behavorial skills to implement their decisions in social situations (Schinke, Gilchrist, & Small, 1979).

Ambivalence is present in many forms. The child mother may have wanted a child, but when the child has problems and the teen sees how difficult it is to parent, she may wish that she had not had a child. Teenagers experience many mixed feelings, and these require time for them to work through and understand. Inconsistent responses indicate the child mother's immaturity. They have good intentions but lack the initiative and commitment to follow through with these intentions. Spietz (1986) found that unless the adolescents felt the need to be responsible, they felt they didn't have to be; they have to be told repeatedly what is expected of them. Teenage mothers respond well to positive feedback but may be expected to continually test limits set by the health professional (Howe, 1980).

In making assessments about the status of teenage parents, the health professional must be genuinely interested in the youth as a person. Questions must be woven into a conversation so that the adolescent does not feel she is bombarded. A checklist in hand with a rote recital will get rote answers, without affect or true feeling. A conversational interview that indicates concern and interest will elicit feelings that may be reflected by tone of voice and body language as well as by spoken words.

The nurse or other health professional also can provide a safe environment for the adolescent to test rules. The teen may not keep appointments; however, the nurse informs the teen that this is permissable as long as the young woman lets her know in advance so that someone else may have the allotted time.

Continuity of care with a known, trusted clinician is important to provide stability in a very unstable adolescent life. The trusted nurse can obtain more accurate information, and the teen will be more likely to listen to her counseling.

It is important to focus on the adolescent mother's potential, what she can do, rather than issuing a lot of "don'ts." Many of the adolescent mothers have little or no self-esteem, and the nurse or social worker may be one of the first adults to indicate confidence in her abilities. Appraisal support is an important form of support. The young women need to hear when they are doing a good job.

The Adolescent's Family

Families are usually the major support for teenage parents. It is important to evaluate family strengths and resources to work with. The teenagers' family is rarely identified as a client, and rarely are services and support directed toward the family, yet the adolescent's opportunity for continued growth is often dependent on family support.

Smith (1983) observed that families incorporate the teenage mother and her infant into the family by one of three ways:

1. *Role Blocking.* The teenager does not assume the mothering role. She either willingly abdicates or a family member takes over. Family dynamics prevent her growth in the mothering role.
2. *Role Binding.* All tasks and responsibilities of mothering are delegated to the teenage mother, and she performs them alone. There is the "you made your bed, and you'll sleep in it" attitude. The teenager is forced into a foreclosed identity as mother.
3. *Role Sharing.* The family shares in responsibilities, enabling the teen mother to grow in other roles as well as in the mother role. The family, through a role sharing process, commits itself to a new system. The pregnancy and, later, the infant are accepted by the

family without stigmatization. A true collaboration occurs as all family members unite to make the best of a difficult situation.

It is important that the adolescent mother's family not be either role-blocking nor role-binding if the young mother is to be able to achieve her adolescent tasks. Knowledge about how the family accepted her pregnancy is important, as is whether the family became committed to a new system of family dynamics for role sharing. Does a family member come with her for prenatal visits? Are family members visiting her at the hospital? What is their response?

Some of this information may be gained directly from family members, such as the grandmother. Appropriate questions include:

What kind of adjustment have you had to make with your daughter getting pregnant?

How is the new baby in the home going to affect your family routine?

It is important for Mary to get back into school; what are the family's plans for helping her with this?"

Body language and affect are very telling about how the family has moved to acceptance over the months of pregnancy. Adult family members may give a more accurate picture of family resources than the teenage mother. Whatever community resources are available need to be shared with the adolescent and adult family members.

Family dynamics have much influence on the teen's ability to achieve the tasks of identity, intimacy, and independence. Anderson and Fleming (1986) found that intergenerational fusion and triangulation (an indication of the adolescent's individuation from the family) were significant predictors of adolescents' identity scores. Individuation was defined as the adolescents' subjective perception of how enmeshed they were in processes of fusion and triangulation within the family (Anderson & Fleming, 1986).

Fusion was defined as the tendency for two family members to merge such that the boundaries between the two become blurred or overlap. One family member may speak for or make decisions for another such that there is a blurring of emotions, including anxieties and tensions, of the two members. Much effort goes into seeking love and approval or attacking the other for not providing it, and the adolescent in a fused relationship has little energy to direct toward self-determined, goal-directed activity (Bowen, 1978). Triangulation is similar to fusion in that both processes indicate a lack of differentiation from the family, but it involves three family members. Three typical modes of expression are found in family triangulation processes. To avoid facing the tension and anxiety that accompany individuation, family members may maintain a conflict-free image by scapegoating (displacing emotional tension or disowned "bad" traits onto a third party, usually a child) (Bowen, 1978). When the adolescent is the person scapegoated in this triangulation process, the adolescent may become emotionally detached or develop a negative identity.

A second form of triangulation involves the adolescent in a stable, cross-generational coalition with one parent against the other parent. In this situation, the adolescent may sacrifice attempts toward individuation and a separate ego identity to continue as stabilizer of her parents' emotional system (Bowen, 1978). A third form of triangulation occurs when a parent demands that the adolescent side with him/her against the other parent. Adolescents in this situation are vulnerable to developing a diffused identity, since commitment to any position may be viewed as disloyalty by either parent.

In a study of unwanted pregnancy and adolescent childbearing within the family system, highly intrusive or enmeshed families were characterized by a preponderance of authoritative statements by parents that were relatively ineffective (Nathanson, Baird, & Jemail, 1986). In intrusive families the adolescent's relationship with the father of the baby deteriorated from pregnancy to 11 months after birth, and the young mother continued to live in the same household. It seemed that for the teen father to negotiate a satisfactory role with his child and with the teen mother, the family's style needs to permit the daughter to disengage from her parental family unit in order to develop as a new family with a partner. Thompson (1986) reported that support from friends and relatives, especially sisters, was associated with higher levels of distress among teenage mothers, but support from a male partner was associated with low levels of distress.

Nonpregnant adolescents who had achieved an identity also had families in which dialogue was greater and the youths were more independent (Bosma & Gerrits, 1985). The adolescent should be able to test family rules such as when she should be in or who she dates. Ideally, the family is a safer environment to test rules and take risks than the community or society, in which repercussions for breaking rules or risk taking are much greater.

Assessment of these family situations are not easily made nor are they easily remedied. They require counseling time with family members, but they are shared here as informational background, since the family is a strong environmental facilitator or deterrent to the teen's movement into adult roles. The clinician who has very limited contact with the young mother either in the postpartal unit or in the clinic can assess indications for referral and the need for public health nurse follow-up in the home to assess the family environment more extensively.

Unfortunately in some situations, the nurse or other health professional may not see any family members. The young mother may be from a single-parent household with the adult parent at work. Or the household may be complex, with stepparents, step-siblings, or alcoholism or other substance abuse, such that there is no stability or any family support that can be depended on consistently. The adolescent mother may be a "throw-away kid," "street kid," "runaway," or otherwise "homeless" young woman. Some general questions that are appropriate to ask the teen mother are:

"Who do you consider your family?"
"How are they available to help you?"
"Who makes the decisions in your home?"
"What happens in the family when something unexpected occurs?"
(For example, expected money does not materialize or a child gets in trouble at school.)
"How do you get along with your parents?" "How do you get along with other kids in the family?"

Roelofse and Middleton (1985) developed an instrument to assess psychosocial health of the family from the adolescent's perspective based on family systems research and adolescent developmental tasks. This measure shows promise for those who wish more formal assessments of family relationships.

The Grandmother: Her Role and Needs

A family member whose alliance is particularly important in working with teenage mothers is the grandmother. Accepting the teenage daughter's pregnancy is not easy for the premature grandmother. The grandmother feels embarrassed and disgraced, especially since her perceived failure as a mother is visible to everyone (Poole & Hoffman, 1981). Yet the grandmother's role is central and cannot be overlooked by the health professional. All research indicates that teenagers seek out health or infant care information from their mothers, in contrast to adult women who look up the information in books or call their physicians (Mercer, 1986a; Vukelich & Kliman, 1985). It is critical to spend time with the grandmother to assess her needs, to update her knowledge, and to discuss how beliefs about infant care and feeding have changed. The grandmother continues in the mothering role for her daughter and as a surrogate mother for the grandchild. She needs to be praised for her help and informed of how important her help is.

Since the grandmother controls the household, nutrition counseling and counseling about providing a safe environment for the growing infant should be shared with the grandmother. Although the teenager's mother may be her greatest source of support, this support may also be a source of conflict (Barrera, 1981). The family may be in a role-blocking or role-binding structure, inhibiting the teenager's achievement of identity, intimacy, and independence. Health professionals can help grandmothers by viewing the pregnancy from the grandmother's frame of reference. Other areas the health professional needs to address in providing care for grandmothers include:

Whether there are support systems in the community available to her
How she is coping, and whether her methods need strengthening or altering
Her feelings about her daughter's pregnancy
Whether her communication with her daughter is open
If group counseling or other grandmothers are available
Whether there is any community assistance available
Her awareness of the young mother's need to continue work on adolescent and young adult tasks

PSYCHOSOCIAL ASSESSMENTS OF THE ADOLESCENT

Knowledge about the young mother's ability to absorb information and health counseling for herself and her infant is essential. The nurse or other health professional needs to know the young mother's cognitive level of functioning and her level of self-esteem and to work with the teen in identifying and enlisting her social support system to become actively involved with her and her child.

Level of Cognitive Functioning

Areas to assess include the adolescent's egocentrism, her present-future orientation, level of abstract thinking or causality, and decision-making skills. These skills are all important for successful parenting and for utilizing anticipatory guidance for child care. Examples of questions to assess each of these skills are given.

Egocentrism

> If your best friend failed a final exam, how do you think she'd be feeling?
> What could you do to make her feel better?
> If your best friend told you she was pregnant, how do you think she'd be feeling? How would her family be feeling?
> When your baby cries, what do you think the baby is feeling?

Present-Future Orientation

> What do you imagine yourself doing 10 years from now?
> Tell me about your plans for finishing high school? For after you finish high school?
> Who is going to help you with the baby? While you are at school? If the baby gets sick?

An additional way of assessing the adolescent's plans or her ability to plan is to ask her to complete three columns on a piece of paper: what my baby and I will need over the next year; what we have; and how we'll get things we don't have. If the young mother cannot read or write very well, the nurse can do this with the teen's verbal input.

Abstract Thinking, Causality

> Would you tell me what the nutritionist told you about the importance of what you eat during pregnancy and after the baby comes?
> What have you heard about what your baby should eat for the first few months?
> Why is it important to take your baby to the doctor if her bowels are running and/or she is vomiting?
> We have been talking about different contraceptives. What have you gotten out of this conversation that will be helpful to you?
> What if a friend asked you to tell her which contraceptive would also help to protect against VD and AIDS, what would you tell her? How does it work?
> If your younger sister or a younger friend wanted to know if she could get pregnant if she didn't have orgasm, how would you explain it to her?

Decision Making

What kinds of things do you decide for yourself without asking
anyone's advice?
How do you go about making an important decision in what you are
going to do—like when you found out you were pregnant?
Whose opinions do you find most helpful to you in making up your
mind?

As the teenager discusses these questions, her cognitive abilities become evident. Use of models and pictures to illustrate points are most
important for this population.

The Teenage Parent's Social Support System

The characteristics of the person (adolescence and parenthood) and of
the situation (home environment, educational and vocational needs)
reflect the social support needed (Norbeck, 1981). The teenage parent's
inability to form friendships or to communicate with and keep friends
may have contributed to the premature parenthood.

Social support is information that leads a person to believe that she is
cared for and loved, esteemed and valued, and belongs to a network of
communication and mutual obligation (Cobb, 1976). Social support has
consistently proven to be a moderator of stress in a variety of transitions over the life course.

Four broad areas of social support have been identified (House, 1981):
emotional support (which includes empathy, caring, love, and trust);
physical support (which includes direct help of money, labor, time);
informational support (which includes receiving the necessary information for coping with personal and environmental problems); and appraisal support (which includes feedback from important persons in the
social network that is necessary for self-evaluation).

The adolescent mother clearly needs all four kinds of social support.
The lack of such social support contributes to higher morbidity and
mortality rates for themselves and their infants. Lack of support pre-
vents adolescent mothers from returning to school; we know that
adolescent mothers who remain in school feel better about themselves
and have more favorable life situations (Colletta et al., 1980).

Peers are important in both emotional and appraisal support. A pow-
erful overall measure of the adolescent's adjustment is the quality of
her peer relationships (Looney, Oldham, & Blotchky, 1978). The adolescent who has at least one same-aged friend is less likely to have
serious psychological problems. In contrast, preference for significantly

older or younger friends, sudden changes in types of friends, being a peer scapegoat, and isolating or maintaining a friendship through a form of antisocial behavior are all indicators of psychological disturbance.

As noted above, either the father of the baby or another male partner is an important source of support to the adolescent mother in many situations. Decisions related to whether the young woman chose to have her baby rather than have an abortion have been related to support from her family (Fischman, 1977). Others observed that the teen father had little influence on the teen mother's attitudes or health behaviors during pregnancy; the teen mother's pleasure with her pregnancy was associated with help from her mother and favorable opinions from friends (Giblin, Poland, & Sachs, 1987). Attendance at postpartum visits were related more to high self-esteem and less to the relationship with the father. Unger and Wandersman (1988) found that the teen mother's behavior toward her infant was associated with her relationships with her male partner.

Kinds of Support Teenage Mothers Will Accept

To learn something about adolescent mothers' sources of and satisfaction with social support, Crockenberg (1986) surveyed adolescent mothers with 2-year-old children. These teen mothers reported that they had received parenting advice from a professional source as well as from their informal network, but the majority indicated that they would like additional parenting advice from other sources such as parenting classes, organized neighborhood groups, visiting public health nurses, and other child development specialists. Almost all (90%) of the mothers thought it would be helpful to have members of their informal support network participate with them in receiving professional services, and 81% thought these individuals would be willing to do so. More than 80% relied on friends and relatives for advice about parenting. This research gives some specific directions as to the kinds of services that adolescent mothers want and would be willing to utilize.

Assessing Social Support

A sociogram that places the adolescent mother in a center circle within four successively larger circles may be used to assess both the density of her support network and frequency of support (Rich, 1978). Moving out from the adolescent, the second circle includes the father of the baby or a selected male partner; the third circle includes her parents and siblings; the fourth circle includes extended family; and the outer circle includes friends, public health nurse, social worker, clinic nurse, Aid to Dependent Children's services, etc. Unbroken lines from the support person or agency to the adolescent may be used to indicate continuous support, and broken lines indicate intermittent support. Lines may be erased or added as social support is no longer available or a new source becomes available. The sociogram also gives a quick view of those in the community who are involved.

Knowledge about the availability of emotional, physical, informational, and appraisal support may be gained by questions such as:

Tell me about your best friend/s. What do you do together? Where do you go?

What do your friends like best about you?

When you are feeling blue, who can usually cheer you up?

If an emergency came up, or if you needed extra money for clothes or something, who would you turn to first? How much help could you expect from them?

Some young people say their brothers and sisters help them out a lot if they don't feel like doing their chores. What is it like in your family?

How do you rate your relationship with your mother on a scale of 1 to 10 with 1 being not so good and 10 being really great? With your father?

What is it like at dinner time at your home?

Who helps you pay expenses for the baby? Who baby-sits for you?

When you are really concerned about something personal, who is able to help you the most?

Who is best at making you feel as if you are a very important person? A very good mother?

When you have an important question about your baby, who do you ask?

Strategies for Providing Support

Unger and Wandersman (1985) designed a program to offer individualized support to isolated, teenage mothers with few resources in which types of supportive intervention were tested. In one group, Resource Mothers, who were experienced mothers and paraprofessionals similar in race and socioeconomic status to the teenager, visited the teenager approximately once a month during pregnancy and the first year following birth with a structured curriculum. The second group contacted the mother once every 3 months merely to note the progress of the mother and her baby and to provide referral when needed.

At 8 months postpartum, visited mothers demonstrated more knowledge about babies, greater satisfaction with mothering, and more responsive attitudes toward their babies than mothers who were contacted only. They were more likely to seek medical care for illness and to talk to the Resource Mother when they had questions about their baby. A higher proportion of visited mothers remained in school. Visited mothers also had fewer low birth weight babies.

Unger and Wandersman also found that perceived support from family and friends was related to mothers feeling satisfied with their living arrangements and with life in general. Family support had particularly strong positive associations with the mother's feeling of adjustment. Child care and perceived support from a substitute father at 8 months postpartum were significantly related to the teen's better mothering and life satisfaction.

Another study found that periodic home visits by nurses greatly enhanced the health and development of disadvantaged mothers and babies; 47% of the women were younger than 19 years (Olds et al., 1986a, 1986b; Olds et al., 1988). The nurses used a curriculum guide but tailored the content of their visits to focus on the family's needs. The nurses focused on parent education, the enhancement of the women's informal support systems, and the linkage of parents with community services. Women who were visited by nurses were less likely to abuse or neglect their infants and were twice as likely to enroll in an educational program or to graduate from high school within 6 months of giving birth. Home-visited adolescents who were younger than 17 had infants who weighed an average of 395 grams more compared to infants of those not visited (Olds et al., 1986a). During the second year of life, infants of all women who were visited by nurses had fewer emergency room visits and were seen by physicians less frequently for accidents (Olds et al., 1986b). During the first 4 years, nurse-visited women had been employed more months, had fewer subsequent pregnancies, and had postponed the birth of a second child an average of 1 year longer (Olds et al., 1988).

Both of these experimental programs had similar positive outcomes; the key intervention was providing support in the home environment and involvement of members of the teens' social network. Referrals to public health nurses for follow-up is critical for teenage mothers. In situations in which the adolescent is alone without family support, community support is vital for the adolescent to help her get her life organized and become self-efficient and self-supporting. For the early and many middle adolescents, this help must be extensive: surrogate parents in a private home or an institution, financial aid, educational counseling, infant day care, and health care for herself and her infant. In other instances, the public health nurse and other health professionals work closely with the adolescent and her parents in helping to evolve realistic plans.

Evaluation of the Adolescent's Self-Esteem

Self-esteem, the acceptance of how others are thought to view her/him (Rosenberg, 1965), is a part of self-concept, which more broadly includes global perceptions of self and the ability to function adequately; there is congruence between self and ideal self such that there is a sense of pride in self (Wylie, 1974). Nurius (1989) referred to self-esteem as the evaluative component of the self-concept.

Much will have been learned about the adolescent mother's self-esteem in evaluating her support system and in learning about who makes her feel good about herself. Her appearance also conveys something about how she feels about herself. Is she well-groomed, alert, and outgoing? Is she depressed? Is she angry at the world? Does she seem to be hostile toward everyone she meets?

Rubin (1964) described aggressive and hostile behaviors during the neomaternal period. Aggressive behavior, such as biting the nurse during labor, represents a desperate quality of behavior, with its purpose to hold on in order to control a desperately painful situation. Aggressive behavior tends to have no time lag between a painful stimulus and the responsive behavior. Following such acts the person is aware of her behavior and feels much guilt and remorse.

Hostility is less acute and tends to be more pervasive and much more sustained; although some guilt or remorse may follow hostile acts, this is not characteristic. According to Rubin, what generally accompanies hostility is a feeling of self-dissatisfaction. The mother feels mean, irritable, and miserable but does not know what is wrong. She hates herself, her behavior, and her inability to control her behavior; she feels miserable about it. Her turmoil wth her inner feelings and her low regard for herself, feed back into her feelings of self-hate, continuing the cycle of hostility. Her behavior reflects the hostility. Attempts to control those around her are symptoms of desperate attempts to gain some stability in her world and are indicative of threatened failure in her exercise of her own capacities to control herself (Rubin, 1964).

At the first detection of hostility, the adolescent should be confronted: "Your behavior indicates that you are very angry and unhappy about something. Can we talk about it? I'd like to help you." Every effort to bolster the adolescent's self-esteem should be made. Until she feels good about herself, she cannot feel good about her infant.

ASSESSMENT OF THE ADOLESCENT'S PARENTING

Adolescent mothering has consistently been associated with mothering difficulties; however, this finding is confounded by life stressors, lack of a supportive environment, and socioeconomic status. The young woman who adapts to the mothering role and shows psychosocial growth in doing so has the following characteristics:

Positive feelings about her infant and past experience in caring for infants

A supportive mate (does not have to be the father of the baby)

A mother who acknowledges her as capable of the role

Hostile feelings about mothering that do not outweigh pleasures in mothering

A supportive family

Cognitive development that permits recognization and understanding of her infant's behavior

An ability and willingness to consider the infant's needs before her own

Initial Adaptation Stage: Birth to 6 Weeks

During this formal stage of maternal role attainment, two phases were observed among adolescent mothers aged 14 to 19: a fairyland phase during the postpartal hospitalization when the attention, praise, and gifts the teenager receives give an initial impression that being a mother is a wonderful experience; and the reality shock phase that seems to peak about the second week when the "cute and precious infant" of hospitalization has to be fed and changed two or three times during the night (Mercer, 1979). The discrepancy between the fairyland and reality shock phases may be met by ambivalence, hostility, and rejection. During the reality shock period, the deprivations of motherhood outweigh the pleasures. However, at 1 month postpartum, teenagers aged 15 to 19 did not differ significantly from women aged 20 to 29 and scored higher than women 30 and older in their gratification in mothering scores; thus the reality shock is not unique to teen mothers (Mercer, 1986).

During hospitalization, teenagers less often than older women describe their infants in terms of unique characteristics or identify features as resembling a family member (Mercer, 1986a). Claiming the infant as a family member is an important part of the acquaintance-attachment process.

How the mother feels about her first act of mothering, her labor and birth experience, should be explored with her as early following birth as possible. The teens's view of the childbirth experience is positively related to her mothering behaviors over the first year following birth (Mercer, 1985b). However, some adolescents are unable to talk about the experience, such as the 14-year-old who did not want to know what happened during the cesarean birth: "I don't want to hear about getting all cut up." The vulnerability of the teenager's body image is evidenced by such responses.

With early discharge from the hospital, the postpartal nurse has little time to assess and counsel the young mother. However, there are signs that the postpartal nurse can observe that indicate whether or not the young mother is proceeding with adapting to her infant in a nurturing and caring way. The initial fuss over a new baby by family members detracts somewhat from the requirements of the teen's new role; however, the family's presence indicates their interest and concern.

The priorities for teaching time should focus on sensitivity to infant cues and needs and knowledge of normal infant development and infant capabilities, since these areas have been identified as those in which teens have the greatest deficits. The physical act of changing a diaper or bathing the infant are concrete behaviors that come easily to her, especially if she has been helping her mother with younger siblings. As one 14-year-old in response to praise about her skill in bathing her infant said, "It ain't no big deal."

The young mother's interest in and excitement about the baby are factors to look for. Some teens want to know whether the infant can see. Discuss the importance of eye contact with the infant, and demonstrate how the infant's eyes will follow the mother's face and voice. Remind the young mother that the infant has been in a snug, warm environment, and that it is important to cuddle and hold the infant for the adjustment to life outside the uterus. An explanation that the infant's initial learning occurs through mouthing and sucking is important. If the teens see these as learning behaviors for the infant, they will less likely label the infant as being bad for sucking the hands and drooling.

The postpartal nurse can intervene in several ways to pique the young mother's interest in her infant. Doing a modified Brazelton examination in which the infant's reflexes are demonstrated usually excites the young mother. The demonstration of the diffuse and undifferentiated motor responses of the newborn may be done by rubbing the abdomen so that the teen can observe the infant curl toward the touch, or by demonstrating the Moro reflex. An explanation that this total bodily response precedes specific response helps teach the teen appropriate expectations of the infant. The nurse can then describe that as the baby's nervous system develops, the infant is able to respond to a stimulus by moving a particular body part rather than the entire body. Describing muscular development as proceeding from the trunk to extremities helps the young parent understand why the infant can't hold a rattle or a bottle until about 4 months of age. Discussion of how infant development proceeds from the head down and that the infant cannot be ready for toilet training until he or she walks well and is able to communicate is important. When possible, involve the grandmother and father in any of these demonstrations.

When young parents understand the process of development and the appropriate stimulation for their infant at each developmental level, they usually participate with much enthusiasm. Explaining normal characteristics of newborns helps to allay anxiety. The diffuseness of the baby's muscular response can be worrisome to the mother who feels the trembling of her baby in response to loud sounds; if she is not told about reflexes, she fears something is wrong. One 16-year-old father was upset that his son's nipples were engorged and wondered whether or not they should be squeezed. He feared that his son might be effeminate. The youth who is just becoming a man is very sensitive to anything that might detract from the masculinity of his son. A planned, intensive acquaintance session for young parents with their infant is very important in helping them become attuned to their infant's needs.

Discussions with the young parents about how crying is the infant's only means of communication and how it takes time to learn the differences between cries are helpful. Demonstration of how the infant becomes alert when held upright and talked to offers the teen a way of engaging the infant before attempting feedings.

Since mothers tend to mother according to their beliefs about child care, it helps to know how teen mothers view children and their care. Questions that determine something about the adolescent's knowledge of infant development include (Barnard & Eyres, 1979):

At what age do you think your baby will start to be aware of his/her surroundings or know what is going on around him/her?
At what age do you think you will start teaching things to your baby?
At about what age do you think your baby will first be able to see objects and people clearly?
At about what age do you think your baby will first be able to hear sounds and voices clearly?

How important do you think it is for you to talk to your baby during
his/her first year?

At what age do you think talking to your baby will be especially
important? (p. 198–199)

Developmental misconceptions may be clarified; however, notation
should be made to repeat the developmental concepts at a later time.
Repetition is important with the teenage mother.

Teenagers' infants tend to have a lower average birth weight (3255
gm compared to 3461 gm) than infants of older mothers (Mercer et al.,
1982). Many infants have to remain hospitalized after the mother's
discharge (up to 25%). When the young woman goes home without her
infant, it is important to stress to the parents that the infant will miss
them and will enjoy having them come in to feed, hold, and talk to her
or him.

Teenagers' less than optimal childrearing attitudes have their impact
on maternal behavior (Mercer, 1986a). A measure of perinatal attitudes—use of a family-centered program, choosing to breast-feed, attending prenatal class, and knowledge of infant competencies—indicated that teens participate less in these areas than do older women.
During the early postpartal hospitalization, perinatal attitudes were
predictive of a more positive perception of the neonate.

Teenagers also report attitudes indicating role reversal and acceptance of harsh or unusual punishment (sadistic) and are less likely to
consider the child's needs and feelings in defining acceptable child
behavior (strict disciplinarian attitudes). At 1 month, negative low
boiling point, sadistic, and strict disciplinarian attitudes were predictive
of less optimal maternal infant attachment, identification of the infant,
and observed maternal behavior (Mercer et al., 1982).

Although teenagers' infants averaged less weight at birth, they averaged a greater weight gain the first month of life (Mercer et al., 1984a).
This may be the result of a different diet or more help from their
mothers. Fewer teens were breast-feeding; although almost two-thirds
initially began breast-feeding, at the end of the first month, only one-
third were breast-feeding. One-third of the teens were also feeding
their infants cereal at 1 month (Mercer et al., 1984a). Their mothers
had told them that this would help their infants sleep through the
night; however, in reality, the teens' infants were not sleeping longer
periods than older mothers' infants. Macknin and associates (1989) also
did not find that cereal fed infants slept through the night more often
than infants who did not receive cereal.

The first 4 to 6 weeks at home appear to go smoothly for the teen
who lives in her mother's home, despite the reality shock. The teenager

as a rule recuperates more easily during the puerperium. She has fewer complaints of fatigue and depression during the first month postpartum (Mercer, 1986a). The lack of time and hectic atmosphere of the first few days home from the hospital are not as overwhelming to teenagers as they are to older women. The resiliency of the more youthful body in recuperating from childbirth cannot be denied.

More teenagers report receiving help from their mothers, and this may also contribute to their easier recuperation (Mercer, 1986a). Help from an experienced mothering person may be important in reducing fatigue and depression during the first month. However, the teenager may also use some denial in regard to emotional feelings such as depression.

Teens' infants also have more episodes of illness the first month following birth. Some of the infants' problems that are reported may reflect some difficulty of the mother in synchronizing her responses to the infant's cues and state (colic, constipation, heat rash, colds) (Mercer, 1980).

Teenagers scored their infants as significantly easier to handle at 1 month than did older women; this probably reflects the greater physical help from their mothers. However, teens, in their immaturity and inexperience, worry about fewer things than do older mothers. The mother in her thirties is concerned about enrolling her infant in preschool and worrying about the correct amount of stimulation to enhance the infant's intellectual abilities; these are quite remote concerns to the present-oriented, more concrete adolescent.

Although the adolescent may have had a substance use history taken during pregnancy and does not seem to be using any substance, it is important to discuss some of the hazards of substance use, since peer pressure may occur at any time. Many drugs are transmitted to the infant through breast milk. If she uses needles, there is a real health danger to her, including hepatitis and AIDS. Instructions for taking a substance use history are outlined in the booklet, *Drugs & Pregnancy: It's Not Worth the Risk*, available from the American Council for Drug Education, 5820 Hubbard Drive, Rockville, MD, 20852 (American Council for Drug Education, 1986). In taking a drug history, as in other encounters with adolescents, it is important to establish trust. It is also important to incorporate counseling with the drug history about the dangers to the young woman and her infant.

Informal Stage: Pleasurable Reciprocal Interchange With Infant (2 to 5 Months)

This period encompasses a give-and-take phase of maternal role attainment identified among teen mothers; a transition seems to occur near

the third month, so that by the fifth month a balance between perceived deprivations and gratifications has occurred (Mercer, 1979). A
restructuring of the young woman's life seems to have occurred toward
the restructuring of her identity. As she has decided what she is willing
to give, she has decided what she is going to take. The young mother
may seek employment or return to school in response to feelings of
boredom and financial need, and a restructuring of role identity apart
from motherhood may be the result. Motherhood, however, contributed to teens feeling they were more responsible and better persons.

For mothers of all ages, a turning point was observed at the fourth
month after birth; because of this, the period was called an *achievement
phase* (Mercer, 1986a). Mothers' descriptions of their infants' accom-
plishments and characteristics indicated their joy in them and sensitivity to their needs.

Teenagers' infants were more advanced in social and motor development and scored higher on growth and development at 4 months than
did infants of older women (Mercer, et al., 1984a). There are several
explanations for this finding. Camp and Morgan (1984) suggested that
high authoritarian attitudes and parenting practices that result from
these attitudes may be a strength the first year of life, but they become
increasingly maladaptive as the child ages. Barnard and Eyres (1979)
reported that mothers' psychosocial assets did not begin to have an
impact on mother-infant interactions until 8 and 12 months. Another
factor may have been the teenagers' higher scores on feelings of satisfaction and gratification in mothering that conveyed a different emotional climate for the infant.

An alternative hypothesis is that an infant profits from polymatric
mothering. Caldwell and associates (1963) studied monomatric mothering (i.e., mothering provided by one person) and polymatric mothering
(mothering provided by more than one person), and their findings did
not support this hypothesis. Infants in monomatric families were more
dependent on their mothers at 1 year, but no significant developmental
differences were observed, although infants from monomatric families
scored higher.

At 4 months postpartum, when describing the most rewarding thing
about motherhood, teenagers more often than older women reported
having someone who wouldn't leave them, someone to keep them
company, something all their own, or someone to play with. These
comments reflect the greater social isolation of teens; they reported
having peers visit with them in their homes less often than did older
mothers.

Continued evaluation of the teen's attitudes toward mothering is
important. For example, the teen's child-rearing attitudes were predic-

tive of gratification in mothering, maternal infant attachment, the infant's growth and development, and observed maternal behavior at 4 months. One way to assess attitudes is to have her list five things an ideal mother does for her infant, then have her list five things an ideal baby does. Teenagers more often focused on activities such as feeding the infant or keeping the infant clean, in contrast to older mothers who more often mentioned playing with, comforting or nurturing, and teaching the infant (Mercer, 1986a).

In order to determine more about the adolescent parent-infant interactions, other questions may be asked (Barnard & Eyres, 1979):

What things are helping your baby to learn at this time?

Some babies seem to enjoy cuddling a lot; others do not care to cuddle at all. How much does your baby cuddle (none, very little, moderate amount, a good bit, a great deal)?

Considering this same scale, how much do you cuddle and sing to your baby?

To what extent has your child affected your lifestyle and home environment?

How has being a mother affected how you feel about yourself?

How do you manage difficult times with your baby?

Describe an usual day for your baby.

Has your infant's cry changed? How?

How long do you wait to respond to crying (minutes)? Hunger ___, wet ___, sleepy ___, angry ___, other ___.

What do you do most often in response to each kind of cry?

What things does your child like for you to do with him/her?

Do you have any concerns about the way your child is growing and developing (physically, socially, intellectually, self-help abilities, speech and language)?

What is your baby eating now?

How are feedings going?

How are bath times going?

How do you teach your baby that something is unsafe?

How do you tell the baby "no" when he/she doesn't need something he/she wants?

Where do you let him/her play? Where do you keep him/her most of the day?

What is the most difficult thing about mothering now?

What is the easiest thing about mothering now?

What is the most rewarding thing about motherhood now?

What are some of your future plans for him/her as far as you have thought about? (pp. 202–210)

Dealing with Infant's Crying

If crying is particularly problematic for the young mother, Newton (1983) offered many helpful suggestions for parents. Talking with the teen mother about how she feels about the infant's crying and where her ideas about crying came from will provide the professional with areas for counseling. Explaining that there is evidence that responding quickly and appropriately to the crying infant helps the infant to develop a more mature system of signals and to cry less as he/she gets older is critical; young parents tend to view prompt responses as "spoiling the infant." Explain that responding promptly to her infant's cry does not always mean holding the baby or immediately feeding. Alternatives that may be suggested include (Newton, 1983):

> Place the infant in an infant seat with a brightly colored toy suspended above.
> Place infant in a swing with soft, soothing music.
> Talk to the crying infant and/or pat the infant gently without moving the infant from bed.
> Take the crying infant for a stroller ride.
> Help the mother understand that her infant will sense and respond to her emotional state.

It is important for the practitioner to emphasize to the adolescent that if the crying makes her angry or emotionally distraught, she must call for help. All mothers need relief at times, whether for an hour to take a walk or for only a few minutes to get out or away. If no person is available to give her relief, there are usually telephone hot-lines for parents to call and talk to another adult until they feel calmer.

Personal Level of Parental Role Attainment: Period of Infant-Directed Activity (5 to 9 Months)

From around the sixth to the eighth month following birth, middle- and late-adolescent mothers began to incorporate the mothering role as part of their identities (Mercer, 1979). With internalization of the maternal role, the young mother also perceives that her personal growth and development are accelerated. She may see herself as more sensitive to others and as having greater skills to care for another. Although the teen will describe the mother role as most difficult, she may not view the premature mother role as handicapping.

However, at 8 months, mothers of all ages reported new challenges in the mothering role that led to this period being called a *disruption phase*

(Mercer, 1986a). Infants were more direct, and their more specific responses were more easily interpreted, but for some teens it was very difficult: an 18-year-old said, "I don't know too much (about mothering). I'm not good. I'm just putting up with it."

Involvement of young fathers with their infants and the mothers of the infants have varied considerably in research reports. Unger and Wandersman (1988) observed that although about half of the biological fathers were no longer involved with the mothers at 8 months postpartum, the teenage mother's relationship to her male partner appeared to play a very important role in affecting her behavior toward her infant; teen mothers with good partner support were less rejecting and punitive with their child care.

Not all relationships with biological fathers are supportive, however. Crockenberg (1981) and we found that some mothers had troublesome relationships with biological fathers in situations in which the young mother had severed interpersonal relationships. These mothers reported the young fathers threatening to sue for custody and making other threats.

At 8 months, lower role strain, greater social support, less marital stress, and greater empathy were associated with teenage mothers' greater gratification in mothering (Mercer et al., 1982). Lower personality disorder, marital stress, sadistic attitudes, and role strain were associated with higher maternal infant attachment. Lower role strain, more optimal boiling point and disciplinarian attitudes, and greater social support were associated with more competent maternal behavior. The young mother's disciplinarian attitudes were predictive of how she handled irritating child behaviors.

At 8 months postpartum, adolescent mothers had more physical health complaints than did older mothers, primarily centering around urinary tract infections and menstrual problems (Mercer, 1986a). The adolescent needs reminding about basic information such as the importance of urinating before and after intercourse to reduce cystitis. A discussion of changes in menstrual patterns while breast-feeding is warranted. Discharges from one's body, particularly blood, arouse much concern in adults, and even more in adolescents.

Discussion of sexually transmitted diseases, including AIDS, is an important part of contraceptive and health counseling. Dysplasia, a precancerous change in cervical cells, has been associated with having sex at an early age and a history of sexually transmitted diseases. There is an association between cervical cancer and the sexually transmitted virus that causes genital warts. Allow time for the adolescent to express any concerns she may have about her health. Use models and visual aids for explanations about her body.

Only one-third of the teenagers reported receiving emotional support at this period (Mercer, Hackley, & Bostrom, 1984b). While one-half reported their mother's or mother-in-law's presence in their social network, one-half also named their male partner. It is important to continue to help the young woman identify persons with whom she can share social support. The lack of emotional support may contribute to their poorer physical well-being.

Reorganization: Infant Concentration On The Mother (9 to 12 months)

Sander (1962) referred to this period as "separating the women from the girls," as mothers must be responsive to the increasing manipulative infant. Teenagers were engrossed in and amazed with the rapid growth and development of their infants during the first year. However, teenagers more often than older mothers reported using physical discipline, and fewer reported using distraction to divert their infants from something they wanted but couldn't have (Mercer, 1986a). When teenagers compared how they disciplined their child with how their mothers had disciplined them, they said that they used more physical punishment than their mothers had. Teenagers' interactions with their infants were also more rigid and more strict than those of older women.

Emotional support received by 39% of the teenagers was significantly related to their child-rearing attitudes. Emotional support was positively related to maternal attitudes regarding control of the child's aggressive responses, encouragement of reciprocity, and appropriate closeness or not seeing the infant as a narcissistic extension of self, and to observed maternal behavior and self-reported ways of handling irritating child behaviors (Mercer et al., 1984b).

Teenagers' infants weighed more than infants of older women, with 60% being above the fiftieth percentile (Mercer, 1984). The question is raised whether this increased weight during infancy begins a life-long trajectory of obesity and hypertension; 41% of the teenagers were black, and blacks have greater problems with hypertension. Nutrition counseling is a must with the youthful mother, both for herself and her infant, and should continue at all contacts with her.

In response to the question about how they coped with difficult times with the infant, teenagers more often said they ignored the infant and stated that they bit or slapped the infant back when the infant bit or slapped. They less often stated that they planned or adjusted their time as a coping strategy. These behaviors can be related in part to less ability to conceptualize abstractly, less experience, and less education, all of which influenced their attitudes.

Ongoing assessment fo the teenagers' parenting practices with their infants is critical. Anticipatory guidance regarding parenting the individuating toddler is important at every contact. Nurses can role-model standards for dependable interpersonal relationships, adult-child interactions, values about child care, and other modes of child care.

Teenagers reported higher stress from negative life events experienced during the first year of motherhood as compared to older women (Mercer, 1986a). This stress was a predictor of maternal role attainment, maternal infant attachment, and infant growth and development. Teenagers also expressed more concern about their future security and reported greater financial stress. Slesinger (1981) found that poor socioeconomic conditions were the most important factor related to the woman's mothering ability and the health of her child. The health professional continues to enlist all community and federal agencies available to provide financial and other support for the teen mother.

SUMMARY

Middle- and late-adolescent mothers, who have advantages at the biological level of adaptation, have disadvantages at the psychological and social levels of adaptation. Their conceptions of ideal mothering behaviors are more focused on caretaking behaviors such as feeding or clothing, and their greater rigidity compared with older women is reflected in their more punitive attitudes toward infants and in their discipline of their infants (Mercer, 1986b). Despite these disadvantages, their infants did exceptionally well during the first year in one study.

The importance of all types of support, especially for the teenager, make it imperative that attention is allotted to helping young women identify potential sources of support and develop social skills in eliciting and maintaining support. It is critical for health professionals to remember that teenagers do not utilize reading materials such as magazines or books in seeking information for problem solving. First, school dropouts probably cannot comprehend the meaning of the pamphlets and other reading materials often passed out to parents, if they are able to read them at all.

The adolescent mother's family, in particular her mother and her male partner, are especially important among low socioeconomic status (SES) black and Mexican American women as a motivation to adopt good health practices (Healthy Mother, Healthy Babies Coalition, 1986). While the father may not be viewed as a good source of health information, his presence, emotional support, and influence have considerable impact on the mother's state of mind and on her assimilation and use of information received from other sources. Teenage mothers rely on family members for health information and problem solving. Thus health professionals must work with male partners and family to disseminate health information.

There is no stereotypical teenage mother; therefore planning and implementation of care systems require creativity and flexibility (Speraw, 1987). Adolescents may well look to health professionals to provide short-term psychosocial support and to provide assistance in planning for the future, along with the direct provision of physical care and education. Special programs work, but enough and strategically placed programs continue to be the challenge. We know mother and infant outcome are both greatly improved through these programs.

Nurses can't correct the problem families, nor can they promise a conflict-free time of motherhood. But knowing how important home visits are to young mothers, public health nurse referrals are a must for all youthful mothers, especially for the low income mothers who have little help from other resources.

5

When Parents Face
an Obstetrical Risk Situation

Pregnancy and childbirth convey specific expectations; women expect that they will be pregnant 9 months, perhaps have some morning sickness, will feel the baby's movement around 4 months, and will become increasingly larger and more awkward until they deliver by their estimated date of confinement (EDC). The expectations are that labor will begin with recognizable cues and that with minimal obstetrical intervention they will deliver a healthy infant. Whenever an obstetrical or medical complication arises to contradict expectations either during pregnancy or childbirth, the expectant mother begins to doubt her abilities as a woman and often her capabilities as a mother. Up to 20% of all pregnancies are labeled as high risk, and this high-risk group accounts for over one-half of all fetal and neonatal deaths (Pernoll et al., 1986). Thus the high-risk label is not to be taken lightly by the pregnant family, as they are faced with uncertainty of outcome. The uncertainty that a family has about outcome has the potential to mediate the extent that social support can contribute to their adjustment (Mishel & Braden, 1987).

Since pregnancy and the approaching birth cause much change for the parents and the family, some stress and anxiety result in normal contexts. With the situation of obstetrical risk, stress increases, and if antenatal hospitalization is required, the stress is heightened even more. Increased stress during pregnancy is associated with poor reproductive outcome (Istvan, 1986; Smilkstein et al., 1984). With increased stress, anxiety and depression are also increased. Anxiety leads to physiological changes such as increased catecholamine levels; anxiety and depression lead to poor health behaviors that contribute to poorer reproductive outcome. Depressive symptoms during pregnancy were associated with greater life stress, less social support, poor weight gain, smoking cigarettes, and the ingestion of alcohol and cocaine (Zuckerman et al., 1989). Maternal anxiety is related to both poorer fetal and newborn health status (Lederman, 1986) and to poorer maternal health (Lederman, 1984b).

This chapter focuses on the impact of high-risk obstetrical situations on the pregnant woman and her family. The impact of a high-risk pregnancy (including challenges of the unique situations of life-threatening emergencies, chronic illness, and obstetrical emergencies during labor and delivery) on the anticipatory stage of parental role attainment is first discussed. This is followed by findings from a study of high- and low-risk women and their partners at the formal, informal, and achievement of parental role identity stages of parental role attainment (Mercer et al., 1987). Chapters 7 and 8, which focus on nursing and health care for infants who are premature and infants with handicaps, are also applicable to many of this group.

IMPACT OF A HIGH-RISK PREGNANCY ON ANTICIPATORY STAGE OF PARENTAL ROLE ATTAINMENT

A high-risk pregnancy changes the way a woman thinks about her unborn child, her pregnancy, her priorities and concerns, her stability of her physical and emotional self, her support system, her body image, sense of control over self and situations, and her family system. The expectant father also experiences many changes with this stressful event but in somewhat different ways. Despite these alterations, most parents in the high-risk situation proceed with the tasks of pregnancy and their anticipatory work of parental role attainment.

Perceptions Of The Unborn Infant

In contrast to parents with an uncomplicated pregnancy who fantasize extensively about the infant's gender, appearance, and other characteristics (Rubin, 1984; Sherwen, 1987), once a high-risk diagnosis is made, the couple worries more and are more anxious about their infant's current and future health and survival (Mercer et al., 1987). High-risk couples often know their infant's gender because of extensive diagnostic tests. The uncertainty of their infant's outcome leads them to cope by hoping for a good outcome, and in terms of the statistical chance of their infants' survival as indicated by their quotes:

(Expectant High-Risk Mothers)

- I want to give her (infant) every day to be that much better. I'm real hopeful.
- I try not to think of it as a person. I don't want to know the sex—a safety valve in case it doesn't make it.
- I can't wait for it to get here. He'd better be healthy. Why is he doing this to me? . . . I'm worried if I should lose him after a couple of months. That would be the worst. I want the best; I'm excited about taking care of him.
- I'm just worrying about the baby's health. I had the fifth transfusion this week. I feel very close to her.
- I really love the baby and want it to be O.K., but I feel like I'm putting a distance between the baby in me in case something happens. Don't listen baby!

(Expectant Fathers with High-Risk Partners)

- I'm looking forward to the birth but am concerned about the baby. Anxious for her to get here. I still worry that something can go wrong.
- I'm hoping that everything turns out O.K. Hoping for a healthy birth. My mind is more on Mary than on the baby.
- I have a strong sense of faith and hope, tremendous anxiety. Stressed, fear but yet optimism. I have never been this stressed in my life.

Uncertainty is pervasive among all high-risk parents. Joan made a statement reflecting the defense of projection to cope with the uncertainty: "I think it is a strong baby. . . . I don't feel as protective toward the baby since I found it was a boy . . . feel it is stronger than me." Anne, a hospitalized woman, said, "Since I've been here, I love it more. A lot of times during the pregnancy, I didn't even think about being pregnant. Now that I'm here, I love the baby more; we're going through something together." This latter comment could in part indicate the defense of rationalization; the hospitalization and risk situation have weakened this woman's control, and by assigning some tangible benefit to the situation, it is easier to continue.

Feelings About Pregnancy

High-risk couples are more anxious, worried, or ambivalent about their pregnancies than low-risk couples; they less often describe feeling great, happy, or that pregnancy is wonderful (Mercer et al., 1987). Curry (1987) reported that hospitalized women wished for the pregnancy to end but quickly added their feelings of guilt about the wish. Curry (1987) also observed that many attempted to justify or make sense of the pregnancy, illustrating how the high-risk situation altered usual expectations of pregnancy such that there was a need to resolve the dissonance.

Partners of high-risk women worry about them, and when the women are hospitalized, men express concern about the separation as well as the difficulty that pregnancy has posed. Men's feelings about the high-risk pregnancy are quite diverse but riddled with uncertainty as indicated by their remark's (Mercer et al., 1987):

- I feel happy about the pregnancy, but still worried and anxious. I worry about how it will change our lives. I worry I didn't discourage her working. I feel a little bit inadequate, about being able to take care of everything besides the financial end—all the intangibles.
- I anticipate the end result. I have financial worries now that the baby is almost here.
- I feel what she (wife) feels—scared, nervous, sad.
- I'm exhausted, working 14 hours a day and racing to the hospital. It is keeping us apart and we can't enjoy our time together.
- I feel a lot more love for my wife; I feel closer to her—sad but hopeful.

A hospitalized woman's ambivalence was evident in describing her feelings about her pregnancy (Mercer et al., 1987):

I feel more negative than positive right now (28 weeks gestation, preterm labor). It's changed my life so much; I feel so tied down. I feel so sick I almost regret being pregnant, yet at the same time want to have the baby. I was less hopeful in the beginning and much more depressed.

Expectant Parents' Priorities And Concerns In A High-Risk Pregnancy

If the couple has other children, their children's care is of great concern, whether the woman is on bed rest at home or in the hospital. The expectant father in high-risk situations is much more focused on his partner's health than the father in low-risk situations. Finances are problematic because of added expenses during pregnancy and the uncertainty of future expenses with a sick or handicapped infant. When asked what would be of most help to their families, many high-risk couples stated, "To win the lottery," (Mercer et al., 1987). As noted above, the infants' health and survival are also of great concern. Anne, a hospitalized high-risk expectant mother described her concerns:

I worry about the long-term effects on my health and my ability to cope. I worry about how I'll feel about the baby, because of the sickness and trouble its caused me. I feel less adequate as a wife because I can't do anything, but I feel thankful that I'm in a supportive relationship. I feel anxious because my role has changed from nurturer to more of a dependent one and have fears about how it'll affect the relationship. I feel guilty and concerned about him (mate) his well being. I feel happy he is supportive, but feel less like a lover in a romantic way than I did about him. This is the biggest stressful event we have faced together in 7 years.

Despite spending greater energy on these stressors and concerns, high-risk women's scores on identification with the motherhood role and relationship with their mother (two tasks of maternal role attainment did not differ from normative samples of low-risk women (Curry, 1987). High-risk women, however, scored significantly lower on acceptance of the pregnancy, indicating that they had not resolved their conflicting feelings.

Stability of Physical and Emotional Self

Physical stability in the high-risk condition makes it easier for the pregnant woman to manage her pregnancy (Corbin, 1987). There is less uncertainty when either the chronic illness of the obstetrical problem stabilizes, and the woman begins to feel a little more in control. Epinephrine levels are positively associated with psychological uncertainty (Delahunt & Mellsop, 1987); thus greater uncertainty among high-risk women increases their risk for higher epinephrine levels. Higher epinephrine levels are associated with longer labors (Lederman, 1984b), decelerated fetal heart patterns, and lower Apgar scores following birth (Lederman, 1986).

Stabilization of the home environment is also central to the high-risk woman's management of the pregnancy (Corbin, 1987). Richardson (1987a) observed that women at risk for preterm labor report increased numbers of conflicts in relationships with persons important to them as their pregnancy progresses. Their method of coping with these interpersonal conflicts—resistance, aggression, or withholding patterns—enhanced rather than resolved the conflicts.

There is less stability in both relationships and emotional responses in high-risk populations. Hospitalized high-risk women differed from low-risk women in their lower level of education, larger number of children, poorer health status, greater stress from negative life events, greater depression and state anxiety, poorer family functioning, and greater received support (Mercer et al., 1987). High-risk women's partners differed from low-risk women's partners in their larger number of children, greater unreadiness for the pregnancy, greater depression and state anxiety, poorer mate relationship, poorer family functioning, and less perceived support (Mercer et al. 1987).

Hospitalized women described their feelings as being on a roller coaster (Curry, 1987). They also experience great stress in their separation from home and family members, their disturbing emotions, changes in their family situations, health concerns, and changing self-image (White & Ritchie, 1984). Hospitalized women and their partners report significantly greater state anxiety and depression than couples experiencing a normal pregnancy; their trait anxiety scores (proneness to anxiety) did not differ (Mercer et al., 1987).

Sense of Control

The more control a woman has of her life, the more positively she views her pregnancy; diminished symptoms of the first trimester of pregnancy meant regaining control of one's body (Gara & Tilden, 1984). Women who see their hopes realized feel more in control; accepting and coming to terms with the pregnancy leads to adjusted or rationalized control (Gara & Tilden, 1984). Perhaps most difficult of all for the high-risk expectant family is their loss of control over their life situation. Their choices regarding the birth and birth environment are severely curtailed. They have a sense of helplessness or powerlessness as they wait for the obstetrical problem to resolve. Anne, the hospitalized woman quoted above, said about her pregnancy:

> I don't like being treated as a sick person. I'm used to treating pregnancy as normal. I'm a very organized person. I like things under *my* control. I didn't plan this (preterm labor)—it's out of my control. I don't have control of my own body; I feel like a victim. I am used to being in control.

Expectant fathers in high-risk situations may feel even more out of control. One man whose wife was hospitalized said, "I have lingering doubts about whether I want to be doing this (having a baby) and who I want to be doing it with." Another man described, "It's a helpless feeling. I'm worried, preparing myself for a possible loss."

The chronically ill expectant woman is likely to be more assertive in the management of her care during pregnancy. Corbin (1987) found that a group of chronically ill pregnant women managed their obstetric risk factors through assessing, balancing, and controlling their conditions; she called this process of management *protective governing*. These strategies (assessing, balancing, and controlling) were used to exert some control over threats to the outcomes of their pregnancies. Conditions influencing the women's ability to govern their pregnancies included the women's agreement with their physician's assessment of their medical and obstetrical risks, their knowledge of the situation, an adequate support system, stability, and their perceived sense of control. Women with a chronic illness did not passively follow medical regimens but assessed the regimens for their potential benefit or harm. They then balanced or modified what they would actually do, maintaining some control.

Social Support

Higher social support was associated with less emotional conflict among pregnant women with a chronic illness (Corbin, 1987). This also holds true for women without chronic illness. Women who later experienced preterm labor described problematic and deteriorating relationships with their partners and parental figures in early pregnancy (Richardson, 1987b). Only 55% of relationships were described as satisfactory prior to the onset of premature labor. In a comparative study, there were no significant differences in high-risk women's rating of their mate relationships from low-risk women's; however, men in high-risk situations viewed their mate relationship poorer than men in low-risk situations (Mercer et al., 1987). Partners in the high-risk situation (96% men, 92% women) more often reported their mates in their social networks than partners in the low-risk situation (79% men, 68% women) (Mercer & Ferketich, 1988). Louise, a hospitalized woman said, "My husband is really the most important to me you know. Our relationship is at the core of all this. If something happens, we still have each other."

Predictors of men's reported mate relationships in high-risk situations were perceived support (23%), relationship with their mothers as teenagers (13%), readiness for pregnancy (13%), weeks gestation they felt fetal movement (4%), current contract with father (4%), and stress from negative life events the previous year (5%), accounting for 63% of the variance (Mercer et al., 1987). Men's unreadiness for the pregnancy seems to place a strain on the couple relationship (readiness for pregnancy also accounted for 9% of the variance for low-risk partners). Only 26% of the variance in high-risk women's reported mate relationship was explained; perceived support explained 8.4% and trait anxiety explained 17.3%.

Wiggins (1983) found that social support was an important predictor of fetal attachment among high-risk women but that the nature of the social support differed by marital status of the women. Among married women, the closeness of their husbands was central, and among unmarried women the support network was important. Received support was a predictor of fetal attachment among partners of hospitalized high-risk women, explaining 6% of the variance; other predictors were family functioning (8%), mate relationship (9%), and help from parents (9%) (Mercer et al., 1988).

Although hospitalized high-risk women reported greater received support than low-risk pregnant women, support received had no effects on anxiety and depression during pregnancy (Mercer & Ferketich, 1988). High-risk women reported greater received and perceived support than their partners, however, and perceived support explained 11% of the variance in men's anxiety and 9% of the variance in their depression.

Curry and Snell (1984) found that high-risk women's relationship with their mothers was positively associated with maternal behavior during pregnancy. More high-risk women (75%) reported their mothers in their support network than low-risk women (61%) (Mercer & Ferketich, 1988). Curry (1987) reported that some hospitalized high-risk women viewed their unborn infant as a member of their support network, and the infant appeared to foster their ability to cope. Joan's and Anne's comments cited above support Curry's observation.

Body Image

The body image, how the body appears to self, evolves from the outward visual appearance of the body, the postural model learned through body positions, and action or motility of the body and body parts (Schilder, 1950). A person's body is heavily invested with emotion and action. The body image is not static but is in a constant state of change (Schilder, 1950), especially during pregnancy.

There is less awareness of the body in a state of complete relaxation, but with movement, a clearer perception of body occurs. Body boundaries are learned through touch. Body orifices are particularly important, as they are more sensitive than other areas of the skin. The high-risk woman on bed rest and tocolytic drugs is immobilized, and assaults to her body intactness and loss of mobility pose threats to her self-image. As her pulse races and she experiences palpitations, headaches, and tremors from the tocolytic drug, her ability to define her body's capabilities and boundaries is threatened. Pain from immobility and bodily intrusions adds to body image distortion. Occasionally, feelings of unreality are so strong that the woman feels as if the experience is happening to someone else, not her. Helen said during her hospitalization, "Nothing like this has ever happened to me before. I am still ambivalent—seems surrealistic—not really happening to me. I know it is."

High-risk women's comments regarding threats to their body image illustrate the impact of the pregnancy and the risk:

- I feel like there must be something wrong with you that you can't have a normal pregnancy. Seems like a lot of women with problems in pregnancy are career women. Now there is a threat of losing ground in my job, position, standing. It is very stressful to stay at home watching TV. Lots of people are competing for your job. After a very stressful business day followed by a night of contractions I ended up in the hospital. I have a loss of self-esteem because part of my self-image is wrapped up in my job.
- I feel more fragile—like pregnancy has taken over my body; whereas before I was in control. There's a little resentment to the child—why is this happening to me?

Family System

In high-risk situations requiring hospitalization, family functioning faces disequilibrium (Mercer et al., 1988; White & Ritchie, 1984). Both high-risk hospitalized women and their partners report poorer family functioning than their low-risk counterparts (Mercer et al., 1988). Perceived support explained 32% of the variance in family functioning, with positive relationship with their mother as a teenager explaining 12% and stress from negative life events explaining 4%, for a total of 48% explained variance among expectant fathers in high-risk situations. For high-risk women, sense of mastery explained 17% unique variance, trait anxiety explained 9%, and relationship with their fathers as children explained 7%, for a total of 33% explained variance in family functioning.

One-fifth of high-risk women were concerned about their roles as wife and mother (Mercer et al., 1987). One high-risk hospitalized woman stated, "I'm not much of a wife now—not contributing much of anything. I feel like a human vegetable or incubator, and I feel unlovable." Another said of her family life, "I'd like to have some kind of my life back. I feel very trapped. Women are already trapped into a life of slavery and poor wages once they're married and pregnant."

The greatest fear in the backs of some women's minds is that they will not survive. Janet summed this fear up: "If I don't make it, I have

two children and a husband. I always think, 'How would they survive?' I
want to see my kids grow up."

Nursing and Health Care For High-Risk Expectant Parents During Pregnancy

Nursing care for the high-risk woman, whether hospitalized or not,
includes assessment and intervention for promoting her work on the
usual maternal tasks of pregnancy in work toward the maternal role
and helping her deal with uncertainty of outcome. If the woman is
hospitalized, nursing care includes, in addition to the above, helping the
woman deal with her loneliness, boredom, feelings of helplessness,
powerlessness, anxiety, depression, and fear, and preparing her for
labor and delivery. The expectant father feels equally as helpless but
often does not receive adequate support from the health professional.

The tasks of pregnancy identified by Rubin (1975), seeking and ensuring safe passage through pregnancy and childbirth, acceptance of
the child by significant others, attaching to the infant, and giving of
oneself, were discussed in chapter 2. They are enlarged here as applicable to the high-risk woman.

Seeking and Ensuring Safe Passage Through
Pregnancy and Childbirth

Rubin (1975) notes that by the third trimester, there is no separation of
self and baby; any danger to one implies danger to the other; there is a
heightened awareness of vulnerability to danger from the environment,
with normal, everyday events becoming dangerous. The high-risk
woman's vulnerability is heightened; she must live with the uncertainty
of the outcome, regardless of her efforts. Her drive to secure a safe
passage accounts for her faithfulness in undergoing screening tests,
numerous laboratory tests, visits to the clinic, complete bed rest, and
hospitalization when necessary. In the work to secure a safe passage,
she willingly alters the family lifestyle and pattern of living. The family
refrigerator is used to store 24-hour (or longer) urine samples. She
takes a leave from her career earlier than planned.

Theories of uncertainty in illness are relevant in considering health
care for the high-risk woman, since she is unable to predict her outcome accurately. Mishel (1988) defined uncertainty as "the cognitive
state created when the person cannot adequately structure or catego-
rize an event because of lack of sufficient cues" (p. 225). Mishel's
theory is utilized to apply to the high-risk woman. In illness, people
who are able to construct a pattern for their symptoms have a clearer

estimation of their status (Mishel & Braden, 1988). Credible authority, such as the health professional, also has a direct negative influence on uncertainty (Mishel & Braden, 1988). Event familiarity, patterns within the health care environment, has a direct effect on reducing ambiguity in a situation (Mishel & Braden, 1988); thus the woman hospitalized for the first time during pregnancy and for a pregnancy-related illness may have higher uncertainty than a woman with a chronic illness.

Health care providers can provide structure through information and social support in addition to trust and confidence as credible authorities. It is important to provide this information to both parents and, when possible, to provide the information to the parents together. The high-risk parent may then appraise the uncertainty as a danger or possible opportunity and mobilize coping strategies to adapt to the situation. The parent may cope by either mobilizing for direct action such as vigilance and information seeking or by affect-management through faith, disengagement, or cognitive support (Mishel, 1988). Uncertainty may be viewed as an opportunity if the alternative is certainty of a negative outcome (Mishel, 1988). The woman in preterm labor at 26 weeks gestation hopes that the labor will be stopped, although she is uncertain whether it will be stopped or not, and this *uncertainty is better than knowing the labor cannot be stopped.*

Taylor's (1983) theory of cognitive adaptation is also helpful to the health professional in understanding the high-risk couple's appraisal of the situation and their behaviors. When a person experiences a threatening event, adaptation occurs through cognitive restructuring of the meaning of life in face of the event; the process of restructuring includes a search for meaning, efforts to gain mastery or control, and an attempt to enhance the self (Taylor, 1983). Taylor proposes that these cognitive restructurings are based on illusions that can protect and lead to constructive action and coping. The high-risk couple faces the real possibility of a preterm infant unable to live or who will have life-long handicaps as a result or of an infant who will have other handicaps. The couple may restructure this possibility by seeing exaggerated health gains for the infant achieved by each added day of gestation (effort to gain mastery), seeing that this trial will bring them closer together (search for meaning), and seeing that if born, their infant will not be as ill as the one they just saw in the intensive care nursery (self-enhancement).

The health professional in gaining the high-risk couple's trust and confidence provides as much information as is available about their situation. Realizing that uncertainty provides the ability to hope, and that hope is a strong coping mechanism; absolute negatives are not introduced unless there is certainty of the occurrence. Possibility of negatives may be introduced without destroying the expectant parents' hope.

High-risk women may feel well except for the pregnancy condition; well people placed in a sick role quickly get frustrated and bored with the hospital routine. It is essential that routines be made more flexible to consider the high-risk woman's needs. For example, does she really need to be awakened at 6:00 A.M. to have her temperature taken?

Childbirth education needs to be expanded to include hospitalized women who also need to ensure their safety through labor and delivery. The content area needs to include the unique needs of the high-risk women (Avery & Olson, 1987). Many have a cesarean birth; preparation for such a birth helps to allay anxiety (Hart, 1980).

Acceptance of Her Infant by Persons Important to Her

The pregnant woman is eager that those close to her show unconditional acceptance of the baby. Her partner's acceptance of responsibility, along with his and others' time, caring, and attention, all reflect acceptance of the mother and her infant.

It is important to assess how others feel toward her infant and whether they are accepting if the infant comes too early or is sick. Conditional acceptance, whether it is of a specific gender or dependent on the infant's condition, is viewed by the woman as implicit rejection (Rubin, 1975).

Attaching to the Infant

High-risk women and their partners score higher in state anxiety during pregnancy (Mercer & Ferketich, 1988), and anxiety about the unborn infant indicated increased attachment postpartally among a low-risk population (Leifer, 1977, 1978). In contrast to earlier beliefs that high-risk women may have more difficulty forming attachments to their unborn infants (Mercer, 1977a, 1977b), research findings indicate that this is not true for the majority. High-risk women score similarly in fetal attachment to low-risk women (Curry, 1987; Kemp & Page, 1987; Mercer et al., 1988). Within the groups of high-risk women, however, there is greater variability in reported fetal attachment.

The uncertainty of outcome may be so great that some high-risk women may hesitate to express their feelings, such as Joan:

> I've had some concerns about whether it's going to be healthy or not. I'm scared to death that it's not going to be healthy. I don't have many other thoughts about it yet.

Similarly, Mary was uncertain, but quite hopeful:

> I guess the baby's doing fine. I can feel it. I just wish he would hang in there and make it. I hope when he comes out, he will have minimal problems. I saw my son last year with all those tubes and IV's, and I don't want to see another baby like that. I hope he's healthy.

Both Joan and Mary have positive concern and anxiety indicating atachment; however, concern for the infant's health outweighs talk of love and closeness to the infant. It is important that frequent opportunities are provided for the mother to talk about her concerns. Concern and worry indicate attachment. Indication of failure to attach was evidenced by Sue:

> The baby blocks, invades my life. I'm not real pleased with the pregnancy or the idea of having the baby. My initial instincts for an abortion were probably the best.

Wiggins (1983) found that maternal health problems were the greatest predictor of fetal attachment among high-risk women; the more maternal health problems, the lower the women's attachment. However, pregnancy risk and health status failed to enter the models predicting fetal attachment for hospitalized high-risk expectant mothers or fathers (Mercer et al., 1988). Educational level had direct negative effects on women's attachment, explaining only 9% of the variance. Predictors explaining 31% of the variance in fetal attachment for men in the high-risk situation were related to support variables as noted above: family function had direct negative effects; mate relationship, received support, and parents' help had direct positive effects.

Hospitalized high-risk women reported significantly greater attachment to their unborn infants than their partners, however (Mercer et al., 1988). The high-risk woman is making a greater sacrifice and investment; it is understandable that to resolve her cognitive dissonance about such a profound investment, a great value is placed on the child. Men who are having less intimate experiences with the unborn infant tend to be more focused on their mates and health threats to them.

Grace (1984) studied whether a mother's knowledge of fetal gender (as many high-risk women have) affected attachment but found no differences between groups of women who knew and who didn't know. Women who had prenatal knowledge of their infants' gender called their infants by name significantly less often than mothers who were unaware of gender, a finding opposite to what was expected.

Discussion of fetal development is important. A visit to the neonatal intensive care unit provides an opportunity for the high-risk couple to see infants approximately the same gestational age as their infant (Perry, Parer, & Inturrisi, 1986). Not only do couples meet those who will be caring for their infant, but they are also able to observe the care that is required.

Giving of Oneself

In giving of oneself, benefits derived from a child are balanced by what is taken away by the child (Rubin, 1975). The high-risk woman gives the ultimate; she may be on bed rest for months, taking drugs that increase her anxiety and her concern for their effects on her infant, and at times she may fear for her own well-being. It is important for the health professional to help the expectant woman enlist support from her partner and family; she must be nurtured during this time if she is to nurture her infant later.

The high-risk woman must see a reason for her giving of self to the extreme. Providing her with accurate information about her and her infant's condition helps to reinforce the value of her sacrifice. While hospitalization is not an attractive alternative, reports of successful outcomes indicate it is worthwhile (Williams, 1986). Putting the high-risk woman in contact with a mother who has had a similar experience is helpful (Snyder, 1988).

If the hospitalized woman feels up to it, it is important for her to have opportunities for creative pursuits to fill her hours. If there is no occupational therapy unit in the hospital, she may be encouraged to have someone bring her handwork or sewing for either her unborn baby or other family member. Special care should be taken to have a program of passive exercises that do not exacerbate her obstetrical problem, since prolonged bed rest tends to lead to weakness.

INITIAL ADAPTATION STAGE OF PARENTAL ROLE ATTAINMENT: IMPACT BY TYPE OF RISK

The impact that a high-risk situation has on the couple varies by the situation in both the morbidity and temporal dimensions. Expectant parents respond differently to maternal life-threatening emergencies, less severe obstetrical emergencies, and the situation of chronic illness or handicap with a pregnancy, and health care is planned accordingly. The nurse and other health professionals have vast opportunities to facilitate early parental adaptation during the formal stage of parental role attainment from birth to 6 to 8 weeks postpartum in situations of obstetrical risk.

Life-Threatening Emergencies

Life-threatening emergencies more often occur around the time of childbirth, whether hemorrhage or pregnancy-induced hypertension is a problem. As normal labor progresses, a woman's ego becomes increasingly constricted, and she is unable to communicate by more than short words, with her temporal focus locked on the present (Rich, 1973). Her anxiety and catecholamine levels increase as her ability to cope decreases (Lederman et al., 1978). Superimpose on this natural physiological and psychological state an unexpected event such as abruptio placentae or internal postpartal hemorrhage. As the expectant mother is rapidly prepped and rushed to the operating room, survival and possible damage to her body are primary concerns. She is lonely and frightened at the metallic sounds of instruments being set up for the surgery. She is in a surrealistic world as she vacillates between consciousness and unconsciousness, never quite sure whether she is dreaming or awake. It can't be real; this floating mass of tissue cannot be her.

Following any birth, ego expansion proceeds from focus on self to the infant, the immediate environment, and to persons and last to events beyond the present (Rubin, 1984). The new mother must regain control of her body before she is able to direct much energy to others.

Nursing and other health professionals are challenged to talk to the women undergoing such an experience by talking to her during the experience (unless she has general anesthesia), telling her that everyone is working to help her through the situation. Touching the woman's arm, shoulder, or face as such reassurance is given helps establish some body boundary and reality to the communication. Zoie described her feelings when she was undergoing emergency surgery and unable to speak:

> I couldn't speak, and I couldn't move in any way to let people know that I knew everything that was going on. I realized they thought I was dying by their frantic rush, by what they were saying, and their sending for the priest. But I knew I was not dying, and I kept trying to open my mouth, but it wouldn't open. I wanted to shout, 'I'm not dying. I am going to live. Please don't give up, please don't quit working with me. I am not going to die!'

In the early postpartum, there is much missing information for the woman who experienced emergency treatment and surgery. She needs help in sorting through and establishing what happened to her. A woman who hemorrhaged following a cesarean birth, had a vaginal packing, and finally a hysterectomy, wanted to know, "How many times was I put to sleep? Why did this happen? I had such an enjoyable pregnancy. It was planned and went well."

Women who have had life-threatening emergencies are weaker and more exhausted than women having a usual delivery. They work hard at regaining control over their bodies and are highly anxious to achieve this control. One woman moving extremely slowly in getting out of bed always insisted, "I'll do it, please let me move at my pace. I'm sorry that I'm so much trouble; I've really caused you a lot of work." The apology indicates that the woman feels inadequate that she is different from other mothers. They need praise for progress and reassurance that they are not trouble, but they are important, recuperating mothers who need rest and nourishment to get well.

Importantly, the partners of women experiencing life-threatening emergencies need extensive support and continual feedback. It is essential that the expectant father be treated as the most crucial support person to the woman and allowed to be with her when at all possible if that is his wish. Being there and witnessing events is usually not as traumatic as the isolation of being sent to a waiting room and treated as an outsider.

Less Severe Obstetrical Emergencies

Situations arise during labor that require a cesarean birth, yet there is no serious threat to the mother's life. Other complications of a non-emergency nature such as a perineal hematoma may be quite painful and demand a lot of the woman's energy that would otherwise be directed toward the new mother role. Sometimes the less severe complications seem to preoccupy the new mother more than severe illness. Perhaps the woman whose life is threatened is so grateful for survival that she forces herself, exhausted as she may be, to focus on events outside herself that she almost missed.

A major premise in either type of event is the sense of loss of expectations and of control. A woman who has diligently prepared for natural childbirth in the birth center faces great disappointment at having to undergo a cesarean birth. Her grief at the loss of expectations and of her control over her birth experience may be expressed with anger and disillusionment with herself as well as with others who were involved in her experience.

Numerous researchers have validated that women view their childbirth experience less positively when it is a cesarean birth (Bradley,

1983; Cranley, Hedahl, & Pegg, 1983; Marut & Mercer, 1979; Mercer, Hackley, & Bostrom, 1983; Padawer et al., 1988). Mothers who had cesarean births also had lower self-esteem (Cox & Smith, 1982). Predictors, in order of their importance of perception of the childbirth experience, were emotional support from mate, time of contact with infant, self-concept, and maternal illness, all of which explained 36% of the variance; informational support, instrumental support, and type of delivery added 3%, but at a nonsignificant level ($p \leq 0.09$) (Mercer et al., 1983). Thus factors other than the surgical delivery are more influential on the woman's satisfaction with her childbirth experience. Control during the childbirth experience is important; women who had spontaneous, unmedicated births also scored higher on perceived control (Hodnett & Simmons-Tropea, 1987). Not all women respond this way. Medically indigent women with minimal childbirth preparation used distancing behaviors prenatally and postpartally to cope with the idea and reality of cesarean birth and were less distraught at having a cesarean birth (Sandelowski & Bustamante, 1986).

Many variables, however, affect the psychological impact of a cesarean birth (Tilden & Lipson, 1981). Variables prior to the birth that affect its impact are birth plans and expectations, the woman's relationship with the physician and hospital, timing of the knowledge that a cesarean would be necessary, and the perceived reason for the cesarean birth. Variables during the birth that affected the impact were the atmosphere in the surgical suite, the presence of the husband, type of anesthesia (some welcomed it, while others were terrified of loss of consciousness or of control of their bodies), and the amount and kind of interactions with their infants at birth. Variables impacting on the cesarean birth postpartally included the amoung and quality of support from nurses, fatigue from labor, and the presence of complications.

Fathers differ from mothers in that they are largely relieved with a cesarean birth (May & Sollid, 1984), with only one-fifth being disappointed or angry. Most of the fathers' negative reactions centered not on the cesarean birth per se but on staff behaviors that ignored their feelings or on policies that excluded their presence at the birth. Fathers need to be treated as knowledgeable persons who are deeply concerned about the outcomes, rather than as "someone in the way, who might faint."

Mothers delivering by cesarean did not differ from mothers delivering vaginally in reported anxiety, depression, or attitudes about the baby (Bradley, Ross, & Warnyca, 1983; Padawer et al., 1988). Conflicting data have been reported about mothering behaviors following cesarean birth. Padawer and associates (1988) reported that women delivering by cesarean birth did not differ in their confidence in mothering (Padawer et al., 1988), whereas Trowell (1982) found that mothers delivering by cesarean were less confident. At 1 year, Trowell observed that mothers who delivered by cesarean maintained less eye-to-eye contact with their infants, reported they felt their baby was a person at an older age, described their experience of motherhood as worse, responded to their infant's crying more slowly, and felt that they had experienced more difficulties and problems than mothers who delivered vaginally. However, there were no differences in the general behavior and development of the two groups of infants (Trowel, 1982). Entwisle and Alexander (1987) found that parents of cesarean-born first and second graders had higher expectations of their children's abilities, and the children also expected and received higher marks in reading and math than children delivered vaginally.

Leonard (1976) found that fathers had more positive feelings toward their infants when the birth as by cesarean. She postulated the reason for this being the father's relief that the infants were out of danger.

Health professionals have an important role in providing parents with the opportunity to discuss their cesarean or emergency birth experience and to fill in any gaps of information. When expectations were not met, understanding the parents' disappointment means more to a parent than a careless comment such as, "You can be thankful you have a live infant." Discussion of vaginal births after a cesarean birth may be helpful to those parents for whom the option is not ruled out.

Providing comfort measures for the mother before she feeds her infant is critical. Pain relief medication, positioning, and inital help getting started are all important. Making all the interactions with her infant as pleasurable as possible will help her dissociate the infant from discomfort. A few women who are insecure may project blame to the infant for her cesarean.

Body image concerns vary, and a scar is viewed differently by mothers. An obese woman who would not look her best in a bikini may be the one who is most concerned about a scar showing if she wears a bikini.

Chronic Illness

The woman with a chronic illness who deliberately chose to have an infant may be dealing with somewhat less uncertainty than women in other high-risk situations. She is more expert in how her body responds to treatment and other medications; she has studied potential outcome of a pregnancy with her condition. The exception is the chronic illness that leads to early maternal death.

In situations of a fatal disease such as acquired immune deficiency syndrome (AIDS), health professionals may harbor resentment that the mother became pregnant, but the woman who hears that there is a 50% chance that her infant will not get the disease may deny the 50% possibility of her infant getting the disease. The woman with AIDS requires extensive help to deal with the uncertainty of her illness and often her living situation. Health professionals and community resources, including mental health and social services, are needed to help families remain functional in such crises (Septimus, 1989).

Mothers with impaired mobility were studied by Kopala (1989), and they also faced a lack of support for their decision to become mothers from both health professionals and their own family. Handicapped mothers, however, are able to see that they spend as much or more time with their children as other mothers and find an increased sense of self-esteem in seeing their healthy child grow up. In addition, having a normal child appears to enhance their own normalcy. Health professionals need to deal with their feelings that run counter to each woman's decision regardless of her situation.

Planning that includes the high-risk couple is important for them to feel some sense of control in a situation where control is lacking. The health professional must accept that the mother's response to her care is based on extensive knowledge of her handicap or disease process, as well as the threat of damage to her body or loss of control over body functions.

A woman who is partially immobilized or on bed rest enjoys back rubs and the gift of time from the nurse who gives them. It provides an intimate time for her to discuss her concerns and feelings. The nurse should organize her activities so that she does not appear rushed. The mother needs to be assured that she and her family, and not the hospital staff, are the ones who are inconvenienced by her risk situation and that the hospital staff are fulfilling their expected roles.

The mother with a health threat in all probability will be depressed at some time. Providing opportunity for her to talk about her concerns is important, and continual assessment of her mental outlook is also important. Referral to mental health professionals is indicated if the depression is affecting her ability to function. A social worker may be able to help work out concerns regarding finances.

Women Hospitalized During Pregnancy for a High-Risk Situation

Birth removes some of the uncertainty for couples with high-risk obstetrical problems; mothers who had been hospitalized and their partners did not differ significantly from low-risk couples in their state anxiety or depression during the early postpartum or at 1 month. High-risk women, however, continued during early postpartum and at

1 month to view their health status less optimally than low-risk women, although 72% were hospitalized for preterm labor (Mercer et al., 1987). Partners of high-risk women, however, did not differ significantly from partners of low-risk women in their reported health status. A mother who had six intrauterine blood transfusions said, "About my health in the future; I'm a little unsure. The thought of AIDS crosses my mind occasionally." At 1 month, mastery, feelings about their pregnancies, dissatisfaction with their birth experience, and how soon the infant was held following birth predicted 42% of the variance in high-risk women's health status. The partners' of high-risk women had 53% of the variance in their health status explained by state anxiety, sex of infant (male infants were associated with better health status), and more positive relationship with their fathers.

During early postpartal hospitalization, high-risk women reported significantly higher infant attachment than low-risk women; high-risk women also reported nonsignificant higher scores at 1 month (Mercer et al., 1987). Partners of high-risk women scored significantly lower than their mates on infant attachment at early postpartum and 1 month; however fathers in both low- and high-risk situations did not differ significantly on their parental attachment scores. The high-risk woman who gave of herself to great extent through antenatal hospitalization tended to place a somewhat higher value on her infant following birth, but this difference began to diminish by 1 month. Irene said during early postpartum, "Though I had a very hard pregnancy and wondered whether it was all worth it, I definitely feel it was now that I have the baby." Kathryn also spoke of her earlier problems in relation to her baby, "After all the problems with premature labor, I truly feel lucky to have my baby." Parents in the high-risk situation did not differ from parents who were in the low-risk situation in their parental competency scores at either early postpartal hospitalization or at 1 month.

Laura described her early mothering:

I feel that being comfortable with parenting is gradual and cumulative. Each day feels better—it doesn't come naturally and people don't automatically know what to do in all situations. It's important and gives me confidence that if there is a problem or question that I have enough resources to find the answers. I feel mixed feelings about staying home with the baby for 6 months. Finances are strained and it's changed our lifestyle.

Lois described a much more hectic early period of mothering:

During the first week of my baby's life, I was elated at having given birth and I felt closer to my husband than ever before. Our happiness, however, was marred by finding out our premature baby had jaundice and would have to return to the hospital for anywhere from 3 days to a week—the time was not specified. The doctors and nurses were very vague about the time involved and the consequences. I guess they didn't want to get our hopes up that we would be able to take the baby home soon. Throughout the whole ordeal we were given the worst possible scenario and were worried to death about the baby possibly needing a blood transfusion. Also, the baby had to have an IV inserted and that was painful—to see him stuck so much. The scare and the fear was 'What if he gets AIDS?' Also, I especially missed the baby tremendously, and my husband missed us both. I spent most of the daytime and every night at the hospital to breast-feed. It was awful.

Fathers also experienced fear and helplessness during the initial adaptation to the infant. Mike shared his feelings:

No one can prepare you for the fear you have when your premature baby stops breathing and changes color from pink to gray. It's a roller-coaster ride from day to day, where you are overjoyed one day and scared to death the next. The hospital care was the best; my only complaint is the lack of information from the doctors. My baby's doctor is the best I could ever want for my son. His tireless hours of work on his days off, as well as his long days when he was working, will make me forever grateful.

The importance of information from health professionals is highlighted by both Lois and Mike.

During this initial adaptation stage of parental role attainment, fathers in high-risk situations rated their couple relationship as significantly less optimal than either their high-risk partners or fathers in low-risk situations. Forty-five percent of the high-risk women had to leave their infants in the hospital on their discharge following birth; at 1 month, 22% still had infants in the intensive care nursery. Although the fathers in the high-risk situation reported less optimal mate relationships (differences were not significant) than the women at the time of hospitalization, the worry about the ill infant no doubt exacerbated any strains. At 1 month, predictors of the fathers' reported mate relationship were self-esteem and perceived and received support, accounting for 48% of the variance. At 1 month, predictors of the mate relationship for high-risk mothers were state anxiety, negative life events stress, fewer weeks gestation at antenatal hospitalization, and greater readiness for the pregnancy, accounting for 29% of the variance (Mercer et al., 1987).

Fathers in high-risk situations reported significantly less received support than mothers during the first week and at 1 month postpartum, although their received social support was not significantly less than that received by fathers in low-risk situations (Mercer et al., 1987). An important role of the nurse in talking with fathers during this time is to discuss their social support networks and help them think about enlisting help from others. Since financial worries are great to fathers at this time, referral to the social worker and providing him with a list of community agencies that may be helpful are very important.

Health professionals have an important role in providing an opportunity for couples to discuss their concerns during the early adaptation stage. Referral to family and or marriage counselors may be indicated, especially if communication between the couple is not open (see chapter 7 for nursing and health care for parents who have infants in the intensive care unit).

INFORMAL STAGE OF PARENTAL ROLE ATTAINMENT: ACHIEVEMENT PHASE

At the informal stage of pleasurable interchange with the increasingly playful infant in which parents feel comfortable with their parenting and parenting style (Mercer, 1986a), high-risk mothers who had been hospitalized were feeling better such that their health status was not significantly different from low-risk mothers (Mercer et al., 1987). Fathers' health status also did not differ from fathers in low-risk situations.

Jane, a high-risk mother who had been on bed rest for 12 weeks during pregnancy, did not feel so strong at 4 months postpartum, however:

> I would like to request that women who are required to be on complete bed rest for more than a couple of weeks to be automatically put on a physical therapy program and closely monitored to provide support for returning to a healthy and strong physical condition. I needed to return to full-time work, and with caring for a baby as well, I'm constantly reminded how truly weak my muscles have become. Yet I'm so tired I lack the motivation to exercise.

Parental role behaviors of parent-infant attachment and parental competence also did not differ between antenatally high- and low-risk mothers at 4 months postpartum (Mercer et al., 1987). Self-esteem and perceived support accounted for 31% of the variance in high-risk mothers' reported competence. High-risk mothers reported significantly higher attachment to their infants than the fathers, contrasted to low-risk couples who did not report significant differences between them. At 4 months, 3% of the high-risk mothers' infants remained hospitalized, but 7% had infants who had been discharged between 1 and 4 months, and these infants continued to have health problems. Only 0.6% of low-risk women had infants with comparable problems. The continued worry and uncertainty about their infants may foster increased attachment among mothers who were high-risk during pregnancy. Parental competence, current contact with their own fathers, and a higher pregnancy risk score were predictive of high-risk women's attachment to their infants, explaining 34% of the variance. For fathers in the high-risk situation, infant attachment (43%) was explained by parental competence and their health problems during the pregnancy. Poorer health during pregnancy among both mothers and fathers was associated with higher parent-infant attachment.

Carla exemplifies the excitement of a high-risk mother at 4 months whose infant was discharged from the hospital at 3 months postpartum:

My baby just came home from the hospital to my great delight. He has a cold now, which worries me because his lungs are scarred and he could get pneumonia. I pray. But he has gained a lot of weight since leaving the hospital and seems to be a reasonably normal baby, a pretty amazing outcome for a boy born at 27 weeks gestation. I've felt pretty well and happy too.

Carla's husband said:

I am very pleased and serene about the baby. It gives me much pleasure to care for him and for her (Carla). Our personal differences do not extend to our dedication to the health and happiness of the baby.

Women who had high-risk pregnancies and were hospitalized did not differ from women who had normal pregnancies in their assessments of their families functioning and their mate relationships (Mercer et al., 1987). Fathers in the high-risk situation, however, rated both their family functioning and their mate relationships as significantly poorer than fathers whose partners had normal pregnancies.

High-risk women need monitoring beyond the puerperium, even though their problem was preterm labor and there is no apparent physical problem. Jane's comment about the physical weakness that occurs following long-term bed rest indicates the importance of more aggressive health care for mothers following birth, and the need for passive exercise during the antepartum on bed rest.

Mothers who have high-risk pregnancies need additional support during this stage of role attainment when other mothers have fewer problems, in part because of continued problems with the infants' health. Fathers in these situations need help in particular in dealing with their frustrations with their family's functioning and their relationships with their mates. Men are often forgotten during this period of parental role attainment, but their need for help is as great as that of mothers; fathers in high-risk situations reported significantly less perceived support at 4 months than fathers whose mates had normal pregnancies (Mercer et al., 1987). Support groups have been helpful to fathers in some situations (Wandersman, 1980).

ACHIEVEMENT OF PARENTAL ROLE IDENTITY

Achieving comfort with one's self in the parenting role and internalizing the parental role identity, usually around 5 to 9 months, coincides with the infant's increasing mobility and beginning individuation. The infant's teething, stranger anxiety, and increased mobility call for different parenting skills and strategies.

High-risk women who had been hospitalized during pregnancy and their partners, however, did not differ from couples who had a normal pregnancy experience in either parental competence or parent-infant attachment at 8 months postpartum (Mercer et al., 1987). Carla, whose son was discharged from the hospital at 3 months after birth, was now comfortable with her role.

> I feel very peaceful now and am growing less fearful all the time about my baby's health. Now I barely worry about it al all. He still uses the apnea monitor at night, but I'm beginning to feel that it's more of a nightmare than a useful precaution. I don't think I'll keep using it much longer. The bills are mind boggling. My boy was horribly sick at first so his expenses were astronomical. But the little one is a joy now, and very well.

Carla's husband wrote:

> I am more pleased each day with baby, Jack. Fatherhood at 50 is rejuvenating.

Mothers who had been hospitalized during pregnancy, however, reported significantly less optimal health status than women who had normal pregnancies (Ferketich & Mercer, 1990a). They also reported significantly more stress from negative life events during the 8 months following birth, and this stress was significantly related to their health status ($r = -0.37$).

Fathers in the high-risk situation reported a higher sense of mastery and higher self-esteem than fathers whose partners had normal pregnancies at 8 months after birth, despite their reported lower received and perceived social support (Mercer et al., 1987). In dealing with their crisis situation in general, these men seemed to have reached a higher level of developmental adaptation. More of the men in the high-risk group were experienced fathers, and this may have contributed to their higher self-esteem and sense of mastery also.

Mothers who were hospitalized scored significantly higher in parent-infant attachment than the fathers (Mercer & Ferketich, 1990a). Depression, parental competence, and number of health problems during the mate's pregnancy accounted for 45% of the variance in fathers' attachment scores. The ultimate giving of self seems to have been a factor in these women's greater attachment. Parental competence and a higher pregnancy risk score were associated with higher parent infant attachment at 8 months and explained 29% of the variance among the high-risk mothers. Low-risk mothers and their partners did not differ significantly in their attachment scores.

Mothers and fathers in high-risk pregnancy situations did not differ from mothers and fathers who experienced normal pregnancies in their parental competence scores at 8 months (Mercer et al., 1989). Fathers did not differ from mothers in their parental competency scores.

At 8 months, women who had been hospitalized did not differ from their mates in their assessments of their couple relationship and family functioning (Mercer & Ferketich, 1990b). As in other studies, some divorces were reported. Partners of high-risk women, however, reported significantly less optimal mate relationships and family functioning than partners of low-risk women. The impact of a high-risk pregnancy was far-reaching; depression and a higher pregnancy risk score were associated with less optimal family functioning among fathers in the high-risk pregnancy situation and explained 47% of the variance. A higher pregnancy risk score was associated with less optimal mate relationships among the women who had been hospitalized and, along with depression and anxiety, explained 52% of the variance.

Follow-up of parents who experience obstetrical complications during pregnancy is important. Their support systems need bolstering, and mothers need attention directed to their physical well-being. Counseling regarding family relationships seems particularly important. Parenting groups are a helpful means for families to exchange ways of coping with various challenges and to learn that their feelings of frustration and, at times, disappointment are not in the minority.

SUMMARY

The couple whose normal process of pregnancy and childbirth is interrupted by an obstetrical risk situation is faced with much uncertainty. In coping with uncertainty, accurate information from a credible authority figure is important.

Couples may be so caught up in the worry about the outcome for the infant that they are unable to deal with usual tasks of pregnancy other than attempts to ensure a safe outcome for mother and infant. When hospitalization is required during pregnancy, the women's separation from her family adds to the disequilibrium within the family. Friends and family tend to provide help as needed from the mother's perspective, but fathers feel a lack of needed support. Fathers feel additional pressures in attempting to maintain the smooth operation of the family, working, visiting the partner and infant at the hospital, and worrying about finances.

The uncertainty about the pregnancy outcome contributes to feelings of powerlessness and loss of control. The couples' priorities and concerns focus on each other and their unborn infant as they work to resolve their crisis.

With instability of both physical being and emotional feelings, much support is needed. Despite these fears and worries, couples in the high-risk situation do not score lower than couples in low-risk situations on attachment to their infant or in their parental competence.

A higher pregnancy risk score was associated with higher maternal infant attachment. However, maternal health status among women hospitalized during pregnancy was below that of women who had normal pregnancies at 8 months.

The response to the obstetrical risk situation is individual. The health professional must allow the patient's definition and response to the situation to be the focus of intervention. The impact of the obstetrical risk situation on the family functioning and, in particular, the mate relationship merit counseling to strengthen these areas.

6

When Parents Have
a Chemical Abuse Problem

Michelle Bushong

In the last decade health professionals in all areas of health care have seen increasing numbers of people suffering from chemical addiction. Between 1968 and 1973 there was a fourfold increase in the number of persons with a chemical dependency problem in the United States (Cuskey, Premkeemor, & Ligel, 1972; Person, Retka, & Woodward, 1977). In 1984 92.8% of young Americans aged 18 to 25 years had tried alcohol; 87.4% had used it the past year, and 71.5% had used it within the past month (National Institute on Drug Abuse, 1986). Ten million people are problem drinkers (Dwyer, 1986). Approximately 20 million persons in the United States have tried cocaine, and 5 million are regular users (Chasnoff, 1987). Approximately 20% to 30% of addicts in concentrated metropolitan areas are women; a study by the Addiction Services Agency in New York City found that 80% of female addicts were between the ages of 15 and 35 years (Burt & Glynn, 1976). Clearly, the vast majority of female addicts are of childbearing age. A study at Harlem Hospital, New York City, reported that 10% of all newborns had urine tests positive for cocaine (Chasnoff, 1987).

Fear of legal reprisals and the social stigma attached to being identified as an addict often keep chemically dependent women from seeking the help they need. Many pregnant addicts do not receive prenatal care, and it is not until their newborns exhibit signs of withdrawal in the nursery that many of these women are identified.

Accepting the parenting role is a strenuous task for the most prepared woman, but the pregnant addict usually does not even begin the early steps of parental role attainment during her pregnancy. She may still be in denial about her chemical dependency problem. The undertaking of the maternal role is most formidable for the chemically dependent woman. Assisting this mother in taking on her new role presents a particular challenge to practitioners who work with her. This chapter is meant to assist practitioners working with chemically dependent parents to understand the disease of addiction and its impact on pregnancy and parenting.

PROFILE OF THE PREGNANT ADDICT

There are several causative theories from which to view chemical or substance addiction. The majority now view addiction as a chronic, progressive relapsing disease. While no genetic link has been identified for this disease, there does seem to be a familial disposition to addiction. Left untreated this disease will progress, often leading to death. Recovery from the disease is a lifelong process but is possible.

Covington (1988) describes addiction as a chronic neglect of the self in favor of something else. In the case of the chemically dependent woman, the self is neglected in favor of the drug of choice. This outward focus becomes more intense as the disease progresses. In the most advanced case the woman may neglect even her physical needs and devote all of her energy to drug-seeking behavior.

Among women who suffer from chemical dependency, there are many variations in personality. Although the practitioner must be cautious of making generalizations, the research to date is clear that there are common characteristics among addicted women. These characteristics differ somewhat from those of the male addict in that the female addict is affected by sex role socialization. Mondanaro (1977) and Rosenbaum (1979) describe women addicts as having learned and continued adherence to strict gender roles. They place themselves in the traditional role of homemaker and mother, subservient to their husbands. They believe they must accept full responsibility for childrearing.

Unlike the male addict, women burdened with chemical dependency are more likely to be suffering from depression (Colten, 1982; Finnegan, 1988). It may be this symptom that often brings the addicted woman into the health care system. Unfortunately, treatment of depression with prescription medications, without attention to the problem of chemical dependency, can lead to a dual addiction. Other psychological problems of the female addict include anxiety, phobias, schizophrenia, and personality disorders (Daghestani, 1988).

The greater majority of addicted women come from families that were dysfunctional in some way (Daghestani, 1988). Women frequently described alcoholism or another type of addiction in one or both parents. In fact, many women reported having received their first drink or "fix" from a parent. The addicted parents of the addicted woman were often unable to provide her with adequate love and nurturing. In addition, because the parents themselves were needy, they had unrealistic expectations of their children. Unable to meet these expectations, the addicted daughter acquired an acute sense of failure at an early age (Mondonaro, 1977). This learned sense of failure is manifest in low self-esteem, feelings of personal inadequacy, and a view of herself as powerless or victimized (Colten, 1982; Daghestani, 1988). Indeed, the women suffering from addiction can often be seen to passively accept whatever comes to her in life. Whitfield (1987) described the woman raised in a dysfunctional family as a "wounded child." The wounded child learned through experience that love is accompanied by abandonment and pain. She has had little, if any, modeling of how to be intimate with a loved one. Thus the addicted woman is often incapable of intimacy.

Physical and sexual abuse are often part of the dysfunctional environment in which the addicted woman was raised (Black & Mayer, 1980). Carr (1977) reported that physical abuse can continue in the adult life of the addicted woman as she tends to remain with an abusive partner. Perhaps having been raised in a dysfunctional family, the partner of the addicted women is often a substance abuser also. Feelings of powerlessness in these males are often soothed by exerting power over their partners and children. This results in his battering both the woman and her children and in the forced social isolation of the woman by her partner.

The chemically dependent woman has developed many mechanisms of coping with her dysfunctional life that are difficult to understand and confusing for the practitioner. Manipulation, defensiveness, and deception are often encountered (Lawson & Wilson, 1980). In an effort to master and control some of her behavior, to alleviate her psychological pain, and to avoid the shame and guilt of her addiction, the woman may completely negate thoughts of her past or her current drug use. Mood altering substances serve to assist her in forgetting past and present hurts and in fulfilling a sense of inner emptiness.

EFFECTS OF COMMONLY ABUSED DRUGS ON THE FETUS AND DEVELOPING CHILD

Establishment of healthy parenting requires the participation of the infant as well as the mother. Therefore it is important for the practitioner to understand the effects of substance abuse on both the mother and her child. The ever-increasing problem of addiction in this country has stimulated much research on the effects of substances on the fetus. However, knowledge about the long-term effects of drugs on the developing child is limited. This chapter focuses on all of the commonly abused substances except tobacco. The major consequences of tobacco use during pregnancy are low pregnancy weight gain, increased perinatal loss, premature birth, and low infant birth weight (Dwyer, 1986); the impact of premature birth is discussed in chapter 7.

Alcohol

Because it is both legally and socially acceptable, alcohol is the substance most commonly abused by pregnant women. Polydrug addiction, or addiction to more than one drug, is being seen more often. When alcohol is not the primary drug used, it is frequently the secondary. Ethanol and its metabolites can alter the growth and development of the embryo. *Fetal alcohol syndrome* is the name researchers have given to a recurring set of abnormalities identified in children exposed to alcohol prenatally.

Fetal alcohol syndrome is characterized by structural abnormalities of the head and face including microcephaly, microopthalmia, a shortened palpebral fissure, a poorly developed philtrum, and flattening of the maxillary area. Intrauterine growth retardation, decreased birth weight, and decreased length may be seen. These children show both early and later developmental delays and intellectual impairment. In addition, neurological abnormalities such as hyperactivity, altered sleep patterns, feeding problems, perceptual problems, impaired concentration, mood problems, and language dysfunction are seen. A child manifesting some but not all of the symptoms of fetal alcohol syndrome is said to have *fetal alcohol effects*.

Fetal alcohol effects are seen three times more often than fetal alcohol syndrome (Weiner & Morse, 1988). Hyperactivity in these children seems to be the most common and persistent neurological handicap (Spohr & Steinhausen, 1984).

The stage of fetal development during which alcohol is used is a determinant in the development of fetal alcohol syndrome and effects. The embryonic tissue is most vulnerable to damage early in the pregnancy when the rapid cell division is occurring. In contrast it is not clear what role the amount of alcohol ingested during pregnancy plays. Fetal alcohol syndrome is seen in infants of 30% to 40% of the women who are chronic, heavy drinkers throughout pregnancy (Weiner & Morse, 1988). However, fetal alcohol effects have been seen in children whose mothers have used varying amounts of alcohol while pregnant, including those who engaged in only occasional binge drinking (Smith, 1979).

Heroin

The effects of prenatal heroin use on the fetus are perhaps the most widely researched, as heroin has been in use since the 1800s. Fetal and infant withdrawal from heroin and the maternal lifestyle have an impact on the fetus and newborn.

Onset of withdrawal symptoms may range from 2 minutes to 2 weeks of life. Symptoms most commonly appear at 72 hours of age. These symptoms, known as neonatal abstinence syndrome, persist for 6 to 8 weeks but may be present for as long as 3 months (Finnegan, 1988). There does not appear to be any direct correlation between extent of the maternal drug use and the severity of the neonatal withdrawal (Phillips, 1986).

Neonatal abstinence syndrome is characterized by abnormalities of the gastrointestinal tract, the central nervous system, and the respiratory system. Gastrointestinal signs included vomiting, abdominal cramps, and diarrhea. These may lead to dehydration and electrolyte imbalance. Neurological signs include irritability, hypertonia, and tremors, which can cause an exaggerated startle reflex. Uncoordinated and ineffectual sucking lead to feeding problems. These neonates have a typically high pitched cry and can be difficult to comfort. Signs of respiratory distress include tachypnea, increased nasal secretions, and intermittent cyanosis. Babies exposed to heroin prenatally are also more likely to succumb to sudden infant death syndrome (Finnegan, 1988).

The lifestyle of the mother using heroin also has an effect on the health of the fetus. Poor nutrition can lead to intrauterine growth retardation and babies of low birth weight. Sharing of needles can expose the mother and her fetus to HIV and hepatitis infections. Many women support their drug habit through illegal means such as prostitution, which can lead to exposure of the fetus to sexually transmitted diseases such as gonorrhea and herpes.

Prescribing methadone in pregnancy may prevent exposure of the fetus to those risks associated with the mother's lifestyle that were described above. However, infants exposed to methadone prenatally may still experience the symptoms of neonatal abstinence. Some research is suggesting that methadone may lead to developmental delays later in childhood (Finnegan et al., 1977). The effects of methadone on the child may be dependent on the dose prescribed during pregnancy and use of other drugs by the mother.

Cocaine

Cocaine use has been associated with preterm labor and delivery, abruptio placentae, and placental insufficiencies leading to fetal distress in labor. There is some evidence indicating that cocaine use during pregnancy may be associated with cardiac arrest and event stroke in the fetus (Chasnoff, 1988; Dixon, 1989). More recent research has shown that cocaine use in early pregnancy may result in urinary tract anomalies (Chavez et al., 1989; Chasnoff et al., 1985).

Evidence also suggests that the nervous system of cocaine-exposed babies may be affected. In addition to hypertonia and hyperirritability, these infants show difficulty in functioning in state control and orientation (Griffith, 1988). Griffith's work with cocaine-exposed babies has shown that these newborns typically remain in a state that will keep them shut off from the environment. Interaction with their environment seems to induce much stress in these babies, as seen by their inability to focus on their mother's face or voice. Transition from one state to another is abrupt and inappropriate for the level of stimulation. Such difficulties may persist for up to 3 months.

Phencyclidine (PCP)

Research is just beginning to disclose the effects of PCP on the fetus. Infants exposed to PCP exhibit symptoms similar to those of infants suffering from narcotic withdrawal, such as hypertonicity, tremors, and hyperirritability (Howard, 1989; Wachsman et al., 1989). In addition, they show rapid changes in level of consciousness and increased sensitivity to aduitory stimuli. Abnormal eye movements such as darting, staring, and nystagmus were also noted. Howard's long-term follow-up of these children revealed that while there were no developmental delays evident in PCP-exposed children, the quality of their gross and fine motor movements seemed abnormal.

Howard and her colleagues (1989) conducted a study comparing children prenatally exposed to drugs (primarily cocaine, heroin, and PCP) to children born prematurely. The developmental scores of the two groups of children were not abnormal, but significant differences were seen between the two groups in the area of unstructured play. The drug-exposed group showed significantly less ability to self-organize, self-initiate, and follow through on a task. Instead of the representational play normally seen in children of the age group studied, much random batting, throwing, and scattering of toys was observed (Howard et al., 1988).

Marijuana

Very little research has been conducted on the effects of marijuana on the fetus. Greenland's (1982) study showed an increase in precipitous labor and meconium staining. Most research demonstrated an increased incidence of maternal anemia, poor maternal weight gain, and greater likelihood of intrauterine growth retardation with continued use of marijuana in pregnancy (Zuckerman et al., 1989). Fried and associates' (1987) research found that marijuana-exposed newborns experienced tremors, hyperirritability, and an increased sensitivity to light. Long-term effects of marijuana on the development of the child deserve much more study, as this commonly used drug has been considered innocuous by its users.

Amphetamine

Amphetamine use in pregnancy is another area in which data are still lacking. Decreased maternal weight gain, increased hypertension, increased prematurity, an increased incidence of fetal distress, and babies small for gestational age have all been noted with prenatal amphetamine use (Dixon, 1989). Eriksson's (1978) study revealed that infants exposed to prolonged amphetamine use in pregnancy often had feeding difficulties. These infants were described as developmentally slow for the first 6 months of life.

MATERNAL ROLE ATTAINMENT
AND CHEMICALLY DEPENDENT MOTHERS

Anticipatory Stage of Maternal Role Attainment

It is a common belief among addicted women that their drug use causes infertility. Indeed, many addicted women do have irregular menstrual cycles, but this is most likely due to their lifestyle and nutritional status and is not directly an effect of the drugs they take. This belief that she cannot get pregnant, accompanied by a chronic neglect of her body, may find the addict many months into her pregnancy before she is aware of it. Thus the addicted woman does not follow the usual trajectory of the anticipatory work of psychologically preparing for the coming baby.

For the pregnant woman who is chemically dependent, pregnancy and the anticipation of parenthood can be overwhelming. Many women have no knowledge about the effects of their drug use on their unborn child. For those women who do know the potential detrimental effects of continued drug use, the shame and guilt that they feel may be so great as to push them further into their denial. Continued denial of the effects of her drug use on the fetus can be a predictor of poor parenting abilities, as this denial is likely to continue postpartum (Mondonaro, 1977).

Most addicted women have unrealistic expectations of what the pregnancy will bring to their lives. The woman may believe that the pregnancy will change her partner, making him more committed and attentive to her and her family. The pregnancy may also be seen as the factor that will bring about a change in her own mother's attitude toward her. Finally, the woman may believe that both she and her partner will be motivated to get into recovery while she is pregnant. Rosenbaum (1979) reported that many addicts get pregnant in order to force themselves to stop using drugs.

Formal Stage of Maternal Role Attainment

By the time the infant is born, the pregnant addict is often already behind in the usual progression of parental role attainment. During pregnancy, her own personal needs and expectations of pregnancy may have interfered with her ability to attach to her fetus. Continued denial and fear may have prevented her from seeking prenatal care or help from any source.

Upon the birth of her baby, the woman enters the formal stage of maternal role attainment. Mondonaro (1977) describes this immediate postpartum period as one of a "collision with reality" for the addicted woman. The mother may continue in her denial, blaming the baby's withdrawal symptoms on the baby being colicky or cold. She may even blame the baby's condition on the staff, whom she believes are giving poor care to her child. In attempting to explain her child's behavior she may view the child as unmanageable or feel that she is incapable of being a good mother.

Most often, the foundation for parenting was never properly established for the addicted woman. Since many women's parents were addicted, the addicted mother quite likely received very little mothering herself. It is difficult for her to learn to give nurturing and affection that she never received herself. Her fear of intimacy may lead to difficulty in bonding with her baby. The addicted woman knows little about finding joy and playfulness without using drugs or alcohol. She may not find interactions with her newborn particularly pleasureable. If the mother continues with her drug use, she will have further difficulty in reading her baby's cues.

Guilt and shame play a large, important role in disturbing this early stage of parental role attainment. The mother may view this fussy and inconsolable baby as a punishment for her drug use (Finnegan, 1988). Partners frequently add to the guilt by blaming the woman for the baby's withdrawal symptoms.

Babies suffering from withdrawal symptoms do not participate in the mother-infant interaction in the same manner as other infants. As described earlier, the infants who are suffering from drug exposure are usually fussy, irritable, and easily disturbed. It would be difficult for any mother to respond to the cues of this infant. Drug-exposed babies have difficulty engaging their mothers, as they cannot tolerate the visual stimulus of the face for any length of time. This behavior is frequently interpreted by the mother as rejection by her newborn. Thus the process of mother-infant attachment is further interrupted.

This fragile bond between the addicted mother and her newborn is often further handicapped by early separation of the mother and child. Close medical attention is frequently needed for these high-risk newborns, requiring that they remain in the nursery. In addition, many communities view the use of illicit drugs by the mother as a legal matter requiring investigation. Drug-exposed babies may be sent to foster care placements for varying lengths of time while an investigation is being completed. This separation of mother and child hampers their already shaky start and delays the mother's process of getting acquainted with, identifying, and claiming her infant.

Informal Stage of Maternal Role Attainment

The lifestyle of the drug using mother is chaotic, lacking in any regular schedule. Drug-seeking behavior demands much of the physical and emotional energy that is needed for parenting. Due to drug-related illnesses, binges, or incarceration, the drug-addicted mother may be separated from her child/children quite often. Her lifestyle may be chaotic enough that she is unable to attend to her infant's physical or emotional needs. Because of this, the chemically dependent mother may be ambivalent about her parental role (Fanshel, 1975); she is unable to enjoy the pleasureable interaction with the infant at this age that low-risk mothers enjoy. Although she may realize she is unable to adequately parent her infant, she may also be very reluctant to give that role to someone else.

Many researchers have examined how the addicted mother evolves her own mothering behaviors in the informal stage of parental role attainment. The drug-addicted woman tends to view her child as a possession whose function is to meet her own needs and demands

(Burns & Burns, 1988; Wellisch & Steinberg, 1980). The mother interprets the infant's growth and development in terms of her own needs
and not those of the infant.

In a study done by Wilson and associates (1979), a comparison was
made between addicted and nonaddicted mothers regarding their perceptions of themselves as mothers and their perceptions of their children. Addicted mothers more often perceived their children as being
difficult and having behavior problems. While addicted mothers expressed concern for their children's safety, they seemed less able to
follow through in providing a safe environment for their children.
Baum and Doherty (1983) described the drug addicted woman as impul-
sive, irresponsible, self-centered, and not oriented toward the intellectual development of her children. She most often takes a threatening
disciplinarian approach to parenting her children.

Achievement of Maternal Role Identity/Personal Level
of Role Acquisition

Eldred et al. (1974) found drug dependent mothers in a treatment
program had abnormally low tolerances for frustration during their
interactions with their children. They observed these mothers to have
unrealistic expectations of their children and to be more comfortable in
expressing hostility toward them that tenderness. Burns and Burns
(1988) described the addicted mother as displaying less attachment to
her children. She interacts inconsistently with her children as she
vacillates between strictness and laxity, blaming and punishing, and
ignoring and loving. Black and Mayer (1980) also described the substance abusing mother as being inconsistent in her discipline techniques and in her attention toward her children.

All researchers noted behavioral problems among children of chemically dependent mothers. Hyperactivity, short attention spans, and
developmental delays were the most commonly reported. As noted
earlier, these symptoms have been suggested as the result of drug
exposure in utero. However, behavioral difficulties render the children
more susceptible to the detrimental affects of suboptimal environmental and social factors, leading to more pronounced developmental delays
and emotional problems (Wilson et al., 1979).

Considering the multiple problems of their infants, their erratic and
inconsistent lifestyles, it would seem most difficult for addicted mothers to move to the personal level of internalizing and achieving comfort
with the maternal role such that it is central to their identity. Both
Mondonaro (1979) and Black and Mayer (1980) described role reversal

in the mother-child dyad, in which the mother is anxious that the child should grow up and assume the parental role of nurturer.

Rosenbaum (1979) portrayed the addicted mother as having two careers: addiction and motherhood. Rosenbaum noted that the longer the woman was participated in the first career of addict, the more difficulty she has with the second career of motherhood. In order to internalize her identity as a mother, the addict must modify her drug use, a task that could prove to be very difficult. The addicted mother's partner, parents, and priends are frequently also substance abusers themselves and offer the mother little guidance in how to balance her addiction and her maternal role. Even her financial status and lifestyle may tie her firmly to her substance use. Unless the woman is first helped into treatment, it is unlikely that she will complete her attainment of the maternal role.

ASSESSING, PLANNING, AND CARING FOR CHEMICALLY DEPENDENT MOTHERS AND THEIR INFANTS

Substance abuse among pregnant and parenting women almost always elicits an emotional reaction from those practitioners involved with the woman and her child. It is easy to feel anger toward a chemically dependent woman when an innocent child is involved. Practitioners may find themselves attaching to the child and having difficulty letting go of their own rescue fantasies. But the nature of the disease of addiction is that recovery, while entirely possible, comes only when the addicted woman is ready for it.

The first step for practitioners in assessing the chemically dependent woman is to assess their own feelings, values, and judgments regarding substance abuse and the addicted mother. Practitioners must identify and claim their anger, their sadness, and their disappointment at the behavior of the substance abusing woman. Anger and judgment in practitioners will be perceived by the addicted woman and breeds mistrust. It is also important for practitioners to assess their own denial. It may be painful for health professionals to accept that a mother has relapsed into using drugs once again. Practitioners may find themselves denying this reality instead of working with the client toward recovery. The process of evaluating their own feelings, judgments, and denial is one that practitioners must repeat at regular intervals while working with these challenging clients.

The substance abusing woman who is still in denial about her drug use is at the highest risk for failing to move through the stages of maternal role attainment. The role of the practitioner working with this client is to assess all of the indicators of substance abuse and present them to the client with the hope of breaking through the denial and motivating the woman to go into treatment. There are many indicators of substance abuse found in the woman's behavior and in her medical, social, and obstetrical histories. These indicators are listed in Table 1.

In addition to obtaining a thorough history, practitioners can use one of the many existing substance abuse assessment forms, for example, American Council for Drug Education (1986). These assessments are designed to measure the extent of the woman's substance abuse. Most of the assessments contain nonthreatening questions that progress slowly from simple to more intimate details of the woman's substance use. Again, practitioners must remember to be nonjudgmental in their administration of such assessments.

When used appropriately, urine toxicology screening can be an useful adjunct to an assessment for substance abuse. Testing may be done on either the newborn's or the mother's urine. The practitioner must be knowledgeable about which substances are excreted by the kidneys and for how long after use they may be found in the mother's and newborn's urine. The woman's permission should be obtained before collecting a urine specimen for a toxicology screen. Performing a urine toxicology screen without the woman's permission would hinder the building of trust and could severely handicap the practitioner in interventions with the mother. In addition, urine toxicology results should be viewed with caution. The results give information only about the woman's most recent drug use. Urine toxicology screens do not reveal alcohol use. They reveal nothing about the woman's pattern of drug use or of her desire to seek treatment or her ability to parent her child.

In working with parents, the practitioner should also be knowledgeable about the many existing instruments to assess a woman's parental attitudes. Both Leif (1985) and Baum and Dougherty (1983) describe tools used to assess attitudes toward parenting. Wellisch and Steinberg (1980) encourage practitioners to include questions in their interviews regarding how the substance abusing mother was parented.

During the assessment process, the practitioner is not only gathering information but is also forming a relationship of trust with the woman. The questions asked during an assessment are of the most intimate nature. They surround a subject about which the woman has much shame and guilt. Practitioners should be careful to assure the client, through their conduct and by establishing a private environment, that the confidentiality of client's responses will be protected.

Table 1 Indicators of Substance Abuse

BEHAVIORAL	Nodding out, slurred speech, hallucinations, blackouts, shaking, irritability, agitation, inappropriateness, mood swings, difficulty concentrating, memory lapses/losses, emotional outbursts, depression, suicidal tendencies, bizarre behavior, reduced motor performance, decreased job performance, marital conflicts, sexual dysfunction, isolation, financial problems, child neglect/abuse, frequent accidents in the home.
SOCIAL HISTORY	Psychiatric problems, frequent use of prescriptive mood altering chemicals, multiple emergency room visits, family history of substance abuse, motor vehicle accidents, arrests, family dissolution, children's problems in school, juvenile delinquency, actions from dependency courts, children placed outside the care of parents, intense daily drama.
MEDICAL HISTORY	Hypertension, gastritis, liver disease, pancreatitis, cardiac arrhythmias, hematological disorders, predisposition to stroke, poor nutrition, sensory impairment, brain damage, sleep disturbance, neurological deficits, seizure disorders, cardiomyopathy, increased incidence of pulmonary disease, problems of sepsis, overdose, AIDS/ARC.
OBSTETRICAL HISTORY	Spontaneous abortion, premature rupture of membranes, premature labor, abruptio placentae, fetal death, low birth weight infant, meconium staining, poor weight gain, inactive fetus, hyperactive fetus, vaginal bleeding, late prenatal care, inconsistent prenatal care, sudden infant death, sexually transmitted diseases.

Jessup and Green (1987) described a five-step process for intervention with the substance abusing woman who may be in denial regarding
her chemical dependence. The goal of such an intervention is to present
the woman with evidence that will help her move beyond denial and
ready herself for treatment. In the steps of this intervention, the
practitioner presents the woman with behavioral, medical, and/or historical indicators of chemical dependence or the results of the toxicology screen. Presentation of the evidence is followed by the suggestion
of treatment options. When presenting the woman with options for her
treatment, it is best to give her phone numbers and, when possible, the
name of a contact person. It should be remembered that the defense
mechanisms of the addicted woman are often denial and manipulation.
While acknowledging the client's discomfort with the intervention process, practitioners should not let themselves become engaged in a
discussion of rationalizing and explaining each piece of evidence presented.

In working with addicted mothers, the practitioner has two clients:
the mother and the child. The addicted woman will need help in resolving her chemical dependency problem as well as her many psychological
problems in order to move on to attaining the role of parent. Therefore
the practitioner may next need to help the mother find an appropriate
treatment program. Issues of child care and transportation should
always be addressed. There are very few drug treatment programs
designed specifically for women, who are pregnant or who have small
children. It may be difficult for the woman to meet her many treatment
program requirements without help in securing child care and transportation.

In the nursery, practitioners caring for newborns should closely
observe the mother's interaction with her infant. As much as possible,
mothers and newborns should be encouraged to remain together to
facilitate the attachment process. The mother may need assistance in
interpreting her infant's cues. She will need to know that her newborn's failure to hold her gaze is the effect of drugs on the newborn's
nervous system and not an indication of rejection. Griffith (1988)
described many unique comforting techniques such as swaddling and
vertical rocking which can be used with the irritable baby in withdrawal. The mother should be taught these techniques to bring her
baby to a quiet alert state. With the infant in the quiet alert state,
Griffith has had success in teaching mothers to interact with their
newborns in measured doses that are tolerable to the infant. The
mother learns to observe the baby and detect the first signs of discomfort and to console the baby before it reaches a crying state. By practicing these simple skills, the mother begins to feel competent, and the

attachment between her and her baby will be strengthened. The practitioner can use the time when she is doing a newborn assessment to point out to the mother her baby's positive attributes and abilities, to praise the mother for her ability to meet the baby's needs, and to model the techniques described above for the mother.

It is important that the practitioner help the mother verbalize her feelings of guilt and shame over the effects of her drug use on her baby. The woman may also need to verbalize her dislike of her newborn's irritable behavior. It is important that the practitioner remain sensitive to the mother's founded and the unfounded concerns. The practitioner's honesty in all matters will encourage the building of a trusting relationship between client and practitioner.

Few researchers have addressed breast-feeding and substance use by the mother. Wilton (1988) reported that almost all drugs have been found in varying amounts in breast milk. Heroin use by the breast-feeding mother can cause prolonged addiction of the infant (Committee on Drugs, 1984). One case study reported an infant developing symptoms of cocaine toxicity while breast-feeding after his mother had used cocaine (Chasnoff, 1987). If the mother is on methadone, the infant should first be withdrawn postnatally (Blinic et al., 1976; Committee on Drugs, 1984). If the mother is taking a dose of 20 milligrams or less of methadone, she can breast-feed her infant. The mother who is on methadone, or who has been using any other drug, and who chooses to breast-feed should be carefully educated as to the potential for the drugs to reach her infant and the signs and symptoms of those drug effects on the baby. The mother who chooses to bottle-feed her infant will continue to need help with learning to hold and cuddle her baby during feeding time.

The infant of any drug using mother should be followed closely for signs and symptoms of both hepatitis B and HIV exposure. If the mother is positive for the hepatitis B surface antigen, the infant will need to receive the hepatitis B vaccine at 1 and 6 months of age. Children with HIV exposure will need to be followed up for antibody testing until at least 2 years of age. The drug lifestyle is often a transient one, making long-term follow-up of these infants very difficult. The practitioner should be sure that the mother and her infant are referred to the public health nursing department in an attempt to assure appropriate follow-up of these health concerns.

Early intervention with drug-exposed children has maximized their potential for normal development (Howard et al., 1989; Weiner & Morse, 1988). Referral to an early intervention child development program is essential. In most of these programs, work is begun with the parents and infant soon after birth. The goal of these programs is to teach the mother to observe her child for developmental delays. The mother is also instructed on how to encourage her infant's development. These basic skills greatly enhance the mother's feeling of competency in her mothering role.

Increased confidence, necessary for moving through the four stages of parental role attainment, is greatly facilitated by acquisition of basic mothering skills. Parenting classes in which mothers are taught such skills as discipline, communication, and nonviolent ways of dealing with their frustrations have proven effective in helping mothers to parent their children successfully (Leif, 1985). These classes need to be comprehensive and longterm. In one program in New York, the Pregnant Addicts and Addicted Mothers Program (PAAM), parenting classes are continuous for 3 years. These classes serve many purposes. They provide the addicted mother with role modeling from the instructors. They provide the practitioner an opportunity to observe the mother interacting with her child and to praise her for appropriate behavior. Providing the mother with information about normal child development helps her to form more realistic expectations of her child. Class participation also helps the mother to experience joy and pleasure from interacting with her child in a drug-free state.

It is crucial to remember that the woman cannot attend to her mothering tasks and role if her basic needs are unmet. The addicted mother will need assistance from a variety of support services, including financial and housing. As mentioned above, she will need help with day care and transportation. She should be provided with contraceptive counseling, pregnancy termination options, and HIV counseling and testing.

Because the addicted woman has difficulty with intimacy, building a trusting and therapeutic relationship with her may require a long period of time. A trusting and therapeutic relationship is essential, however, for successful intervention with the addicted woman. Others discussed the need for a primary practitioner in working with substance abusing mothers (Eldred et al., 1974; Howard et al., 1988). The consistency of a single health care provider aids in the building of trust. It is this provider who can help interpret the mother's needs to other staff.

The best approach to working with substance abusing mothers is through the use of a multidisciplinary team. Since the woman will likely be involved with a drug treatment program, an early intervention developmental program, public health nursing, and social services, it is important for all of the agencies dealing with the client to work together to achieve common goals. The multidisciplinary team is also essential in helping individual team members cope with their feelings of anger and frustration and in identifying their biased judgments. Continued education about addiction and its effects on the mother and her child is important for health professionals. The many specialists in the multidisciplinary team are the perfect resource for providing this information for other team members.

SUMMARY

It is apparent from the literature that the woman entrapped in substance abuse is tremendously handicapped in attaining her maternal role. Many factors combine to handicap the mother and child in this task. There is an intergenerational style of inadequate parenting in the family of the addict (Moise, Reed, & Connell, 1981). Therefore the mother suffers not only from the emotional problems of having been raised in a dysfunctional family, but she also lacks an appropriate parental role model.

The infant is unable to offer the mother appropriate cues and rewards for the development of continued and strong attachment. Finally, both the physical and the social environment of the mother offer her poor support for overcoming the problems she encounters in accomplishing the tasks of motherhood.

Practitioners who work with the substance abusing mother are faced with a difficult challenge. They need to possess a unique set of qualities. Personal maturity and inner strength are needed when confronted with the deep denial of these clients. Practitioners need to be realistic in presenting the client with the consequences of her drug abuse while being creative in helping the mother to explore all of her options for recovery. A sense of hope and a belief that recovery is possible is essential even with the client who is seemingly hopeless.

PART III
INFANTS WITH
A SPECIAL CHALLENGE

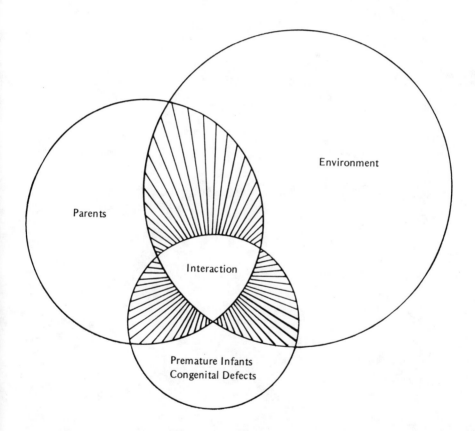

FIGURE 3
Interactive model adapted from *Child Health Assessment Part 2: The First Year of Life,*
p. 132, by Kathryn E. Barnard and Sandra J. Eyres, DHEW Publication
No. HRA 79-25, Hyattsville, MD: U.S. Department of Health, Education, and
Welfare. Copyright 1979 by Kathryn E. Barnard. Reprinted with permission of
Kathryn E. Barnard.

7

When the Infant
Is Born Prematurely

Dramatic changes in perinatal care have occurred over the past 15 years. Along with the great technological advances in providing care and saving smaller and more immature infants, there have been many human advances. As a result of earlier research that found a disproportionate number of abused children had also been born prematurely and, as a result, experienced long-term separation from their parents, hospital policies were changed to encourage opportunities for families to become acquainted with and attached to their high-risk infants. Parents are encouraged to visit and to participate in care as much as is possible. This openness in the neonatal intensive care unit (NICN) has enabled parents to see infants less ill and more ill than their own, to observe the outcomes of other infants, and to become somewhat familiar with their infants during the worst of times. As a consequence, parents' concerns and preoccupations during the early postpartum days focus more on their infant and less on introspection in dealing with their losses of expectations. Three decades ago, Kaplan and Mason (1960) posed four psychological tasks for mothers of premature infants: preparation for possible loss of the infant; acknowledgement of her failure to deliver a full-term infant; resumption of maternal-infant relationships on the infant's discharge from the hospital; and learning how premature infants differ from term infants in their needs and growth patterns. Advanced technology allows parents to have greater hope for their infants' survival, and the encouragement of ongoing parent-infant interactions in the NICN permits ongoing parental relationships with their infants. Research findings are encouraging about long-term development of the preterm infant. Extent of illness rather than immaturity is the stronger variable in affecting later infant behavior (Holmes et al., 1982; Plunkett et al., 1986), and maternal responsivity (Greene, Fox, & Lewis, 1983). The very sick immature infant who experiences numerous complications may develop life-long chronic problems requiring specialized medical and physical care.

This chapter focuses on parental concerns and responses to premature birth, responses to homecoming without the baby, the premature infant's homecoming, and parenting challenges during the stages of parental role attainment. Comparative studies contrasting the development of premature infants with term infants and the mothering of these infants provide an informational base for health promotion and intervention with families facing the crisis of premature birth. Suggestions for interventions are incorporated within these topics.

PARENTAL CONCERNS AND RESPONSES TO PREMATURE BIRTH

During pregnancy the high-risk parent dealt with extensive uncertainty about the pregnancy outcome. With the birth, much uncertainty is relieved; both mothers who had been hospitalized for preterm labor and fathers of premature infants had significantly less anxiety following birth (Aradine & Ferketich, 1990).

During the first postpartal week, mothers of preterm infants had greater anxiety and depression than mothers of term infants, but no differences were observed from the second through the sixth week (Gennaro, 1988). The level of maternal anxiety did not differ between mothers of infants in the highest, high, or median neonatal risk categories, but mothers with higher problem-solving abilities tended to report greater anxiety (Gennaro, 1986). However, if the infant is very immature and small and/or very ill, much uncertainty continues. The very low birthweight immature infant is more subject to anoxia and complications such as necrotizing entercolitis (requiring surgery) or intraventricular or other intracranial hemorrhage (with possible sequelae of cerebral palsy or other complications from brain damage).

Women who are hospitalized or treated at home on bed rest for several weeks or months during pregnancy have some psychological preparation for a preterm birth. Others may have no warning; labor begins and delivery is quickly over. The couple are in a state of shock with the untimely onset. The aura of tension during preterm labor (PTL) is directed to the well-being of the unborn preterm infant. Throughout the labor, the mother's reactions or needs may be noted secondarily, increasing her anxiety about herself as well as about her infant.

In addition to heightened anxiety for her unborn infant, the woman may express guilt and anger. Mae, in active labor at 23 weeks gestation, illustrates both of these emotions:

> Maybe I've been too active. Maybe I shouldn't have come here (from out of state to visit friends). Why did this happen to me? My husband and I want a child and are able to take good care of a child.

The expectant father may also feel guilty. If the membranes happened to have ruptured shortly after the couple made love, he may feel directly responsible. In a situation that isn't secure, one partner may accuse the other of behavior that initiated the untimely labor. All of these responses indicate the beginning psychological work of dealing with failure to deliver a term infant.

The expectant mother may be afraid and feel shame that her body is not performing as it should. One woman stated that she felt "betrayed" by her body's inefficiency. She may wonder what bodily defect led to an incompetent cervix, premature contractions, or premature ruptured membranes. Previous abortions or unsuccessful pregnancies add to the stress of a premature labor and reinforce feelings of inadequacy. One husband told his wife who delivered premature twins following an 8-year fertility problem and an abortion, "There's something wrong with you. You are not a normal, *whole* woman."

The primacy of the baby's welfare is expressed by June. June, who was admitted to the hospital at 31 weeks gestation for preterm labor, had delivered a week later. She described her experience:

> It really was pretty good, the actual delivery that is. Labor was rough; I had constant pain under my right rib. The contractions started and got worse, and they took me off ritodrine. I tried to relax, and they kept happening. The pediatricians checked him, and I held him. All of the problems with the pregnancy weren't what I expected, but the labor and delivery was O.K. He's (baby) beautiful. He's got pneumonia and all the tubes, but he is improving. It's tiring and scary too. It is tiring recuperating from all that I went through, all of the waiting and not knowing. Scary to see him there with the tubes, but I know he's getting better. Tiring too because it seems all I have time for is resting and going over to the ICN to see him. When I come back, I'm exhausted. My prominent concern now is about the baby; my concerns in this order are, the baby, money, and my recuperation.

When asked if she would change anything about her labor and delivery, June replied, "Nothing I could have done differently really. What happened, happened; everyone was supportive." June appears to have a realistic appraisal of the situation, including the physical condition of her infant which she rated as "fair." There is no indication of guilt or grief at the loss of a normal pregnancy and well full-term infant by her comments; however, the intense fatigue she feels may in part reflect her unexpressed grief.

Parents without warning are much less prepared for the early birth. In either situation, one can assume that much of the preparation for the birth was not accomplished, and in each situation, there has been a great loss of expectations. However, although parents are emotionally upset during the mother's early postpartal hospitalization, their concern is directed toward their infant's survival rather than to their loss of a normal pregnancy or normal childbirth experience (Pederson et al., 1987).

The premature infant's condition greatly affects parental response. When responses of mothers of ill prematures were contrasted with those who were well, many differences emerged (Pederson et al., 1987). Significantly, more mothers of ill prematures were emotionally upset (95% versus 68%), crying (41% versus 16%), disappointed with baby (33% versus 11%), uncertain about the baby's survival (78% versus 24%), concerned about the infant's long-term prognosis (38% versus 15%) and need for special preparations for the infant after discharge (83% versus 52%). Among mothers of ill prematures, 56% felt alienated from their infants; 32% of mothers of well prematures felt alienated.

Alice, a mother of two sons, had been hospitalized for 2 weeks prior to her daughter's premature birth at 35 weeks. She expressed some of the alienation she felt initially:

> She didn't look like a girl. Looked like a stranger at first. Now I feel closer to her. It's not a reality really yet. Hard to call her by name yet. The same feelings I had with my son. I felt closer after about 3 days. She has a low sugar level; she's jittery. They are watching her in the nursery.

Alma, who at 24 weeks gestation was admitted for preterm labor and delivered 5 weeks later, felt alienation from her tiny infant more acutely:

> Emotionally it's been real up and down—mostly down. Mainly because I can't have her with me. I can't do all the normal things. It's made me real cranky and I've made other people miserable. It feels at times that she's the hospital's baby more than mine.

Alma described her terrifying birth experience:

> It was very fast. I watched the baby's monitor and it got all jerky and went from 156 to nothing. I got frantic and called the nurse and they took me to

the delivery room real fast. By then the heart rate was O.K. But then it went down again. They put me on oxygen and I was really crying. I thought she was dying. I yelled for them to put me out fast so they could save her. The doctor didn't even have time to scrub my stomach.

Alma had an illusionary projection of her daughter's physical condition (Taylor (1983) described that maintaining illusions helped in cognitive adaptation to a crisis); Alma rated her infant's overall health as very good; however, the interviewer noted that her anxiety indicated a more realistic appraisal:

> Under the circumstances, she's doing really well. Compared to the others in the ICN she's a lot stronger. To me, she looks really tiny, so fragile. She's just started moving now, before she had no control at all. She's doing well enough that I feel pretty optimistic about it, but it will be a while before she'll be able to come home.

High-risk women who had been hospitalized during pregnancy focused somewhat more on their infant and infant care and less on overall family maintenance than their partners (Mercer et al., 1987). The concern most frequently voiced by high-risk mothers was about their baby's health; other concerns in order of their frequency were their own health or their breast-feeding; being a good mother; how they would manage another child or the other child's reaction to the baby; career, school, work, or finding day care; finances; and family stability. Fathers' concerns, in order of frequency expressed, were their infants' health; their partner's health; miscellaneous concerns relating to housing, cars, time, and recreation; finances or how they could provide for the family; family stability and getting on with life; and being a good father.

Many parents tended to be coping with their premature infants through maintaining illusions about the welfare of their infants such as Alma described above. When asked to rate their infants' health from poor to very good, very small two-pound infants were rated as having very good health. Physicians and nurses were credible authority figures who provided information that their infants were doing well and this appeared to be an enormous facilitator of parental coping (see chapter 5 for discussion of Mishel's theory of coping with uncertainty). Parental comments about these small infants included:

- The pediatrician said he was O.K., so I'm not worried.
- He's very good, compared to his size or infants his age.
- He's in very good health, just small (2 pounds).

- They (twins) are beautiful; they are little fighters.
- He came out screaming, spunky little guy. He's perfect. Nurses said he was great.
- She's bigger than I thought. She is not as bad as I had thought.

Thus for some there was relief in seeing the infant.

In contrast, when the prognosis is poor, the physician may be encountered by denial and hostility; parents reported that if they did not maintain hope, they feared that the physician would give up (Waller et al., 1979). Waller and associates (1979) provided guidelines for presenting poor prognoses: parents will be more likely to hear information about prognosis when they request it; keep in mind that no one can see into the future with certainty (miraculous recoveries have occurred); when parents need information that they seem ready for, it must be presented honestly with commitment to continuing to do everything possible; have parents describe what they have already been told before answering their questions in order to build on what they know and determine whether denial is operative; seek counsel from members of the NICN team; and the professional needs to determine whether the pain of his or her limitations is interfering with ability to be supportive to the parents.

The assumption cannot be made that because no concerns about self are expressed (Pederson et al., 1987), these will not arise once the emergency nature of their infant's births and conditions subside, and the infant is discharged from the hospital. Snyder (1988) described the need for high-risk mothers to get together and share their common experiences, "We just had to get our stories out." Topics Snyder described as coming up frequently included how to cope with being confined either at home or at the hospital, how to get good health care, concern over future pregnancies, grief over childbearing losses, loss of social support systems during pregnancy, and the alienation that can come with being a high-risk mother.

CHARACTERISTICS OF THE PRETERM INFANT

An overview of the premature infant's characteristics, and the special challenges such infants present to parents provides a baseline for helping parents realize differences between preterm and term infants. It is critical for parents to realize that preterm infant responses are a result of immaturity; otherwise they may think they are doing something wrong.

The healthy newborn's temperature control, digestive, respiratory, and cardiac functioning are stable soon after birth; the normal newborn is able to achieve smooth state transitions, to pay attention to a voice or face in the alert state, and to integrate and regulate motoric and other physiologic functioning into self state regulation and differentiation of the alert state (Als & Brazelton, 1981). The infant's level of organization, degree of subsystem differentiation within that level, and degree of modulation is an index of the infant's competence and functioning (Als & Brazelton, 1981). Als & Brazelton (1981) used case studies to compare behavioral organization of preterm and term infants that provide insight into differences in behavior, although the observations cannot be generalized. During the newborn period the premature infant, in contrast to the term infant, was more easily strained by environmental manipulations, more fragile, and able to achieve low-level alertness only when physiological and motor integration were externally maintained. Although preterm infants showed an increase in alertness and stability at 3 and 5 months, they continued to be strained by face-to-face interaction. They had a sober affect, with few smiles and then only when their eyes were averted. Unlike the term infant who engaged in interactional play in face-to-face situations, the preterm infant protested through frantic arching and flinging movements. At 9 months, the preterm infant continued to be less social and to need caretaker's assistance for social interactions. Field (1981) found that preterm infants' gaze aversion was associated with the extent of stimulation provided by the interacting partner; they tended to show less gaze aversion with a moderately active partner (mother) than with minimally active partners (sibling or infant peer) or the excessively active partner (father). Although health professionals have almost constant contact with infants in the NICN, their interactions are largely nonsocial (Weibley, 1989); thus the first weeks (and, for some, months) of the very small preterm's life are spent receiving treatments and medications more than in social interaction.

Holmes et al. (1982) also observed that preterm infants showed less motor maturity, more deviant reflexes, and a general flattening of affect at the time of discharge from the hospital than term infants. However, these deficits were associated with illness, gender, hospitalization, and obstetrical complications rather than immaturity per se.

In studying preterm infants from 32 weeks gestational age to term, significant developmental gains were observed with age; individual stability of performance was also observed along with the developmental changes (Korner et al., 1989). This is in contrast to how preterm infants are usually viewed; however, infants born after 32 weeks gestation are far more mature and experience fewer complications than infants who are born earlier (e.g., 22–32 weeks gestation).

Gorski, Davidson, and Brazelton (1979) identified three stages of behavioral organization in high-risk neonates that are helpful guides to professionals working with their parents. The first stage is that of physiologic organization or "in-turning." During this first stage, infants must develop sufficient internal stability and integrity before they are able to use caregiver support and input. Handling may disturb the infant's physiological state; resultant disorganized behavior (e.g., pallor, cyanosis, respiratory distress) contributes to parental feelings of inadequacy and seeing the infant as unrewarding. The nurse may show how swaddling and using a pacifier can help the infant to reach a quiet, alert state.

The second stage of behavioral organization is that of organized behavioral responsiveness or "coming-out." The second stage begins when the baby is no longer acutely ill and is able to breathe effectively and to absorb calories and gain weight. Many infants are unable physically to tolerate eye-to-eye contact or close cuddling in the early weeks. Spacing and timing of feedings are important for successful absorption of calories. In addition, a quiet environment and distancing the infant from the caregiver during the feeding helps.

The third stage of behavioral organization is that of reciprocity between the infant and the social environment. This third stage occurs when the infant is strong enough to breathe without help, feed, and respond to caregiver behaviors in a predictable way; the infant continues to be handicapped, however. If the environment becomes overstimulating, the infant may withdraw from the overload. The infant is difficult to rouse and, when aroused, presents unrewarding responses to parents. It is important to reassure the parent that this disorganization is in the baby and is unrelated to their behavior. If the infant's uncontrolled activity or startles interfere with holding or the quiet alert state, swaddling may be helpful. It is best to use spontaneous alert periods for interactive play and to gradually try to stretch these periods. It is important for parents to allow the unconsolable baby to use self-quieting mechanisms. Throughout the preterm infant's three stages of behavioral organization, it is essential that the health professional encourage parents to express their feelings about their interactions.

Preterm Infant's Physical Appearance

The infant's appearance is frightening to some parents, while other parents express relief that their preterm infant looks better than anticipated. Fathers and mothers use similar terms to describe their small infants, with fathers tending to focus somewhat more on the infant being strong, eating well, and having open eyes and somewhat less on signs of health problems (Mercer et al., 1987). Almost all parents focused on their preterm infant's health; the majority of the comments about the infant's health were focused on problems such as bruises, jaundice, and hematomas, with fathers more often mentioning blood gases and whether the infant was on or off the ventilator. Positive comments about their infant's health included "a miracle," "she's all there," "perfect," and "strong." In order of their frequency other areas of focus on preterm infants included size (such as tiny, small, or "little doll") or actual weight; positive adjectives (such as beautiful, gorgeous, cute, or pretty); characteristics suggestive of temperament (such as alertness, responsiveness, and ease of comforting); and negative adjectives (such as scrawny, funny-looking, or fuzzy). Only the mothers talked about whether the infants were easy to care for and used such terms as "a real good baby," and "not a crier." Characteristic mothers' descriptions of their infants included:

- I was real sick and in the ICU; I had a clot in my lungs during labor. It is kind of depressing the baby is so small, has lots of tubes. The two of us have been through so much already. He is tiny, scrawny, looks helpless. Doesn't look very comfortable with tubes all over.
- I felt less worried after seeing the babies. I feel a lot of love for them. I just stare at them, a miracle, I cry at how small they look.
- He's a little peanut—3½ pounds. Pretty long for a premie; he is healthy except he's not eating. They found some blood in his stool today so they will try to feed him later.

Characteristic fathers' descriptions included:

- She has progressed from 100% oxygen, now just in isolette. Small—3¼ pounds. She is doing quite well. I am very optimistic. There is a possibility of brain damage hanging over us until we know for certain.
- This is the most wonderful, cute baby ever. He is really small, has a squeaky cry. Has much more of a personality than people say a 2-day-old baby has. I'm really excited about watching his grow up. He's a real healthy, robust little guy.
- He's a little tiny peep of a baby born at 26 weeks. He has lost 10 gm since birth. There's no permanent damage yet. So many things could happen.

- He looks good. Looks like our daughter and me. Has a full head of
  hair. He's active; they say he'll lose weight. The doctor say he is
  doing fair; I think he looks good. Kind of touch and go here. He has
  a tube in so he doesn't breathe on his own.

A comparison of maternal perceptions of their preterm neonates
within 48 hours of delivery, at time of infants' discharge from the
hospital, and 2 to 3 weeks after discharge from the hospital revealed
that mothers viewed their premature infants more positively than they
viewed an average infant at all three times (Koniak et al., 1985). As the
mothers became better acquainted with their infants through caretaking, they began to view their infants as having difficulty in establishing
predictable patterns of behavior similar to average infants. This finding
illustrates that the mother's need to maintain illusions about the preterm infant for coping decreases as her infant's survival becomes more
of a certainty. Others who compared mothers' ratings of preterm
infants with respiratory distress syndrome with trained clinicians' ratings using an adaptation of the Brazelton scale 5 weeks following birth
found that mothers' ratings did not differ significantly from clinicians
(Field et al., 1978).

Regardless of parents' perceptions of their infants in the NICU, in
the years following, these children are not perceived differently than
children in the general population (Philipp, 1983). Mothers and fathers
were in agreement in their perceptions of their children who had been
in the NICU from 6 months to 14 years earlier. They compared their
children favorably to other children their age; extreme prematurity had
not had a long-term disruptive effect on their lives.

THE FORMAL STAGE OF PARENTAL ROLE ATTAINMENT:
PARENTING A PREEMIE

The formal stage of parental role attainment, when parenting behaviors reflect what the experts prescribe, may extend beyond the usual 6
to 8 weeks following birth when the infant is preterm. In addition, with
the very small premature infant, uncertainty about survival and chronic
health problems may continue throughout this period; thus the progression through parental role attainment will vary by the infant's
wellness and length of the hospitalization.

For the very small preterm infant weighing less than 500 gm, parental support is critical. Kavanaugh (1988) points out that despite aggressive treatment, most infants this small die within the first 24 hours of
life. Kavanaugh stresses that it is important to create the infant's

reality and to provide supportive counseling, anticipatory guidance, and follow-up phone calls and visits. It is important that grief counseling extend beyond the hospital.

Other researchers observed that when ill newborns were transferred to a regional center, parents experienced grief reactions similar to parents whose infants do not survive the newborn period (Benfield, Leib, & Reuter, 1976). The level of anticipatory grief was not associated with the severity of infant illness. Fathers were faced with great interruptions in their daily lives since their wives and infants were in separate hospitals, and they had to maintain family stability during the crisis.

Homecoming without the Baby

Discharge from the hospital without her baby increases the mother's feelings of emptiness and sadness. She has watched other mothers ceremoniously dress their infant for the homecoming event. Special sensitivity to and support for perterm mothers' discharge is important.

There is uncertainty as to when the baby will be able to go home. Both parents are concerned about getting the baby home so that the family can adjust to the infant and get back to a normal routine. It is hard to acclimate young siblings until the infant is discharged. All family members are handicapped in the initial identification of the infant, and claiming the infant as a family member may not be completed until the infant is safely home. Getting the infant home also seems to be equated with ending much of the uncertainty about survival, "Once she is home, I'll feel better. I'm concerned that something might go wrong with her."

Women who were transported to a Level III hospital for antepartal hospitalization and delivery were concerned about spending much time with their infants hospitalized several hours drive away from their homes. Lois said, "I want to be with the baby, and it'll be hard from where I live. I want to talk to him, to bond, to do all those things." Lois was concerned about her son's health and when she could take him home, yet had not been to the NICN to see him:

I'm waiting for my husband to go with me. I'm kind of scared to go by myself to see him with the tubes and all, would feel stronger going with someone. I worry every night, how long he'll be here (hospital). When I go home, people will ask, 'Where's the baby?'

Women also do not want to take their infants home before they feel ready, as evidenced by Jean, a primipara, "I am worried about taking the baby home before I feel ready to handle a little tiny baby." Molly, who had been hospitalized for PTL at 28 weeks was successful in carrying her baby that she referred to as "him" for 8 additional weeks. Although she had a 1-year-old daughter at home, Molly was very apprehensive:

> I'm really tired. I don't really know what to do with her (baby). She doesn't want to eat. She is a lot less alert than my first baby. I'm concerned about how to handle both children and getting to know the baby. I'm scared that she will be less appealing than my first. I'm used to more feedback and interaction. I'm feeling depressed, but don't know why. I wanted the pregnancy over but didn't realized I'd have to start caring for the baby right away. I wasn't ready. I feel like I need to get myself back together before I can mother.

Helping Parents Parent Their Preterm Infant in the Hospital

During the first week after birth of the preterm infant, parents cried more, felt more helpless, were more worried about their ability to cope and about future pregnancies, and wanted to talk to hospital staff more than mothers of term infants (Trause & Kramer, 1983). These responses are expected and realistic. A videotape describing the NICN and equipment, presenting staff, and discussing parental reactions to the birth of high-risk newborns is inexpensive to produce and can be helpful to parents (Perez, 1980).

Because of the mothers' fatigue and some pain (many are also recuperating from cesarean births), it is important to take them to the NICN in a wheelchair. They can then walk to a chair placed next to their infant. Even if the mother is ambulatory, the grief she feels adds to her fatigue, and walking any distance contributes to shakiness and increased discomfort from the exertion, making it difficult for her to interact with her infant.

The mothers' activity level with her infant (looking, touching, smiling, vocalizing, and looking en face) increases over time, with a gradual increase in length of the mother's visiting time (Minde et al., 1980). This activity level or maternal behavior was positively related to the mother's interactive behavior with her infant during the first 3 months at home. All consistently low-activity level mothers had poor relationships with their mothers and their partners. Maternal behavior was explained largely by the mother's relationship with her mother, relationship with the father of the baby, and whether she had had a previous abortion. Of special interest was the failure of the maturational status of the infants to contribute to differences in observed maternal behavior.

Fathers play a meaningful role with their preterm infants during the hospitalization, although mothers more often demonstrate nurturant behavior during the initial visit (Marton, Minde, & Perrotta, 1981). After the first visit, mothers and fathers do not differ in their interactions with the infant, indicating that the environment of the NICU presents similar opportunities for both parents.

The nurse and other health professionals have enormous impact on parents during this formal stage of parental role attainment. In helping them to maintain their hope and receive positive feedback, the parents' attention must be directed to the smallest change in their infants; these observed changes may then be used for projecting realistic goals. Newman (1980) pointed out that parents quickly learn that their expectations must be lowered, with the smallest clinical and developmental change being salient.

Schraeder (1980) projected three stages of parenting behaviors in the NICN: Stage I includes touching, stroking, holding and studying infant en face, and fondling, holding or talking to; Stage II is the caretaking stage when the mother may diaper, feed, perform other caretaking tasks; and Stage III identity is the stage when the parent takes photographs, brings toys, makes a special bonnet or bootees, and moves from focus on physiological parameters to focus on the child.

Parents may need encouragement to take snapshots of their preterm infant; if they do not have a camera, a camera should be purchased for the nursery for such purposes. A snapshot gives parents something concrete to show friends who ask about the infant and enables the mother to continue identification of her infant at home. Huckabay (1987) studied black and Hispanic low SES mothers of preterm infants, giving one group a snapshot of their infant and not giving a snapshot to a control group. Both groups of mothers had comparable bonding behaviors prior to their discharge. Four weeks after their discharge from the hospital, mothers who received a snapshot of their infant had significantly higher bonding behaviors with their preterm infants than mothers not receiving a snapshot.

If a mother wishes to breast-feed, she should be encouraged to express her milk and bring it into the nursery for her infant. This contributes to the mother's self-esteem, because she is contributing to her infant's care in a way that no one else can. A mother's tendency to feel that the infant "is more the hospital's than hers," can be changed by encouraging her participation in her infant's care in any way possible. If the infant is being tube-fed, she can help by holding the syringe or, more importantly, a pacifier for her infant (if the infant is able to suck) during tube-feeding.

White-Traut and Nelson (1988) tested two interventions among mothers with premature infants who were 28 to 35 weeks gestation and off ventilation support within 24 hours of birth: a control group received routine care; one group talked to their infants; and one group used interactive intervention (massage, talking, eye contact, and rocking). The talking and interactive interventions were administered within 24 hours after birth; maternal infant interaction was tested during a feeding period prior to the infants' discharge from the hospital. Mothers in the control group who did not receive an intervention scored lower than other mothers in total maternal behavior but did not differ significantly from the talking group. Mothers in the interactive intervention group scored significantly higher. Infant behavior was significantly different between the talking and routine care group, with the talking and interacting group not differing from each other. Thus both interventions were beneficial in enhancing maternal behavior.

Marino (1980) warned against nurses giving the illusion of competing with parents. Nurses' expert skill in caring for the infant overwhelms parents. Nurses buying clothes and toys for special infants may give the appearance to the mother that the nurses are claiming her infant as their own. Marino provided three objectives for nursing care without competing with the mother: (1) foster the attachment process between parent and child by encouraging skin-to-skin contact as early and as often as possible, teach parents how to get the baby to an alert state, point out the baby's unique characteristics and ask the parents what they have noticed, and provide parents privacy to interact with their infants when possible; (2) deal with ambivalent feelings that contribute to a competive atmosphere such as avoiding unfavorable comparisons of the baby's response to parent caretaking with theirs, encourage parents at a quiet time to talk about their hopes and fears, and facilitate parents' groups; and (3) provide parents with opportunities to learn to care for their infant.

Jean illustrated how mothers feel abut the nurse's expert skill: "You have so much more time to spend with her and know her so much better than I do. She likes and knows you better than me." The nurse can tell the mother, however, that her infant knows her voice because she heard it in utero, and her relationship is much stronger because of this pregnancy time. Point out any infant response to the mother to reinforce their developing relationship.

If the nurses are aware when parents are coming for a visit, they can make a small sign to put on the isolette or bed that says something like, "Hi, I'm Judy and I'm happy today. I gained two ounces and my mommy and daddy are coming to visit me tonight." Such notes take little time but help assure parents the importance of their visits.

If the parents live some distance away and are unable to visit often, it helps to photograph their infant dressed in parent's gifts of clothing or with toys brought by parents. Notes on postcards may be written daily with comments about weight gains or other observations. The mother can address a stack of cards and leave them with the nurse to write daily notes as she completes her charting for the day.

Mothers of preterm infants, as other mothers, experience much conflict in return to careers or other employment. Finding a caretaker who will be sensitive to an infant whose cues are not always distinct is worrisome to parents. Collins and Tiedje (1988) describe a working mothers' group program consisting of six sessions held after delivery but before the mother returns to work. The program provides an opportunity for women to discuss concerns and develop positive feelings about themselves.

Preparing Parents for the Preterm Infant's Discharge

Consolvo (1986) described a program in which mothers were allowed to live in the hospital with their infant prior to discharge. Mothers who participated in this care program had decreased anxiety about their infants' illness. When possible to plan, this type of live-in program is preferrable to special structured teaching programs. Special preparation is imperative for parents who take their infants on apnea monitors, and special treatment regimens home.

Harrison and Twardosz (1986) tested the effects of a structured teaching program by comparing a group of women receiving such a program with a group who received routine care and a group in which mothers were provided the opportunity to discuss nonmedical concerns about their infants or their situations. No group differences were observed in maternal perceptions or maternal infant interaction behaviors at 2, 4, and 8 weeks following discharge from the hospital. These findings speak well for the NICN nurses who routinely provide the kind of noncompetitive nursing care suggested by Marino (1980). Also, short-term instruction is probably not remembered. If mothers feel stressful, it is difficult to attend to programs of instruction. Cagan and Meier (1983) developed a form to use with families of high-risk infants in discharge planning; the form covers salient areas of infant care and parental concerns. Censullo (1986) also outlined a guide for nursing strategies in helping families plan home care of their high-risk newborn with four foci: counseling to facilitate grieving and crisis resolution and to promote self-esteem; education in infant behaviors and responses; improving communication between hospital, clinic, and community; and referrals for special care programs (infant stimulation) and parent support groups.

Elsas (1981) proposed a psychosocial risk inventory to alert health professionals to parents who need more extensive help in making a

healthy adaptation in their family. The infant who is socially unresponsive does not alone predict whether abuse and neglect will occur, but
other factors interact with the infant's response, such as the mother's
environmental support, general education, ability to separate herself
from her infant, and her preparation for the infant (Egeland, Breitenbucher, & Rosenberg, 1980). Abusive parents are less satisfied with
their children and view child rearing as more difficult and unenjoyable
(Trickett & Susman, 1988).

Family characteristics that are "red-flag alerts" for additional help
include social isolation, family history of abuse and neglect, serious
marital problems, apathetic and dependent personality styles, low self-
esteem, and unwanted pregnancy (Altemeier et al., 1982; Anderson,
1987; Hunter et al., 1978). Individuals and families with these characteristics need mental health and/or family counseling and extensive
social support from community resources. Affleck and associates (1986)
reported that when the infant's postdischarge status was more severe
(more likely to have future developmental and/or health problems),
maternal adaptation was positively associated with satisfaction with
emotional, informational, and tangible support received during the
hospital-to-home transition.

THE INFORMAL STAGE OF PARENTAL ROLE ATTAINMENT WITH A PRETERM INFANT

The informal stage of parental role attainment, during which parents
have mastered tasks of caring for small infants and developed their own
style and which is a time of pleasurable reciprocal interchange with the
infant, has greater variability among parents of preterm infants. The
informal stage, usually achieved within 2 to 5 months after birth,
occurs at some time after the preterm infant's discharge from the
hospital.

The first few days at home are highly anxious days, although parental anxiety is less than during the hospitalization for preterm labor
(Aradine & Ferketich, 1990). Mothers of preterm infants expressed
more concerns and worries than mothers of term infants at 2 and
6 weeks after their infants' discharge from the hospital, however
(Goodman & Sauve, 1985). While no mother of a term infant was
concerned about her infant's appearance, mothers of preterms were
concerned about the shape of or shaved head, dusky color, or skin
abrasions. A public health or visiting nurse referral is very supportive
help for many to help allay these and other concerns, especially during
the first weeks at home. Very low birth weight infants have done well

when discharged early with nurse specialist home follow-up (Brooten et al., 1986).

Trause and Kramer (1983) reported that preterm mothers were crying less and not wanting to be left alone less often than mothers of term infants 1 month following discharge, however. The researchers attributed this to their supervised child care experiences in the NICU. Others found that mothers who blamed their antepartal behavior as causing their infant's high-risk status had more positive mood states and anticipated less difficulty than mothers who blamed others (Affleck et al., 1982).

Mothers search for mastery, meaning, and protection from future harm in adapting to their high-risk infants following their discharge for the NICN (Affleck, Tennen, & Gershman, 1985). Primary control, the mother's view of how much her infant's recovery and future development depended on her actions, and secondary control, whether mothers perceived gains or advantages from the experience of having a high-risk infant, were both related to their adaptational outcome as reflected by mood states.

Preterm mothers' infants were less alert and less focused than term infants during feeding time the first 4 weeks after discharge (Minde, Perrotta, & Marton, 1985). Perhaps in order to try to compensate for this behavior, preterm mothers work harder; they looked at their infants using the en face position more at both 4 and 8 weeks after the infant's discharge. Preterm infants continued to have feeding problems 3 months after their expected date of birth. Health problems (e.g., colds, eye and ear infections, thrush, colic, rashes) during the first 3 months did not differ between preterm and term infants (Minde et al., 1985).

Others observed that immaturity was evident among preterms 3 months postterm in motor performance and automatic regulation, but their orientation behavior and state regulation were affected by postnatal illness (Greene et al., 1983). Preterm infants looked at their mothers less often.

Mothers of premature infants also spent more time in proximity to their infants, held them a larger portion of time, and tended to use more tactile-kinesthetic stimulation at 1, 4, and 8 months following their discharge (Crnic et al., 1983). The mothers of preterm infants smiled less often than mothers of term infants, suggesting that their interactions were not as pleasurable. The preterm infants also smiled less often and averted gaze from their mothers more often than term infants, so their mothers did not receive the positive feedback.

Fathers and mothers demonstrated similar patterns of interaction in face-to-face play 3 months following preterm infants' discharge from the hospital, but mothers introduced caretaking into the play situation more often (Marton et al., 1981). As the preterm infant began to catch up with the term infant, fathers tended to decrease their involvement.

Both stress and social support appear to mediate maternal attitudes and behavior at 1 and 4 months. Mothers experiencing greater stress had less positive attitudes and behavior, while those with greater social support responded more positively (Crnic et al., 1983).

Mothers of preterm infants reported significant improvement in parental competence from 1 to 4 months after delivery (Aradine & Ferketich, 1990). However, the impact of the mate relationship and family functioning is evident, with decreases in both observed during that time. Trause and Kramer (1983) reported, however, that preterm parents became increasingly sensitive to each other over time.

The health professional's major role during this period is to promote the parents' pleasure in interacting with their infants and to reinforce the parents' positive behaviors. Observation during feeding periods is helpful to determine whether the still somewhat immature infant is being held too closely or moved too much (the automatic rocking, jostling type of behavior that may be a parental tendency) to accommodate. Parents can be helped to give the infant some distance (e.g., feeding the infant in an infant seat) and to understand that the infant is too immature to handle excessive movement. Let parents know that you understand the extraordinary time and work that are needed to help their infants gain control and to learn.

It is important for the nurse or other health professional who sees the mother for follow-up to assess the mother's adaptation to the infant. Her behavior as she interacts with her infant and talks about her gives cues about her feelings about the child and her relationship to her. Is she able to enjoy the infant? Does the mother smile spontaneously at her infant? Does she respond warmly and appropriately? Is she sensitive to the infant's cues indicating sensory overload? Is the father also involved with the infant? If the answer to these questions is yes, the parent is attached to her infant and feeling good about mothering. If, in contrast, the mother continues to express fear of the baby's responses, doubts her ability to care for and avoids handling the baby, and feels alone in her role, there is need for intensive work with the family.

If problems arise that suggest that either parent needs help to resolve them, a question such as, "Have you thought about seeing a family counselor?" or "How have you thought about handling this situation?" may provide impetus for their seeking help. Since poorer mate relationships and family functioning tend to occur over time, it is important to encourage parents to keep communication open and talk over their concerns. Telephone hotline numbers of agencies in the community and other resources that are available should be left with parents, in the event they decide to seek help later.

PERSONAL LEVEL OF PARENTAL ROLE ACQUISITION

The personal level of parental role attainment, internalizing the parental role as part of one's identity, most often occurs from 5 to 9 months. There is no evidence to suggest that most parents of preterm infants do not achieve this level within this time period. Research findings suggest that mothers of preterm infants are ahead of mothers of term infants in some areas. If the preterm infant has a chronic health problem and/or handicap such as cerebral palsy, the information in Chapter 8 is applicable to these situations.

Mothers' achievement of the maternal role during this time may be tied to prenatal events and stressors following birth. Mothers who had more extensive mood disturbance around the time of the infant's discharge from the hospital had greater problems in caretaking at 9 months following discharge (Affleck et al., 1982). Six months following hospital discharge, mothers who did more to prevent unfavorable outcomes, were more optimistic about their pregnancy outcomes, and saw their infant's complications as more avoidable, reported greater mood disturbance (Affleck, Tennen, & Rowe, 1988). The researchers suggest that health professionals in their counseling often discourage self-blame to help lessen the mother's guilt, but the guilt may help give the woman a sense of personal control over future birth outcomes. Mothers who saw their problem as more avoidable indicated a lower risk for and were more optimistic about future births.

By toddlerhood (12 to 36 months), no differences were observed between mothers of term and preterm infants for maternal confidence (Gross, Rocissano, & Roncoli, 1989). Predictors of maternal confidence in the preterm group of mothers were prior experience in childcare, birth order, and whether the infant had cerebral palsy. Preterm mothers with higher maternal confidence had greater experience in child care prior to becoming a parent, were parenting their first child, and their child did not have cerebral palsy. Term mothers with greater maternal confidence had greater prior experience in child care, were older, and had toddlers with higher birth weights. Prior experience in the tasks of the mothering role were important to all mothers in predicting their maternal confidence.

Over 6, 8, 10, and 14 months, preterm infants who weighed less than 1850 gms at birth behaved increasingly like term infants, and observed differences between them disappeared, except that preterm infants continued to vocalize less (Crawford, 1982). Crawford noted that mothers of preterm infants demonstrated more caretaking and affectionate behavior toward their infants. Barnard, Bee, and Hammond (1984) also found that by 8 months, preterm infants less than 34 weeks gestation who had no central nervous dysfunction or assisted respiration did not differ from term infants in task involvement. Preterm infants' mothers demonstrated higher levels of stimulation at 4 months when their infants showed lower levels of responsiveness, and at 8 months, when their infants had caught up, they continued either with the same or declining levels of stimulation. Mothers of term and preterm infants were more similar at 2 years, except that mothers of preterms were less positive in a teaching task and described themselves as less involved.

Developmental scores of preterm infants are influenced by their interactions with caregivers and their ordinal positions in their families. Firstborn preterm infants receive more stimulation through their first 2 years; at 1 and 3 months firstborns receive more responsive care and social stimulation than later born infants, and at 8 months they receive more verbal and object stimulation (Sigman et al., 1981).

Infants with moderate to lengthy hospitalizations due to respiratory illness displayed a pattern of attachment that was more anxious-resistant than infants who were healthy preterms (Plunkett et al., 1986). Plunkett and associates' study indicated that infants who remained at risk into their second year were at greater risk for developing relationships that reflect a difficult to care for infant whose parents' had difficulty in overcoming an early need to avoid attaching for fear the infant would not survive. They suggest intervention by helping parents to read and respond to their infant's cues accurately, to initiate pleasurable interactions with the infant, to provide a secure base for the toddler's exploration, and to comfort the toddler when stressed. It is consoling to parents to know that differences between securely and insecurely attached infants appear to disappear in childhood (Weitzman & Cook, 1986) and that at 3 years of age, preterm infants' social abilities are unaffected by birth status (Bakeman & Brown, 1980).

Professional support continues to be critical during this period; at 8 months, professional support was positively correlated with the quality of home environment, greater maternal satisfaction with parenting, and more positive assessment of infant temperament (Crnic, Greenberg, & Slough, 1986). Stress measured at 1 month after the infant's discharge from the hospital was associated with less positive maternal attitudes and mother-infant interactive behavior and less secure infant-maternal attachment. Intimate support provided by the mother's husband or partner was the greatest predictor of both maternal and infant functioning at 8 and 12 months. Crnic and associates suggest that both mothers and infants may be more sensitive to the impact of stress and more responsive to social support because of their infant's and their own vulnerability. Health professionals' support, along with traditional sources of support, plays an important role in both infant development and in parenting.

The outcome of a transitional consultation program (TCP) conducted by nurses to prepare parents for the infant's transition from hospital to home was compared to routine care among mothers of high-risk infants (Affleck et al., 1989). The range of consultants' behavior included listening to mothers' feelings and concerns, providing information about typical and atypical infant characteristics, calling attention to infant's developmental change, mutual problem solving, role modeling therapeutic and caregiving procedures, and preparing mothers to deal with problems when on her own. The medical severity and the mothers' need for support moderated the effects of the TCP. A higher than average medical severity was associated with increased positive mood among the TCP mothers, but with below average medical severity, the TCP had negative effects on mothers' mood states. When there was an above average need for support, the TCP had negative effects on mothers' mood states. When there was an above average need for support, the TCP was associated with increased maternal responsiveness and sense of competence, but with below the average need for support, the effects of the TCP were negative. Although mothers who needed more support were more distressed, they were more responsive in their interactions with their infants and seemed to enjoy them more. These findings indicate the importance of the health professional's assessment of need for support with the parents of high-risk infants. Mothers who had a greater need for support appear to have been more receptive to and/or to have made better use of support.

Another tested intervention by health professionals is demonstration of the Brazelton Behavioral Assessment Scale. Szajnberg and associates (1987) used the Brazelton Scale with a group of mothers of ill preterm infants at 34 weeks gestational age and a routine physical examination with another group. Pre- and posttests were given. Both groups of preterm mothers' attitudes were also compared to a group of mothers of term infants. At 34 weeks and at 6 months (corrected age), preterm mothers indicated greater adaptation to their infant's symbiotic needs and tended to be less worried about the infant's curiosity than mothers of term infants. Thus before the preterm mother has benefit of extensive contact with her infant, she is prepared for greater sensitivity as opposed to learning her sensitivity from infant feedback. Preterm mothers had greater conflict about femininity (willingness to forego body image and sexuality concerns temporarily for the sake of child-bearing/rearing) than mothers of term infants, indicating that earlier stress may force them to postpone these needs longer than term mothers. The intervention of the demonstrated Brazelton had the positive effects of that group of mothers visiting the NICN more frequently the week following the demonstration rating their infants as temperamentally easier 8 months later, and having more positive attitudes toward the baby's exploration and toward the baby demanding exclusive attention (focalization on the mother). There appears to be some continuity from 6 to 42 months in maternal sensitivity, with discontinuity resulting in situations of loss and relationship problems, hard to teach infants, and less emotional support (Pianta, Sroufe, & Egeland, 1989).

Another type of intervention program of 11 sessions emphasized maternal sensitivity and responsiveness to infant social signals; seven were conducted the week prior to the infant's discharge from the hospital, and four were conducted at home during the 3 months after discharge (Nurcombe et al., 1984). At 6 months the group receiving the intervention was more confident, satisfied, and positive toward child rearing than the preterm group not receiving the intervention. Mothers receiving the intervention viewed their infants as more adaptable, happy, and approachable and less easily distressed.

THE HEALTH PROFESSIONAL IN THE NICN

No other position is more demanding than that in an NICN. Several have written about "burn-out" to describe the high turnover of personnel working there. Marshall and Kasman (1980) define burn-out as the loss of motivation for creative involvement, characterized by deterioration of well-being, chronic fatigue and exhaustion, frequent minor incapacitating ailments, depression, hostility, overinvolvement, scapegoating, and the detached lonely individual who takes work conflicts home. There are several causes of burn-out in the NICN. Among these are the complexity of the emotional issues, the frequency of death indicating personal failure, ethical issues, challenges of working with highly stressed families, state-of-the-art technology, interdisciplinary and intradisciplinary conflicts, chronic patients who may live for months then suddenly die, and in general the frenetic environment (Marshall & Kasman, 1980).

There are both individual and organizational strategies that may be used to combat burn-out. It is important for individuals to leave the

NICN area completely for breaks and meals. A support person who is acceptable to staff should be available for individuals to discuss their feelings; group sessions led by the support person are helpful when a special problem arises. Marshall and Kasman (1980) suggest a routine after work that helps separate the pressures of the NICN from home life such as walking or jogging, developing outside interests or hobbies, and taking vacations and mental health days.

In working with highly stressed families with multiple problems, Bolton (1983) emphasizes that it is time that health professionals are relieved of the burden of the expectation that all families can change. Just as many of the frequent deaths are unpreventable, many of the dysfunctional family relationships that are dealt with cannot be resolved within the period of time the family is available to NICN professionals.

Most hospitals provide an extensive orientation program for nursing staff; new house staff also need a similar orientation. Interdisciplinary conflict may be decreased by having all disciplines take part in the orientation. As noted above, support groups are important for health professionals. Weekly interdisciplinary meetings with an ethicist and other professionals to discuss cases are a means of a regular channel that provides an opportunity for individuals to raise questions and voice opinions.

SUMMARY

The handicaps of preterm infants in interacting with their parents present challenges that most parents seem to prepare for. Research findings indicate that parents are able to overcome their initial grief in delivering a preterm infant and to learn to relate to an infant who in no way resembles the parents' prebirth "fantasy" infant. The one consistent finding is that preterm infants who smile less also have parents who show less positive effect. Health professionals' greatest challenge is in helping parents enjoy interactions with their difficult infants.

To avoid a competitive air with parents, clinicians must recognize the unique styles of parent–infant interaction along with their priorities and concerns. Harrison (1989) suggested that in some cases the nurse's efforts to teach developmental stimulation may indicate that the nurse sees them as unable to meet their infant's needs; emphasis must be on the parents as those who can most effectively respond to the infant's behavioral cues and need for stimulation. Giving the reason for stimulation enables parents to be creative in moving into their informal stage of parental role attainment. Mentioning different ways of handling situations allows parents to feel in control of selecting and creating their own style.

Although preterm infants are greatly handicapped at birth, it is reassuring that toward the last half of their first year they catch up. At ages 13 and 20 months, very low birth weight infants who had no evidence of severe intraventricular hemorrhage or cerebral palsy did not differ from term infants in their security, temporal stability, and similarity of attachment to their parents (Easterbrooks, 1989).

Research focused on the impact of the infant with severe medical and physical problems on parenting and the family is badly needed. Evaluation of ongoing parent–infant interactions is important to ascertain continued parental adaptation. In situations of family stress and deprivation, the clinician's assistance in coordinating a social support network with tangible physical help is critical.

8

When the Infant
Has a Congenital Defect

The often-asked questions immediately following the birth of an infant, "Is he all right?" and "Does he have all of his fingers and toes?" convey the anxiety with which parents have been anticipating their child's birth. At that moment, when the infant appears healthy and all right, staff relay that message with joy, "You have a beautiful boy" or "a lovely girl," and quickly hold the infant up for the mother and father to see. In contrast, when a defect is readily evident, the mother's anxious question is usually met by momentary silence. A quick exchange of glances among those attending her asks, "Are you going to tell her? Do I have to be the one to tell her?" A mother who asked, "Is he all right?" remarked, "I saw the nurse's eyes, and then I knew. I knew without a doubt that something was wrong."

Birth defects are a major child health problem. Approximately 250,000 infants are born each year with handicaps diagnosed at birth (Raff, 1986). Although many defects are diagnosed prior to birth, many are not. In those situations, the health professionals are also temporarily stunned as are the parents. Many factors may account for the shock that staff seem to experience when a child with a defect is born. There may be unconscious denial that the predicted rate of birth defects will occur, strong identification with the parents, a displaced sense of guilt for behaviors or comments made in earlier interactions with the parents, or fear of inability to deal with the parental grief.

Thus health professionals as well as the parents are disappointed and experience shock when an infant enters the world with an unanticipated abnormality. Both the professional and the parent are experiencing a stressful situation because of the loss of the desired normal infant and the happiness that accompanies deliveries of healthy, whole infants. In this chapter parental responses to the birth of a child with a defect are discussed and suggestions are provided for dealing with the situation and assisting parents at the time of birth and in the early months of parenting.

PARENTAL RESPONSES

The birth of an infant with an anomaly has an immediate and pervasive impact on the parents. The event consumes enormous amounts of energy, inflicts great mental pain, and demands immediate restructuring of family plans and goals and parents' physical and social worlds. The crisis extends from self to family, to friends, and to the community; it is rather complex or may be viewed as several crises precipitated by one enormous crisis. There is a crisis involving self-identity: "Who am I?" or "What kind of person am I to produce a defective child?" There is a crisis of social stigma: "How do I cope with the curious glances or expressions of pity?" There is a crisis of unforeseen expenses: "How can we afford the type of care, surgery, and/or treatments required for this child?" There is the crisis of loss: "I wanted a beautiful, normal little girl, not a mentally retarded, deformed little boy." There is the crisis of family strain in dealing with the problems: "How will this affect my husband? My other children? My parents?" In resolving each crisis, many decisions and adaptations must be made.

Many of these crises confront the mother following exhausting labor to bring the infant into the world. The father may be equally exhausted from his lack of sleep, anxiety, and concern for his wife in their mutual work. Few events could be more disappointing or heartbreaking, or follow more painful work, than the birth of an infant with a defect.

Older parents seem to have more difficulty with the crisis; parents with more education seem to handle the crisis better but have more difficulty with adapting socially (Leifson, 1980). Palfrey and associates (1989) found that in families in which mothers had more education, stress from a child's disability was greater; black families (in contrast to white and Hispanic families) and larger families reported less impact on the family from a handicapped child. There were no differences in impact of a handicapped child on the family composition in terms of natural parents, reconstituted families, single parents, or grandparents.

Responses by Type of Defect

Parental anxiety about their child with a defect may in part be related to the threat of their loss of standing in the community (Waechter, 1970).

Both family and society in general are more rejecting of facial and genital defects (Easson, 1966).

The face, readily visible to everyone, is a hallmark of identity; persons with unusual facial characteristics are recipients of many jokes and cruel remarks, even when they have no deformities (e.g., hose-nose, elephant ears). Infants and children with craniofacial deformities were rated at the bottom of an attractiveness scale by adults and children (Barden et al., 1988a, 1988b). Mothers of facially deformed infants scored more negatively on 26 out of 27 possible mother-infant interaction behaviors, although they contended they were more satisfied with parenting than mothers of normal infants (Barden et al., 1989). Maternal nurturance/responsiveness was also lower among mothers with infants with minor facial deformities (Field & Vega-Lahr, 1984).

Gender is at the core of a person's identity. A child is socialized either as feminine or masculine from birth. Parents interact with and handle girls differently than boys; as the child develops sexually, social interactions give feedback that affect the child's body image. The first question asked by friends is, "Was it a girl or a boy?" Genital abnormalities are difficult for parents to explain or discuss. Visible genital defects at birth more often occur in males (Schultz, 1984). The rarest genital defect is hermaphroditism; however, gender is not in question in the more common congenital defects affecting approximately 20,000 newborn males per year (e.g., hypospadias, epispadius) (Schultz, 1984). Any defect of the genitals, however slight or operable, arouses deep-seated emotions in both parents and child in regard to sexual identity and role.

Parents want information about the time and prognosis for corrective surgery in genital anomalies. Surgical timing is important, since children react differently to corrections of anomalies at different developmental stages. Both the impact on the child and the time period of coping with an unrepaired anomaly must be considered (Schultz, 1984).

Some parents tend to monitor their child's genitals more than is the case with normal children when there is a genital anomaly. Parents who are extreme in their monitoring or in their focus on their child's genitals need teaching about normal sexual events during infancy; referral for psychological counseling may be indicated (Schultz, 1984).

Reparable and Irreparable Defects

Health professionals often have difficulty understanding why parents' initial response to having a baby with a cleft lip differs little from parents' response to an infant with Down syndrome, since the cleft lip is easily repaired and the infant has promise for a normal future. Parents, however, are initially as upset when a child's fingers are missing as they are when a limb is missing (Setoguchi, 1968). Whether it is the shock that something is wrong or the narcissistic wound that one's child is not perfect is a moot point. The initial impact of the baby with a defect is one of profound disappointment; any defect is unacceptable. This was illustrated by Mrs. Jones when she was told that cleft lips were very common, and she retorted, "Not in my family, they're not!"

Over a 3-month period, emotional adaptation to infants with a birth defect did not differ by whether the defect could be repaired, except between 2 to 4 weeks following birth, when parents of infants with irreparable defects had three times the emotional adaptation responses of other parents (Mercer, 1977a). During this period, the initial adjustment in the home setting and the first trips out into the community are occurring. The mother's fear of social rejection in these early exposures to outsiders may account for some of the increase in emotional response. Possibly, it takes at least 2 weeks for the parent to absorb the information that the child will never be normal.

Cognitive adaptation responses of determining a cause of the defect, resolving conflicting information, and planning for the future were greater for parents of infants with irreparable defects as would be expected (Mercer, 1977a). Social adaptation responses of determining others' response to their infants also were much higher for parents of infants with irreparable defects.

Each time a child faces a surgical procedure, parents experience an exacerbation of all of the early feelings and emotions during the first week following birth. Parents report that they relive all of the early moments following the news of their child's defect as they wait during the surgical event. Parents have great fear of their child's death during or after surgery, especially if they earlier wished for the child's death as resolution to their problems.

The parents with a child with an irreparable defect have no time limit to their plight. The chronicity of their situation necessitates permanent alteration of roles and goals. There is no magic of surgery to transform their child to a normal child; they have no escape except their own or their child's death. The lifelong commitment for parents is awesome when they realize that their child can never achieve independence. While most couples look forward to the years when their children mature, become independent, and leave home, the couple with a child with a permanent defect have no such reprieve from child care chores. Rather, child care may become more laborious as the child grows and becomes stronger and the parents age and become less robust. This reality alone has an enormous and disquieting impact on parents' lives, as they worry about who will care for their child when they are unable to.

Time and Manner of Being Told

Learning about the baby's condition early helps to relieve some of the mother's frustration; most mothers feel that the shock may be less the earlier they are told and that they are able to adapt more easily (Murphy & Pueschel, 1975). Mothers are also able to sense that something is wrong by others' interactions with them. A few mothers, however, do not feel the need to be told early; some have reported that they wish the baby's diagnosis had been delayed until they had recuperated from the delivery (Cowie, 1966). Ideally both parents should be present when told about the infant's defect; mothers in particular note that they need their partners at this time. If possible, the explanation is made while showing the couple their baby; visualization at the time permits realistic input rather than frightening fantasy.

The manner and content of the information are thought to be more important than the timing by some parents. Parents report vivid memories about being told the infant's diagnosis over a period of several years (Barsch, 1968). Parents are most appreciative when a sympathetic approach is used and the prognosis is not presented as either overly pessimistic or overly optimistic (Carr, 1970; D'Arcy, 1968). When such critical information is conveyed in a terse, uncaring manner, the impact seems much greater. The telling should not be rushed; adequate time for parents to ask questions and express their feelings is important. If both parents are in the delivery room and they see the infant at once, the physician should spend time with the couple in privacy as soon as the delivery process is completed to provide them with an opportunity to express their concerns and to ask questions.

Parental responses of adaptation to the impact of the birth of an infant with a defect occur within three major areas: emotional, cognitive, and social adaptation. These emotional, cognitive, and social areas of adaptation are not discrete entities, however. There is cognitive work in the social behavioral adaptation, but in the social adaptation, the work must be done in interaction with another person or persons.

Emotional Adaptation Responses

Emotions reflect the parents' intrapersonal state and are a cue as to their internal organization. Emotional responses are more often researched than other responses, but emotional adaptation responses were less apparent than cognitive and social adaptation over a 3-month period following birth (Mercer, 1975). A wide range of emotional responses are notable: shock, anger, fear, guilt, anxiety, and depression. These may be viewed within the framework of the grief process, which is discussed following the overall emotional, cognitive, and social adaptation responses.

Shock

Shock is the initial response to the birth of a defective baby; it is accompanied by expressions of disbelief that this event has actually occurred. "I just can't believe it," or "you just never think that this will happen to you," are examples of shock responses. One father fainted when he first saw his son with a facial defect.

Shock reactions appear to be self-limiting and time-specific, terminating during the first week following the birth. A restriction of thought and concern for self are often expressed in shock responses. Although parents express shock at the birth of a baby with a defect, they sometimes make comments that indicate the event was not totally unexpected. Comments such as, "I had an intuition that something was wrong with the baby all through this pregnancy," or "We worried more about the pregnancy this time," reflect parental fears during pregnancy that became reality.

The shock of this crisis event is of such impact that one mother described it as crossing into a world that was completely different from any she had ever known (Daniels & Berg, 1968). The intense emotion felt at this initial impact is remembered for years.

Anger

Anger is one of the predominant and more pervasive of the emotional responses to the birth of a baby with a defect. Anger responses are seen in fault-finding, condemning behavior, and expressions of bitterness or resentment. Anger may be directed toward self, family members, visitors, or medical personnel but is seldom directed toward the baby.

Anger responses occur early regarding the immediate situation, the labor experience, or the new role as mother or father of an infant with a defect. Problems arising from situations ensuing from the infant's birth continue to evoke anger over a long period of time. An example of the temporal range of anger expression was shown by an 86-year-old mother who expressed anger that she had not been prepared for her first viewing of her daughter who had been born with a cleft lip and palate some 60 years earlier. She refused to read a publication on the topic, because she did not wish to "reexperience those feelings." This mother had not had benefit of professional counseling to allow her to work through her anger and resolve her feelings; she had not adapted to the event, despite the fact that her daughter was essentially normal following corrective surgery as a toddler.

Fear

Parental responses of fear may be observed as expressions of apprehension of what must be done in the immediate or distant future. Early fears seem to center about realistic factors (e.g., surgeries on the baby, complicated health care, and concern for the child's potential in adult years). Rather than decreasing, fear responses seem to increase as parents become increasingly familiar with and attached to their handicapped child. Perhaps some of the parents' fear results from their anger about the event, and parents feel something will happen to the baby in retribution for their anger.

Early responses sometimes reflect a death wish for the infant, for the infant's death would erase all of the problems (Daniels & Berg, 1968; Freeston, 1971). However, after becoming attached to the infant, there is a real fear of the infant's death. The fear of losing the infant becomes paramount each time the child faces corrective surgery.

Guilt

Guilt is an adaptive response that may be observed by statements reflecting a feeling of personal responsibility for the defect through failure to follow good health practices or by some past error or sin. Remarks such as "I can't help but think of the glass of wine I drank," or "Even though the doctor said my feelings didn't cause the baby to be like this, I still feel guilty." Expressions of guilt are observed more often during the first month (Mercer, 1973). It seems that when self-blame occurs, adaptation moves more smoothly, since that means self-control over the event recurring (Affleck et al., 1985; Horan, 1982). Guilt as an emotional response overlaps with the search for mastery of control in the situation, a cognitive behavior.

Depression and Anxiety

Anxiety and depression accompany the response to the event, the parental fears, and wish for the infant's death. Depression is evidenced by covert behaviors, facial responses, crying, and statements such as, "It's just terrible, I don't know how I can stand it," and "The baby is such a disappointment."

Depressed parents retreat from contacts, relationships, social situations, or painful conflicts. Parents withdraw by limiting the duration of a conversation by abruptly changing to a topic other than the baby, by closing their eyes to close out another's presence, or simply by pulling the curtains around their bed to avoid seeing or being seen.

Withdrawal provides a temporary retreat from painful reality or a means to limit exposure to the stressful situation. Parents use withdrawal to limit intake of information to a level that is tolerable for them, or at times as a defense of flight. All parents of an infant with a defect seem to use withdrawal at some time in their adaptation to and coping with the situation.

Depression recurs periodically, and in the event of mental retardation or irreparable defects, the sorrow is chronic (Olshansky, 1962). Adaptation differs for mothers and fathers, but nearly all describe chronic sorrow. Fathers described their adjustment to children with Down syndrome as a gradual, steady recovery, while mothers described ups and downs with periodic crisis patterns (Damrosch & Perry, 1989).

Cognitive Adaptation Responses

Parents' cognitive adaptation reflects the hard work of absorbing the reality, gathering information to make an appraisal, and making plans to deal with their situation of having an infant with a defect. Cognitive adaptation includes parents' sorting of their knowledge, beliefs, and wishes in order to make choices from alternatives available to them in planning their future.

Parents are often confused about the facts relating to their child. Their mental discord or cognitive dissonance commonly derives from conflicting data from authoritative sources. Conflicting data may be related to the diagnosis, observation of, or other information about the baby. Examples of dissonance are: "The minister said it was God's will, but I don't think God would deliberately make a baby like that," and "The doctor who delivered the baby said he couldn't be sure the baby is mongoloid, but the pediatrician said that there is no doubt."

Cognitive dissonance is observed more often during the first couple of weeks than later (Mercer, 1975). This suggests that parents work hard very early at sorting out facts in attempts to achieve a good fit with reality. It could be that parents gain sophistication from having to extract explicit, accurate information. When parents are involved with numerous health professionals where there is no collaboration, such as when some may be in different cities, the parent is the authority who must describe the infant's status, what other persons have said, and the treatment regimen of other health professionals. The parents are the experts in both the knowledge of the defect and of their child's progress and development. The question is raised as to whether this is a natural outcome or whether this is placing undue responsibility on parents as coordinators of their child's health care.

Search For Cause Of Defect And Mastery

A major cognitive response is the search for a cause of the infant's defect or any factor that could have led to the baby's defect. Mothers actively sift through events of their entire pregnancy for any behavior, medication, or treatment that could be the culprit. Both parents search for similar conditions within their immediate and extended families. Parental ability to modify the situation varies in inherited and uninherited attributions; attribution of blame to a genetic transmission represents an inherent part of self that cannot be changed, and the only control to prevent recurrence is to avoid future pregnancies (Horan, 1982). Self-blame due to a cause that cannot be changed leads to greater helplessness and depression and is a blow to the parent's self-esteem (Horan, 1982). Sometimes parents blame the child's defect on the genetic background of the spouse (Mercer, 1977a).

All parents seem to carry on this meticulous search, which ends largely around the end of the first month after birth. Most mothers come up with theories as to the cause of the defect that imply parental guilt (Johns, 1971). The thoroughness of the parents' search for a cause indicates that this is a strong need. Gardner (1969) suggested that guilt reactions that come with assuming responsibility for a mishap give the person some feeling of control over an otherwise uncontrollable situation. Horan (1982) proposed that the greater the extent of perceived ability to prevent a similar recurrence of the birth defect (e.g., avoid exposure to rubella while pregnant), the more rapid the parent will adapt to the infant's defect.

Shapiro (1989) observed that both meaning attribution and support group participation were associated with mothers' decreased levels of stress and depression. The meaning of their childrens' developmental delays was also associated with increased emotion- and problem-focused coping. Assigning meaning led to seeing the child's health condition as a challenge in which mothers were confident that their actions could make a difference in the child's outcome.

In the search for mastery, meaning, and protection from future harm, cognitive adaptations include parental orientation to primary and/or secondary control in the situation (Affleck et al., 1985). Cognitive behaviors related to primary control include parental efforts to alter the environment and maintain the belief that a recurrence and/or the outcome of their infant with an anomaly are under their personal control (Affleck et al., 1985). Secondary control cognitions are in the form of the parent adapting to the environment and viewing the catastrophe as serving a positive purpose in their lives (Affleck et al., 1985). Both primary and secondary control cognitions were positively associated with mothers' adaptation.

Review Of A Successful Past

Mothers exhibited a strong need to review in memory past events relating to a former self before the birth of their infant with a defect in their cognitive adaptation to the birth (Mercer, 1975). The historical review focused on successes and happy times. Previous pregnancies, labors, and deliveries, mothering activities, other children's behavior, pleasant vacations with husbands, and their husbands' responses to other normal children were all reviewed. This historical review appeared to be a retreat that was needed to momentarily bolster self-esteem sufficiently to be able to confront and deal with having a less than perfect baby. By reaffirming success in other roles with other family members, the mother could then move to the disappointing and challenging role of mothering an infant with a defect. This need to reassure themselves and any listener that they were normal, capable, and efficient persons who had normal experiences up to this point in time may have also been an effort to soften societal stigma.

The mothers' review of the past may also provide continuity of self at a respectable level of self-esteem. Importantly, it appeared to provide an opportunity for the mother to marshall her forces in the brief retreat, and to provide the reassurance that she was capable of meeting the challenge of mothering a baby with a defect.

Hope

Parents express their deepest longing and wishes through dreams, fantasies, or statements. The striking characteristic of the dream and fantasy wishes is the theme of physical or geographic flight from the painful situation. Mothers frequently tell of dreaming of having a healthy, normal infant only to awaken and face the reality of their anomalous infant.

The wishes reflecting parents' hope indicate their belief or expectancy that the best possible outcome for the baby will occur. Hope is important, as it seems to be an energizer that provides motivation to continue the difficult task of adapting to the infant with an anomaly.

Statements of hope are often followed by statements of intended behavior to provide for or to do for the baby. The hope of improvement or
progress serves as the springboard for action. Parental responses of
hope are realistic. Terms such as "achieve his potential," or "I can only
hope for the best," show that parents are not hoping for the impossible.
Much of parental hope is anchored in a belief in the miracles of modern
science; surgery possibilities especially offer extensive hope.

Planning For The Future

Closely associated with hope is the planning for the future; planning
begins early as parents project arrangements that must be made for
themselves, their baby, and the rest of their families. Making plans
involves choice of alternatives. Parents' planning begins with the immediate and extends to the far, far future. "How does this baby affect my
life and expectations?" The immediacy of the situation demands the
planning for the incorporation of the defective baby into their personal
and social systems.

Early, during the first week, the mothers' planning tends to center
around themselves, indicating a degree of egocentricity (Mercer, 1975).
The need to assume a new identity as mother of a baby with a defect
involves a change in self-concept that is stressful.

Necessary treatments and care require that parents begin making
decisions and arrangements. Depending on the nature of the defect, the
amount of planning may vary considerably. During the early months
when so much of the parents' energy is directed to making necessary
plans for the baby's care and incorporation into the family, other family
members receive less attention than usual. Most of the attention that
older siblings receive is directed toward preparing them for the baby's
homecoming.

Social Adaptation Responses

Social adaptation responses include identification of the social definition of the new role as parent of an infant with a defect and social
acceptance and support for self and the baby. All overt and covert
behaviors of any person interacting with the parents are examined
minutely for any nuance of avoidance, withdrawal, rejection, repul-
sion, or acceptance. These social responses usurp the majority of parental responses in adapting to an infant with a defect (Mercer, 1975).
Having a baby is a social activity; assuming a new role is a social
activity.

Evaluation of Others' Reactions To Their Infant

Of all specific adaptive social responses, evaluation of others' reactions to their babies is by far the most frequently observed (Mercer, 1975, 1977a). When the baby has an obvious defect, defining one's role as parent of such a baby is a frightening experience. Perhaps for the first time a parent experiences social aversion from total strangers. If the defect is less obvious, the parent deliberately confronts many persons with her infant to "test" for social stigma. One mother who had an infant with Down syndrome took him to shopping centers, amusement parks, and church when the infant was just a couple of weeks old. Her comments following the trips were, "No one knew anything was wrong," and "They all said what a pretty baby." This seemed to comfort and assure her that she and her infant would be accepted by society, at least temporarily. Darling (1979) referred to this type of behavior as passing (as normal).

Another mother used the nurse to observe others' responses to her daughter with a facial defect. The mother asked the nurse to go with her to the plastic surgeon's office, "to hold the baby while she drove the car." Upon arrival at the plastic surgeon's office, the mother did not offer to hold her baby but sat as an observer accompanying the nurse. The baby cried, and the nurse readied the bottle for the feeding as the 1-month-old baby squirmed, but the mother did not offer any help. As they left the office, the mother remarked, "No one seemed to even notice that the baby had anything wrong with her." This mother had deliberately posed as an outsider (the nurse was dressed in street clothes and appeared to be the mother of the baby) to determine social response to her infant.

If a person does not seem to reflect either a positive or negative response, mothers ask direct questions to clarify any implications of stigma. All mothers observe their husbands closely for their reactions to their baby with a defect. The father plays an important role in setting the example for the child's acceptance or rejection in the family (Meyer, 1986), in addition to fostering the mother's ability to cope with the situation (Bristol & Gallagher, 1986). Examples of mothers' evaluations of their husbands' reactions during the first days following the birth are:

- I don't know if that's the real reason (had work to do) he didn't stay to feed him.
- It seems harder on my husband. With men I guess it is harder on them. Perfection means so much to them. That sperm has just got to be perfect.

Mothers seem to look for the fathers' responses to the baby quite thoroughly, especially during the first week (Mercer, 1975, 1977a). The father's acceptance of their baby seems to also indicate to the mother that he also accepts her, even if she did not produce a normal baby.

Reactions of the family (other children, parents' siblings, in-laws, and extended family) assume much greater importance during the first few weeks the baby is in the home setting (Mercer, 1975, 1977a). If family members can accept the baby as an individual, the parents are better able to accept and plan for the baby. One mother was particularly relieved to hear her 7-year-old son tell a friend, "His fingers will grow later," in reference to the infant's webbed fingers. Her son's friend accepted the explanation matter-of-factly and replied, "He's real neat."

As the mother regains her strength and expands her social sphere of interaction, reactions from persons other than the family become more important to her. One mother felt relief when her pediatrician told her in a very accepting manner that he had about 20 children with Down syndrome in his practice. She said, "He didn't use the word 'enjoy,' but he indicated that he liked working with these children. In other words, he isn't repulsed by them." Darling (1979) reported that parents' most common complaint was that the medical treatment for their children was rude and dehumanizing. However, the physicians' medical competence was not questioned, only their lack of compassion and concern for parents' feelings. Darling (1979) noted that beginning in infancy, parents of children with defects had to search and fight for services that other parents take for granted, such as health care, social acceptance, freedom of movement, and education.

Attitudes toward the body or body parts are determined to a great extent by the interest, actions, and attitudes of others; beauty and ugliness are social phenomena (Schilder, 1950). Social phenomena influence parental adjustment to the baby with a defect. Society is very ambivalent in its attitudes toward the child with a handicap, imposing additional conflicts for parents that contribute to their feelings of frustration, anger, and guilt (Zuk, 1962).

The ambivalent attitude of society is reflected in works that question the life-saving efforts to save the infant with gross anomalies (Haynes, 1971; MacKeith, 1971). The ethical problems posed in painful dilemmas have been guided by the federal regulations requiring treatment for all newborns with anomalies and the President's Commission for the Study of Ethical Problems in Medicine (Drane, 1984). Nursing ethics committees have considered such perplexing ethical dilemmas as whether anencephalic infants should be used as organ donors (Koenig, 1988).

Ambivalence is further portrayed by physicians who are uncomfortable in listening to parental concerns and by nurses who push infants with a defect to the rear of the nursery where they can't be viewed from the window. The mother feels ostracized if health professionals avoid her and her infant.

Self Appraisals for Their New Role

Self-appraisals are a continuous process for mothers. The first week following the birth of their infant with a defect, self-appraisal reflects much displeasure and criticism. The criticisms range from not liking one's name to current coping abilities. As the mother's social sphere expands, her self-appraisals increase. As each new situation is encountered, she tests her self in the new role as mother of an infant with a defect. It has been proposed that the mother may feel defective through her identification with her infant and is attempting to determine that she isn't (Gordeuk, 1976).

Social interactions are critical for parents in defining their roles and in assimilating cues for their planning and expectations. Mothers' apraisals of their environment for acceptance of their babies and of themselves are a priority that consumes much of their time.

Grief Process

Parents are faced with several losses through the loss of a normal infant: a lifetime of dreams or the hope of their child reaching or going beyond their own level of achievement. No one relinquishes a desired or valued object without a protest and painful, reluctant withdrawal of attachment from the lost object. All of the unconscious and conscious behaviors or responses to having a baby with a defect may be viewed from the framework of the grief process, a painful process that involves very hard work in achieving a level of adaptation compatible with the parents' lifestyle.

Many writers have described the grief process experienced by parents who have a defective child. An important difference in grieving over the loss of a normal baby and other kinds of losses is that the defective baby exists as a never-ending reminder of the baby that was hoped for. With the loss of the normal baby, parents also lost the role as parent of a normal baby.

Mercer (1973) reported four phases of the grief process following the birth of an infant with a defect. The initial phase of numbness or shock was time-limited, ending by the sixth day following the defective child's birth. The second phase, protest and yearning, was observed over the first 3 months, with a peak occurring at 1 month. Protest and yearning reflected a objection to the loss of a normal baby and a longing for the normal baby. A third phase, disorganization, reflected by despair, depression, and chaos, was largely limited to the first 2 months; however, disorganization was neither time- nor phase-specific. The fourth phase, reorganization, reflects a taking-hold in the crisis situation and accommodating the lifestyle to the baby with a defect. The reorganization phase was neither time- nor phase-specific; these behaviors made up the majority of observed behaviors at each observation period over 3 months following birth and made up two-thirds of all grief process behaviors.

Drotar and associates (1975) proposed a model showing the overlapping sequence of parental rections to the birth of an infant with a defect in 5 stages: shock, denial, sadness and anger, equilibrium, and reorganization. They noted that some parents may obtain equilibrium within a few weeks following birth while other parents take many months.

The necessity of incorporating the baby into the family system presents an inescapable urgency to plan for and prepare for the baby. Mothers' adjustment to the event of having a baby with a defect was evidenced by their increasing behaviors directed toward a reformulation of their expectations, hopes, wishes, and ideas in accord with their situation with their babies. Less than one-third of their behaviors were directed toward their lost normal babies (Mercer, 1973). The reorganization behaviors that were observed to begin shortly following their child's birth speaks to the strength of parents facing this dilemma. Immediate constructive forward movement may provide some release of tension and anxiety. In any event the defective child, the replacement of the parents' lost normal child, does not permit or allow parents to completely immerse themselves in their grief. This factor may contribute to prolonged or delayed grief, as was the case with the 86-year-old mother described above. In situtations of irreparable defects, however, chronic sorrow or grief is more descriptive of the process (Olshansky, 1962).

Defense Mechanisms

Because of the feelings of failure at having created a defective baby and of the psychological threat in finding acceptance for themselves and their baby, all parents use defense mechanisms to protect their ego during their adaptation to the event. Denial has been reported as the most commonly used defense (Rozansky & Linde, 1971). Two-thirds of the parents of mentally retarded children expected their child to become normal, regardless of the severity of the retardation (Wolfensberger & Kurtz, 1971). Parents tend to reject the diagnosis of mental retardation initially. Denial appears to serve a constructive function for parents by allowing them to delay a more realistic acceptance until they are able to cope with the problem. Two-thirds of the parents who were told of possible brain damage to their child at birth denied that they had ever been told (Drake & Ober, 1963). Barden and associates' (1989) hypothesis that mothers of facially deformed infants would demonstrate strong denial on self-report measures such that they appeared unaware of or unwilling to admit the stress inflicted by the infant was supported.

Although defenses are unconscious responses, I have observed a form of denial that appears to be in part a conscious effort of parents to convince themselves and others that they are maintaining control in the stressful situation. Examples of this form of denial are: "I was upset yesterday, but I am all over it now;" "I've accepted what's wrong with the baby and I've gotten over it (second day after birth);" and "I don't care what people say."

A few parents see themselves as chosen as special persons to care for a handicapped child, a form of rationalization, and demonstrate extreme devotion and dedication to the child's care. Another extreme observed is the situation of parents acting out hostility toward the child with a defect by painful ministrations, supposedly for the sake of the child (Ross, 1964). Sublimation by overzealous participation in parents' groups and rationalization seem to help soften the realistic blow of the defect for some parents (Ross, 1964).

The birth of a child with a defect also triggers dormant anxieties in parents leading to the use of the defense of displacement (Cohen, 1963). Dissatisfactions with their marriage are displaced onto the handicapped child; parents quarrel about the child's needs rather than about their shortcomings.

LONG-RANGE IMPACT ON THE FAMILY AND INDIVIDUALS IN THE FAMILY

The birth of a baby requires alterations in any family constellation. There are increased numbers of interactions, new roles, new routines, and habits that have to be altered or adopted. When the infant has a handicap, the adaptation to absorb the baby into the family is much more difficult.

Although placement is very difficult, a few parents may elect not to parent their child with a defect and seek institutionalization. This is a decision that parents must weigh for themselves according to their unique situation. Resource persons who are knowledgeable about institutional conditions, situations, and alternatives and who are skilled in having parents express their feelings openly with each other must be available to parents at such a time. While the decision and consequences rest solely with the parents, skilled consultation and counseling are vital to parents for making a decision they can live with comfortably.

When a child has a birth defect, there are additional and usually more complicated routines for child care that must be mastered to assure smooth functioning of the family and members of the family. The dwindling of social support systems for families as mothers return to their homes, still somewhat on shaky ground as far as having developed adequate coping mechanisms, exacerbates the possibilities for strained husband-wife, parent-in-law, or parent-child relationships.

Mothers often express concern that they are neglecting their other children because of the extra care and energy directed toward the baby. The father's support is crucial to the mother at this time. If the husband is immature and unable to be supportive, this intensifies the wife's burden. Wives often report that they have to be strong to support their husbands. Fathers of handicapped children tend to withdraw from the ongoing care of the children and experience more emotional disturbance and stress than fathers of normal children (Palfrey et al., 1989). Wives reported poorer mental and physical health in a study of parents of mentally retarded, physically impaired, and developmentally at-risk children (Dunst, Trivette, & Cross, 1986).

Few studies have been done regarding the economic burden to families with handicapped and chronically ill children, yet the few that have been done verify the cost is great (Jacobs & McDermott, 1989). As would be expected, single parents experience the greatest financial problems (Dunst et al., 1986; McCubbin, 1989). In attempts to compensate for the handicapped child in the home, parents go to great lengths to change the environment to normalize the child's self perception (Krulik, 1980).

Siblings of retarded children have been identified as a population at risk; this is thought to be a result of the excessive parental attention to the retarded child at the expense of the siblings, sibling identification with the retarded child's behavior, and the normal child's anxiety about the sibling's retardation in relation to his own sexual and aggressive fantasies (Martino & Newman, 1974). Although Beavers and associates (1986) reported siblings of a retarded child often assumed a more responsible and caring role, the majority of research indicates the difficulty that siblings of handicapped children have (McAndrew, 1976; Vadasy et al., 1984). Anger, jealousy, and resentment may be observed among healthy siblings as they see the handicapped child receive the attention and care; this may be followed by guilt (Futcher, 1988).

Siblings of children with a chronic illness performed poorer in school and experienced many health problems (McKeever, 1983). Parents may expect normal siblings to assume adult behavior (Cirillo & Sorrentino, 1986). Brothers exhibited more symptomatic behavior than sisters in one study of sibling response to chronically ill siblings (Lavigne & Ryan, 1979).

Although parents of handicapped children report higher levels of marital stress, divorce rates were not found to be substantially higher than in families with normal children (Leventhal & Sabbeth, 1986). Parents usually subordinate their needs to those of their handicapped child (Sabbeth & Leventhal, 1984).

Families with handicapped children also reported compromise of their employment situation (Palfrey et al., 1989). In addition, the choice of the family house, community, family friends, and vacation plans are limited when the child has physical/multiple problems. Rearing a handicapped child is a complex, dynamic process, and the parents' stress cannot be isolated from the status of the child (Murphy, 1982).

PARENTAL ROLE ATTAINMENT WITH AN INFANT WITH A DEFECT

Formal Stage of Parental Role Attainment: Birth to 8 Weeks

During the formal stage of infant role attainment when parents of normal children are following advice of professionals in how to parent, parents of infants with congenital defects are in a stage of shock, denial, and disorganization in dealing with their feelings about the defect. They want and need advice from professionals in great detail. During this period, parents need health professionals who can respond with caring and understanding. Parents in one study offered specific advice for physicians and nurses: have a positive attitude; listen attentively and objectively to what parents say; know how to treat the child or refer elsewhere; have up-to-date knowledge; communicate freely with telephone numbers regarding agencies and resource in the community; and just "be there" for them (Leifson, 1980). Parents stress the need for accurate information that does not deprive them of all hope.

If health professionals are to provide this warm, supportive care, some introspection is necessary. Health professionals entered the profession to help others; as a caring person the professional experiences feelings of disappointment, failure, helplessness, and grief when a baby with a congenital defect is born. Although at a much lower level of self-involvement, the professional's defenses and emotions are similar to those experienced by the parents. Health professionals feel grief, are depressed, experience anger, hostility, and guilt, and have a desire to withdraw—all at the time they are the supportive person. It is important to face the fact that these are human responses and that a support system for the professional is a necessary and important part of providing care for parents.

Warm, caring responses are remembered as a support to coping with the stressful situation; these responses may be conveyed in many ways. One may simply sit quietly nearby. Some persons respond well to touch; placing a hand on the mother's arm and simply saying, "I'm sorry," communicates caring. The professional may be afraid of crying; however, tears connote deep caring and empathy.

Parental anger is difficult to deal with in the early days following birth. It is difficult for clinicians to remember that the anger is not directed at them personally but is a healthy protest about a fate over which the parent has no control. It is helpful to reply to a hostile remark with understanding, "You must be terribly hurt and disappointed that this has happened to you." Platitudes or reassurances that "everything will turn out for the best," are troublesome burdens to the already overburdened parent who knows that "things did not turn out for the best." Factual information that provides some hope helps parents to make realistic plans.

It is important to respect a parent's need for withdrawal during the first few days and neither push nor press the parent. Tactics of delay or refusals to participate in the infant's care may indicate the parent's need for more time; the parent needs to retain autonomy in such decisions. The nurse is usually the one who can determine the mother's readiness for additional information or for increased involvement with her child. Mrs. Bennett is an example of withdrawal until she was able to interact with her child. She asked that her baby be kept in the nursery for one day, that the nurse feed the baby for the next 2 days in her room, and that on the fourth day, the nurse stay with her while she fed her baby. This request was followed except for two breakdowns in communication. A person who assumed the mother had to accept reality immediately through confrontation with the infant took the baby to the mother's room on the first day. Mrs. Bennett denied her child, "That is not my baby, take her out." She later told another person, "I knew that was my baby, but I was not ready to look at her." Four days later the baby was taken to Mrs. Bennett and left with her alone for the feeding. She panicked, became very upset, and could not feed her baby; she rang for the nurse to take her away. Although this mother had to temporarily withdraw from interaction with her infant, she formed a very strong attachment for her during the first 2 weeks and became an excellent, caring, nurturing mother. But she had to move at her own pace—a pace with which her inner resources could cope.

Sensitivity to the parents' responses and awareness of progress is vital, however, because there is a point at which withdrawal, depression, fear, or guilt indicate a need for psychiatric or psychological consultation. A useful guide in assessing these behaviors is noting a parent's progress or lack of progress. Behavior is not static, and if there is not movement toward acceptance and adaptation, consultation becomes indicated.

Most parents display some rejection of the infant with an anomaly initially (Freeston, 1971; Johns, 1971; Mercer, 1974). A healthy, thriving infant promotes a mother's self-confidence, just as an unhealthy infant may make a mother feel unsuccessful and frustrated (Benedek, 1959). A mother's feelings of failure and frustration can result in maternal aggression toward the infant, her own mother, and, by identification with both, toward herself. Threats of failure may also lead to self-imposed requirements in an effort to achieve an ideal. Mothers' initial rejection of handicapped infants may be a defensive attempt of their ego to maintain an unblemished self-image.

Mothers have difficulty touching and handling their infants with defects the first few days following birth, as was the case with Mrs. Bennett (Mercer, 1974); to move the infant's arm, they may tug at the infant's sleeve. Mothers are seldom comfortable touching the actual defect during the first few days. Two-day-old infants with facial deformities were held less closely and received less ventral contact than normal infants (Langlois & Swain, 1981). Mrs. Day was unable to bathe her infant with a myelomeningocele for months.

The expectation would be that attachment behaviors would show an increase in mothers' interactions with their defective infants over time. However, attachment and aversion behaviors remained constant over a 3-month period; 75% of mothers' behaviors indicated attachment to their infants, and 25% indicated aversion or avoidance (Mercer, 1974). This avoidance behavior must tend to carry over for years. Four-year-old subnormal children received less stimulation and affection than normal children in a nursery class (Jeffree & Cashdan, 1971).

In instances that require surgery for the survival of the infant with a defect, parents may refuse permission when the infant's condition precludes the ability to function mentally or physically in any capacity. Many unresolved issues revolve around such circumstances. The Baby Doe legislation has removed most life-and-death decisions from the hands of both parents and physicians. Ethical problems surrounding such decisions are formidable and continue to be debated. Ethical rounds are an important part of the health care team in all large centers with neonatal intensive care units.

Fear, hope, and withdrawal reappear whenever a threatening event occurs such as surgery, examinations, or rehospitalization of the child. Additional supportive help is important at those times.

Fost (1981) offered several approaches for health professionals to take in helping parents in their process of early adaptation. First, information about the reality of the situation must be repeated over and over, and over a long period of time. Fost notes that counseling during the phase of shock is usually not effective. However, consoling and listening are much more effective during the early days and weeks following birth; parents reported a need to talk with informed and sympathetic professionals. Parents should be informed and see the infant as early as possible following birth. Importantly, urgent decisions should be separated from nonurgent and reversible decisions. Parents are burdened at times thinking they have to make many long-term decisions such as foster care or institutionalization for the child, at a time of mental turmoil. At times decisions are made by medical caregivers, such as transporting the infant to another medical facility and using diagnostic and therapeutic interventions to support the infant, leaving parents with a feeling of helplessness (Lynch, 1989). Parents should be consulted about all decision making regarding their infants; despite their grief-stricken state, they are capable of making logical decisions concerning their infant's care (Penticuff, 1988), especially if they are kept informed with accurate information (Harrison, 1986).

Great care should be taken in giving information to parents to avoid giving conflicting information that results in dissonance for the parents. Parents do ask the same questions over and over. Sometimes they simply cannot hear the answer due to their shock. Sometimes they do not like the answers and are subconsciously seeking answers that they do like. It is far better to say, "I don't know, but I'll find out," than to provide incorrect information. To get an idea of how information has been interpreted, before giving further information, it is best to ask the parent, "Can you tell me what you were told about this earlier?"

The most effective support for the parent who needs to review her past and/or her labor and delivery experience is sensitive, reactive listening. Mother's cues alert the nurse to points for positive reinforcement, such as, "You really managed that situation well." Such comments reinforce the mother's self-image and let her know that a person whose opinion she values recognizes her strengths.

When parents are searching for a cause for their baby's defect, many "old wives's tales" need to be discounted (e.g., having a tooth pulled did not cause the cleft palate). Some couples may blame each other. This may be an indication of their usual reaction to stress, or it may reflect marital discord. Solidarity between the partners should be promoted. One way of facilitating communication between parents is by talking to them together. Once the husband realizes it is acceptable to express his emotions or fears, the wife usually feels more understanding toward him. In a large number of cases, the cause of the defect is unknown, and it is important that this be shared.

Part of the parents' search for a cause of the birth defect may be their desire to avoid having another child with a defect. Genetic counseling is important for all parents who have an infant with a congenital defect so that they can receive accurate information as a basis for decisions to have another baby. If the defect is diagnosable by chorionic villi or amniotic fluid sampling, parents may be willing to try again, and if diagnosis of a defective infant is made, they may elect to have an abortion. Other parents may choose sterilization to avoid the possibility of recurrence.

In their search for a cause of the defect, parents also wonder whether their normal children are apt to have children with a defect. Parents need information regarding hereditary transmission clarified. For example, in the case of hereditary transmission by recessive genes in which the probability is one in four that a future child will have a specific disease, some parents assume that since they had a child with the defect that the next three children will be normal. Interpretation of the chances of one in four applying to each infant of each pregnancy is necessary.

Parents face the real meaning of their infant's handicap during the early weeks at home, particularly those handicaps that require special care from birth. There is the possibility that they will focus on the handicapped infant to the exclusion of their partner or other children. There is a risk that they may be overprotective as a result of the anger and guilt. Occasionally, another child or the mate may become a scapegoat for the disappointment felt about the infant.

Parents of infants with defects carefully observe the clinician's facial expressions and comments for indication of acceptance or rejection of the child. It is important to become acquainted with the infant prior to interacting with the infant and the mother. By completely undressing and inspecting the infant closely for any other defects and noting unique normal characteristics, the nurse or other clinician can later point these out to the mother. It is important to respond to the infant as an infant who happens to have a defect rather than as a defective infant. By talking to the infant, smiling at and cuddling the infant, the clinician is able to show acceptance of the infant and provide a role model for care.

Parents are also sensitive to any treatment of their infant that differs from that observed in the care of other infants. One mother asked why her son's hands were covered with his shirt (he had webbed fingers). When told that he was scratching his face, she said, "Oh, I thought maybe it was to hide his hands."

Another mother remarked after she had gone home that she wanted to take her son back to the hospital to see the nurses because they were interested in him and attached to him. She observed, "They seem to love these babies extra." She proudly took her son back for the staff to see and received reinforcement for the mothering job she was doing with her son. The staff in this situation had been very successful in seeing an infant with a defect and a mother with the same needs as any other mother-infant pair.

Parents are quick to see those who are uncomfortable in talking with them. One mother said about her priest who had come to visit, "I was relieved when he finally left. He fidgeted from one foot to the other and didn't know what to say."

During the early days and weeks parents are not usually concerned with hearing about other infants with defects that are much worse than their child's. Some persons think that it is helpful for parents to hear about persons who are worse off than they. This is a fallacy. Mrs. Bennett stated, "I don't have the energy to think about all the deformed children. My baby is all that I am able to think about now." Later parents do benefit from exchanges with other parents with similar experiences and in knowing that they are not alone in their experience. Experienced parents are able to offer hints about practical matters such as feeding, baby-sitters, and handling careless remarks from others. The parents with a new problem, however, pace their readiness for seeking out parents with similar problems. It takes time for them to identify with parents of a child with a defect. Lists of resources along with phone numbers of any organizations that may be helpful should be kept available to hand out to parents to take home with them.

Transition from the hospital to home is particularly difficult. Support persons who accepted their infant have provided parents with some security in the hospital. Leaving the hospital is frightening because this is the parents' first interaction with their child in the community on their own. If the child needs constant close observation and complex care, it is important in discharge planning to help parents obtain funding for trained home care nursing and/or respite care providers (Freitag-Koontz, 1988).

Follow-up care following discharge from the hospital is an important role for health professionals (Fost, 1981). Guidelines for the development of a bereavement follow-up program after perinatal loss (Ilse &

Furrh, 1988; Maguire & Skoolicas, 1988) may be utilized for parents with an infant with a congenital defect by adapting the content to deal with grief of a handicapped child.

The extra work of caring for a handicapped infant falls unequally on the mother. It is no surprise that mothers and fathers report a different pattern of adjustment. Mothers report greater chronic sorrow, negative affect, and self-blaming (Damrosch & Perry, 1989). Mothers voice a greater need for opportunity to express their feelings and in particular need praise and recognition for their role; they particularly find that encouragement of their expressions of sadness and weakness and positive feedback on how they are handling the situation are useful (Damrosch & Perry, 1989). Fathers need special support and counseling in dealing with their feelings to help them be able to interact with and enjoy their handicapped child; fathers play fewer parent-child games with a handicapped child than mothers (Dunst et al., 1986).

Attainment of the Informal Stage of Role Attainment: 2 to 5 Months

The informal stage of pleasurable interaction and play with the infant in which parents develop their own style of parenting is hampered by the sadness of chronicity with permanent handicaps. However, since parental expectations for infants are not so great prior to 6 months, especially with the wide range of time in development of mobility, parents with handicapped infants see fewer differences during this period of time. When Down syndrome infants were compared to normal infants over a 2-year period, their social environments were similar at 6.5 months; however, by 17 months, mothers of normal children spoke more often about the environment, gave more definite directions, and provided more attention to their infants than the mothers with Down syndrome children (Smith & Hagen, 1984). Retarded infants' growth rates slowed markedly as age advanced. Of interest was that medical complications were unrelated to the quality of the infants' home environment.

Mothers of facially deformed infants who averaged 17.2 weeks of age engaged in less tactile-kinesthetic stimulation with their infants, touched their infants affectionately less often, maintained less en face contact, and were less responsive to their infants' behavioral cues than mothers of normal infants (Barden et al., 1989). Barden and associates raised the question of whether these less optimal interactions began with the infant's characteristics, the mother's reactions, or a combination of interactional processes.

Darling (1979) identified phase of parental entrepreneurship with a child with a congenital defect. The first phase, anomic, includes the postpartal period when first information is given and the need for information, emotional support, power in and control over their situation is greatest. This phase occurs during the formal stage of parental role attainment. The second phase, seekership, is the period when parents often encounter rude and dehumanizing care and usually begins during the informal stage of parental role attainment; parents are avid researchers in exploring resources for information and guidance at this time. The third phase of parental entrepreneurship in the revelation phase when solutions are discovered; this is characteristic of the informal stage of parental role attainment. The fourth and fifth phases occur during the personal level of parental role acquisition: normalization, which includes establishing a normal routine for the family, and the crusader phase, which is an attempt to change society when no solutions are found.

Health professionals are challenged to emphasize the importance of providing a stimulating environment for handicapped infants even though the infants are unable to respond with the vigor of normal infants. Parents seemed to ignore the extent of developmental delay with Down syndrome infants during the first 6 months; thus it is critical to begin very early in training parents to provide the compensatory training needed (Smith & Hagen, 1984).

During this period finding competent baby-sitters is important so that parents resume a normal social life. This is a particular problem for parents who have an infant who is difficult to care for. Often, where nuclear families are isolated, there are senior citizens who would like an useful role. A service to both parties occurs in such instances when they can be brought together. Connecting with parents' groups also provides a network for finding available help.

Achievement of Parental Identity as Parent with Handicapped Child

During this stage when the parents have internalized and achieved comfort with the role of parent of an infant with a defect, they have also achieved Darling's (1979) normalization and crusader phases described above. The work of normalization is described as an ongoing process of actively accommodating to the changing physical and emotional needs of the handicapped child or adolescent (Deatrick, Knafl, & Walsh, 1988). The process of normalization begins at birth from practical necessity as a conscious effort to treat the infant with a defect the same as other children, yet still provide for any special needs. A study of mothers with children aged 1 to 4 years with cystic fibrosis found that problems they reported did not predict their child's competence scores; however, mothers' perception of ideal parenting style predicted the child's competence (Stullenbarger et al., 1987). This finding was attributed in part to the normalization phenomenon. Deatrick and associates (1988) suggest that normalization proceeds at an unknown cost as family members balance demands of the handicapped child with goals of parenting the child normally and having a normal family life.

Long-term follow-up and social support are important. Referral to the public health nurse provides a source of help that is unique, as the nurse is able to assess the home setting and offer practical advice in day-to-day care and in community resources.

As parental grief diminishes, parents are increasingly able to work productively and cooperatively with health care providers in solving problems related to their child's treatment and care (Monsen, 1986). Many setbacks are common for families with children with long-term disabilities, but the nurse or other clinician can serve as consultant, support person, and family advocate.

SUMMARY

Parents who have an infant with a congenital defect react to their loss of the desired perfect baby with angry, protesting, and disorganized behaviors that are atypical of their usual patterns of behavior. Because their assumptive world and their egos are threatened, they respond defensively. Health care professionals may respond to the stressful situation similarly; they, too, are powerless to change the event, and their professional goal of achieving optimal health or functioning for all clients is thwarted. No one accepts loss graciously or calmly, and everyone needs supportive help within the social structure to cope and to adapt.

Definitive behaviors occur and may be viewed within the framework of a grief process, although phases of the grief process are not time-specific for parents of an infant with a congenital defect. When a defect is irreparable, chronic grief is the result.

Major challenges to the health professional are to provide parents with an environment in which they can express their feelings and concerns, help the parents become acquainted with their infant, and provide accurate information about the defect, its etiology, treatment, and/or care, along with comprehensive information about community resources, federal agencies, and other possible social support.

Sharing information about care, treatments, improvisions, and practical ways other families have dealt with similar problems is important. Referral to support groups is not usually accepted until parents have become comfortable with their identity as parent of a child with a handicap. Public health nurses and social workers are important persons to work with parents who have an infant with a congential defect in long-term follow-up from birth.

PART IV

SPECIAL CHALLENGES IN THE ENVIRONMENT

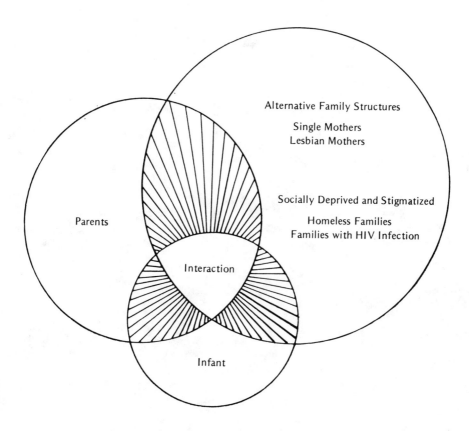

Figure 4
Interactive model adapted from *Child Assessment Part 2: The First Year of Life*, p. 132, by Kathryn E. Barnard and Sandra J. Eyres, DHEW Publication No. HRA 79-25, Hyattsville, MD: U.S. Department of Health, Education, and Welfare. Copyright 1979 by Kathryn E. Barnard. Reprinted with permission of Kathryn E. Barnard.

9

Parenting in Alternative Family Structures

Traditionally, the childbearing family has been headed by a married father and mother. An analysis of the changing norms and values about family life in the United States from the late 1950s through the middle 1980s revealed basic shifts in attitudes about marriage, divorce, having children, gender roles, and nonmarital sexual experience over those decades (Thornton, 1989). These changes in attitudes are evidenced by less strong needs to marry, stay married, to have children, or to maintain a strict division of labor between women and men. The trend toward greater acceptance of cohabitation without marriage during the 1980s has probably been a factor in the greater numbers of infants being born to unmarried women.

The number of infants born to unmarried women in 1987 (933,013) was 40% greater than the number reported in 1980 (665,747); this is nearly twice the increase that is reported for married women (23%) (National Center for Health Statistics, June, 1989). Over two-thirds of these births to unmarried women were to women 20 years and older. Women of this age have had an increasing number of marriages end in divorce, and many have postponed marriage to advance their careers and continue their education.

The percentage of children living in families headed by nonmarried women has increased from 9% in 1960 to 20% in 1985 (U.S. Bureau of Census, 1988). If this trend continues, approximately one-half of all children born after 1975 will reside in a mother-only family during a part of their childhood (Bumpass, 1984).

Approximately 1.5 million parents are gay or lesbian, and up to one-third of lesbians are mothers (Johnson, Smith, & Guenther, 1987). The number of lesbian women opting to become mothers through alternative (artificial) insemination is increasing (Pies, 1985).

Father-only headed families are in the minority; too few were found in the Kellam et al. (1977) study for a separate analysis of that group. An increase in the number of children living with and being reared by grandmothers is occurring, however (Kennedy & Keeney, 1988). This phenomenon was observed more often among mothers who were the youngest or only child in their families of origin; a variety of circumstances had occurred during the daughter's childhood or adolescence that resulted in the daughter being irresponsible when she became a parent.

This chapter focuses on family structures in which the mother is the only biological parent present: the nonmarried heterosexual mother and the partnered lesbian mother. These families face greater social discrimination and a more hostile environment than other types of family structures. A major theme emanating from the unsupportive environment is directed toward health care providers. Health professionals must examine their own biases and beliefs and deal with these in order to care for nonmarried heterosexual mothers and lesbian mothers with respect and sensitivity to their special needs.

Father-only family structures are not discussed here; these situations are rare, especially during the period of infancy. This chapter does not deal with the experience of lesbians who had children while in heterosexual relationships, although much of what is stated can apply to their situation.

IMPLICATIONS OF FAMILY STRUCTURE

The family structure is defined as those persons living together as a family and the roles that each person enacts as a member of that family group. Research findings have identified family structures more vulnerable to having very low birth weight infants who are also likely to be handicapped by lifelong chronic conditions. The family environment as the major source of social support during child rearing impacts on both the child's and the parent's health over time.

Impact on Children

Brown and associates' (1989) profile of familes having very low birth weight infants was characterized by unmarried mothers with less education, poorer living conditions, and greater numbers of people living in the household; very few nuclear families were in their sample. The majority (79%) lived in the inner city; 25% changed residence during an

18-month study period, with 7% changing residence three or more times.

Family structure has been related to children's mental health (Kellam et al., 1977), with children who are in mother-alone families being at greatest risk of social maladaptation and psychological problems. Six major family types were analyzed in a sample of first grade children: mother-alone, mother/father, mother/grandmother, mother/step-father, mother/other, and mother-absent families (Kellam et al., 1977). The mother/father and mother/grandmother families had fewer children classified as socially maladapted than other family types, indicating that it was not father absence that was associated with the children's social maladaptation but lack of maternal support.

A review of published research found that partnered lesbians had greater emotional and economic resources and provided children with a richer family life than heterosexual or lesbian women living alone (Kirkpatrick, 1987). Studies comparing lesbian mothers with divorced heterosexual mothers have found more similarities than differences in their children's acquisition of sex role behavior (Hoeffer, 1981), with no differences in children's gender development (Kirkpatrick, Smith, & Roy, 1981).

Children who grow up in mother-only families are more likely to drop out of school and to be poor as adults (McLanahan & Booth, 1989). This is due in large part to the economic deprivation in their family of origin; there simply are no resources or money for extracurricular school and other enriching activities.

Impact on Parents

The focus on the nonmarried mother as parent emphasizes the environmental factors that add to her stress and challenge her parenting. One-half of all single mothers live below the poverty line due to the mother's low earning capacity, lack of support from the nonresidential father, and few benefits provided by the state (McLanahan & Booth, 1989). In addition to income insecurity and erratic work patterns, these stressed single mothers change residence more frequently, thus leading to less social integration and potential support from neighbors. Although relatives provide physical support, relatives also are likely to interfere with the mother's parenting role leading to conflict that may increase her stress (McLanahan & Booth, 1989).

Women's salaries continue to be far below those of men's and single parent families are more likely to be on welfare (Sandler, 1980). Thus the environment of poverty has major impact for the single mother.

The environment of low income mothers is rife with crime and violence as they face persistent economic worries along with rampant discrimination because of their sex, race, single parent status, and other personal attributes (Belle et al., 1980). Single mothers identified several who had discriminated against them: the welfare department, rental agents, employers, restaurants, schools and teachers, sales persons, patrolmen, social workers, and taxi drivers (Belle et al., 1980). A study of public health nurses from five agencies found that nurses held more favorable attitudes toward married mothers than single mothers, irrespective of the mothers' race (Morgan & Barden, 1985).

In addition to the stigma and discrimination facing nonmarried mothers, lesbian mothers "raise their families in a larger society that is hostile and uncomprehending and that fails to provide role models and adequate legal protection" (McCandlish, 1987, p. 23). There is no inherent pathology in lesbian mother families; it is the profound impact of a homophobic culture that increases lesbians' challenges in parenting (Pennington, 1987). Lesbian women's health needs are the same as those of other mothers; their additional needs are provoked by the largely homophobic environment in which they live (Green, 1987). Motherhood is the prominent identity among lesbian mothers (Kirkpatrick, 1987). Rivera (1987) notes that gay parents "exist in the shadow of a legal guillotine that lingers until the eighteenth birthday of their children" (p. 199); at any time the parent-child relationship may be severed by the court.

Long-term single parenting was found to be a chronic stressor for women who were the only adult in the household during their children's grade school through adolescent years (Thompson & Ensminger, 1989). Single mothers faced the dual hardship of structural isolation and the absence of social support. Low education was the most important predictor of the mother's initial risk of early psychological distress. Having another adult in the household was the critical factor in the mothers' well-being, as opposed to the other adult specifically being a spouse, indicating that it is social isolation rather than the absence of a husband that places the single mother at risk. Events that were particularly stressful for mothers were death of a family member or close friend and residential moves. Emotional support and social integration contributed to mothers' well-being; a relationship with a close confidant was associated with less sadness and tension. Those who attended church regularly also reported less tension.

THE NONMARRIED HETEROSEXUAL MOTHER

Beginning with pregnancy, the single mother faces decisions and challenges that the married mother does not have to worry about. These challenges continue during parenting. The discussions of the formal, informal, and achievement stages of maternal role attainment include qualitative data from interviews over a 1-year period of 28 nonmarried mothers who participated in a larger study (Mercer et al., 1982; Mercer, 1986a). These 28 nonmarried mothers were an average age of 25 years, with a range from 20 to 39 years; whereas some women in the larger study were unmarried at the time of birth but married later, these 28 women did not. One-half of the group had a high school diploma, 21% had some college, 18% had not graduated from high school, 4% had grade school education only, and data were missing for 7%. These nonmarried mothers also reported annual incomes that assured financial struggles in paying rent, buying food, clothes, and medical care for themselves and their infants: 7.1% reported incomes from 0 to $2,000; 3.5% $2,000 to $4,000; 14.3% $4,000 to $6,000; 10.7% $6,000 to $8,000; 3.5% $8,000 to $10,000; 3.5% $10,000 to $12,000; 7.1% $12,000 to $14,000, 14.3% $14,000 to $18,000; 14.3% $18,000 to $22,000; and 3.5% $28,000 to $34,000. Data were missing for 18%.

Five different family structures or living arrangements were prevalent among this group of nonmarried mothers; they lived either alone with the infant (21%), with a male partner (25%), with her parent/s (21%), with other relatives (14%), or with an adult woman who shared the household work and expenses (18%). A nonmarried mother from each of the living arrangements is presented as a case example at each of the three stages of maternal role attainment following birth to illustrate major concerns in those family structures.

Anticipatory Stage of Maternal Role Attainment: Pregnancy

In a study comparing single and partnered women during the second trimester of pregnancy, Tilden (1983) found that all women worked on the major tasks of pregnancy: accepting the pregnancy and forming an attachment to the unborn baby, seeking safe passage for both themselves and their infant, assuring acceptance of the child by others, and developing their capacity to give (Rubin, 1975). Single women differed in four additional areas of concern during their pregnancies—decision making, disclosure, social support, and legal issues.

Decision Making

Two-thirds of the single women (aged 20 to 35) had gotten pregnant accidentally in contrast to one-fourth of the partnered women (Tilden, 1983). The single women spent much time in deciding about whether

or not to continue their pregnancy based on their beliefs about parenthood and abortion, earlier experience with abortion, familiarity with
single parent role models, and their sense of readiness for an infant at
this particular time in their lives. Their relationships with the father of
the infant was not a factor in their decision making.

Role models for the single women deciding to continue their pregnancies were their parents or surrogate parents who had raised them
and their siblings alone. Whether or not this was the right time in their
lives to be pregnant was related in part to their financial situations and
age; 60% of the women were approaching age 30.

Disclosure

Randell (1988) found that first-time partnered mothers-to-be 30 and
older made quite elaborate plans for celebrating the disclosure of their
pregnancies to their parents, other family, and friends. Special dinners
and special cards were used to announce the happy occasion. In contrast, single women reported disclosing their pregnancies to their families as particularly difficult; they faced negative reactions to their pregnancies that contributed to feelings of anxiety, depression, and lowered
self-esteem (Tilden, 1983). Fathers of the single women's infants also
reacted to news of their pregnancies negatively; their major concern
was the women's expectations of them as fathers.

Social Support

Whereas partnered women readily list their partners as their major
source of support, single women listed their mothers or sisters and
friends as major sources of their support (Tilden, 1983). Single women
seemed to become aware of the need for increased support and sought
this out; health professionals were frequently named in their support
system. While single women did not differ significantly on emotional
and informational support, they had less tangible or practical help than
partnered women (Tilden, 1984).

Legal Issues

Legal issues that predominated for the single mother included the
baby's last name, completion of the birth certificate (naming the baby's
father), the father's legal rights and responsibilities, and legal guardian-
ship of the infant if something should happen to the mother. Most of
the single women in Tilden's (1983, 1984) study opted to give the baby
their own last name. The legal consequences of naming the father on

the birth certificate aroused much anxiety, particularly about future demands the father might make.

Summary

The added tasks facing single women during pregnancy are anxiety provoking. Single women experience higher life stress, less tangible support, and higher state anxiety but report no significant differences in trait anxiety, depression, or self-esteem than partnered women (Tilden, 1984).

The special needs of the single mother-to-be necessitate special counseling and health care. Continuity of care is especially important for the single mother. Referral to a social worker and legal consultation are also important. Single women may need encouragement to ask their mothers to participate in childbirth classes and to be present during the delivery (Brazelton, June 13, 1989). During pregnancy it is also helpful to encourage the single mother to think about how she will handle her and her child's feelings about their different family structure; facing such questions ahead of time allows the mother mental rehearsal of how she will respond and will help her to reassure herself of her own feelings without being apologetic or defensive (Brazelton, June 13, 1989).

Formal Stage or Initial Adaptation and Physical Recovery Phase of Maternal Role Attainment

During the period from birth to 6 to 8 weeks when mothers tend to model their mothering according to professionals' advice, there were no significant relationships between marital status and mothering behaviors among women aged 20 to 29 and women aged 30 to 42 years (Mercer et al., 1982). The only demographic or psychosocial variables significantly related to marital status among women aged 20 to 29 were age, negative life events stress, general support, educational level, and number of infant illnesses. Single mothers tended to be younger, have greater negative life events stress, more general support from others, and less education, and their infants tended to have more illnesses. Among 30- to 42-year-olds, the only significant relationships with marital status were physical support from the father of the baby and maternal illness; older single women tended to have less help from the father of the baby, as would be expected, and more illness complaints.

Single adult mothers do not differ from married women in their early interactions with or feelings about their infants. Single mothers 30 and older reported more maternal illness, while single mothers in their 20s reported more illnesses among their infants (Mercer et al., 1982). In general, children in single-parent families miss more school and mothers miss more work because of illness; single-parent families also report a greater frequency of needing health care and not obtaining it (Moreno, 1989).

The qualitative analysis of the single mothers' interviews implicated specific stressors that may have contributed to a higher incidence of illness among this population. These nonmarried mothers reported a general lack of physical help during their recuperation from birth, concern about going back to work, needing money, concerns about their relationship with the father of their babies, and a lack of care or help with the physical health and recuperation from birth problems. Fatigue was central, along with their worries of how competent they would be as single mothers; one voiced concern about what would happen to her infant if she died. In addition, their mothering practices were criticized by family members or their infant's fathers. Whereas all mothers had severe fatigue during this physical recuperation period, the nonmarried mothers were worried about their abilities as single mothers, and their support systems validated for some that they were lacking in competency.

The case examples include Deloris, who was living with her sister; Janet, who was living with her mother and father; Denise, who was living alone; Jane, who was living with the father of her baby; and Joyce, who shared a home with another woman and her two children.

Deloris (Living with Adult Sister)

Deloris, a 39-year-old African American with some college, was living with her sister and 10-year-old niece. Because of uterine fibroid tumors, she did not know she was pregnant for 3 months. She described herself as looking forward to motherhood and felt that she would be a good, old-fashioned mother. Her son was born by cesarean delivery. During the first month at home, he had a little cold and cough, and Deloris expressed concern about his crying and jerking in his sleep. She complained of numbness in her fingers on both hands since her son's birth.

Deloris was breast-feeding her son without any difficulties and had already introduced him to cereal and applesauce at 1 month. Deloris noted that her sister and a girlfriend had bolstered her morale and provided her with important advice from things they had learned. In addition they gave her several baby items such as a bassinette.

Deloris's major concerns at this stage were an upcoming move to another apartment, whether she would be a good mother, and what would happen to her and her baby financially. She had not talked much with the father of her son and was not aware of his concerns.

Janet (Living with Mother and Father)

Janet, a 20-year-old Caucasian, had attended college and lived with her mother, father, and sister. Her son was delivered by low forceps, and she described being very frightened during the birth, although her mother was with her. She said she did not want her son to grow up to be dependent on her, although he needs her. Janet also said she was very glad that she did not have a girl, since she wouldn't want to be in the labor room with her in 20 years the way her mother had to be with her. Janet had to leave her son in the hospital for a day after she was discharged because of jaundice; she said that she cried and got hysterical, despite the explanation, because she was so scared.

Janet's baby's father visited the hospital daily, and Janet said the baby looked like his father. She added that they would be getting married eventually.

At 1 month, Janet complained that she was not getting enough sleep, although she was really enjoying motherhood. She indicated that she had thought she would be looking forward to going back to work, but now she didn't want to leave her son. She wondered whether she was doing things right for her son and said that he slept with her.

During the first month home, Janet's son had a cold and stopped breathing and turned blue. She said that she blew in his face and got him to start breathing again. The entire family took him to the hospital and waited during numerous tests, but the diagnosis was a cold, and in 2 weeks he was over it.

Janet said she asked her mother or a friend for advice because of the way they had treated their own kids. Her mother watched her son for her while she napped when she became exhausted, but Janet noted that she had less help than she needed. Her breast-feeding was going well; Janet said that she nursed her son every 2 hours. Her son's father was supporting her emotionally along with her mother and sister, and he also contributed to the baby's care financially. The baby's father was seeing his son about three times a week.

Janet had left her son with her sister once to go out and called her every 10 minutes while out; she didn't want to leave the baby. Her major concern at 1 month was her son's health and whether he would develop normally. She said the father's major concern was the baby's health and whether he would continue to look like him.

Denise (Living Alone)

Denise, aged 25, lived alone in an apartment. Her daughter's father was with Denise during labor and the spontaneous birth. She described her pregnancy as "horrid." Denise was nauseated for 5 months, then later developed preeclampsia and false labor 3 weeks prior to birth.

Denise said that being a mother meant having someone to share with, that she wouldn't be alone again. She said it was a nice feeling to be needed.

At 1 month, Denise described having been sore for 3 weeks after birth. She was still trying to get her routine down and was finding herself quite busy but missing her quick pace of life. She indicated she was anxious to go back to work but worried about her daughter "developing bonds with others." Denise said that her daughter had vomited one night and she called everyone she knew; they all reassured her that babies do throw up.

Denise voiced worry about her daughter developing normally without a father image; the father came only every other week. She was also concerned about a rash on the baby's face. The breast-feedings were going well. She said she never let her daughter cry but picked her up immediately if she cried.

Denise reported no help with infant care of household chores during her first month home; the baby's father and a girlfriend provided emotional support. The baby's father gave her financial support and bought outfits for the baby but did very little in taking care of the infant. She reported she made all of the decisions about the baby and baby's care. Her primary concerns at this period were leaving the baby with a sitter on a daily basis, being able to provide for her adequately, the daughter's development without a positive father image, and getting accustomed to a new schedule when she had to go back to work.

Jane (Living with Father of Baby)

Jane, a 23-year-old caucasian, was living with the father of her daughter. She described her pregnancy as an easy one and noted that she had worked until the ninth month when her blood pressure went up and her feet began swelling. Her labor was a long 30 hours, but she delivered her daughter spontaneously.

Jane was excited about her daughter during the hospitalization and was looking forward to mothering: "I think it's going to be fun. I'm looking forward to taking her to the park and for walks."

At 1 month, Jane was exhausted; she had severe hemorrhoids, had mastitis the first week home, and had a cold and sore throat for the last week. The first week at home had been so difficult that Jane felt that she didn't want her daughter; she needed to feed her often, and she didn't feel free to do anything. She was still finding it difficult to get used to the constant demands of breast-feeding. She added that the baby's father was expecting a lot of her and was being very perfectionistic, correcting her constantly to be sure she did everything exactly right.

Jane said that she took care of the baby, but the baby's father helped with household chores. Despite his being a perfectionist, Jane said her partner was her major source of support: "He loves me and takes care of me whenever he can."

Her daughter had an eye infection, and Jane was scheduled to see an orthopedic doctor about her daughter's hip. Jane's primary concern at 1 month was whether things would ever get back to normal and comfortable again. Her partner's major concern was for them financially.

Jane felt she had not been prepared for after the baby came—the breast engorgement problems, intercourse, and other physical concerns. Her physical discomfort had been intense during this stage of formal role attainment.

Joyce (Living with Another Woman)

Joyce, a 21-year-old African American, lived with another woman and her two children. Joyce had a high school education. Her pregnancy "was miserable, bad morning sickness, spotting and cramps, colds, flu, and at 33 weeks went into preterm labor and was hospitalized for 8 days. I never felt too good and never felt normal." Her son's father was with her during labor and the spontaneous birth.

While in the hospital, Joyce noted that she thought being a mother would be "fun, but it will have its bad points too. I think I'm ready to deal with it. I think about the responsibility his whole life."

At 1 month Joyce was feeling rather well and enjoying motherhood. She had left her son with her mother for the first time and missed him very much. She was thinking about going back to work and dreading it but had to because she needed the money.

Joyce consulted her mother or the baby's father's mother when she had a problem or concern about his care. She had just introduced him to the bottle after breast-feeding exclusively for the first month. She said her partner and his mother had been the most helpful to her the first month, both with physical help and in teaching her about the baby. Her major concern was finding a good baby-sitter for when she returned to work.

Summary

The nonmarried mother was beginning to worry about leaving her child to go back to work and finding adequate child care for her to do so, about finances, and about father role models for the child during the formal stage of maternal role attainment. The importance of providing information about recuperation during the puerperium was highlighted by the mothers' severe physical discomforts and lack of knowledge about sexual activity at this time.

Follow-up of the single mother and her infant is critical during her physical recovery period to enable her to begin parenting under the best circumstances possible. Overall these nonmarried mothers, despite having a social support network, did not report having enough help. Encouraging the single mother to establish a network of friends with whom she can share child care is also important; friends who may be called on for assistance sometimes work out better than family members (Colletta, 1979), who tend to be more critical of the inexperienced mother's attempts.

McLanahan, Wedemeyer, and Adelberg (1981) found that single mothers' role orientation determined whether social networks and the type of support the network offered buffered any negative effects of stress on their mental health. The two major role orientations observed were stabilizers who wanted to maintain their predivorce roles and changers who were attempting to establish a new identity; women established and thrived in different social networks according to their role orientation. McLanahan et al. observed that family support tends to isolate women from community support and new social experiences; in addition, women who were distressed had unusually large networks, indicating attempts to establish security by expanding the number of network members. Barrera (1981) suggested that the size of the network may be a barometer of the extent of experienced stress.

Informal/Achievement Stage or Pleasureable Reciprocity with the Infant: 2 to 5 Months

During this period in which mothers master the tasks of caring for a small infant and are able to receive much pleasure in their interactions with their infants, marital status was not related to adult women's gratification or satisfaction in the mothering role or to their feelings of love for their infants (Mercer et al., 1982). Among 20- to 29-year-old women, there was a significant relationship between marital status and observed maternal competency behaviors ($r = 0.34$), with no significant relationship observed among 30- to 42-year-old women. For women in their 20s, being married was associated with more competent mothering behaviors. Among women in their 20s a very low, but significant correlation between marital status and infant growth was observed ($r = -0.19$; $p = 0.04$), but with the tendency for infants of single mothers to exhibit greater growth. No significant relationship between marital status and infant growth was observed among women 30 and older.

The older the adult single mother, the more secure she may be in other roles such as her career; usually she has had greater opportunity to and has secured more education. It is no surprise that she was also able to assume the mothering role with fewer difficulties than younger women. Women in their 30s spoke of greater readiness in general for the mothering role (Mercer, 1986).

Becker (1987) compared adult single mothers (aged 20 to 28 years) with teenage mothers aged 15 to 17 years; all had infants up to 12 weeks of age. The adult mothers did not differ significantly in stressful life events, but adolescents listed more good life events, especially in relation to social support. The community may be more supportive to the very young single mother. There were no age differences in the mothers' assessment of expected infant developmental behavior overall; the adult mothers were more able to see their infants as capable of regulating their behavioral state (Becker, 1987).

Interviews with the 28 nonmothers reflected both pleasure in their infants and, for many, pain in relationships with the father of their infants. Some were breaking up with their boyfriends and/or moving out. A glimpse of the situations of case study mothers in each of the five different family structures provides insight to their special challenges at this time.

Deloris (Living with her Adult Sister)

At 4 months, Deloris was feeling good; her only physical concern was her weight. She wanted to lose some weight.

Deloris felt very positive about motherhood after initially being scared. She asked her friend who had a baby 2 months older than hers about any concerns. "I feel good about motherhood. I'd like to have another one if I could afford it. I see my family more but don't go out as much." Aside from her friend who answered her questions and her sister who baby-sat, Deloris described herself as being alone in caring for her son. She was giving him the bottle, cereal, and fruit in addition to breast-feeding.

When asked to rate herself in the mothering role on a scale of 1 to 10 with 10 being excellent, she did not hesitate to rate herself as a 10. Her major concerns were to continue to have good health and live to see her son grow up.

Deloris demonstrated great pride and delight with her son, despite the very tight finances and her having to work and care for her son. The movement of this 39-year-old woman into the maternal role was with much self-assurance.

Janet (Living with Mother, Father, Sister)

Janet reported motherhood to be a lot easier and a lot more fun at this achievement stage. "I never thought I'd enjoy it this much. He fills my day. I used to sit home and watch TV. I have more of a purpose. I am a lot more responsible and I've matured a lot since I've become a mother."

Janet did not mind the changes that the baby had brought in her life, adding that the changes were all for the better. She had not had to go to work but was planning to go back to college in 4 months.

Janet's mother had been the person who had helped her most during the last 4 months, but she rated the amount of help she received as less than she had needed. Her son was now on the bottle and had no problems in switching from the breast.

She viewed the most difficult thing about motherhood at 4 months as "the responsibility of wondering what type of parent you'll be and the responsibility of controlling someone else's life." She rated herself as 7.5 in the mothering role. One of the most rewarding factors in motherhood at 4 months was watching her son grow and being able to see day-to-day changes in him. Her primary concern was seeing that her baby has everything that he needs. The baby's father was not involved in child care, and Janet preferred it this way. Without the pressures of needing to go to work, and by living in her parent's home, Janet was moving into the mothering role with less financial strain than other nonmarried mothers.

Denise (Living Alone)

At 4 months, Denise was upset that she had lost her job as a secretary; however, she was interviewing for another job. She also was receiving unemployment compensation. She was tense and appeared rather insecure.

Denise had a uterine infection when she went for her postpartum checkup, but described her health as very good. She said that she loved motherhood and was quite animated about it. Denise also noted that she respected herself more now that she was a mother and was not as self-destructive as she had been before (drinking and partying).

Denise said that no one had helped her in the day-by-day situations in mothering, and that she cared for her daughter all of the time except when she worked, and a baby-sitter cared for her then. Her daughter was being bottle-fed; she had given her some mashed potatoes but felt badly after the daughter had a constipated stool.

Denise said the most difficult thing about motherhood at 4 months was dealing with her emotions when her daughter's father left (he visited them bi-weekly), adding that both would be depressed, and her daughter did not smile for 2 days after he left. Despite all of the stressors in her life, Denise was very pleased and happy about the mothering role; she rated herself as an 8, indicating that maybe she was not quite as perceptive as she could be. Finances were a major concern, and her baby's father's major concern was how to deal with being a father.

Although Denise expressed delight in her daughter, she was experiencing strain in the role because of lack of social support and financial help.

Jane (Living with Father of Her Baby)

Jane was feeling much better than at 1 month; her hemorrhoids were no longer problematic, and she felt in control of her emotions. Although she had had a couple of colds, she was feeling rested after spending a couple of weeks with her mother. Jane described motherhood:

> It's nice now. She's doing so much—rolling over, smiling, laughing, talking. I feel like a mom. I'm enjoying it. I'm not anxious to have another one right away, but I am enjoying her. She keeps me company. I feel more insecure in some ways. I need to watch myself so that I can be a good mother—not be so grumpy and always do the right thing. It's wonderful to have someone love me so unconditionally. She loves me no matter what.

The major change resulting from the baby's birth seemed to be the financial pressure; she and her partner wanted financial security more strongly. They also felt a lot of pressure to get married that they had not felt prior to the baby's birth. Jane said they didn't feel the need to get married although at times she wished they would. Other times she didn't feel they need to get married. Since they were living on their savings, finances were a great strain to them.

Major helpers for Jane had been her partner, mother, and a friend with a 15-month-old toddler. The baby's father was unemployed, so he helped a lot with the baby.

Jane was continuing to breast-feed and did not give her daughter any other food. For Jane, the greatest difficulty in mothering was lack of time to do the things she wanted to do, such as reading or baking. She found playing with her daughter the easiest. She rated herself as 7 in the mothering role, and noted that her lack of patience was her reason for not giving herself a 10.

Major concerns during this achievement stage were finances, going back to work, and being a good mother. She added that mothers had to keep their sense of humor and needed some time for themselves. Just a few hours away from her daughter relieved much tension for Jane. Strain was becoming evident in the relationship with the baby's father because of increased financial pressure.

Joyce (Living with an Adult Woman)

Joyce had bought a car and was enjoying her work at 4 months, although she felt guilty initially when she left her son with a baby-sitter. She was annoyed that the sitter had not called her at work when her son cried all day; he had an ear infection. Her menstrual periods were more frequent than they should be, and she had a cold she couldn't shake. She wondered whether her energy level would ever be the same as before pregnancy.

Her son's father was bothered that she didn't pay as much attention to him as she did prior to birth, and queried her, "Don't you need me anymore?" She said she had quit trying to make him understand, as she was a more responsible person now.

Motherhood at 4 months was described by Joyce as different; in some ways it was a good feeling and in other ways it was not. Joyce was excited that she had always wanted to do something with her life, and now she felt she must do things and organize her life for the baby's sake. She added that it was a good feeling to "know you're needed; I appreciate myself more."

Although Joyce named her sister as the person most helpful to her during this stage, she also listed her mate, mother, coworkers, and other family members. She felt she had as much help as she needed at this time.

Joyce had just weaned her son from the breast at 4 months and bottle feedings were going well. She was feeding him everything—meats, vegetables, fruits, all strained baby foods.

The most difficult thing about mothering was not knowing what was wrong with her son—there was so much to do. She noted that she had taken him to the doctor twice before an ear infection was discovered. She felt taking general care of him was easiest, but rated herself as 6 to 7 in mothering. Seeing her son grow and be healthy, do things, and his alertness were most rewarding for Joyce.

Summary

Although nonmarried mothers were enjoying their infants very much, they continued to have concerns about their care. Overall, the transition to motherhood was viewed as self-enhancing. Giving up bad habits, becoming more organized, and caring for an infant all meant they were more responsible adults. They enjoyed this improved image of themselves. Reinforcing these positive feelings and good mothering behaviors is an important role for health professionals, especially since many of the nonmarried mothers continued to work at relationship problems with their male partners.

Those nonmarried mothers not living with parents or a family member were most often dealing with concerns and problems emanating from their infant's father. Denise reported both she and her daughter were upset for a couple of days after a visit by the daughter's father. Jane felt pressure to get married, yet the relationship with her boyfriend was increasingly more strained due to financial pressures. Joyce's boyfriend was feeling left out due to her attention to the baby and felt unneeded.

Helping the nonmarried mother gain aid from community resources is important. Their continued financial strain and concerns about babysitters as they returned to work were paramount.

Achievement of Maternal Role Identity

Achievement of a maternal identity added dimensions of richness and responsibility to the 28 nonmarried mothers' self-image such that they felt and described the transformation rather graphically. Their lives overall were less chaotic and more orderly; although finances were problematic, their infants were their priority, and they felt the struggles were well worth it. The rewards of motherhood were in pleasureable interactions with their infants, and in the joy of watching their infants' growth and development.

One-third of the nonmarried mothers achieved comfort with the maternal role from 6 to 12 months, with one woman noting that she did not feel confident in the role at 1 year. Two of the women said that they had achieved the role during pregnancy, 29% felt confident and comfortable with the role after birth and the first couple of days, 10% said they had felt comfortable with the role when they went home from the hospital, and 14% felt they had achieved the role between 1 and 6 months.

Friends ($N = 10$) were named more often than mothers ($N = 9$) as role models for the maternal role. Seven of these 28 nonmarried women (25%) said they had not had role models; one who had no models had used TV and books. Grandmothers were listed by two of the women as role models.

This period of the infant's beginning to separate from the mother and increasing directed activity is a time when parents need to be comfortable with themselves as mothers and their plans for disciplining their child. There is a strong need for the pediatrician's or nurse practitioner's support during this period. Two kinds of support are particularly crucial for the nonmarried mother; they need the professional's help with issues concerning discipline since they are the only disciplinarian, and they need help in letting the infant become independent (Brazelton, June 6, 1989).

Having a partner appears to contribute to a mother's competence during this stage. At 8 months following birth, low but significant relationships between marital status and maternal competency were observed among women in their 20s ($r = 0.20$) and women 30 and older ($r = 0.24$). Women who were single tended to score somewhat lower than women who were married.

When their infants were 1 year old, there was a significant correlation between marital status and the way mothers who were aged 30 and older handled irritating child behaviors ($r = -0.35$), ($p = 0.007$), but not among women in their 20s (Mercer et al., 1982). Single women tended to score themselves as handling irritating child behaviors less optimally than married women. No other maternal role behaviors were significantly related to marital status. Without an adult to share the responsibility, the single women may have judged themselves more harshly, or their less optimal handling of irritating behavior may have been a result of the additional stresses facing single parents. The case examples of the nonmarried women from this larger study verify that both of these factors are operative. As the infant becomes more manipulative and directive, having a partner seems to be more important for the parenting role.

Many problems with boyfriends were evident for the 28 nonmarried mothers, however. Emotional and physical abuse was experienced by some of these women. One mother, Zoie, who lived with her brother, had been hospitalized for 4 days following a beating by her daughter's father who had fractured facial bones and caused her to have double vision. She was afraid of this man, who said he wanted to "come back to her," yet had other women in three different localities. She had to go back to the hospital for some surgical repair. At the 1-year interview, Zoie was 2 months pregnant by this man who had beaten her and fathered her first child. Four (14%) of the nonmarried mothers were pregnant at the 1-year interview. Glenda had married a man she met at church (not the father of her baby) who molested her infant daughter on at least 3 occasions as evidenced by bloody diapers and lacerations found on physician's examination; she left him and was seeing her daughter's father again. Ellen left the father of her baby, who had not yet divorced his wife but who was seeing other women while he lived with her; she found out he had been doing so since her pregnancy. One infant's father was letting him touch his hot cigarette and get burned as a way of teaching him to avoid unsafe things.

Although there seems to be greater societal acceptance of nonmarried mothers, this is not always true on an individual basis. Linda, a 32-year-old single mother, noted that one of her major worries was peoples' responses to her as a single parent. She said she met other mothers in the park and other places who would be friendly until they discovered she was not married.

Studies of single parents of preschool children have identified other environmental stressors that add to the difficulty in parenting. Single women reported more stressful life events that center around employment issues, living conditions, or personal goals, while married women reported fewer life changes and changes that center around the home and family (Weinraub & Wolf, 1983). Importantly, however, no significant differences were observed in the parenting of single or married mothers of preschool children, despite a less stable and consistent social network and less emotional support (Weinraub & Wolf, 1983). Single parents were in general more socially isolated and worked longer hours; they also had more physical help with child care. Weinraub and Wolf concluded that single parents may be as successful as married parents during the child's preschool years.

Others found that the lack of a close friend or persons to call on for everyday help were related to problems for single women in parenting (Norbeck & Sheiner, 1982). Availability of persons to call on for practical help was more important as opposed to having actual help with household or parenting.

A study of kindergarten through third grade childen referred by teachers as having adjustment problems identified that older siblings and a family with two parents served to moderate the stress reported by the children (Sandler, 1980). Single parents appeared to handle ordinary stressors fairly well, but the more aversive events were problematic. Sandler urged that community psychologists augment the natural support systems within families and avoid interventions that may displace the role of these systems.

A study of single-parent and married employed women found that single women were somewhat more depressed but did not report lower self-esteem; single women were more committed to work, worked longer hours, and experienced greater work-family role strain (Keith & Schafer, 1982). Single parents who had less depression had nontraditional sex role attitudes, longer work hours, higher income, lower work-family strain, and higher self-esteem.

Single parents have demonstrated the impact of a retarded child on their family is not greater than for other family structures; however, they do not attend educational conferences for their children as often (Palfrey et at., 1989). This is probably a result of their career roles and lack of a partner to share these responsibilities. Although single-parent families are less well off financially and the mother's coping is less effective in maintaining family integration, these families are higher on family adaptability because of greater flexibility in family rules and role relationships than two-parent familes (McCubbin, 1989).

A look at the case examples of the nonmarried mothers from different family structures indicates how their concerns differed and how they were similar during the stage of maternal role achievement.

Deloris (Living with Adult Sister)

Deloris was working and felt she was keeping up with the pace at 8 months. Her son was really good, except for colds, which responded well to the vaporizer. Motherhood made her feel better about herself, and she expressed a desire to go back to school and get a better job.

Deloris's sister and a girlfriend continued to be her major support. The father of her baby was doing very little in regard to taking care of the infant, and she was receiving less help than she needed.

Deloris noted that she was not as active as she had been a year ago and was just beginning to get her vigor back at 8 months. Her son was eating solids well and continued to be bottle-fed. When he reached for something he shouldn't have, Deloris said, "No," and slapped his fingers; she also offered something else to distract him or at times let him cry.

The most difficult thing about mothering at 8 months was the lack of time for everything. Playing with her son was considered the easiest part, and the most rewarding was to see her baby happy. She rated herself as 9 in the mothering role. Deloris's major concerns at this time were to go to school to get a better education so that she could get a better job, along with finances. Finances were a worry.

At the interview when her son was a year old, Deloris reported having had a hysterectomy (fibroid tumors) 2 months earlier. Both she and her son had had the flu but were well at the time. Deloris's mother came to take care of her and her son following her surgery. She said that financially things were a lot tighter; her annual income was between $12,000 and $14,000. Her son's father was not helping out as much as she needed financially; he had not worked steadily and was going to school.

Deloris observed that her son was stubborn and had a temper and that discipline would be more difficult now. She rated herself as an excellent mother (10). Having to take time off from work for her surgery was the most difficult event for her over the first year of motherhood. The most unexpected event was her son's umbilical hernia. She said her advice to other new mothers would be "Read all the literature. Get as much information as you can, go to classes. Call friends with children for their experiences."

When asked when she felt that she had assimilated the role of mother, Deloris replied, "When we came home from the hospital." Despite her surgery, Deloris looked rested and vibrant; her mother was continuing to stay with her and help them. The father of the baby visited less often with her mother there, but that did not seem problematic to Deloris. She had moved into the mothering role with ease despite her concerns about going back to school and finances.

Janet (Living with Mother and Father)

At her 8-month interview, Janet said that she loved being a mom but that her health had gone down the drain; she had had strep throat and tonsilitis. In describing how motherhood affected her, Janet said:

> Things change a lot. I think it's the best thing that's happened to me. I didn't feel that way when I was pregnant. I'm changing in my attitudes. I get along better with children and other people too. Being a mother makes you take a longer look at yourself as a person. You try to better yourself. Your attitudes toward life are going to be transmitted to the child. I used to have a devil-may-care attitude toward what others thought of me. I appreciate my own parents more than I ever have.

> I am just friends with the baby's father now. I was very resentful at first; now I've handled it out of my son's need to be close to his father.

At the 1-month interview, Janet had indicated that she and the father of the baby would get married eventually, and the dissolution of that possibility was hard for her. Janet reported that her friend, a neighbor with children, had been the most helpful to her during the past months. She had provided Janet with a lot of moral support and helpful advice about babies. Once every other week Janet was taking her son to visit his father and remained during the entire visit.

Janet was teaching her son that things, such as a heater, were unsafe by letting him feel the warmth, then pulling his hand away and saying, "hot." She gave him something to distract him when he couldn't have an object, and said, "no" forcefully to the off-limits object.

Janet wondered whether she had provided enough for her son, whether he was missing out on something, and whether she had given him enough time and attention. She enjoyed the feeling of accomplishment when she played with him, and he obviously had fun. She rated herself as 6 in the mothering role, saying, "No matter how much time I spend, there is always something I could be doing more; a little guilt creeps in."

Janet said her primary concerns were her son and how things will affect him—where she takes him and who she associates with and what examples were being set for him. "It's funny how much a baby can change your life. They are depending solely on you, and you'll do anything for them."

At the 1-year interview, Janet reported a continuance of illness with strep throat. She said:

> I've been trying to be both mom and dad to him. I wore myself out and got real depressed. I felt guilty about leaving him so I didn't have any career plans. My grandmother sent me a ticket to go visit her. She helped me a lot. She sat me down and talked to me. She told me I wouldn't be neglecting him by going on with my life. I was so emotionally drained by not ever being away from him. I was laying down with him so he'd go to sleep— totally involved with him. For a whole month she set up things to keep me busy with time for myself. I felt so much better. After I got home, I decided to go back to school. I'm taking a beauty course 4 days a week now. I exchange babysitting with friends. He's doing fine and so am I.

Obviously, Janet identified her grandmother as the person most helpful to her during the last quarter of her first year of motherhood. "My grandmother made me realize I was trying to be too much to him; she took away all my guilt."

Her son visited with his father twice a week for about 5 to 6 hours. He occasionally took care of him when Janet had a night class. However, Janet did not feel that he was doing enough for her son saying, "As a typical man he's torn between his own life and remembering he has a son. It is easy for him to forget. We don't have a relationship, but he does have a son. I want to maintain that contact as much as possible. He criticizes me as a mother and that makes me furious since I am the one who takes care of him all of the time." The father was not contributing financial support, although at 1 month Janet had indicated he contributed some. Janet said she didn't want him to, since she felt it would be a bind on her and make her indebted to him. She did not complete the item regarding her annual income.

Janet was having problems with discipline. She described her son as a suicide child. A week earlier when her sister was baby-sitting while she was at school, he got shocked from the cable TV; he was on the floor, stiff, blue, and not breathing. She breathed in his face, splashed water on his face, ran outside, and screamed for help. This enabled him to wake up. They took him to the doctor and found that his mouth was burned.

Janet said she tried to divert his attention when he was fussy, but she was concerned that he bit other children maliciously and beat up 2-year-olds. For this behavior she spanked him, slapped him in the mouth, flicked him with her finger, or squirted him with water. She noted that her parents had been very strict with her and that everything had to wait until she was 18; she left home at that time. It was ironic that she had returned home; Janet at 20 was immature and still adolescent in many ways. She indicated that she had been sheltered as a child because of her father's strictness. Her grandmother, more than her parents, appeared to provide her with nurturance that she needed as a mother.

She laughed and rated herself as 20 (10 as excellent) in the mothering role, and then said 9½. "I think I'm a damned good mother."

The most difficult time during the year had been when her son fractured his skull when he fell and hit his head. She said that she had to sleep under his crib she was so worried. (The reader will recall that her son had an incident prior to 1 month of age when he had quit breathing and was rushed to the hospital.)

The most unexpected event of the year was her feeling of contentment. She hadn't expected to feel so sure of herself and to experience all of the changes. Her advice to other mothers was, "not to let guilt trips get to you. Love them, spend time with them, but don't forget yourself."

Janet's major concern at 1 year was that her son's dad would try to fight for custody of him. She said that she had worried all year about this. She was also concerned about trying to get back into a career.

Janet reflected that there was never any information provided about raising a child alone, that most materials were directed toward married couples. She saw a large need for single parent's feelings to be addressed. Her feelings as a single parent centered around whether she was adequate and doing a good job. This process changed a lot for her over the year.

Janet also shared that she had not assimilated the mothering role until 1 year after birth. At this time, "I was used to being a mother, more settled in, more confident, and realized that I was pushing too hard. A mother does not equal slave. I realized I was spoiling him. I wasn't letting either one of us be a person in our own right." Janet's insecurities in the maternal role were reflected in what she called her son's "suicide" behavior. Hopefully, she will be able to convey some of her newly acquired confidence to her son.

Denise (Living Alone)

At 8 months, 25-year-old Denise was seeing a chiropractor because she had been hit when in her car. However, her morale was high. She was effusive about motherhood:

> I'm loving it more as she gets older. I like it more because she is respond-
> ing. It is more work, but there is more fulfillment. I'm happier than I've
> ever been. I'm more responsible—a different attitude. I feel a lot of satis-
> faction that I've had her. I feel more sure of myself and my judgment. On
> the way to work, I drop her off at the baby-sitter, and pick her up after
> work. I drop her off when I go to school. I get up at 4:00 A.M. if need be.

Denise named a girlfriend who was the person most helpful to her. This friend listened to her complaints, was very supportive, and baby-sat for her when she went to school. She also read a lot of books for information.

Her daughter had had a intestinal infection and a cold, but was better. Denise was feeding her daughter foods that had been put in the blender, and the bottle. To teach her something was unsafe, she explained in a stern voice what would happen: for example, "If you pull on the plug, it'll fall on your head." Denise added that she did not want to say, "Don't," all of the time.

The most difficult thing for Denise was providing for the two of them, and concerns about the future. She rated herself as excellent (10) in the maternal role. She said she had begun potty training and that as soon as her daughter was potty trained she could go to nursery school. Denise's primary concerns at 8 months were finances; she added, "What a guilt trip."

At 8 months, her daughter's father was no longer involved in their lives. She mentioned someone else whom she was dating. Despite her financial concerns and busy schedule of work and school, Denise enjoyed her daughter, and her interactions with her were warm, affectionate, and nurturing.

When her daughter was 1 year old, Denise said she was down to her normal weight, working, and had completed three semesters of school; her life could not be better. She stated, "I don't know what I did without her. I can't believe how much of a difference she's made on my attitude. I'm more responsible than before. I have to have more forethought in everything I do." She continued to name her girlfriend as the person most supportive to her, both emotionally and time-wise, and said she was exceedingly generous at birthdays and Christmas.

Denise stated that her daughter's father was not contributing financial support, and any time spent with the child had been at his convenience. She was attempting to work out set times at which he could visit.

Denise was teaching her daughter that something was unsafe by telling her that it was "hot," for example; at times, her daughter touched the hot area anyway, but she learned from it. She spoke in a stern voice to her, and this was effective; occasionally she slapped her hand when the stern voice didn't work.

Denise stated that she first felt as if she were a mother during her pregnancy. She continued to rate herself as an excellent mother. Her daughter's sicknesses had been the most difficult event over the first year. Seeing her daughter grow up and learn to respond were the most rewarding pleasures of motherhood. Her primary concern, however, was "money." Her income during the past year had been between $14,000 and $18,000.

Denise's advice to other mothers was, "Give them space to grow. Listen to them; they have a lot to say."

Jane (Living with Father of Baby)

At 8 months, Jane had just found out that she was 8 weeks pregnant. She was feeling comfortable with motherhood, saying that it got easier all of the time and that it was a lot of fun. Jane added:

> I feel shocked. Motherhood has enriched my life. She's a part of me. She belongs with me. I had a hard time accepting the mothering role. I don't feel like I'm just a mother. I'm me, a person who happens to be a mother. It comes naturally. I'm no longer a "working woman" or a "sexy person." I had planned to go back to school, but that's out now. I guess there really isn't a convenient time to have a second baby. We'll just have this one, then I'll have my tubes tied. I'm still nursing, but the doctor said it would be too hard to be pregnant and nursing too.

Jane noted that the baby's father had been the most helpful to her. He entertained the baby when she got particularly tired. She noted that she was tired a lot but attributed the fatigue to her pregnancy. She rated herself as 8 in the mothering role. She was primarily concerned about moving and avoiding fatigue. She added that she and her partner would handle this second baby by sticking together and keeping their sense of humor. Jane stated that she was upset by negative remarks from others about her pregnancy and wanted this baby to be as special to everyone as her first was.

At the 12-month interview Jane had had the flu. Pregnancy was difficult, since she got the flu in the middle of moving to a new residence.

Jane said she was more confident about herself, and that five extra pounds didn't matter since she was out of the sexual competition. Her partner was accepting this second pregnancy a lot better than she. He was helping her more with the first baby now.

Fatigue was continuing to be a problem for Jane when her daughter was a year old, as she was 7 months pregnant. Her daughter had had bilateral ear infections over the first year with some hearing loss; Jane was concerned how this would affect her balance and the development of speech. She rated herself as 9 in the mothering role and noted that she felt confident in the mothering role sometime between 4 to 6 months following birth.

The most difficult thing about motherhood over her first year had been the loss of freedom to come and go as she pleased. She had lost her expectation of going back to work, but was content to stay home.

Jane's primary concern, however was finances; "I'd like to be able to support them well—house, food, clothes—always enough, not indulged, but cared for." Jane listed her annual income as between $6,000 and $8,000. She added that the baby's father was also concerned about finances.

Jane's advice to other mothers was, "Don't isolate yourself as you are going through the mothering process. Talk with other mothers."

Joyce (Living with Another Woman)

At 8 months, Joyce said that her body was finally feeling normal again, although she had had flu, two colds, sore throat, and a kidney infection. She felt that she was better organized and was adjusting. She was still somewhat unsure in her mothering role, however:

> I love it, but it is scary sometimes. I look at other kids and wonder what I'm going to do. I enjoy him, but sometimes he fusses and I can't satisfy him, and I don't know what to do. I do feel better about myself. I feel needed. I have a clear purpose for living, and I feel confident about that. I work a lot more. I care more. I get to work on time. I am more responsible and more stable. I feel closer to my mate—increased harmony.

Joyce said that discipline was the most difficult for her, "I don't know what to do. He doesn't understand yet, and I can't hit him, and he needs to explore, and I don't want to put everything away." Loving her son was the easiest thing for her. She rated herself as 7 in the mothering role saying, "I'm not bad, I just know I could do better. I doubt myself a lot." Her primary concern was to own a home, and her mate's major concern was in providing for his family.

At the 1-year interview, Joyce's health was better; her only health problem had been a cold. Joyce continued to see the transformation in her identity:

> It is a sense of accomplishment that he is good and healthy. It is nice to have someone dependent. I feel better about myself. I am doing something worthwhile. Before I felt I was wasting my life. I feel now I'll try to achieve my goals sooner. Before him (baby) I loved to get high; now, I rarely want to. The things I do are done only if he'll enjoy them. I think of him before me.

Joyce confided that she was not as close to her son's father as she had been earlier, noting that they argued a lot and that he was jealous. Money was a frequent subject for argument. Joyce said that she basically was supporting both the baby and herself (her annual income was reported as between $18,000 and $22,000). She added, "He doesn't understand why I don't have money and why I'm always broke. He sometimes feels that I should drop everything when he wants something. Child care is expensive ($250.00 per month); I have a car, I wash more clothes, and things are expensive. I am surprised that he and his mother don't understand." When a phone call was made to Joyce regarding completing a questionnaire, she advised the interviewer that she was filing rape charges against her baby's father. She didn't want to see him anymore but had to because of the baby. She was given a brochure about family counseling services and was advised that they could help her set limits for herself and her son's interactions with the father.

Joyce, although reporting uncertainties during early motherhood, said that she had felt like a mother and comfortable with her decisions as mother since her son's birth. She rated herself as 8 at 1 year, saying, "I doubt myself so much. I do what I think is best." The most difficult event during her first year of motherhood had been the relationship with the baby's father; this was also the most unexpected event—"that I would go through this." Seeing her son happy was the most rewarding aspect of motherhood, and playing with him was the easiest part of mothering for her.

Summary

Mothers as single parents are handicapped by their lower socioeconomic status and greater numbers of life stressors. Despite wider social acceptance of single parenthood, nonmarried mothers continue to face much social stigma and discrimination in all arenas, including health care. As Belle and associates (1980) had observed, several of these mothers and/or their infants suffered violence from their partners.

During pregnancy the single expectant mother has additional tasks to resolve that coupled mothers do not. Whereas disclosure of the pregnancy is usually a joyous occasion for family members, single pregnant women find disclosure as painful. Professional support is particularly important in helping these expectant mothers to resolve legal issues around naming and planning for future care of their children.

Nonmarried mothers' support system is particularly important as their infants age, and they need sanction for their disciplining and child care methods. As Tilden (1983) discovered was the case during pregnancy, family and friends were also the major source of support for the nonmarried mothers during their first year of motherhood. Although the majority of the 28 nonmarried mothers were involved with their infant's father to some extent over the first year of motherhood, the majority of these relationships were problematic.

The themes of being needed and of being transformed into a more responsible person who was able to organize and care for a dependent child were specific self-image enhancers. The nonmarried mothers enjoyed their children and were rewarded by their interactive responses just as other mothers. (See Mercer, 1986a, for discussions of the concerns of all first-time mothers during the first year of motherhood.)

The health care system focuses largely on partnered women in traditional nuclear families; this focus must be broadened to include the nonmarried mother, regardless of her family structure. The nonmarried mother continues to doubt herself and needs continued reassurance about her mothering.

THE LESBIAN MOTHER

Saralie Bisnovich Pennington

The possibility for women who are openly lesbians to have foster children, formally adopt children and to have alternative insemination (formerly referred to as artificial insemination) represents a revolutionary change in the expectation of who has the right to parent. This change provides a freedom of choice for millions of women who approximately a decade ago felt they had no choice.

Lesbian mothers bring an unusual amount of planning to their pregnancies. The very nature of their situation, not being with men as sexual partners, requires a consciousness that is not part of the heterosexual experience of pregnancy. Their preparation process for pregnancy includes use of both directed and leaderless support groups, class and discussion groups, counseling and psychotherapy, reading existing literature pertinent to their situation, and becoming familiar with the medical options, medical practitioners, and available facilities. This section of the chapter will be dealing with the experiences of lesbian mothers who chose to have children in the context of a lesbian identity and for the most part in the context of a lesbian relationship. Following the presentation of five lesbian mother families, published research regarding lesbian mothers' maternal role attainment and implications for health professionals will be presented.

Making The Decision and Preparing For Motherhood

The 18 lesbian mothers who provided information for this chapter section had several things in common. All who were in couple relationships considered themselves to be co-mothers to their children, had achieved or were in the process of achieving legal rights and responsibilities or adoption for the nonbiological mother, with one exception had been in the relationship for at least 5 years prior to becoming pregnant, were over 30 years of age when they had their first child (most in their late 30s or early 40s), were middle or upper middle class, spent several years preparing themselves emotionally and financially prior to actively making the decision to become pregnant, spent from 1 to 3 years trying to become pregnant, and had used alternative insemination as a means of becoming pregnant. Some of the women actively involved the biological father as part of the family, and all voiced the desire for the child to be able to locate the biological father after the age of 18 a part of the insemination agreement. For some of the children, locating the father will not be an option, as his anonymity was also part of the insemination agreement.

The extensive preparation done by these women regarding parenthood could be likened to that done by heterosexual women pursuing adoption with several important differences: these women are creating family constellations that are considered abnormal and unnatural by the larger society and need to prepare themselves and, ultimately, their children for the potential lack of support and possibly outright hostility from family, acquaintances, neighbors, child care providers, schools, other children, other institutions, and the medical and general community. This is a mighty task requiring a high level of self-awareness, stability, maturity, and the ability to utilize personal and community resources.

Lesbians using alternative insemination are creating many possibilities for their family structures. There are lesbians who chose to co-parent with a man who may or may not be the biological father, and the biological parents may or may not choose to live together. There are lesbians who are co-mothers and are involving the biological father and his male partner as co-fathers in the family structure. In this latter situation the child has the potential for having four active parents. In all of the situations that I have examined, all of the involved fathers have been either gay or bisexual. This is not to say that a heterosexual man could not be involved. The risks inherent in these new family situations (or, rather, unique to them) are at this point hypothetical. One could easily argue that having three or four involved parents harkens back to and improves on earlier forms of family life where the child-rearing practices were not so privatized and considered to be the domain of the two-parent nuclear family. The lesbian mothers interviewed for this chapter are raising their children for the most part in traditional two-parent, two-mother families where the two mothers are the two parents.

Special Risk Factors For Lesbian Mothers

The risk factors for single lesbian mothers (e.g., mothers raising children without partners) are the same as those for single mothers in general, with the added stressors and risk factors of lesbian mothers in general. Major risk factors cited by lesbian mothers include abandonment by and loss of support from family friends and the community. These factors can result in denial of sexual orientation; denying the nature of the lesbian couple/family relationship publicly; hypervigilance about safety and security for the child; psychosocial isolation from the extended family and family of orientation; physical/medical problems related to stress, bias, and mistreatment by health professionals; and increased expense to insure legal protection for an alternative family unit. Added to these responses are the fear of custody problems and the need to restrict their environment for the health and safety of the family unit.

All women who shared their experiences were acutely aware of these risk factors and recognized the stress on them as individuals and on their partnerships associated with dealing with the pressures from a hostile environment. Thus it is evident that the risks for these women are external and do not originate from an internal condition. The risk comes from the unpredictable reactions over which they have no control.

Unique Pregnancy and Early Parenting Issues for Lesbian Mothers

The desire to become pregnant and achieving this desire are times of positive anticipation for a woman, her partner, family, and friends. It is a time for significant people in the woman's life to be interested, supportive, and joyful, and in short, a time for the family/friendship network to rally around the woman and her mate in a positive, loving manner. What in reality happens to a lesbian who desires pregnancy and achieves this state? The great majority of informants had support from family and friends, and those with mates had the support of the mate and the mate's extended family. For those who did not have this support, a look at the nonsupport and how it affected the woman and her partner is important.

Departure from the Cultural Norm

Pregnancy for lesbian mothers can represent to many in our society a violation of a cultural norm that lesbians do not have children. That lesbians do become pregnant may be viewed as an affront to or a violation of "normal family life." When the lesbian mothers' family members evidence these feelings, especially the mother's and her partner's parents, this negative response can tax the self-esteem, sense of competence for the parental role, maternal confidence, and possibly the physical and mental health of the mother(s). As was stated in chapter 1, maternal anxiety is associated with greater neonatal and maternal risk, greater depression, and less confidence in coping and parenting abilities. Mothers with higher anxiety during pregnancy were more hostile and interacted less positively with their children at 8 months following birth than mothers who had lower anxiety. It is also noted in the chapter that maternal depression is associated with fewer affectionate maternal-infant interactions and vocalizations and that depressed mothers neither adapted their behavior in synchrony with their infants' changing behavior nor responded spontaneously to their infants' vocalizations.

In the population I interviewed, where there was an absence of support from the maternal family of orientation, the mothers prepared themselves for the situation. Strong support situations such as soliciting other family members, friends, and positive associations with individuals from the childbirth preparation and medical communities helped these women maintain a cohesive sense of self-esteem. Social support from the environment was seen as crucial by and for these mothers; during their pregnancies they felt they received it unequivocally as long as they were careful to whom they revealed their lesbian identities. This of course added another stress in terms of the concern over when "to come out" and feeling guilty or disloyal over "passing" as straight. Case examples of lesbian mother families are presented later that illustrate these feelings.

Acceptance of the Infant by Significant Others

One of the issues faced by lesbian mothers is the quality of acceptance afforded the child of the biological mother by the family of the nonbiological mother. If two lesbians in a relationship both have children, how do they deal with the situation of acceptance of the child by one set of grandparents of the daughter's partner, and the relative noninclusiveness or rejection by the other set of grandparents in the same situation? There is the potential for both tremendous family support and recognition and for extremely painful rejection and family isolation.

Family nonsupport can range from declaring the lesbian mother "unnatural in her desire to have a baby" and "selfish" in terms of fulfilling her own maternal needs at the expense of an innocent child to threats to take the child away from the "evil influences" of an unnatural family or ignoring that the pregnancy is happening. Some families accept the pregnancy and ask the mother to hide that she is a lesbian. When there is a partner involved, it may be asked of her that she identify herself as a good friend who is helping out, as opposed to being a co-parent or other mother. How does this outright rejection, request for identity distortion, ignoring, and general invalidation present risks for the mother, for her partner, and for the unborn child?

When the single mother or couple do not receive the emotional and increased closeness of social relationships of extended family (as is the case for the majority of heterosexual mothers), the usual anxiety, normal concerns about pregnancy and mothering, normal ambivalence, and health issues can become exacerbated. The lesbian couple or individual can become isolated, both physically and emotionally. More stress can be placed on the nonpregnant partner and the relationship itself can be in jeopardy. Even when all issues are well thought out beforehand, when the reality of rejection hits, the ensuing anxiety and depression can be overwhelming.

Such intense stress can be hypothesized to contribute to miscarriage, and women gave examples of developing serious blood pressure problems, intestinal disturbances, and other stress-related conditions resulting from the rejection and harrassment of extended family. Either the biological or nonbiological mother coming out to her family has caused negative shock waves with the potential for hostile realignment and readjustment of family relationships. The individual and/or couple face even greater stress following birth when tangible and emotional help is not forthcoming, which can inhibit their ability to function. The effects on self-esteem, the ability to care for oneself and a newborn, and the effects on the parents' changing relationship or on the single-parent mother can be devastating. The bonding process between mother and child may be affected, and familial bonds may be negated. The couple or individual may feel as if they are swimming alone upstream.

Community Nonsupport Issues (Including Friends, Coworkers, Work Situations, and Schools)

Another major area of stress that can put the lesbian mother at risk comes from outside the immediate family. All lesbian mothers who were interviewed identified environmental factors that were outside of their control as posing the greatest threat to themselves, their children, and their family life. Lesbian mothers coming from nurturing family environments have many issues to consider. Once they leave their family and encounter the outside world, they have choices of how to present themselves and their situation. Some of the questions a mother or a couple must ask themselves are: Who do I tell and what are the risks in telling that I am a pregnant lesbian, a lesbian mother, or the nonbiological lesbian mother? When do I choose anonymity and when do I choose to pass as heterosexual or do so by default?

Universally, the women stated that the world outside their families and friendship groups made the heterosexual assumption that they were straight while pregnant and/or once they had the child. They constantly found themselves in the position of having to come out as lesbian or feel as if they were lying about their identity. Supermarkets, playgrounds, day care centers, and schools afford the opportunity for anyone to ask about the child's father or the person's husband. Jane explained:

> This was the first time in my adult life that I recognized what heterosexual privilege was all about. Having a child brought me into an intimate contact with institutions and situations that I was protected from in terms of homophobia and in some cases forced me back into the closet. Every day I am challenged in some way when I am out in the world with my child. This situation is quite complex when coming out can mean dealing with having to educate or deal with hostility or anything other than the acceptance that other mothers take for granted.

To fail to come out takes its toll in guilt, anxiety, and an ongoing fear of being found out. Coming out as the nonbiological mother also has problems, since she is not afforded the legitimacy given to the other parent because of her gender.

The risks posed by a hostile community push the family constellation or single lesbian mother back on themselves and their own communities to become more isolated and insular, and they are deprived of the general support granted newly pregnant women and new mothers. Depending on the strength of the individual or the couple, this can have differing results.

The issue of the nonbiological parent being accorded time off in a work situation after the birth of the baby is an example of another source of stress. The partner had added stress if she had to act as a buffer or protector for her pregnant spouse or the new mother. A nonbiological mother described some of the decisions she had/has to make:

> Do I want to be intimate and personal on the playground or in the supermarket, in the neighborhood, or in the various child care situations in terms of providing information about my child's parenting? When do I make the decision to say Michael has two mothers? We are paranoid about being out as lesbians. There is stress of working overtime as a parent in terms of feeling the need to be extra protective and vigilant about the child's safety and security. We have to make concerted efforts to find non-homophobic environments and have to avoid certain activities (certain family gatherings and vacations with people where my family constellation will be invalidated or criticized or where I will be subjected to hostility about other gay people or feel silenced about my sexual orientation). Nothing is automatic, and everything has to be conscious. Every time something new comes up, we have to deal with our child's reactions and new explanations have to be given. We have to be the educators, which is a drag. We feel like we are always breaking ground.

Legal Issues

Some specific concerns related to lesbian family issues affect their future lives rather than the immediacy of pregnancy and infancy. As with single heterosexual mothers, lesbian mothers have legal choices and legal expenses that do not face married women. Concerns regarding when and how to tell the children about the nature of their conception and the potential for legal problems and related custody concerns such as what will happen to the child if the biological mother should be unable to care for the child or should die are other serious concerns.

Case Histories Illustrating Issues and Concerns of Lesbian Mothers

Five case histories of families who live in the San Francisco Bay Area illustrate some of the major issues and concerns with which lesbian mothers must deal. The Bay Area is probably the most supportive or as supportive as any area in the United States of alternative family structures. This is not to suggest that homophobia is not a problem in this locale, simply that it is easier to live as a lesbian mother in communities in the Bay Area; perceived and actual risks to the mothers and children are not as great. These five families are representative of a nonclinical sample of mothers and illustrate what very high-functioning women have to deal with when they challenge what is considered to be normative child-rearing/family structure. Some of the informants utilize psychotherapy to help them deal with their issues and to aid them in the parenting process. There is not a large enough known clinical population of pregnant and early (first year of the baby's life) mothers from which to generalize. Lesbian mothers that I have seen in my practice reflect the same concerns in terms of their identity as lesbian mothers as do the nonclinical population. Names of women and infants have been changed as well as identifying information to protect the confidentiality of participants.

Alice and Vicky's Family

Alice is the nonbiological mother, and she has received complete acceptance in her role as mother from her parents and siblings. She stated that her partner of 10 years, the child's biological mother, did not receive such acceptance from her own family of origin:

> Vicky's parents had a party to introduce their grandchild to the family, but they refused to acknowledge me as the other parent; rather, they chose to identify me as a very good friend who is helping Vicky raise the baby. This felt like a terrible invalidation of the family unit. I wept for hours and knew that I would never again hide the nature of our relationship. At a particularly vulnerable time in our union, the birth of our child, I was asked to deny my identity, connection, and contribution. It would have been easier if I had not been there.

Vicky feels it is better that she, Alice, and their two children (they have had a second child since this incidence occurred) do not live close to her family:

> It is easier for me to be in a lesbian relationship, especially with children, and live far away. My extended family and my parents' close friends think I

decided to have a baby on my own, got tired of waiting for the right man, and decided on artificial insemination.

The insemination process was difficult for Vicky. She had concerns about AIDS; however, she found her only option was to use an anonymous donor. Approximately 7 years ago, only two out of the five doctors recommended to her would inseminate unmarried women. Vicky found much more liberal attitudes from doctors when she was inseminated 2 years ago for her second child. Vicky noted:

> I am very uncomfortable talking to doctors. I had a serious condition that was misdiagnosed during my pregnancy, because my doctor felt my symptoms had to do with my ambivalence about being a pregnant lesbian. It got in his way of taking a proper history. When one of our children had to be cared for in the intensive care nursery, Alice was allowed in by special permission and not because she was being validated as our child's other mother.

An issue both women will have to deal with in an outgoing way is their concern that their children cannot know their biological fathers, as that was a condition for insemination. When their oldest child was around a year old, he showed a preference for Alice, the nonbiological mother (a time when children use their second parent in separating from their primary parent). Vicky stated:

> I felt as if I had lost something special and was angry, upset, and confused. I had questions about my ability to be a mother. We utilized counseling to help us with our dilemma and achieved a positive resolution. It is still difficult at times to deal with the reality that I am not the only mother, that I am not *it*. Of course, there are definite bonuses to our situation.

Both women would like to move to a more suburban environment and plan to join a gay/lesbian support group in the suburban community they have chosen in order to have a better idea of what lies ahead. If the move will mean that their children will face increased homophobia, they will not make the move. They fear a suburban lifestyle will not include the diversity that fits in with their needs as a "different family." They are specifically concerned about the hostile attitudes their children will get from other children and from teachers in public schools outside of the San Francisco Bay Area. Alice legally adopted both children, which involved both legal expense and much emotional trauma. Alice summed up their experience by saying, "We always have to think about everything. We don't have the choices and the mobility of straight families."

Deanna's Family

Deanna chose to have a baby on her own. They have been living with Deanna's partner since her son was a year old; he is now 6. Deanna's comments reflect the existential dilemmas faced by lesbian mothers and their children, even in the most supportive circumstances:

> I have an unusually wonderful and supportive family and job. My family was excited that I wanted to have a baby, even though I was single at the time. I chose a lesbian doctor for myself and my baby as I didn't want my son to experience negative judgments about lesbians having babies. However, when I am questioned by relative strangers or acquaintances about my child's father I end up feeling like a fake if I go along with their heterosexual assumptions. When people ask, "Where's his dad?" or say, "He must look like his dad," I can't tell the truth unless I make the decision to come out as a lesbian or a lesbian mother. Everything you do with or about your child involves heterosexual assumptions and unless you are in an all gay/lesbian, mixed gay/heterosexual situation, or a rare supportive heterosexual situation, you have to live a lie. Everything you do in a community with other families results in you and your child having to deal with potential ostracism and hostility.

Rena and Bonnie's Family

Rena began:

> When I decided to begin the process of becoming pregnant, I knew health care would be an important issue. I was aware I had a tremendous choice of gay/lesbian sensitive health practitioners. The Bay Area is really different in this respect, and gays move here for this reason. Pregnancy gave me a window on heterosexual privilege. I received concern and consideration from men I had never received before. Chivalry replaced hostility or sexual vibrations. A grief reaction ensued, and I asked myself, "Why aren't people like this all the time?" Heterosexual privilege began with the pregnancy and extended into having a young child. My former alienation from the culture has changed, and the change is alienating. Every minute of every day I am challenged with, "Do I come out?"

Rena is referring to the fact that others assume that a person is heterosexual if she is a mother or if she is pregnant. Rena continued:

When I am asked about the existence of a husband or a father, I am in conflict between maintaining the pretense that there is a father in my son's life or risking the hostility that would come from disclosure of my lesbian identity. I used a donor for insemination who was willing to be identified when my son is 18; however, my son's other parent is his other mother.

Bonnie, who is the other mother, also deals with heterosexual assumption when she is out alone with the child, and everyone assumes she is the only mother. When she is asked about "her" labor, delivery, husband, child's father, etc., she faces the dilemma of what to disclose as well:

Do I tell the person I am the child's mother, explain my relationship to his biological mother, or do I lie? Our child takes us into the heterosexual world where we have to ask ourselves, "Do we want to share personal information with people on the playground, in the supermarket, or in various other neighborhood or child care situations, about our child's parenting?" The dilemma remains. When do you say, "Seth has two mothers, or his other mother is Bonnie?"

Both mothers expressed paranoia about "being out" as a lesbian parent. They feel the stress of working over time as a parent in terms of feeling the need to be extra protective and vigilant about the child's safety and security. Rena stated:

I have to make a concerted effort to find non-homophobic environments, and I have to avoid certain activities, such as family gatherings and vacations with other people, where my family constellation will be invalidated or criticized or where I will be subjected to hostility about other gay people and will feel silenced about my sexual orientation.

This couple both reported complete family support for their relationship and their parenting.

Meg and Josie's Family

Meg and Josie both had and continue to have an extremely supportive family situation. Josie's mother was present at the birth and stayed on to help her daughter and family in the first few weeks. They stated that they felt they had an unusual situation and that some of their friends had encountered nonsupport and hostility from families of orientation and extended families when they had babies as lesbian mothers.

This couple was aware, however, that some distant family members looked on their situation as abnormal. Some of the insensitive attitudes they are aware of personally and professionally include:

- Lesbians having children is selfish (i.e., dragging innocent children into a sick situation and an abnormal context).
- They are satisfying maternal needs without questioning the effect on a child.

Meg and Josie see as a major concern during pregnancy the temptation to stay "with your own kind" out of fear of negative community attitudes. They feel that there are not many options other than living in the San Francisco Bay area to avoid these attitudes.

They continue to say that it is difficult to be open with who they are, as they are afraid that their child could be physically snatched from them:

If you are openly gay, then you and your child could be a target for anything, as any nut can come after you. If you are famous you may have to hide the identity of your child. Can you imagine running for a public office and saying on television, or in your campaign literature, "Hi, I'm Jane and I'm a family women," alongside pictures of you, your female partner, and your children?

Meg and Josie feel that mothers with male children are more at risk because they have to face accusations that they are raising the child to hate men or to be a wimp. The ultimate insult is that any other woman would be a better parent as long as she isn't a lesbian.

Meg and Josie also described the financial and legal ramifications of homophobia, such as increased expenses to draw up protective documents, custody, and adoptions, all of which create financial pressures. There can be issues with the medical profession. "We feel we always have to be on the defensive. There is tremendous pressure to be a perfect parent. It can be summed up by stating that there is hostility and fear versus a bottom line of loving and caring for the community."

Nan and Ruth's Family

Ruth, the nonbiological mother spoke first. Her first concern was:

Will I be perceived by others as a member of the baby's family? My situation is different from that of some of the other lesbian mothers in that our daughter has an involved biological father, so I was concerned as to what role I would have. We have had no problem with the baby's father in terms of my role with the baby. He is very secure with Nan and me. In terms of medical care pre- and postpartum, we have had complete acceptance from our doctors for all procedures, including amniocentesis, labor, and delivery. Our childbirth preparation classes were successful in terms of professional attitudes, and everyone accepted our three-parent constellation. In short, we were treated as if our family was a natural one. I was given the power to make all medical emergency decisions, and of course we had medical care from a sophisticated place and by sophisticated doctors. We only had one questionable experience, and that was from our acupuncturist who could not accept the idea of me being the baby's other mother.

Nan's family is very comfortable with our relationship. Her nieces wanted to know what the baby would call me; they wanted to know out of curiosity, and they are completely comfortable with our relationship.

I came out to my family 2 years ago in preparation for becoming pregnant now and having the baby. My mother and sister were horrified. It was a nightmare, and the baby was a nonevent because it wasn't my baby. The denial was devastating—there was no reciprocal acceptance for my sister regarding my child when I had been such a devoted aunt to her children. I felt disappointed and abandoned. I wrote to my father, mother, and sister individually at the time of the birth. I told them, "I am adopting a baby." The baby has both our last names, that is, both Nan's and my last names, and I told my family that both Nan and I want children and decided on alternative insemination and to have the child together. My father, from whom I had been alienated in the past, responded positively, sending cards, letters, and presents. He definitely considers himself to be the grandfather, is a newsbearer to the rest of the family, and is confronting my mother and sister about their denial and avoidance. After a few months, they, too, began to acknowledge the baby's existence.

What seemed to be so helpful to this family was having community support and knowing they had a network of supportive people. Nan's family is part of the network; unfortunately Ruth's family, with the exception of her father, felt that what Ruth and Nan were doing was "sick," and they felt sorry for the baby being raised in a "sick environment." Ruth acknowledged, "I wish they were sending us joy and health. I'm glad I started the coming out process 2 years ago and did not wait until the baby was born. Our neighbors are part of our support network, and we would like to know other gay/lesbian parents and couples with children."

Ruth and Nan's baby's father is less involved in the decision-making process for the baby's needs than they are. They are the primary parenting unit and have this documented in a legal contract. The baby's father currently spends a block of time with his daughter twice a week and drops by almost every day to see her. Eventually they plan that he will have the baby at his home one night a week. The baby has the mothers' names and not the father's name for three reasons: the mothers are the primary parenting unit, future adoption issues, and in the event of emergency, it would be too complicated if the child did not have the nonbiological mother's name, in terms of medical release and responsibility.

They feel restricted as to where they can live due to homophobia and discrimination:

> Medically, we have had no problems with our pediatrician in terms of attitudes toward our family unit. We are most worried about the cruelty of other children and others in general and the ensuing possibility of discrimination.
>
> We have a very comfortable relationship with the baby. She has a different relationship with each of us. Nan is clearly the nursing mother, and they have a blissful union. Ruth is the soothing mom, and we feel it is easy to joke about who is the favorite mother. There were more feelings of competition for Ruth with the baby's father. However, they are knitting a close family and feel much closer to the baby's father now that the baby is here. Our roles are clear, and we really care about each other. We'd like our daughter to be athletic and have music lessons. We would like her to be interested in the arts and sports and hope she will strive academically and play the piano or cello and tennis. We all have our fantasies and dreams.

Lesbian Women's Anticipatory Stage of Maternal Role Attainment

As described above, the lesbian woman's decision to become a mother is very carefully planned. The lesbian woman's reasons for becoming pregnant as opposed to adopting a child include a desire to have the personal experience, the difficulty in adopting, and the desire to raise a newborn (Harvey, Carr, & Bernheine, 1989). In Harvey and associates' study, the average age of 35 biological mothers was 33.7 years, with almost 60% having graduate or professional degrees; 89% worked during pregnancy, and 60% of those worked until or through the ninth month of pregnancy. Friends and published materials were more important sources of information on how to conceive than were health professionals. The majority (82.8%) became pregnant by alternative insemination, with two-thirds opting to use an unknown donor. Of the 17% (six) who became pregnant through sexual intercourse, only two informed the men of their intention.

In McCandlish's (1987) study of five lesbian families, the decision to have a child was made out of caring for the partner as opposed to the desire to become a nonbiological parent. In two families the nonbiological parent was uncomfortable with the inability to legally adopt the child and lack of parental rights that are converse to the larger cultural norm where biological fathers obtain custody and their children bear their names.

Almost all of the women (94.3%) in Harvey and associates' (1989) study sought prenatal care during the first trimester of pregnancy, with the remaining obtaining care during the first 16 weeks. Almost one-half (48.6%) utilized nurse-midwives or lay-midwives, and four lesbian women were refused services by a health care practitioner. Almost all (91.4%) disclosed their lesbian identity to their health care providers. The women's commitment to participate in the experience was evidenced by 88.6% attending childbirth classes. The majority were critical of health professionals' knowledge of and sensitivity to lesbians' health care concerns, although the majority were satisfied with their obstetrical care providers.

Wismont and Reame (1989) applied the major tasks of pregnancy as outlined by Rubin (1984) to the assessment of the pregnant lesbian couple. As is evidenced in the interview data described above, others' acceptance of the pregnancy requires careful negotiation by the pregnant couple. Wismont and Reame suggest that legal issues involving lesbian parenting may interfere with the mother's ability to achieve full social acceptance of her pregnancy. To achieve the task of assuring safe passage for the mother and infant, the lesbian couple often spends much time finding an accepting health care environment and health professionals who do not invalidate their unique family structure. The discrimination and stigmatization facing lesbian pregnant women have the potential to increase her ambivalence about the pregnancy and could theoretically make binding-in to the infant more difficult, as was discussed earlier. The task of giving of oneself is costly to the lesbian mother; in experiencing social hostility and discrimination, the gift is costly. Wismont and Reame suggest that the expected child becomes more highly valued, and the child might take on a more significant role in meeting the mother's emotional needs.

The Formal Stage of Initial Adaptation of Maternal Role Attainment

Although all five nonbiological parents felt excluded during the pregnancy, they all attended the birth and were surprised at their immediate attachment to their infants (McCandlish, 1987). McCandlish (1987) reported that during the early symbiotic period the biological mother and child were very close; all mothers nursed their infants. All lesbian mothers in the Harvey et al. (1989) study also breast-fed their infants for 1 month; 80% breast-fed for at least 6 months.

At the time of birth McCandlish reported that all biological mothers took from 2 to 3 months off from work with partners taking no more than 2 weeks off. Nonbiological mothers were clearly attached to the child but expressed anxiety about whether the child was attaching to them; they provided from 40% to 50% of the child care.

As with heterosexual couples, lesbian couples reported changes in their relationships after the birth of the first child (McCandlish, 1987). A reduction in sexual intimacy was a concern; role differences and increased partner needs were additional stressors, as is the case with heterosexual couples.

The Informal Stage of Maternal Role Attainment

As in all areas of early lesbian mothering, additional research is needed regarding the informal stage of maternal role attainment in which the mother is comfortable with her decisions and mothering and able to enjoy the interactions with her infant. During this stage, the nonbiological mother is able to see that the infant is attached to her also, and this relieves some of her anxiety in this area (McCandlish, 1987).

From my interview data, during this stage of achievement for heterosexual mothers, the indications are that the lesbian mother must continue to be hypervigilant in dealing with the social environment. Who she comes out to and the answers she gives to strangers in the community regarding the infant's father all must be carefully weighed. The spontaneity of joyous sharing with interested strangers is absent. The strain of hiding parts of her identity can lead to a pile-up of resentment (Green, 1987). Mental health problems of lesbian mothers stem from their interface with the nonsupportive environment rather than from intrapsychic problems (Green, 1987).

Role models for mothering are often chosen from the lesbian community (Wismont & Reame, 1989). As in the situation of heterosexual mothers, mothering behaviors are learned from a variety of persons.

Achievement of Maternal Role Attainment

The highly committed lesbian woman who chooses to mother also places her child's well-being as a priority in considering all social interactions (McCandlish, 1987; Pennington, 1987). The maternal identity is the salient identity for lesbians as for most other mothers (Kirkpatrick, 1987). Research is lacking in this area, however.

McCandlish (1987) reported that around the age of 14 months, the child made a clear move from the biological mother toward the nonbiological mother. In two of five cases, the biological mother was uncomfortable with the child's rapprochement phase (a subphase of separation-individuation in which the infant is aware of the power and ability to physically move away from the mother); this was the case with Vicky cited above.

Implications for Health Professionals Caring for Pregnant or New Lesbian Mothers and Their Families

Culturally sensitive care for lesbians by clinicians who understand the cultural experience of being lesbian and how lesbians perceive illness and wellness is central (Stevens & Hall, 1988). Stevens and Hall describe the meaning of illness and wellness as linked to lesbian identity, a quality that is central to and differentiates the self, with a core cultural experience being stigmatization. The implications of this stigmatized identity must always be considered by lesbians in all arenas of their life, including seeking health care, as was evidenced in the case studies. The challenge of coping with stigma seems to promote the development of a strong self-concept, but the extent a lesbian believes her identity is revealed may affect how she views her body image and self and may contribute to the stress she experiences. Almost three-fourths (72%) of 25 lesbians studied reported negative responses such as ostracism, invasive personal questioning, shock, embarrassment, condescension, and fear from health professionals once their identity was known (Stevens & Hall, 1988). These negative responses and the fear of actual harm seem to be factors in 84% of the self-identified lesbians' describing a reluctance to obtain health care (Stevens & Hall, 1988).

It is important for the clinician not to assume that all clients are heterosexual, and patients and clients do need to feel comfortable enough to talk about their sexual orientation and lifestyle if they are to achieve the best possible care and treatment. In order to do this, it is essential that health professionals assess their own attitudes toward lesbian mothers and their level of comfort in working with them. If health professionals cannot resolve their own homophobia, they should not serve this population. It is crucial to be aware of this populations' special needs and to be sensitive to the stressors from the culture in which they live rather than seeing the woman's problems as a result of her sexual orientation.

Referrals to appropriate services when indicated are important, and these referrals to support groups, therapists, or family counselors should be to those who are sensitive to issues faced by lesbian mothers. As health professionals are the first line of care for pregnant women, their responsibility is to look at their own attitudes and to educate themselves to be sensitive to the lesbian mothers' different needs. The hostility and stigma that the lesbian mother faces in her social environment increases her anxiety and may potentially affect her usually strong self-esteem. In most metropolitan areas there are groups of gay and lesbian physicians and nurses, and such groups may be invaluable sources of information and referral for providing sensitive, nonjudgmental care. If no such group exists, it is necessary to become acquainted with current literature to become as informed as is possible.

It is crucial that the lesbian parent or lesbian couple and their child or children are seen as a viable parenting and family unit. When this attitude prevails, the patient, the family unit, and the community as a whole are strengthened. With the tremendous concern that is being generated about the disintegration of the family, the more supportive the society and its subcommunities are toward alternative family forms, the stronger and more productive these families and their individual members will be. They in turn will add to the strength of our community, our society, and our world.

SUMMARY

In a heterosexual situation families respond with increased support and affirmation and bonding around the birth of a baby, which is generally the opposite experience for families of lesbians. When there isn't a male in the picture, the assumption in a heterosexual situation is that the mother can always have as a goal finding a male to be a father to the child.

The lack of support for the lesbian couple along with the normal changes during the perinatal period contribute to the many stressors for the couple. In the best of circumstances the birth of a baby may be traumatic to the parents' relationship. Harrassment, hostility, judgmental attitudes, and anger toward the mother-to-be, as opposed to family support and confirmation, can lead to physical risks such as colitis and ulcers during pregnancy and the postpartum periods. This negativity from families is especially difficult, as mothers normally have ambivalence while pregnant, and during early mothering are less equipped to deal with and are more vulnerable to hostility. The pregnant woman's partner has the added stress of having to act as a buffer and protector of her partner against this hostility.

An important role of the health professional is to be aware of community support systems for lesbian families and to help clients become linked with these systems.

10

Parenting in Acutely Socially Deprived and Stigmatized Situations

Mary Margaret Gottesman

Homeless families and families with AIDS constitute two of the most socially deprived and stigmatized groups in the United States today. Homeless women and infants are also likely to be women and infants at risk for AIDS (Novello, 1989). The economic and social circumstances of homelessness often lead women to engage in behaviors such as prostitution and intravenous drug use (IVDU), which place them at risk for acquiring HIV infection. Prostitution and intravenous drug use together account for over 80% of the HIV infections in women (Novello, 1989).

Homeless parents and parents at risk for AIDS face multiple challenges to safe and successful childbearing and childrearing. Their complex needs require thorough asessment and intensive intervention (Ramey, Sparling, Bryant, & Waski, 1982). Intervention with multiproblem families builds upon knowledge of the parent's adaptation and style, the child's adaptation and temperament, and the characteristics of the parent and child's environment (Barnard & Douglas, 1983).

HOMELESS FAMILIES

In a 29-city study conducted by the United States Conference of Mayors (1987), over one-third of the homeless population surveyed were homeless families. Families are also the fastest growing group among the estimated 250,000 to 3,000,000 homeless (Institute of Medicine, 1988). The increase in the number of people living in poverty has

244

parallelled the decrease in funding for social welfare programs at the federal level (Wilson, 1987). The number of persons living in poverty in the 5 largest U.S. cities rose by 58% between 1970 and 1980 (Ruggles & Marton, 1986). During that same time period, the number of persons living in areas of extreme poverty increased by 182% (Schorr, 1988). Thirty-six percent of those living in extreme poverty are children.

Homeless Mothers: Adaptation and Style

The characteristics of homeless families in the United States vary by region. Over two-thirds of homeless families are headed by single women (U.S. Congress, House of Representatives, Committe on Ways and Means, 1985). The remaining homeless are 2-parent families. There are more 2-parent families in the Midwest and West and more single parent families in the South and the East. Homeless mothers are typically high-school educated or less and in their late twenties. Most have little or no employment experience. Teen mothers form at least 20% of all homeless, single mothers.

The ethnicity of homeless families also varies by region. Black families dominate inner city populations in the East and South. White families dominate all rural homeless populations as well as the urban homeless populations in the Midwest and West. Little is known about the size and characteristics of homeless Hispanic families. However, a recent report places the poverty rate for Hispanic children at 39.69% suggesting that many are at risk for homelessness or marginal housing (U.S. Congress, House of Representatives, Select Committee on Children, Youth, and Families, 1987b).

Data from McChesney's (1987) study identify 4 types of homeless families based on descriptions of their descent into homelessness. The 4 types are: unemployed couples; mothers leaving relationships; mothers receiving Aid for Families and Dependent Children (AFDC); and mothers who were homeless teens.

Unemployed couples tend to be headed by men with either obsolete, little or no job skills, who sometimes work and sometimes do not. The shift in the economy from reliance on unskilled and semi-skilled labor to high technology has left many of these men unemployable at jobs which would enable them to support their families. These families tend to have a traditional family structure where the men are the principle bread-winners and the women care for the home and children.

Mothers leaving relationships did so because of divorce, separation, or death of a spouse or partner. These women tend to be better educated and to have stronger employment histories than other homeless women. Women also report leaving relationships because of abusive conditions for themselves, their children, or both (Boxill & Beatty, 1987; McChesney, 1986b). In Bassuk, Rubin, and Lauriat's (1986) study of homeless families, 36% of the women reported having lived in battering relationships. A far larger percent of homeless mothers across all studies report being abused physically, sexually, or both as children.

Mothers in the AFDC group include all families where the customary source of income was AFDC payments for one year or more. They are largely single women without a high school education and little or no employment experience.

Finally, mothers who had been homeless teenagers form a particularly vulnerable and needy group. These mothers are often the victims of physical and sexual abuse in both their families of origin and their foster families (Bucy, 1987). In addition, most are not high school graduates. Prostitution is one of the few avenues for survival open to these women. Thus, they are at high risk for contracting AIDS as well as sexually transmitted diseases.

Homeless women face many barriers to accessing health care (Coalition for the Homeless, 1985). While families qualified for AFDC are automatically eligible for Medicaid, applicants must have an address to qualify for AFDC. Thus, the neediest of families are excluded from the two largest social welfare programs created to help them. Even if women secure Medicaid coverage, they must often rely on public transportation for care at distant facilities and for which there is often a lengthy wait (Kozol, 1988a). If she has other children, they must often accompany her since child care is largely unavailable. This requires the expenditure of scarce cash resources as well as jeopardizing the mother and her children's access to adequate food at soup kitchens and timely arrival for shelter in the evening.

Studies of homeless mothers show that they frequently suffer from chronic illness, depression, personality disorders, and mental illness (Wright, 1989). The incidence of alcohol and drug abuse is also greater in this population than in housed impoverished families. Thus, homeless families are often multiproblem, dysfunctional families (Wilson & Neckerman, 1986).

Impaired physical and mental health reduce the mother's ability to meet the safety and growth needs of her child. Of equal importance is impairment of the mother's ability to be psychologically available to her child, a factor critical to child development (Bornstein, 1985). Research shows that mere physical presence of the mother is insufficient for a healthy mother–child relationship. Rather, the mother's ability to relate contingently and appropriately to the child is the critical element for the normal child's development (Estrada, Arsenio, Hess, & Holloway, 1987).

Severely limited financial resources, substance abuse, absence of shelter, physical and sexual abuse during childhood, poor maternal education level, and impaired psychological functioning are each documented risk factors for adaptation to the demands of parenting (Heinicke, Beckwith, & Thompson, 1988). Homeless mothers typically possess more than one of these risk factors (U.S. Congress, House of Representatives, Select Committee on Children, Youth, and Families, 1987a). Thus homeless families are among those most in need of supportive and therapeutic interventions.

Homeless Children: Effects on Their Adaptation

Children in the United States now constitute 40% of persons in poverty. They are the only poverty level group growing in size (Schorr, 1988). Moynihan (1986) notes that children replaced the elderly as the nation's poorest group in 1974. According to a congressional study, by 1980, preschool children became 6 times more likely to live in poverty than the aged (U.S. Congress, House of Representatives, Select Committee on Children, Youth, and Families, 1987b).

Children under 5 years of age comprise from 46.5% to 65% of the samples of children in various studies of homeless families. Infants under a year of age form at least 13.2% of all homeless children. School-aged children comprise 53.5% of homeless children with 12- to 17-year-olds comprising 11.7%. Research by Bassuk and Rubin (1986), McChesney (1987), and others provide a description of homeless children.

Homeless infants are likely to be high-risk infants physiologically as well as environmentally (Escalona, 1982). This is often a consequence of little or no prenatal care (Institute of Medicine, 1985). Currently, prenatal care available to the indigent and uninsured is inadequate to meet the demand (Hughes et al., 1987).

The toll of little or no prenatal care is an increase in the number of low birthweight infants. Chavkin, Kristal, Seabron, and Guigli (1987) report that the infant mortality rate (IMR) was 24.9 for infants born to mothers living in New York's welfare hotels. This is more than double the national IMR for the United States of 10.6. Low birthweight is associated with learning disabilities, mental retardation, and greater physiological vulnerability (Fanaroff & Martin, 1987).

If the infants of homeless mothers are born at term and healthy, their postnatal health is likely to suffer from malnutrition and anemia. A survey by Dehavenon (1985) found that 56% of welfare mothers diluted their infants' formula. At least 17% had no refrigeration for formula or other foodstuffs. Lack of refrigeration increases the risk for gastroenteritis with resultant diarrhea, dehydration, and hospitalization.

Regular health care is virtually nonexistent for these infants (Egbuonu & Starfield, 1982). Therefore, many health problems which would benefit from early identification and treatment are unattended. Homelessness also renders infants vulnerable to upper respiratory infections from exposure to the elements or crowded shelter conditions, repeat ear infections from inadequate treatment, skin rashes from poor hygiene and infrequent diaper changes, and a host of infectious conditions such as impetigo, pediculosis, and scabies. Nearly 75% of homeless children are underimmunized or not immunized at all (U.S. Congress, House of Representatives, Select Committee on Children, Youth, & Families, 1987a). Bassuk and Rubin (1986) found that chronic health problems such as asthma were also more prevalent among the homeless children.

More importantly, higher rates of failure to thrive and developmental delay are found among homeless infants (Bassuk & Rubin, 1986; McChesney, 1986a; Whitman & Thornton, 1986). Parents describe high levels of behavioral problems and school failure for their children over five years of age (Bassuk, Rubin, & Lauriat, 1986). In Bassuk and Rubin's (1986) study, over 50% of children 5 years of age and older were clinically depressed on a standardized measure of childhood depression. Many of these children also reported suicidal thoughts.

Poor physical health, anemia, hunger, depression, and behavior problems interfere with the ability of children to relate in a positive, interactive manner with their parents, peers, and teachers (Wilson & Neckerman, 1986). These problems also impair the child's ability to achieve competence in social environments important to normal growth and development: the family, the school, and friendships. Thus, the vulnerability of infancy stretches into childhood and adolescence creating young adults ill-prepared for employment and the parenting of their own children.

The Environment of Homelessness:
Inanimate, Animate, and Support Characteristics

Numerous reports in journals and newspapers detail the squalid, crowded, oppressive conditions in the majority of welfare accommodations accepting the homeless. Kozol (1988a, 1988b) poignantly described the sense of isolation, darkness, and hopelessness one experiences upon entering such places. Plumbing is often nonfunctional or communal in nature. Rats and roaches heavily infest all areas. Few rooms have or are permitted to have even a hot plate for cooking. Few have adequate refrigeration. Many are dirty, in ill repair, and contaminated with lead-based paint. Children are, therefore, at risk for disease, accidental injury, and lead poisoning.

In addition, children lack safe play areas, age appropriate toys, and the privacy to rest and study. The absence of the opportunity and materials for play contribute to the substantial developmental delays seen in these children. Inadequate sleep and study time jeopardize successful learning and, in part, account for the high rate of school failure among homeless children.

Shelter conditions are generally cleaner. However, most shelters have large, crowded dormitory areas with high noise levels, little space per family, and virtually no privacy. Such an environment makes sleep difficult. It also adds to the stress of parenting. Boxill & Beaty (1987) described the strain of "public parenting." Every word, every behavior of a parent and child are subject to the scrutiny and judgment of strangers. This increases the pressure on mothers in a chaotic environment to demonstrate adequate parenting skills in order to avert the placement of their children in foster care.

The length of time families can stay in shelters is usually limited. Most shelters require families to leave early in the morning, thus, necessitating waking the children from sleep. With little or no day care available, children and their parents face unpredictable daily schedules and a steadily increasing level of sleep deprivation (Kozol, 1988a).

Homeless families tend to be without support from family and friends (Bassuk & Rubin, 1986; Boxill & Beaty, 1987; McChesney, 1986a). Thirty percent of homeless New York mothers (Molnar & Klein, 1988) and 25% of the mothers Bassuk, Rubin, and Lauriat (1986) interviewed were unable to name any supportive person. Twenty-six percent of the New York mothers identified their children as their support. Thirty percent of the women in McChesney's (1986a) study had deceased mothers and 35% had deceased fathers. Families often live at such distances from siblings and parents that they are effectively cut off from this source of support. Support may also be withdrawn because of alcohol and drug abuse. As already mentioned, a large percentage of homeless mothers, particularly homeless teen mothers, are victims of physical abuse, sexual abuse, or both in their families of origin. Such abusive families are unlikely to offer assistance or to be sought for assistance.

Abused mothers are more likely to abuse their children (Labell, 1979). It is not surprising then, that many homeless families are clients of the child welfare system. Even those who are not live in fear of losing their children if they are judged neglectful (Bassuk, Rubin, & Lauriat, 1986).

The circumstances of homelessness also make it difficult to maintain friendships. Frequent moves, limited access to phones, no mailing address or letter writing materials contribute to the isolation of the homeless from friends (Kozol, 1988a, 1988b).

The environment of homelessness has few positive role models to offer children. Physical abuse, the victimization of others, alcohol and drug abuse are daily examples of adult coping styles encountered by homeless children.

While a "social safety net" exists supported by government and philanthropic resources, it is unable to effectively meet the needs of multiproblem families such as the homeless (Institute of Medicine, 1988). This is due as much to bureaucratic barriers to access for services as it is to the inadequacy of the help offered (Schorr, 1988). The inadequacy of services is compounded by the fragmentation among many agencies. Homeless families are in need of shelter, food, education, job training, employment, health care, and counseling. However, the 1980s have seen a steady decrease in the amount of support in all of these areas even as the need has increased (Institute of Medicine, 1988). Data also show that homeless families are the least likely to receive social welfare benefits (Freeman & Hall, 1986).

The Interaction of Homeless Mother, Child, and Environment

The cumulative effect of the social and environmental conditions of homelessness are devastating for children and mothers. Mothers are often unable to meet either the psychological or physical needs of their children. Thus, they experience little gratification and confirmation of personal value from their primary role as parents. Children, in turn, experience little of the nurturance and affirmation of self-worth which is critical to developmental competence. Their physical health and growth are often impaired from unsanitary living conditions, malnutrition, lack of health care, as well as lead and asbestos exposure.

All of these factors lead to a vicious cycle of failure, frustration, and abuse handed from one generation to the next. As Schorr (1988) noted, the plight of the homeless is societal, and not just individual and personal. The declining numbers of births and the increasing number of children living in poverty's devastating environment demand complex and comprehensive approaches to the care of homeless families.

FAMILIES WITH HIV INFECTION

Women and children form the fastest growing segment of persons with AIDS (Rogers, 1989). A woman's diagnosis of HIV infection often means the diagnosis of a family with HIV infection. Prior to 1988, women and children were each 7% of all AIDS cases. In 1988 they were each 10% of all cases reported to the Communicable Disease Center

(CDC). Estimates for 1992 predict 32,000 AIDS cases among women and from 10,000 to 20,000 cases among children. This is a dramatic increase when compared to the 453 pediatric cases reported to the CDC in March 1987.

Profile of Mothers with AIDS and Their Adaptation

Most women ($\geq$ 78%) with AIDS are in their childbearing years, 13–39 years of age (Rogers, 1989). They are disproportionally members of minority groups. Approximately 51% are black, 20% Latino, and 29% white or other. Most are from the ranks of the urban, inner-city poor. Over 50% do not have a high school education. Health care providers on the east coast estimate that at least 15–30% of women with AIDS are homeless (Mitchell, 1989).

Drug use overwhelms all other contexts in which AIDS in women and children occurs (Rogers, 1989). Twenty-five percent of HIV infected women are daily cocaine users. Many others are daily alcohol, marijuana, and polydrug abusers. Intravenous drug use and sexual promiscuity are the primary etiologic factors for HIV infection in 81% of women with AIDS (Novello, 1989). Approximately 52% of these women are IVDUs themselves. Another 18% are the sexual partners of male IVDUs, and 11% are the sexual partners of other high risk males.

Homeless teen mothers are a special concern (Hein, 1989). Approximately one in every 1000 homeless teen mothers 15 years of age or less tests HIV antigen positive. This number jumps to one in 100 among homeless teen mothers 16–19 years of age. The number of infected women 15 years of age or less is expected to grow as men seek younger homeless women for sex-for-pay in the hope of finding uninfected partners.

The parallels between homeless women and women with AIDS are numerous. Women with AIDS are among the most disadvantaged (Mitchell, 1989). They are largely isolated with little or no supportive network of kin and few material or financial reserves with which to meet their minimum daily needs or those of their children. Health care providers and others often perceive these women primarily as vectors of infection to children and men. Thus, with the diagnosis of HIV infection, they are made to feel further stigmatized and unwelcome (Novello, 1989).

With so few personal resources and so little social support, these women often cope with the diagnosis of HIV infection by using fatalism or denial. Neither of these strategies enable women with HIV infection to participate in complex supportive, protective, and palliative care plans for themselves and their children.

Impact of AIDS on Infants and Children

Since 1988, perinatal transmission has accounted for 95% of all new AIDS cases in children 13 years of age or less (Rogers, 1989). Perinatal transmission occurs through intrauterine exposure to HIV, intrapartal contact with infected maternal blood, and consumption of the HIV infected breast milk (Landesman, 1989).

The demographic characteristics of children with AIDS are those of their mothers (Mitchell, 1989; Novello, 1989). Approximately 80% are black or Latino children, 55% of whom are males. Most live in households headed by single mothers reliant on public assistance programs. Many are clients of the child welfare system as a consequence of family violence or neglect.

One of the most frustrating aspects of perinatal care for the HIV infected woman is the inability of available serologic tests to distinguish between newborns who are HIV infected and those who are unaffected and simply carrying passively acquired maternal HIV antibodies (Martin, Katz, & Miller, 1987). Because all newborns of HIV infected mothers are seropositive, recommendations are that the clinical and serologic status of these infants be followed indefinitely (Andiman, 1989). Thus, although 75% of infants lose maternal antibodies by 9 to 10 months of age, parents and providers may not know whether the infant is infected for 15 months or longer.

Infants infected with HIV are at high risk for developing AIDS (Martin, Katz, & Miller, 1987). By 5 months of age 83% of infants born with HIV infections are symptomatic. Over 90% are symptomatic by 1 year of age. The average length of survival after the onset of symptoms is 6.5 months and 68% die before 2 years of age. Infants with early onset of symptoms often present with failure to thrive, developmental delay, and encephalopathy (Oleske, 1989).

Loss of an intact central nervous system impairs the infant's ability to interact with the mother. This deprives the mother of behavioral cues which enable her to recognize the infant's needs and to respond in a contingent and appropriate manner (Brazelton, Koslowski, & Main, 1974). As the child's developmental disability becomes more pronounced, the mother may experience intensified feelings of anger, failure, and loss, further impairing her ability to care for her child.

The age of onset of symptoms is the best indicator of a child's prognosis (Oleske, 1987). Early onset of symptoms, particularly when it is accompanied by Pneumocystis Carinii pneumonia (PCP), is often associated with a fulminant course of illness and death for 85.7% of these children. Researchers believe that most of these infants contracted HIV during intrauterine life resulting in a critical impairment of the immune system during their development (Katz, 1989).

Children with late onset of symptoms, at a median age of 13.5 months, and who develop Lymphoid Interstitial Pneumonitis (LIP) rather than PCP, live longer (Oleske, 1987). Although their overall mortality rate is a relatively low 25.7%, their morbidity is substantially greater. They are subject to repeat bacterial infections, progressive neurological disease, seizure disorders, multiple blood dyscrasias including anemia, renal failure, and cardiopathy. Thus, AIDS is a chronic disease with multiorgan involvement.

Environment of Families with AIDS: Inanimate, Animate, and Supportive Characteristics

Women and children with AIDS live in much the same environment as homeless women and children—urban, inner city poverty areas. The dirty, crowded, and physically hazardous environment in which they live is particularly consequential for women and children with HIV infection and, therefore, impaired immune responses. It places them at high risk for many forms of infection. Buildings in poor repair increase the risk of respiratory infections from aspergillus, asbestosis, and legionella. The higher incidences of reportable communicable diseases due to under-immunization, sexual promiscuity, and untreated tuberculosis cases place children at risk for life threatening illnesses from measles, polio, pertussis, and Mycobacterium avii intracellulare. Sexually transmitted diseases, such as herpes and syphilis, increase the susceptibility of high risk women and infants to HIV infection (Oleske, 1989).

When a diagnosis of HIV infection is made, women and their children often experience the fear and rejection of others, including health care providers (Flaskerud, 1987; Lawrence & Lawrence, 1989). For women and children with restricted social support resources, this is devastating as even their few supports are withdrawn out of fear and ignorance. Families of children with AIDS and HIV infected women poignantly describe their sense of isolation, stigmatization, and emotional distress as they experience rejection by their schools, communities, and even health care facilities (McGonigel, 1988). A survey of New York abortion clinics open to women with limited resources showed that 75% refused services to women identifying themselves as HIV positive (Mitchell, 1989).

The situation is further complicated when considering the consequences of society's negative perception of these women, who are often prostitutes, IVDUs, or both. Negative social perceptions frequently translate into negative self-perceptions and hence, low self-esteem (Coopersmith, 1967). Further, contacts with child welfare authorities exacerbate feelings of low self-esteem as they confirm a woman's failure in her fundamental role as mother (Chodorow, 1978).

Women and children with HIV infection and AIDS require numerous services and intensive health care management. However, these families, like the homeless, are often the families who are not enrolled in even basic public assistance programs (Freeman & Hall, 1986).

The Interaction of Mother, Child, and Environment for Families with ADIS

Women and children with perinatally acquired AIDS comprise the most disadvantaged and disenfranchised group in the United States today. Not only do they have inadequate housing, food, health care, and education, they typically have few social supports and virtually no recognition of value and worth to the society in which they live. Their lives are almost certain to be shortened by HIV infection and its consequences. The quality of life for the children may be even further diminished by encephalopathy and developmental delay.

Each of these facts alone poses a barrier to successful enrollment and cooperation in a quality plan of care. However, all of these facts together pose nearly insurmountable difficulties for poorly educated women of few resources. Despite their limited resources, parents with HIV infection must plan for the welfare and care of their healthy and infected children even as they themselves may be ill with AIDS. This is likely to be a particular source of anguish and frustration for parents, since there may be few, if any, options available which the parents would consider acceptable. At the same time, children face separation from and loss of their parents, an uncertain future, and, if they are ill with AIDS, the stress of multiple medical therapies.

ASSESSING, PLANNING, AND CARING FOR THE HOMELESS FAMILIES AND FAMILIES WITH AIDS

The characteristics of effective health care services for homeless and HIV infected families are similar across all stages of parental role attainment. However, each stage also presents unique challenges to health care providers.

Homeless families and families with AIDS require comprehensive, coordinated, community-based, and family-centered care offered by providers who convey concern and respect for their clients. All needed services should be available to both adults and children in one place, at the same time, and coordinated by one responsible professional for each family. Care for adolescents from high risk environments should not require parental permission (Melton, 1989). This reflects the model of care found most helpful for children with chronic illness and their families (Shelton, Jeppson, & Johnson, 1987).

The element of provider caring and respect deserves special emphasis (Septimus, 1989). Homeless families and families with AIDS receive very little caring and respect in their daily lives. While the majority of homeless families in one study rated their contacts with public assistance programs as "not at all helpful," they rated contacts with shelter providers as "helpful" to "very helpful" (Bassuk, Rubin, & Lauriat, 1986). The element of personal caring and respect is critical to successful efforts to assist families. Providers caring for populations at high risk for AIDS, consistently link the success of their efforts to the genuine caring staff convey to clients (Morrison, 1987).

Successful programs demonstrate the need for services to be easily accessible to clients (Fraulino & Simpson, 1989). This may require the location of health care and social service agencies in urban poverty areas. Hours of operation must also be tailored to the daily living patterns of the clients. This may mean early hours, late hours, and weekend operation. These factors make attracting competent staff difficult. Nevertheless, effective demonstration projects prove that it can be done with significant benefits for needy families.

The availability of free food, clothing, and child care items is an important draw for these mothers whose efforts are centered in the care of their children. Access to free cosmetics, perfumes, and other items appealing to women are another way to entice women to maintain contact with providers. Respite child care services, tied to attendance at parenting classes, provide the opportunity to enhance the mother's knowledge of child development and parenting skills. Such classes also offer an opportunity for women to support one another and decrease their feelings of isolation.

It is imperative that providers be familiar with the full range of public assistance programs and community services available to these women. It is just as important that professional staff be available to assist women with applying for these resources.

Initial assessment should include careful sexual, social, and substance abuse histories in addition to a personal and family medical history. This will identify the full range of each woman's needs and direct the selection of appropriate interventions. The low education and high stress levels of these women require that health care information be simple and clear.

Women of unknown HIV status whose histories place them at risk for HIV infection require counseling and the opportunity for testing. Special attention should be given to arrangements for sharing test results in a supportive environment (Holman et al., 1989). The diagnosis of HIV infection is often an overwhelming experience. Professional support should be readily available.

Compliance with measures to reduce the acquisition and transmission of HIV infection is difficult to achieve. Uninfected women often face battering and abandonment by their sexual partners if they try to introduce the use of condoms (Novello, 1989). Infected women also fear abandonment by sexual partners who learn of their HIV status (Mitchell, 1989).

Families with HIV infection have identified the need for a sense of hopefulness from the providers (McGonigel, 1988). Interventions should emphasize the preventive and palliative measures women can implement to enhance the quality of their lives and their children's lives.

The Anticipatory Stage of Parental Role Attainment

Pregnancy for homeless women and women with AIDS poses challenges for both themselves and their providers. Prenatal care offers clinicians a valuable opportunity to intervene in the lives of these women. Most women, whatever their circumstances, desire to care for their children well, born and unborn. Providers often note that high risk women will do for their children what they will not do for themselves (Mitchell, 1989).

Because pregnancy represents an altered state of immunity, there is concern among obstetricians that maintenance of pregnancy may result in a more rapid progression of HIV illness (Landesman, 1989). Preliminary data from Minkoff cited by Landesman (1989) indicate that T_4 cell values below 300 T_4 cells/μL are associated with increased maternal morbidity due to infections.

Women who test HIV positive should receive abortion counseling (Holman et al., 1989). Most women who choose abortion will not return for follow-up care, therefore, it is important to provide a maximum of information and resources during each contact.

Women who continue their pregnancies require careful and frequent assessment for symptoms of progressing HIV infection. These include persistent bacterial pneumonia, resistant vaginal monilial infections, and weight loss or poor weight gain beyond the first trimester (Mitchell, 1989). Persistent colds merit a chest x-ray to rule out pneumonia. Women with symptomatic HIV infection may also benefit from prophylactic antibiotic and antifungal therapy.

Surgical delivery does not decrease the risk of infant HIV infection. Therefore, the diagnosis of HIV infection does not preclude a vaginal delivery. However, HIV positive women should not breast-feed since breastmilk serves as a means of viral transmission.

Working with the symptomatic perinatal AIDS patient is one of the most difficult tasks faced by providers. Even as providers strive to maintain the pregnancy, they assist the mother in preparing for her own death and the uncertain future care of her infant.

Achievement of the best possible perinatal outcomes for the mother and infant is an important goal. However, health care for these women is incomplete without efforts directed towards the long term goal of creating a functional family unit. Establishing a bond of trust and respect with the client is crucial to ongoing intervention. Discussions which focus on the woman, her hopes and dreams are important to creating a lasting relationship. Care which ignores the individual and focuses only on the woman's weaknesses will not sustain a long term therapeutic relationship.

The Formal Stage of Parental Role Attainment

Homeless women and women with AIDS often receive late or no prenatal care. The opportunity for intervention, therefore, occurs at the time of delivery and without the opportunity to establish a trusting relationship beforehand.

Early postnatal assessment and intervention should be directed towards the mother's physical recovery. Psychosocial interventions should consider the mother's need for rest, nutrition, and comfort measures. A tired, hungry, uncomfortable mother is unlikely to enjoy her infant or to participate meaningfully in plans for discharge.

Caregivers should also assess for barriers to continued physical recovery after discharge. This would include whether or not she has access to shelter, food, clothing, hygiene products, and follow-up care for herself and her infant as well as the availability of help with child care. Since the majority of these women are single mothers, even the minimum support of the infant's father will be unavailable to most.

The constant effort required to meet basic daily living needs, often combined with the poor mental health of these women, robs them of the energy to invest in developing the prenatal maternal–child relationship. Because this prenatal relationship lays the foundation for the postbirth relationship, culturally appropriate assessment of the early maternal–child relationship is critical as are interventions to promote an early positive experience between mother and infant. Appropriate interventions include: assisting women to explore their feelings about the new infant, helping them understand their infant's behavioral cues and the need to respond contingently, and assuring the opportunity for frequent mother–infant contact during hospitalization.

Women whose infants are HIV infected may experience difficulty in claiming their infants for many reasons. The child may be small for gestational age and disappoint her expectations. If the infant is born neurologically impaired, the infant is often difficult to feed and unresponsive, making it difficult to experience satisfaction in caregiving. These mothers will need special assistance in learning caregiving strategies which will promote optimal infant nutrition and development. They must also learn necessary protective measures and symptoms of illnesses common to infants with AIDS.

Most importantly, the mother may fear rejection of herself and her child by significant others when they learn of the child's and, therefore, the mother's diagnosis. Mothers may benefit from role playing how they will share information on their HIV status and that of their child with others. Finally, providers should assist women with identifying alternative sources of support for themselves and their child.

Informal Stage of Parental Role Acquisition

Although this period, around 2 to 5 months following birth, is usually one of pleasure for functional families, the everyday lives of homeless women and women with AIDS offer few opportunities for pleasurable exchange between mother and child. While many women achieve feelings of competence during this time, homeless women and women with AIDS are often unable to meet their infants' needs for food, clothing, cleanliness, safety, and health care. In addition to limited resources, the woman may suffer from anemia, sleep deprivation, depression, and AIDS, all of which limit the mother's ability to care for and respond to her child.

This is also the period when the normal, healthy infant strives to engage the mother in play. This normal behavior may be viewed by the stressed mother as an unreasonable demand for attention and provoke negative maternal behavior. Parent–infant interaction may be further impaired by the infant's inability to produce engagement behaviors due to the stress of an irregular schedule, overstimulation from the environment, sleep deprivation, illness, neurological impairment, or a combination of these factors (Als, 1982).

This is the period during which many HIV infected infants become symptomatic (Oleske, 1989). Women and infants with progressive AIDS illness will require more intensive intervention. Providers face the challenge and the necessity of striking a balance between honestly confronting the reality of the mother and infant's eventual death and maintaining hope. Both mother and child need coordinated prophylactic and supportive medical care.

The Personal Level of Parental Role Acquisition

Many homeless mothers and mothers with AIDS are likely to view their infants as central in their lives as are mothers in low risk samples. The parental role is often their only source of social status and opportunity for feelings of personal satisfaction (Bassuk, Rubin, & Lauriat, 1986). Certainly these mothers experience many barriers to parenting. Some are more successful than others and some will not succeed at all in parenting their children.

Mercer (1986a) noted that at 8 months even well adjusted mothers experience an increased level of stress in adapting to their increasingly active infants. This is even more likely to be true for the high risk woman. The difficult circumstances in which most of these women will continue to live will also continue to drain them of energy and time for parenting their children. At the same time they must often restrain and quiet their normal active 8-month-olds in crowded shelter and hotel environments.

A more disquieting finding by Barnard and Eyres (1979) is that 8-month-old infants of unresponsive mothers appear to give up their efforts to engage their mothers in interaction and cease to respond to any of their efforts. This reinforces the absolutely critical need to focus intervention efforts on the maternal–infant relationship. However, these efforts are not likely to be successful if the basic needs of these families are unmet and if they remain in the chaotic environment of extreme poverty. This emphasizes the need for ongoing, intensive intervention from a multidisciplinary team.

Finally, this is the period when most infants with symptomatic AIDS illness will die. Most will die in hospitals. Providers familiar to the mother and child can do much to assist staff in helping the mother to feel welcomed and valued as a participant in her child's care. Most mothers will need assistance with burial arrangements. All mothers will need the opportunity for grief counseling. With the death of her child, a mother may now terminate her contact with providers.

SUMMARY

The numbers of homeless families and families with AIDS grow each year. They present caregivers with a host of complex problems, the consequences of individual vulnerabilities interacting with poverty's environment. Effective care for these families calls for creativity, flexibility, and commitment from their providers. Such care should be family-centered, community-based, coordinated, and provided by a multidisciplinary team in an easily accessible location.

Families are the womb of society's future. When families are unable to nurture healthy, competent children, society suffers along with the individual. As Schorr (1988) notes, both the problems and their solutions are known. Skilled providers can make a difference in the lives of the acutely socially deprived and stigmatized.

References

Abernethy, V. D. (1973). Social network and response to the maternal role. *International Journal of Sociology of the Family, 3*, 86–92.

Adams, G., Adams-Taylor, S., & Pittman, K. (1989). Adolescent pregnancy and parenthood: A review of the problem, solutions, and resources. *Family Relations, 38*, 223–229.

Affleck, G., Allen, D., McGrade, B. J., & McQueeney, M. (1982). Maternal causal attributions at hospital discharge of high-risk infants. *American Journal of Mental Deficiency, 86*, 575–580.

Affleck, G., Allen, D. A., McGrade, B. J., & McQueeney, M. (1982). Maternal caretaking perceptions and reported mood disturbance at hospital discharge of a high risk infant and nine months later. *Mental Retardation, 20*, 220–224.

Affleck, G., Tennen, H., Allen, D. A., & Gershman, K. (1986). Perceived support and maternal adaptation during the transition from hospital to home care of high-risk infants. *Infant Mental Health Journal, 7*, 6–18.

Affleck, G., Tennen, H., & Gershman, K. (1985). Cognitive adaptations to high-risk infants: The search for mastery, meaning, and protection from future harm. *American Journal of Mental Deficiency, 89*, 653–656.

Affleck, G., Tennen, H., & Rowe, J. (1988). Adaptational features of mothers' risk and prevention appraisals after the birth of high-risk infants. *American Journal on Mental Retardation, 92*, 360–368.

Affleck, G., Tennen, H., Rowe, J., Roscher, B., & Walker, L. (1989). Effects of formal support on mothers' adaptation to the hospital-to-home transition of high-risk infants: The benefits and costs of helping. *Child Development, 60*, 488–501.

Ainsworth, M. D. (1964). Patterns of attachment behavior shown by the infant in interaction with his mother. *Merrill-Palmer Quarterly, 10*, 51–58.

Als, H. (1982). Toward a synactive theory of development: Promise for the assessment and support of infant individuality. *Infant Mental Health Journal, 3*, 229–243.

Als, H., & Brazelton, T. B. (1981). A new model of assessing the behavioral organization of preterm and fullterm infants. *Journal of the American Academy of Child Psychiatry, 20,* 239–263.

Als, H., Tronick, E., Lester, B. M., & Brazelton, T. B. (1979). Specific neonatal measures: The Brazelton neonatal behavior assessment scale. In J. D. Osofsky (Ed.), *Handbook of Infant Development* (pp. 185–215). New York: John Wiley & Sons.

Altemeier, W. A., O'Connor, S., Vietze, P. M., Sandler, H. M., & Sherrod, K. B. (1982). Antecedents of child abuse. *The Journal of Pediatrics, 100,* 823–829.

American Council for Drug Education. (1986). *Drugs & Pregnancy.* New York: The American Council for Drug Education.

Anderson, C. L. (1987). Assessing parenting potential for child abuse risk. *Pediatric Nursing, 13,* 323–327.

Anderson, S. A., & Fleming, W. M. (1986). Late adolescents' identity formation: Individuation from the family of origin. *Adolescence, 21,* 785–796.

Andiman, W. A. (1989). Virologic/serologic aspects of HIV infection. *Seminars in Perinatology, 13,* 16–26.

Antonucci, T. C. (1985). Social support: Theoretical advances, recent findings, and pressing issues. In I. G. Sarason & B. R. Sarason (Eds.), *Social Support: Theory, Research and Applications* (pp. 21–37). Boston: Martinus Nijhoff.

Aradine, C. R., & Ferketich, S. (1990). The psychological impact of premature birth on mothers and fathers. *Journal of Reproductive and Infant Psychology.*

Asch, S. S. (1968). Crib deaths: Their possible relationship to postpartum depression and infanticide. *Journal of the Mount Sinai Hospital New York, 35,* 214–216.

Averill, J. R. (1973). Personal control over aversive stimuli and its relationship to stress. *Psychological Bulletin, 80,* 286–303.

Avery, P., & Olson, I. M. (1987). Expanding the scope of childbirth education to meet the needs of hospitalized, high-risk clients. *Journal of Obstetric, Gynecologic, and Neonatal Nursing, 16,* 418–421.

Bakeman, R., & Brown, J. V. (1980). Early interaction: Consequences for social and mental development at three years. *Child Development, 51,* 437–447.

Baldwin, B. A. (1978). A paradigm for the classification of emotional crises: Implications for crisis intervention. *American Journal of Orthopsychiatry, 48,* 538–551.

Ballou, J. W. (1978). *The Psychology of Pregnancy.* Lexington, MA: Lexington Books.

Barden, R. C., Ford, M. E., Wilhelm, W. M., Rogers-Salyer, M., & Salyer, K. E. (1988a). The physical attractiveness of facially deformed patients before and after craniofacial surgery. *Plastic and Reconstruction Surgery, 82,* 229–235.

Barden, R. C., Ford, M. E., Wilhelm, W. M., Rogers-Salyer, M., & Salyer, K. E. (1988b). Emotional and behavioral reactions to facially deformed patients before and after craniofacial surgery. *Plastic and Reconstruction Surgery, 82,* 409–416.

Barden, R. C., Ford, M. E., Jensen, A. G., Rogers-Salyer, M., & Salyer, K. E. (1989). Effects of craniofacial deformity in infancy on the quality of mother-infant interactions. *Child Development, 60,* 819–824.

Barnard, K., & Eyres, S. J. (1979, June). *Child Health Assessment, Part 2: The First Year of Life.* (DHEW Publication No. HRA 79-25). Hyattsville, MD: U.S. Department of Health, Education, and Welfare, Public Health Service, HRA, Bureau of Health Manpower, Division of Nursing.

Barnard, K. E., & Douglas, H. B. (1983). *Child Health Assessment, Part I: A Literature Review.* Seattle: NCAST Publication.

Barnard, K. E., Bee, H. L., & Hammond, M. A. (1984). Developmental changes in maternal interactions with term and preterm infants. *Infant Behavior and Development, 7,* 101–113.

Barnett, B., & Parker, C. (1986). Possible determinants, correlates and consequences of high levels of anxiety in primiparous mothers. *Psychological Medicine, 16,* 177–185.

Barrera, M., Jr. (1981). Social support in the adjustment of pregnant adolescents. In B. H. Gottlieb (Ed.), *Social Networks and Social Support* (pp. 87–89). Beverly Hills, CA: Sage Publications.

Barrera, M., Jr. (1986). Distinctions between social support concepts, measures, and models. *American Journal of Community Psychology, 14,* 413–445.

Barsch, R. H. (1968). *The Parent of the Handicapped Child: A Study of Childrearing Practices.* Springfield, IL: Charles C Thomas.

Bassuk, E. L., & Rubin, L. (1986). Homeless children: A neglected population. *American Journal of Orthopsychiatry, 57*(2), 279–286.

Bassuk, E. L., Rubin, L., & Lauriat, A. S. (1986). Characteristics of sheltered homeless families. *American Journal of Public Health, 76*(9), 1097–1101.

Baum, P., & Dougherty, F. (1983). Drug addicted mothers' parenting and their children's development. *International Journal of Addictions, 18,* 291–302.

Beavers, J., Hampson, R. B., Hulgus, Y. F., & Beavers, W. R. (1986). Coping in families with a retarded child. *Family Process, 25,* 365–378.

Becker, P. T. (1987). Sensitivity to infant development and behavior: A comparison of adolescent and adult single mothers. *Research in Nursing & Health, 10,* 119–127.

Bee, H. L., Barnard, K. E., Eyres, S. J., Gray, C. A., Hammong, M. A., Spietz, A. L., Snyder, C., & Clark, B. (1982). Prediction of IQ and language skill from perinatal status, child performance, family characteristics, and mother-infant interaction. *Child Development, 53,* 1134–1156.

Bee, H. L., Hammond, Mary A., Eyres, S. J., Barnard, K. E., & Snyder, C. (1986). The impact of parental life change on early development of children. *Research in Nursing & Health, 9,* 65–74.

Belle, D., Longfellow, C., Makosky, V., Saunders, E., & Zelkowitz, P. (1980). Income, mothers' mental health and family functioning in a low-income population. Paper presented at the American Academy of Nursing Annual Meeting, Dallas, September 29, 1980.

Bell, R. Q. (1974). Contributions of human infants to caregiving and social interaction. In M. Lewis & L. S. Rosenblum (Eds.), *The Effect of the Infant on Its Caregiver* (pp. 1–19). New York: John Wiley & Sons.

Belsky, J. (1984). The determinants of parenting: A process. *Child Development, 55,* 83–96.

Belsky, J., Lang, M., & Huston, T. L. (1986). Sex typing and division of labor as determinants of marital change across the transition to parenthood. *Journal of Personality and Social Psychology, 50,* 517–522.

Benas, E. (1975). Residential care of the child-mother and her infant: An extended family concept. *Child Welfare, 54,* 290–294.

Benedek, T. (1959). Parenthood as a developmental phase. *Journal of the American Psychoanalytic Association, 7,* 389–417.

Benfield, D. G., Leib, S. A., & Reuter, J. (1976). Grief response of parents after referral of the critically ill newborn to a regional center. *New England Journal of Medicine, 294,* 975–978.

Bettes, B. A. (1988). Maternal depression and motherese: Temporal and intonational features. *Child Development, 59,* 1089–1096.

Bibring, G. L. (1965). Some specific psychological tasks in pregnancy and motherhood. *1 Congress International de Medecine Psychosomatique et Maternite* (pp. 21–26). Paris: Gauthier-Villars.

Bibring, G. L., Dwyer, T. F., & Valenstein, A. F. (1961). A study of the psychological processes in pregnancy and of the earliest mother-child relationship. *Psychoanalytic Study of the Child, 16,* 9–24.

Black, R., & Mayer, J. (1980). Parents with special problems: Alcohol and opiate addiction. *Child Abuse and Neglect, 4,* 45–54.

Blinick, G., Jerez, E., & Wallach, R. C. (1976). Drug addiction in pregnancy and the neonate. *American Journal of Obstetrics and Gynecology, 125,* 135–139.

Blos, P. (1962). *On Adolescence.* New York: Free Press.

Blos, P. (1979). *The Adolescent Passage.* New York: International Universities Press.

Blumberg, N. L. (1980). Effects of neonatal risk, maternal attitude, and cognitive style on early postpartum adjustment. *Journal of Abnormal Psychology, 89,* 139–150.

Bolton, F. G., Jr. (1983). *When bonding fails: Clinical assessment of high-risk families.* Beverly Hills, CA: Sage Publications.

Bornstein, M. (1985). How infant and mother jointly contribute to developing cognitive competence in the child. *Proceedings of the National Academy of Science, USA, 82,* 7473–7476.

Bosma, H. A., & Gerrits, R. S. (1985). Family functioning and identity status in adolescence. *Journal of Early Adolescence, 5,* 69–80.

Boudreaux, M. (1981). Maternal attachment of high-risk mothers with well newborns. *Journal of Obstetric, Gynecologic, and Neonatal Nursing, 10,* 366–369.

Bourne, E. (1978). The state of research on ego identity: A review and appraisal. Part I. *Journal of Youth and Adolescence, 7,* 223–251.

Bowen, M. (1978). *Family Therapy in Clinical Practice.* New York: Jason Aronson.

Bowlby, J. (1960). Grief and mourning in infancy and early childhood. *Psychoanalytic Study of the Child, 15,* 9–52.

Bowlby, J. (1969). *Attachment and Loss, vol. I. Attachment.* New York: Basic Books.

Bowlby, J. (1977). The making and breaking of affectional bonds I. Aetiology in light of attachment theory. *British Journal of Psychiatry, 130,* 201–210.

Boxill, N. A., & Beaty, A. L. (1987). *An Exploration of Mother/Child Interaction Among Homeless Women and Their Children Using a Public Night Shelter in Atlanta, Georgia.* Atlanta: Atlanta Task Force for the Homeless.

Bradley, C. F. (1983). Psychological consequences of intervention in the birth process. *Canadian Journal Behavioral Science/Revue Canienne Sciences Comportement*, *15*, 422–437.

Bradley, C. F., Ross, S. E., & Warnyca, J. (1983). A prospective study of mothers' attitudes and feelings following cesarean and vaginal births. *Birth, 10,* 79–83.

Brazelton, T. B. (1973). *Neonatal Behavioral Assessment Scale.* Philadelphia: J. B. Lippincott.

Brazelton, T. B. (1989, June 6). Single moms need caring, support. *San Francisco Chronicle*, B, p. 4.

Brazelton, T. B. (1989, June 13). Single mothers need support in childbirth. *San Francisco Chronicle*, B, p. 4.

Brazelton, T. B., Koslowski, B., & Main, M. (1974). The origins of reciprocity: The early mother-infant interaction. In M. Lewis & L. Rosenblum (Eds.), *The Effect of the Infant on Its Caregiver* (pp. 49–76). New York: John Wiley & Sons.

Bristol, M., & Gallagher, J. (1986). Research on fathers of young handicapped children. In J. Gallagher & P. Vietze (Eds.), *Families of Handicapped Persons* (pp. 81–100). Baltimore: Paul H. Brookes.

Bronfenbrenner, U. (1977). Toward an experimental ecology of human development. *American Psychologist, 32,* 513–531.

Broom, B. L. (1984). Consensus about the marital relationship during transition to parenthood. *Nursing Research, 33,* 223–228.

Brooten, D., Brown, L. P., Munro, B. H., York, R., Cohen, S. M., Roncoli, M., & Hollingsworth, A. (1988). Early discharge and specialist transitional care. *Image: Journal of Nursing Scholarship, 20,* 64–68.

Brooten, D., Kumar, S., Brown, L. P., Butts, P., Finkler, S., Bakewell-Sachs, S., Gibbons, A., & Delivoria-Papadopoulos, M. (1986). A randomized clinical trial of early hospital discharge and home follow-up of very-low-birth-weight infants. *New England Journal of Medicine, 315,* 934–939.

Brown, L. P., Brooten, D., Kumar, S., Butts, P., Finkler, S., Bakewell-Sachs, S., Gibbons, A., & Delivoria-Papadopoulos, M. (1989). A sociodemographic profile of families of low birthweight infants. *Western Journal of Nursing Research, 11*(5), 520–526.

Brown, M. A. (1986). Social support, stress, and health: A comparison of expectant mothers and fathers. *Nursing Research, 35,* 72–76.

Bucy, J. (1987). Runaway youth. (Prepared Statement). In U.S. Congress, House of Representatives, Select Committee on Children, Youth, and Families. *The Crisis in Homelessness: Effects on Children and Families.* Washington, DC: U.S. Government Printing Office.

Bumpass, L. L. (1984). Children and marital disruption: A replication and update. *Demography, 21,* 71–82.

Burns, W., & Burns, K. (1988). Parenting dysfunction in chemically dependent women. In I. J. Chasnoff (Ed.), *Drugs, Alcohol, Pregnancy and Parenting* (pp. 159–171). United Kingdom: Kluwer Academic Publishers.

Burt, M., & Glynn, T. (1976). *A Follow-up Study of Former Clients of New York City's Addiction Services Agency*, vol. 2. Bethesda, MD: Burt Associates.

Cagan, J., & Meier, P. (1983). Evaluation of a discharge planning tool for use with families of high-risk infants. *Journal of Obstetric, Gynecologic, and Neonatal Nursing, 12,* 275–281.

Caldwell, B. M. (1962). The usefulness of the critical period hypothesis in the study of filiative behavior. *Merrill-Palmer Quarterly, 8,* 229–242.

Caldwell, B. M., Hersher, L., Lipton, E. L., Richmond, J. B., Stern, G. A., Eddy, E., Drachman, R., & Rothman, A. (1963). Mother-infant interaction in mono-matric and polymatric families. *American Journal of Orthopsychiatry, 33,* 653–664.

Camp, B. W., & Morgan, L. J. (1984). Child-rearing attitudes and personality characteristics in adolescent mothers: Attitudes toward the infant. *Journal of Pediatric Psychology, 9,* 57–63.

Campbell, S. B. G. (1979). Mother-infant interaction as a function of maternal ratings of temperament. *Child Psychiatry and Human Development, 10,* 67–76.

Campbell, S. B. G., & Taylor, P. M. (1979). Bonding and attachment: Theoretical issues. *Seminars in Perinatology, 3,* 3–13.

Caplan, G. (1959). *Concepts of Mental Health and Consultation.* Washington, DC: U.S. Dept. of Health, Education, & Welfare.

Caplan, G. (1981). Mastery of stress: Psychosocial aspects. *American Journal of Psychiatry, 138,* 413–420.

Caplan, G., & Grunebaum, H. (1967). Perspectives on primary prevention. *Archives of General Psychiatry, 23,* 365–374.

Carey, W. B., & McDevitt, S. C. (1978). Revision of the infant temperament questionnaire. *Pediatrics, 61,* 735–738.

Carr, J. (1970). Mongolism: Telling the parents. *Developmental Medicine and Child Neurology, 12,* 213–221.

Carr, J. N. (1977). Psychological aspects of pregnancy, childbirth, and parenting in drug dependent women. In J. L. Rementeria (Ed.), *Drug Abuse in Pregnancy and Neonatal Effects* (pp. 82–91). St. Louis, C. V. Mosby Company.

Cavanaugh, R. M., Jr. (1986). Obtaining a personal and confidential history from adolescents. *Journal of Adolescent Health Care, 7,* 118–122.

Censullo, M. (1986). Home care of the high-risk newborn. *Journal of Obstetric, Gynecologic, and Neonatal Nursing, 15,* 146–153.

Chao, Y. M. (1979). Cognitive operations during maternal role enactment. *Maternal-Child Nursing Journal, 8,* 211–274.

Chao, Yu-Mei (Yu). (1983). Conceptual behaviour of Chinese mothers in relation to their newborn infants. *Journal of Advanced Nursing, 8,* 303–310.

Chasnoff, I. J. (1987). Perinatal effects of cocaine. *Professional Education Reprints.* White Plains, NY: March of Dimes.

Chasnoff, I. J. (1988). Cocaine: Effects on pregnancy and the neonate. In I. Chasnoff (Ed.), *Drugs, Alcohol, Pregnancy and Parenting* (pp. 97–103). United Kingdom: Kluwer Academic Publishers.

Chasnoff, I. J., Burns, W. J., Schnoll, S. H., & Burns, K. A. (1985). Cocaine use in pregnancy. *New England Journal of Medicine, 313,* 666–669.

Chasnoff, I. J., Lewis, D. E., & Squires, L. (1987). Cocaine intoxication in a breastfed infant. *Pediatrics, 80,* 836–838.

Chavez, G., Mulinare, J., & Cordero, J. F. (1989). Maternal cocaine use during early pregnancy as a risk factor for congenital urogenital anomalies. *Journal of the American Medical Association, 26,* 795–798.

Chavkin, W., Kristal, A., Seabron, C., & Guigli, P. E. (1987). The reproductive experience of women living in hotels for the homeless in New York City. *New York State Journal of Medicine, 87*(1), 10–13.

Chodorow, N. (1978). *The Reproduction of Mothering.* Berkeley, CA: University of California Press.

Cirillo, S., & Sorrentino, A. M. (1986). Handicap and rehabilitation: Two types of information upsetting family organization. *Family Process, 24,* 283–292.

Clewell, B. C., Brooks-Gunn, J., & Benasich, A. A. (1989). Evaluating child-related outcomes of teenage parenting programs. *Family Relations, 38,* 201–209.

Coalition for the Homeless. (1985). *A Crying Shame: Official Abuse and Neglect of Homeless Families.* New York: Coalition for the Homeless.

Cobb, S. (1976). Social support as a moderator of life stress. *Psychosomatic Medicine, 38,* 300–314.

Cohen, P. C. (1963). The impact of the handicapped child on the family. *Social Casework, 43*(3), 137–142.

Cohen, R. L. (1966). Pregnancy stress and maternal perceptions of infant endowment. *Journal of Mental Subnormality, 12*(22), 18–23.

Cohen, R. L. (1979). Maladaptation to pregnancy. *Seminars in Perinatology, 3,* 15–24.

Cohen, S., Mermelstein, R., Kamarck, T., & Hoberman, H. M. (1985). Measuring the functional components of social support. In I. G. Sarason & B. R. Sarason (Eds.), *Social support: Theory, Research and Applications* (pp. 73–94). Boston: Martinus Nijhoff.

Cohn, J. F., & Tronick, E. Z. (1983). Three-month-old infants' reaction to simulated maternal depression. *Child Development, 54,* 185–193.

Coley, S. B., Jr., & James, B. E. (1976). Delivery: A trauma for fathers? *Family Coordinator, 25,* 359–363.

Coll, C. T. G., Hoffman, J., & Oh, W. (1987). The social ecology and early parenting of Caucasian adolescent mothers. *Child Development, 58,* 955–963.

Colletta, N. D. (1979). Support systems after divorce: Incidence and impact. *Journal of Marriage and the Family, 41,* 837–846.

Colletta, N. D., Gregg, C. H., Hadler, S., Lee, D., & Mekelburg, D. (1980). When adolescent mothers return to school. *The Journal of School Health, 50,* 534–538.

Collins, C., Tiedje, L. B. (1988). A program for women returning to work after childbirth. *Journal of Obstetric, Gynecologic, and Neonatal Nursing, 18,* 246–253.

Colten, M. (1982). Attitudes, experiences, and self perceptions of heroin addicted mothers. *The Journal of Social Issues, 38*(2), 77–92.

Committee on Drugs. (1984). The transfer of drugs and other chemicals into the human breast milk. *Perinatal Press, 8*(5), 67–75.

Compton, P. (1989). Drug abuse: A self-care deficit. *Journal of Psychosocial Nursing, 27*(3), 22–26.

Conger, R. D., Burgess, R. L., & Barrett, C. (1979). Child abuse related to life change and perceptions of illness: Some preliminary findings. *Family Coordinator, 28,* 73–78.

Consolvo, C. A. (1986). Relieving parental anxiety in the care-by-parent unit. *Journal of Obstetric, Gynecologic, and Neonatal Nursing, 15,* 154–159.

Coopersmith, S. (1967). *The Antecedents of Self-Esteem*. San Francisco: Freeman Press.

Corbin, J. C. (1987). Women's perceptions and management of a pregnancy complicated by chronic illness. *Health Care for Women International, 8*, 317–337.

Covington, S. (1988). *The Chemically Dependent Women: Who is She?* A collection of unpublished papers. La Jolla, CA.

Cowan, P. A., & Cowan, C. P. (1988). Changes in marriage during the transition to parenthood: Must we blame the baby? In G. Y. Michaels & W. A. Goldberg (Eds.), *The Transition of Parenthood: Current Theory and Research* (p. 114–154). Cambridge, England: Cambridge University Press.

Cowie, V. (1966). Genetic counseling. *Proceedings of the Royal Society of Medicine, 59*, 149–150.

Cox, B. E., & Smith, E. C. (1982). The mother's self-esteem after a cesarean delivery. *MCN, The American Journal of Maternal Child Nursing, 7*, 309–314.

Cox, M. J., Owen, M. T., Lewis, J. M., Riedel, C., Scalf-McIver, L., & Suster, A. (1985). Intergenerational influences on the parent-infant relationship in the transition to parenthood. *Journal of Family Issues, 6*, 543–564.

Cranley, M. S. (1981a). Development of a tool for the measurement of maternal attachment during pregnancy. *Nursing Research, 30*, 281–284.

Cranley, M. S. (1981b). Roots of attachment: The relationship of parents with their unborn. *Birth Defects: Original Article Series, 20*, 59–83.

Cranley, M. S., Hedahl, K. J., & Pegg, S. H. (1983). Women's perceptions of vaginal and cesarean deliveries. *Nursing Research, 32*, 10–15.

Crawford, G. (1985). A theoretical model of support network conflict experienced by new mothers. *Nursing Research, 34*, 100–102.

Crawford, J. W. (1982). Mother-infant interaction in premature and full-term infants. *Child Development, 53*, 957–962.

Crittenden, P. M., & Bonvillian, J. D. (1984). The relationship between maternal risk status and maternal sensitivity, *American Journal of Orthopsychiatry, 54*, 250–262.

Crnic, K. A., Greenberg, M. T., Ragozin, A. S., Robinson, N. M., & Basham, R. B. (1983). Effects of stress and social support on mothers and premature and full-term infants. *Child Development, 54*, 209–217.

Crnic, K. A., Greenberg, M. T., Robinson, N. M., & Ragozin, A. S. (1984). Maternal stress and social support: Effects on the mother-infant relationship from birth to eighteen months. *American Journal of Orthopsychiatry, 54*, 224–235.

Crnic, K. A., Greenberg, M. T., & Slough, N. M. (1986). Early stress and social support influences on mothers' and high-risk infants' functioning in late infancy. *Infant Mental Health Journal, 7*, 19–33.

Crnic, K. A., Ragozin, A. S., Greenberg, M. T., Robinson, N. M., & Basham, R. B. (1983). Social interaction and developmental competence of preterm and full-term infants during the first year of life. *Child Development, 54*, 1199–1210.

Crockenberg, S. (1981). Infant irritability, mother responsiveness, and social support influences on the security of infant-mother attachment. *Child Development, 52*, 857–865.

Crockenberg, S. B. (1986). Professional support for adolescent mothers: Who gives it, how adolescent mothers evaluate it, what they prefer. *Infant Mental Health Journal, 7,* 49–56.

Cronenwett, L. R. (1982). Father participation in child care: A critical review. *Research in Nursing & Health, 5,* 63–72.

Curry, M. A. H. (1979). Contact during the first hour with the wrapped or naked newborn: Effect on maternal attachment behaviors at 36 hours and three months. *Birth and the Family Journal, 6*(4), 227–235.

Curry, M. A. (1987). Maternal behavior of hospitalized pregnant women. *Journal of Psychosomatic Obstetrics and Gynaecology, 7,* 165–182.

Curry, M. A., & Snell, B. J. (1984). *Antenatal Hospitalization: Maternal Behavior and the Family.* Final Report of Grant 1 R01 NU 00939, Nursing Research and Analysis Branch, Division of Nursing, Bureau of Health Professions, HRSA, USPHS. Portland, Oregon: Department of Family Nursing, The Oregon Health Sciences University.

Cuskey, W. R., Premkeemor, R., & Ligel, L. (1972). Survey of opiate addiction among females in the U.S. between 1950 and 1970. *Public Health Review, 1,* 8–39.

Daghestani, A. (1988). Psychological characteristics of pregnant women addicts in treatment. In I. J. Chasnoff (Ed.), *Drugs, Alcohol, Pregnancy, and Parenting* (pp. 7–16). United Kingdom: Kluwer Academic Publishers.

Damrosch, S. P., & Perry, L. A. (1989). Self-reported adjustment, chronic sorrow, and coping of parents of children with Down syndrome. *Nursing Research, 38,* 25–30.

Daniels, L. L., & Berg, C. M. (1968). The crisis of birth and adaptive patterns of parents of amputee children. *Clinical Proceedings of Children's Hospital, Washington, D.C. 24,* 108–117.

D'Arcy, E. (1968). Congenital defects: Mother's reactions to first information. *British Medical Journal, 3,* 796–798.

Darling, R. B. (1979). *Families against society: A study of reactions to children with birth defects.* Beverly Hills, CA: Sage Publications.

Davids, A., Holden, R. H., & Gray, G. B. (1963). Maternal anxiety during pregnancy and adequacy of mother and child adjustment eight months following birth. *Child Development, 34,* 993–1002.

Davidson, B., Balswick, J. O., & Halverson, C. F. (1980). Factor analysis of self-disclosure for adolescents. *Adolescence, 15,* 947–957.

Deatrick, J. A., Knafl, K. A., & Walsh, M. (1988). The process of parenting a child with a disability: Normalization through accommodations. *Journal of Advanced Nursing, 13,* 15–21.

Dehavenon, A. L. (1985). The tyranny of indifference and the reinstitutionalization of hunger, homelessness, and poor health: A study of the causes and conditions of the food emergency in 1.506 households with children in East Harlem, Brooklyn, and the Bronx in 1984. Paper prepared for the East Harlem Interfaith Welfare Committee. New York: East Harlem Interfaith Welfare Committee.

Delahunt, J. W., & Mellsop, G. (1987). Hormone changes in stress. *Stress Medicine, 3,* 123–134.

DeLozier, P. P. (1982). Attachment theory and child abuse. In C. M. Parkes & J. Stevenson-Hinde (Eds.), *The Place of Attachment in Human Behavior* (pp. 95–117). New York: Basic Books.

Deutscher, M. (1970). Brief family therapy in the course of first pregnancy: A clinical note. *Contemporary Psychoanalysis, 7*, 21–35.

Deutscher, M. (1981). Identity transformations in the course of expectant fatherhood. *Contemporary Psychoanalysis, 17*, 158–171.

Dixon, S. (1989). Effects of transplacental exposure to cocaine and methamphetamine on the neonate. *Western Journal of Medicine, 150*, 436–442.

Drake, M. E., & Ober, G. (1963). Parental medical histories of mental retardates as compared and evaluated against newborn and hospitalization records. *American Journal of Mental Deficiency, 67*, 688–690.

Drane, J. F. (1984). The defective child: Ethical guidelines for painful dilemmas. *Journal of Obstetric, Gynecologic, and Neonatal Nursing, 13*, 42–48.

Drotar, D., Baskiewicz, A., Irvin, N., Kennell, J. H., and Klaus, M. H. (1975). The adaptation of parents to the birth of an infant with a congenital malformation: A hypothetical model. *Pediatrics, 56*, 710–717.

Dunn, J. F. (1975). Consistency and change in styles of mothering. In Ciba Foundation Symposium 33, *Parent-Infant Interaction* (pp. 155–176). New York: Elsevier.

Dunst, C. J., Trivette, C. M., & Cross, A. H. (1986). Mediating influences of social support: Personal, family, and child outcomes. *American Journal of Mental Deficiency, 90*, 403–417.

Dyer, E. D. (1965). Parenthood as crisis: A re-study. In H. J. Parad (Ed.), *Crisis Intervention: Selected Readings* (pp. 312–323). New York: Family Service Association of America.

Dwyer, D. (1986). Substance abuse in pregnancy. *Public Health Currents, 26*(1), 1–6.

Easson, W. M. G. (1966). Psychopathological environmental reaction to congenital defect. *Journal of Nervous and Mental Disease, 142*, 453–459.

Easterbrooks, M. A. (1989). Quality of attachment to mother and to father: effects of perinatal risk status. *Child Development, 60*, 825–830.

Egbuonu, L., & Starfield, B. (1982). Child health and social status. *Pediatrics, 69*, 550–557.

Egeland, B., Breitenbucher, M., & Rosenberg, D. (1980). Prospective study of the significance of life stress in the etiology of child abuse. *Journal of Consulting and Clinical Psychology, 48*, 195–205.

Eldred, C., Grier, V., & Berlinger, N. (1974). Comprehensive treatment for heroin addicted mothers. *Social Casework, 55*, 1450–1477.

Elkind, D. (1980). Strategic interactions in early adolescence. In J. Adelson (Ed.), *Handbook of Adolescent Psychology* (pp. 432–444). New York: John Wiley & Sons.

Elsas, T. L. (1981). Family mental health care in the neonatal intensive care unit. *Journal of Obstetric, Gynecologic, and Neonatal Nursing, 10*, 203–206.

Elster, A. B., & Panzarine, S. (1980). Unwed teenage fathers. *Journal of Adolescent Health Care, 1*, 116–120.

Emde, R. N. (1980). Emotional availability: A reciprocal reward system for infants and parents with implications for prevention of psychosocial disorders. In P. M. Taylor (Ed.), *Parent-Infant Relationships* (pp. 87–115). New York: Grune & Stratton.

Engstrom, L., Geijerstam, N. G., Holmberg, N. G., & Uhrus, K. (1964). A prospective study of the relationship between psycho-social factors and course of pregnancy and delivery. *Journal of Psychosomatic Research, 8,* 151–155.

Enright, R. D., Shukla, D. G., & Lapsley, D. K. (1980). Adolescent egocentrism-sociocentrism and self-consciousness. *Journal of Youth and Adolescence, 9,* 101–116.

Entwisle, D. R., & Alexander, K. L. (1987). Long-term effects of cesarean delivery on parents' beliefs and children's schooling. *Developmental Psychology, 23,* 676–682.

Entwisle, D. R., & Doering, S. G. (1981). *The First Birth.* Baltimore: The Johns Hopkins University Press.

Erikson, E. H. (1959). Identity and the life cycle. *Psychological Issues, 1*(1), 5–171.

Erikson, E. H. (1968). *Identity, Youth, and Crisis.* New York: W. W. Norton.

Erickson, H., & Swain, M. A. (1982). A model for assessing potential adaptation to stress. *Research in Nursing and Health, 5,* 93–101.

Eriksson, M., Larsson, G., & Zetterstrom, R. (1978). The influence of amphetamine addiction on pregnancy and the newborn infant. *Acta Paediatrica Scandinavica, 67*(1), 95–99.

Escalona, S. K. (1982). Babies at double hazard: Early development of infants at biologic and social risk. *Pediatrics, 70*(5), 670–676.

Estrada, P., Arsenio, W. F., Hess, R. D., & Holloway, S. D. (1987). Affective quality of the mother-child relationship: Longitudinal consequences for children's school relevant cognitive functioning. *Developmental Psychology, 23*(2), 210–215.

Fanaroff, A. A., & Martin, R. J. (Eds.). (1987). *Neonatal-Perinatal Medicine* (4th ed.). St. Louis: C. V. Mosby.

Fanshel, D. (1975). Parental failure and consequences for children: The drug abusing mother whose children are in foster care. *American Journal of Public Health, 65,* 604–612.

Farber, E. A., Vaughn, B., & Egeland, B. (1981). The relationship of prenatal maternal anxiety to infant behavior and mother-infant interaction during the first six months of life. *Early Human Development, 5,* 267–277.

Fedele, N. M., Golding, E. R., Grossman, F. K., & Pollack, W. S. (1988). Psychological issues in adjustment to first parenthood. In G. Y. Michaels & W. A. Goldberg (Eds.), *The Transition to Parenthood: Current Theory and Research.* Cambridge, England: Cambridge University Press.

Fein, R. A. (1976). The first weeks of fathering: The importance of choices and supports for new parents. *Birth and the Family Journal, 3*(2), 53–57.

Feiring, D. (1976). *The Influence of the Child and Secondary Parent on Maternal Behavior: Toward a Systems View of Early Infant-Mother Attachment.* Unpublished doctoral dissertation, University of Pittsburgh, Pittsburgh. (University Microfilms No. 76-347).

Felton, G. S., & Segelman, F. B. (1978). Lamaze childbirth training and changes in belief about personal control. *Birth, 5,* 141–150.

Ferketich, S. L., & Mercer, R. T. (1989). Men's health status during pregnancy and early fatherhood. *Research in Nursing & Health, 12,* 137–148.

Ferketich, S. L., & Mercer, R. T. (1990). Effects of antepartal stress on health status during early motherhood. *Scholarly Inquiry for Nursing Practice An International Journal,* 4(2).

Field, T. (1981). Gaze behavior of normal and high-risk infants during early interactions. *Journal of the American Academy of Child Psychiatry, 20,* 308–317.

Field, T. M., Hallock, N. F., Dempsey, J. R., & Shuman, H. H. (1978). Mothers' assessments of term and pre-term infants with respiratory distress syndrome: Reliability and predictive validity. *Child Psychiatry and Human Development, 9,* 75–85.

Field, T., Sandberg, D., Garcia, R., Vega-Lahr, N., Goldstein, S., & Guy, L. (1985). Pregnancy problems, postpartum depression, and early mother-infant interactions. *Developmental Psychology, 21,* 1152–1156.

Field, T., & Vega-Lahr, N. (1984). Early interactions between infants with cranio-facial anomalies and their mothers. *Infant Behavior and Development, 7,* 527–530.

Figley, C. R. (1983). Catastrophes: An overview of family reactions. In C. R. Figley & H. I. McCubbin (Eds.), *Stress and the Family, vol. II. Coping With Catastrophe* (pp. 3–36). New York: Brunner/Mazel.

Finnegan, L. (1988). Drug addiction and pregnancy: The newborn. In I. J. Chasnoff (Ed.), *Drugs, Alcohol, Pregnancy, and Parenting* (pp. 59–71). United Kingdom: Kluwer Academic Publishers.

Finnegan, L., Schut, J., Flor, J., & Connaughton, J. (1977). Methadone maintenance and detoxification program for the opiate dependent woman during pregnancy: A comparison. In J. Rementeria, J. (Ed.), *Drug Abuse in Pregnancy and Neonatal Effects.* St. Louis: C. V. Mosby.

Fishbein, E. G. (1984). Expectant father's stress—due to the mother's expectations? *Journal of Obstetric, Gynecologic, and Neonatal Nursing, 13,* 325–328.

Fischman, S. H. (1977). Delivery or abortion in inner city adolescents. *American Journal of Orthopsychiatry, 47,* 127–133.

Flaherty, J., & Richman, J. A. (1986). Effects of childhood relationships on the adult's capacity to form social supports. *American Journal of Psychiatry, 143,* 851–855.

Flaskerud, J. H. (1987). AIDS: Psychosocial aspects. *Journal of Psychosocial Nursing, 13*(1), 2–6.

Fleming, A. S., Flett, G. L., Ruble, D. N., & Shaul, D. L. (1988). Postpartum adjustment in first-time mothers: Relations between mood, maternal attitudes, and mother-infant interactions. *Developmental Psychology, 24,* 71–81.

Fost, N. (1981). Counseling families who have a child with a severe congenital anomaly. *Pediatrics, 67,* 321–324.

Fraulino, L. J., & Simpson, B. J. (1989). The AIDS epidemic: Developing an institutional response. *Seminars in Perinatology, 13*(1), 44–48.

Frazier, D. J., & DeBlassie, R. R. (1982). A comparison of self-concept in Mexican American and non-Mexican American late adolescents. *Adolescence, 17*(66), 327–334.

Freeman, R. B., & Hall, B. (1986). *Permanent Homeless in America: Working Paper No. 2013.* Cambridge, MA: National Bureau of Economic Analysis.

Freeston, B. M. (1971). An enquiry into the effect of a spina bifida child upon a family. *Developmental Medicine and Child Neurology, 13,* 456–461.

Freitag-Koontz, M. J. (1988). Parents' grief reaction to the diagnosis of their infant's severe neurologic impairment and static encephalopathy. *Journal of Perinatal and Neonatal Nursing, 2*(2), 45–57.

Freud, S. (1937). Mourning and melancholia. In J. Rickman (Ed.), *General Selection From the Works of Sigmund Freud.* London: Hogarth Press.

Freud, S. (1959). *The Complete Psychological Works of Sigmund Freud,* vol. 20. (J. Strachey, translator) London: Hogarth Press.

Freud, A., & Burlingham, D. (1944). *Infants Without Families.* New York: International Universities Press.

Fried, P. A. (1980). Marijuana use by pregnant women: Neurobehavioral effects in neonates. *Drug and Alcohol Dependency, 6,* 415–423.

Fried, P. A., Watkinson, B., & Willan, A. (1987). Neonatal neurological status in a low risk population after prenatal exposure to cigarettes, marijuana, and alcohol. *Journal of Developmental Behavior in Pediatrics, 8,* 318–326.

Frommer, E. A., & O'Shea, G. (1973). Antenatal identification of women liable to have problems in managing their infants. *British Journal of Psychiatry, 123,* 149–156.

Futcher, J. A. (1988). Chronic illness and family dynamics. *Pediatric Nursing, 14,* 381–385.

Gabriel, A., & McAnarney, E. R. (1983). Parenthood in two subcultures: White, middle-class couples and black, low-income adolescents in Rochester, New York. *Adolescence 28*(71), 595–608.

Gara, E. O., & Tilden, V. P. (1984). Adjusted control: An explanation for women's positive perceptions of their pregnancies. *Health Care for Women International, 5,* 427–436.

Gardner, R. A. (1969). The guilt reaction of parents of children with severe physical disease. *American Journal of Psychiatry, 126,* 636–644.

Gennaro, S. (1986). Anxiety and problem-solving ability in mothers of premature infants. *Journal of Neonatal, Gynecologic, and Obstetric Nursing, 15,* 160–164.

Gennaro, S. (1988). Postpartal anxiety and depression in mothers of term and preterm infants. *Nursing Research, 37,* 82–85.

Gerzi, S., & Berman, E. (1981). Emotional reactions of expectant fathers to their wives' first pregnancy. *British Journal of Medical Psychology, 54,* 259–265.

Giblin, P. T., Poland, M. L., & Sachs, B. A. (1987). Effects of social supports on attitudes and health behaviors of pregnant adolescents. *Journal of Adolescent Health Care, 8,* 273–279.

Gilligan, C. (1982). *In a Different Voice: Psychological Theory and Women's Development.* Cambridge, MA: Harvard University Press.

Gladieux, J. D. (1978). Pregnancy—the transition to parenthood: Satisfaction with the pregnancy experience as a function of sex role conceptions, marital relationship, and social network. In W. B. Miller & L. F. Newman

(Eds.), *The First Child and Family Formation* (pp. 275-295). Chapel Hill, NC: Carolina Population Center, University of North Carolina.

Glazer, G. (1980). Anxiety levels and concerns among pregnant women. *Research in Nursing and Health, 3,* 107-113.

Gloger-Tippelt, G. (1983). A process model of the pregnancy course. *Human Development, 26,* 134-148.

Goffman, E. (1963). *Stigma.* Englewood Cliffs, NJ: Prentice Hall.

Goldberg, S. (1978). Prematurity: Effects on parent-infant interaction. *Journal of Pediatric Psychology, 3,* 137-144.

Goldberg, S. (1979). Premature birth: Consequences for the parent-infant relationship. *American Scientist, 67,* 214-220.

Goldberg, S. (1983). Parent-infant bonding: Another look. *Child Development, 54,* 1355-1382.

Gonik, B., & Creasy, R. K. (1986). Preterm labor: Its diagnosis and management. *American Journal of Obstetrics and Gynecology, 154,* 3-8.

Goodman, J. R., & Sauve, R. S. (1985). High risk infant: Concerns of the mother after discharge. *Birth, 12,* 235-242.

Gordeuk, A. (1976). Motherhood and a less than perfect child: A literary review. *Maternal-Child Nursing Journal, 5*(2), 57-68.

Gorski, P. A., Davison, M. F., & Brazelton, T. B. (1979). Stages of behavioral organization in the high-risk neonate: Theoretical and clinical considerations. *Seminars in Perinatology, 3,* 61-72.

Gould, R. L. (1972). The phases of adult life: A study in developmental psychology. *American Journal of Psychiatry, 129,* 521-531.

Govaerts, K., & Patino, E. (1981). Attachment behavior of the Egyptian mother. *International Journal of Nursing Studies, 18,* 53-60.

Grace, J. T. (1984). Does a mother's knowledge of fetal gender affect attachment? *MCN The American Journal of Maternal Child Nursing, 9,* 42-45.

Green, G. D. (1987). Lesbian mothers: Mental health considerations. In F. W. Bozett (Ed.), *Gay and Lesbian Parents* (pp. 188-198). New York: Praeger.

Greenberg, M., & Morris, N. (1974). Engrossment: The newborn's impact upon the father. *American Journal of Orthopsychiatry, 44,* 520-531.

Greene, J. G., Fox, N. A., & Lewis, M. (1983). The relationship between neonatal characteristics and three-month mother-infant interaction in high-risk infants. *Child Development, 54,* 1286-1296.

Greenland, S., Statisle, D., Brown, N., & Gross, S. J. (1982). The effects of marijuana use during pregnancy. *American Journal of Obstetrics and Gynecology, 143,* 408-410.

Griffith, D. (1988). The effects of perinatal cocaine exposure on infant neurobehavior and early maternal-infant interactions. In I. J. Chasnoff (Ed.), *Drugs, Alcohol, Pregnancy, and Parenting* (pp. 105-113). United Kingdom: Kluwer Academic Publishers.

Gross, D., Rocissano, L., & Roncoli, M. (1989). Maternal confidence during toddlerhood: Comparing preterm and fullterm groups. *Research in Nursing & Health, 12,* 1-9.

Grossman, F. K., Eichler, L. S., Winickoff, S. A., Anzalone, M. K., Gofseyeff,

M. H., & Sargent, S. P. (1980). *Pregnancy, Birth, and Parenthood*. San Francisco: Jossey-Bass, Inc., Publishers.

Hardy, J. B., & Duggan, A. K. (1988). Teenage fathers and the fathers of infants of urban, teenage mothers. *American Journal of Public Health, 78*, 919–922.

Harriman, L. C. (1983). Personal and marital changes accompanying parenthood. *Family Relations, 32*, 387–394.

Harriman, L. C. (1986). Marital adjustment as related to personal and marital changes accompanying parenthood. *Family Relations, 35*, 233–239.

Harrison, H. (1986). Neonatal intensive care: Parents' role in ethical decision making. *Birth, 13*, 165–175.

Harrison, L. L. (1989). Teaching stimulation strategies to parents of infants at high risk. *MCN, The American Journal of Maternal Child Nursing, 14*, 125.

Harrison, L. L., & Twardosz, S. (1986). Teaching mothers about their preterm infants. *Journal of Obstetric, Gynecologic, and Neonatal Nursing, 14*, 165–172.

Hart, G. (1980). Maternal attitudes in prepared and unprepared cesarean deliveries. *Journal of Obstetric, Gynecolgic, and Neonatal Nursing, 9*, 243–245.

Harvey, S. M., Carr, C., & Bermheine, S. (1989). Lesbian mothers: Health care experiences. *Journal of Nurse-Midwifery, 34*, 115–119.

Hatcher, D. L. (1976). Understanding adolescent pregnancy and abortion. *Primary Care, 3*(3), 407–425.

Haynes, W. S. (1971). Preservation of the unfit. *Medical Journal of Australia, 1*(Pt.1), 650–651.

Healey, G. W., & DeBlassie, R. R. (1974). A comparison of Negro, Anglo, and Spanish-American adolescents' self concepts. *Adolescence, 9*(33), 15–24.

Healthy Mothers, Health Babies Coalition. (1986). *Healthy Mothers, Healthy Babies: A Compendium of Program Ideas for Serving Low-Income Women*. Washington, D.C.: U.S. Dept. of Health and Human Services [Publ. No. (PHS) 86-50209].

Hein, K. (1989). *Adolescent AIDS: The Next Wave of the HIV Epidemic*. Paper presented at the Fifth Annual Pediatric AIDS Conference, September, Los Angeles, CA.

Heinicke, C. M., Beckwith, L., & Thompson, A. (1988). Early intervention in the family system: A framework and review. *Infant Mental Health Journal, 9*, 111–141.

Helfer, R. E. (1973). The etiology of child abuse. *Pediatrics, 51*(Suppl), 777–779.

Hill, R. (1965). Generic features of families under stress. In H. J. Parad (Ed.), *Crisis Intervention: Selected Readings* (pp. 32–52). New York: Family Service Associaton of America.

Hobfoll, S. E. (1985). Limitations of social support in the stress process. In I. G. Sarason & B. R. Sarason (Eds.), *Social Support: Theory, Research and Applications* (pp. 391–414). Boston: Martinus Nijhoff.

Hobbs, D. F., Jr., & Cole, S. P. (1976). Transition to parenthood: A decade replication. *Journal of Marriage and the Family, 38*, 723–731.

Hodnett, E. D., & Simmons-Tropea, D. A. (1987). The labour agentry scale: Psychometric properties of an instrument measuring control during childbirth. *Research in Nursing & Health, 10*, 301–310.

Hoeffer, B. (1981). Children's acquisition of sex-role behavior in lesbian-mother families. *American Journal of Orthopsychiatry, 51*, 536–544.

Holman, S., Berthaud, M., Sunderland, A., Moroso, G., Cancellieri, F., Mendez, H., Beller, E., & Marcel, A. (1989). Women infected with human immunodeficiency virus: Counseling and testing during pregnancy. *Seminars in Perinatology, 13*(1), 7–15.

Holmes, D. L., Nagy, J. N., Slaymaker, F., Sosnowski, R. J., Prinz, S. M., & Pasternak, J. F. (1982). Early influences of prematurity, illness, and prolonged hospitalization on infant behavior. *Developmental Psychology, 18*, 744–750.

Horan, M. L. (1982). Parental reaction to the birth of an infant with a defect: An attributional approach. *Advances in Nursing Science, 5*(1), 57–68.

House, J. S. (1981). *Work, Stress and Social Support.* Menlo Park, CA: Addison-Wesley.

Howard, J., Beckwith, L., Rodnig, C., & Kropenske, Y. (1989). The development of young children of substance abusing parents: Insights from seven years of intervention and research. *Zero to Three Bulletin of the National Center for Clinical Infant Programs, 9*(5), 8–12.

Howard, J., Kropenske, V., & Tyler, R. (1988). The long term effects on neurodevelopment in infants exposed prenatally to PCP. In D. Clout (Ed.), *Phencyclidine: An Update.* National Institute on Drug Abuse Research Monograph Series, No. 64.

Howe, J. (1980). *Nursing Care of Adolescents.* New York: McGraw-Hill.

Huckabay, L. M. D. (1987). The effect of bonding behavior of giving a mother her premature baby's picture. *Scholarly Inquiry for Nursing Practice: An International Journal, 1*, 115–129.

Hughes, D., Johnson, K., Rosenbaum, S., Simons, J., & Butler, E. (1987). *The Health of America's Children: Maternal and Child Health Data Book.* Washington, DC: Children's Defense Fund.

Hunter, R. S., Kilstrom, N., Kraybill, E. N., & Loda, F. (1978). Antecedents of child abuse and neglect in premature infants: A prospective study in newborn intensive care unit. *Pediatrics, 61*, 629–635.

Ilse, S., & Furrh, C. B. (1988). Development of a comprehensive follow-up care plan after perinatal and neonatal loss. *Perinatal and Neonatal Nursing, 2*(2), 23–33.

Institute of Medicine. (1988). *Homelessness, Health, and Human Needs.* Washington, DC: National Academy Press.

Istvan, J. (1986). Stress, anxiety, and birth outcomes: A critical review of the evidence. *Psychological Bulletin, 100*, 331–348.

Jacobs, P., & McDermott, S. (1989). Family caregiver costs of chronically ill and handicapped children: Method and literature review. *Public Health Reports, 104*, 158–163.

Janis, I. L. (1982). Decisionmaking under stress. In Goldberger, L., & Breznitz, S. (Eds.), *Handbook of Stress: Theoretical and Clinical Aspects* (pp. 69–87). New York: Free Press.

Jeffcoate, J. A., Humphrey, M. E., & Lloyd, J. K. (1979). Role perception and response to stress in fathers and mothers following pre-term delivery. *Social Sciences & Medicine, 13A*, 139–145.

Jeffree, D. M., & Cashdan, A. (1971). The home background of the severely subnormal child: A second study. *Journal of Medical Psychology, 44,* 27-33.

Jessup, M., & Green, J. (1987). Treatment of the pregnant alcohol dependent woman. *Journal of Psychoactive Drugs, 19,* 192-203.

Johns, N. (1971). Family reactions to the birth of a child with a congenital abnormality. *Medical Journal of Australia, 1*(Pt.1), 277-282.

Johnson, S. R., Smith, E. M., & Guenther, S. M. (1987). Parenting desires among bisexual women and lesbians. *Journal of Reproductive Medicine, 32,* 198.

Josten, L. (1981). Prenatal assessment guide for illuminating possible problems with parenting. *MCN, The American Journal of Maternal Child Nursing, 5,* 113-117.

Josten, L. (1982). Contrast in prenatal preparation for mothering. *Maternal-Child Nursing Journal, 11,* 65-73.

Kagan, S. L., & Seitz, V. (1988). Family support programs for new parents. In G. Y. Michaels & W. A. Goldberg (Eds.), *The Transition to Parenthood: Current Theory and Research* (pp. 311-341). Cambridge, England: Cambridge University Press.

Kantor, D., & Lehr, W. (1975). *Inside the Family: Toward a Theory of Family Process.* New York: Harper & Row.

Kaplan, D. M., & Mason, E. A. (1960). Maternal reactions to premature birth viewed as an acute emotional disorder. *American Journal of Orthopsychiatry, 30,* 539-552.

Katz, B. Z. (1989). Natural history and clinical management of the infant born to a mother with human immunodeficiency virus. *Seminars in Perinatology, 13*(1), 27-34.

Kavanaugh, K. (1988). Infants weighing less than 500 grams at birth: Providing parental support. *Perinatal Neonatal Nursing, 2,* 58-65.

Kegan, R. (1982). *The Evolving Self.* Cambridge, MA: Harvard University Press.

Keith, P. M., & Schafter, R. B. (1982). A comparison of depression among employed single-parent and married women. *Journal of Psychology, 110,* 239-247.

Kellam, S. G., Adams, R. G., Brown, C. H., & Ensminger, M. E. (1982). The long-term evolution of the family structure of teenage and older mothers. *Journal of Marriage and the Family, 44,* 539-554.

Kellam, S. G., Ensminger, M. E., & Turner, J. (1977). Family structure and mental health of children. *Archives of General Psychiatry, 34,* 1012-1022.

Kemp, V. H., & Page, C. K. (1987). Maternal prenatal attachment in normal and high-risk pregnancies. *Journal of Obstetric, Gynecologic, and Neonatal Nursing, 16,* 179-184.

Kempe, C. H., Silverman, F. N., Steele, B. B., Droegemueller, W., & Silver, H. K. (1962). The battered child syndrome. *Journal of the American Medical Association, 181,* 17-24.

Kennedy, J. F., & Keeney, V. T. (1988). The extended family revisited: Grandparents rearing grandchildren. *Child Psychiatry and Human Development, 19,* 26-35.

Kirkpatrick, M. (1987). Clinical implications of lesbian mother studies. *Journal of Homosexuality, 14,* 201-211.

Kirkpatrick, M., Smith, C., & Roy, R. (1981). Lesbian mothers and their children: A comparative survey. *American Journal of Orthopsychiatry, 51,* 545–551.

Klaus, M., Kennell, J., Plumb, N., & Zuehkle, S. (1970). Human maternal behavior at the first contact with her young. *Pediatrics, 46,* 187–192.

Koenig, B. A. (1988). Should anencephalic infants be used as organ donors? *California Nurse, 84*(2), 8–9.

Kohlberg, L. (1964). Development of moral character and moral ideology. In M. L. Hoffman & L. W. Hoffman (Eds.), *Review of Child Development Research, vol. 1* (pp. 383–431). New York: Russel Sage Foundation.

Kohlberg, L., & Gilligan, C. (1972). The adolescent as a philosopher: The discovery of self in a post-conventional world. In J. Kagan & R. Coles (Eds.), *12 to 16: Early Adolescence* (pp. 144–179). New York: W. W. Norton.

Koniak, D., Ludington-Hoe, S., Chaze, B. A., & Sachs, S. M. (1985). The impact of preterm birth on maternal perception of the neonate. *Journal of Perinatology, 5,* 29–35.

Kopala, B. (1989). Mothers with impaired mobility speak out. *MCN, The American Journal of Maternal Child Nursing, 14,* 115–119.

Korner, A. F., Brown, B. W., Jr., Dimiceli, S., Forrest, T., Stevenson, D. K., Lane, N. M., & Constantinou, J. (1989). Stable individual differences in developmentally changing preterm infants: A replicated study. *Child Development, 60,* 502–513.

Kozol, J. (1988a). *Rachel and Her Children: Homeless Families in America.* New York: Crown.

Kozol, J. (1988b). The homeless and their children—I. *The New Yorker,* January 25, 65–84.

Kronstadt, D., Oberklaid, F., Ferb, T. E., & Schwartz, J. P. (1979). Infant behavior and maternal adaptations in the first six months of life. *American Journal of Orthopsychiatry, 49,* 454–464.

Krulik, T. (1980). Successful "normalizing" tactics of parents of chronically ill children. *Journal of Advanced Nursing 5,* 573–578.

Labell, L. (1979). Wife abuse: A sociological study of battered women and their mates. *Victimology, 4,* 258–267.

Lamb, M. E. (1974). A defense of the concept of attachment. *Human Development, 17,* 376–385.

Lamb, M. E. (1982). Early contact and maternal-infant bonding: One decade later. *Pediatrics, 70,* 763–768.

Lamb, M. E. (1983). Early mother-neonate contact and the mother-child relationship. *Journal of Child Psychology and Psychiatry, 24,* 487–494.

Landesman, S. H. (1989). Human immunodeficiency virus infection in women: An overview. *Seminars in Perinatology, 13,* 2–6.

Langlois, J. H., & Swain, D. B. (1981, April). Infant physical attractiveness as an elicitor of differential parenting behaviors. Paper presented at the Society for Research in Child Development biennial meeting, Boston, MA.

LaRossa, R., & LaRossa, M. M. (1981). *Transition to Parenthood.* Beverly Hills, CA: Sage Publications.

Lavigne, J., & Ryan, M. (1979). Psychologic adjustment of siblings of children with chronic illness. *Pediatrics, 63,* 616–627.

Lawrence, S. A., & Lawrence, R. M. (1989). Knowledge and attitudes about acquired immunodeficiency syndrome in nursing and nonnursing groups. *Journal of Professional Nursing, 5*(2), 92–101.

Lawson, M., & Wilson, G. (1980). Parenting among women addicted to narcotics. *Child Welfare, 59*(2), 67–79.

Lazarus, R. S., & Folkman, S. (1984). *Stress, Appraisal, and Coping.* New York: Springer Publishing Company.

Leavitt, M. B. (1982). *Families at Risk: Primary Prevention in Nursing Practice.* Boston: Little, Brown, & Co.

Lederman, R. P. (1984a). *Psychosocial Adaptation in Pregnancy: Assessment of Seven Dimensions of Maternal Development.* Englewood Cliffs, NJ: Prentice-Hall.

Lederman, R. P. (1984b). Anxiety and conflict in pregnancy: Relationship to maternal health status. *Annual Review of Nursing Research, 2,* 27–61.

Lederman, R. P. (1986). Maternal anxiety in pregnancy: Relationship to fetal and newborn health status. *Annual Review of Nursing Research, 4,* 3–19.

Lederman, R. P., Lederman, E., Work, B. A., Jr., & McCann, D. S. (1978). The relationship of maternal anxiety, plasma catecholamines, and plasma cortisol to progress in labor. *American Journal of Obstetrics and Gynecology, 132,* 495–500.

Leif, N. (1985). The drug user as a parent. *The International Journal of the Addictions, 20,* 63–97.

Leifer, M. (1977). Psychological changes accompanying pregnancy and motherhood. *Genetic Psychology Monographs, 95,* 55–96.

Leifer, M. (1980). *Psychological Effects of Motherhood: A Study of First Pregnancy.* New York: Praeger.

Leifson, J. (1980). Handicapped children: Parental reactions and coping behaviors. Paper presented at Western Interstate Commission Higher Education, Communicating Nursing Research, 13th Annual Conference, April, 1980.

LeMasters, E. E. (1965). Parenthood as crisis. In H. J. Parad (Ed.), *Crisis Intervention: Selected Readings* (pp. 111–117). New York: Family Service Association of America.

Leonard, S. W. (1976). How first-time fathers feel toward their newborns. *MCN, The American Journal of Maternal Child Nursing, 1,* 361–365.

Lester, B. M., Hoffman, J., & Brazelton, T. B. (1985). The rhythmic structure of mother-infant interaction in term and preterm infants. *Child Development, 56,* 15–27.

Leventhal, J. M., & Sabbeth, B. F. (1986). In M. Yogman & T. B. Brazelton (Eds.), *In Support of Families.* Cambridge, MA: Harvard University Press.

Levinson, D. J., Darrow, C. N., Klein, E. B., Levinson, M. H., & McKee, B. (1978). *The Seasons of a Man's Life.* New York: Alfred A. Knopf.

Lewis, C. C. (1981). How adolescents approach decisions: Changes over grades seven to twelve and policy implications. *Child Development, 52,* 538–544.

Lewis, J. M., Owen, M. T., & Cox, M. J. (1988). The transition to parenthood: III. Incorporation of the child into the family. *Family Process, 27,* 411–421.

Lindblad-Goldberg, M., & Dukes, J. L. (1985). Social support in black, low-income, single-parent families: Normative and dysfunctional patterns. *American Journal of Orthopsychiatry, 55,* 42–58.

Lindemann, E. (1944). Symptomatology and management of acute grief. *American Journal of Psychiatry, 101,* 141–148.

Loevinger, J. (1976). *Ego Development.* San Francisco: Jossey-Bass, Inc., Publishers.

Looney, J., Oldham, D., & Blotcky, M. (1978). Assessing psychologic symptoms in adolescents. *Southern Medical Journal, 71,* 1197–1202.

Lynch, M. E. (1989). Congenital defects: Parental issues and nursing supports. *Journal of Perinatal and Neonatal Nursing, 2*(4), 53–59.

MacKeith, R. C. (1971). A new look at spina bifida aperta. *Developmental Medicine and Child Neurology, 13,* 277–278.

Macknin, M. L., Medendorp, S. V., & Maier, M. C. (1989). Infant sleep and bedtime cereal. *American Journal of Disease of the Child, 143,* 1066–1068.

MacNamara, M., & Goodavage, M. (November 27, 1988). Young and on the street. *This World, San Francisco Chronicle,* 9–10.

Maguire, D. P., & Skoolicas, S. J. (1988). Developing a bereavement follow-up program. *Journal of Perinatal and Neonatal Nursing, 2*(2), 67–77.

Majewski, J. L. (1986). Conflicts, satisfactions, and attitudes during transition to the maternal role. *Nursing Research, 35,* 10–14.

Marcia, J. E. (1980). Identity in adolescence. In J. Adelson (Ed.), *Handbook of Adolescent Psychology* (pp. 159–187). New York: John Wiley & Sons.

Marino, B. L. (1980). When nurses compete with parents. *Journal of Association for Care of Children in Hospitals, 8,* 94–98.

Marshall, R. E., & Kasman, C. (1980). Burnout in the neonatal intensive care unit. *Pediatrics, 65,* 1161–1165.

Martin, K., Katz, B., & Miller, G. (1987). AIDS and antibodies to human immunodeficiency virus (HIV) in children and their families. *Journal of Infectious Diseases, 155,* 54–59.

Martino, M. S., & Newman, M. B. (1974). Siblings of retarded children: A population at risk. *Child Psychiatry and Human Development, 4*(3), 168–178.

Marton, P., Minde, K., & Perrotta, M. (1981). The role of the father for the infant at risk. *American Journal of Orthopsychiatry, 51,* 672–679.

Marut, J. S., & Mercer, R. T. (1979). Comparison of primiparas' perceptions of vaginal and cesarean births. *Nursing Research, 28,* 260–266.

May, K. A. (1980). A typology of detachment/involvement styles adopted during pregnancy by first-time expectant fathers. *Western Journal of Nursing Research, 2,* 445–461.

May, K. A. (1982). Three phases of father involvement in pregnancy. *Nursing Research, 31,* 337–342.

May, K. A., & Sollid, D. T. (1984). Unanticipated cesarean birth from the father's perspective. *Birth, 11,* 87–95.

Mawson, D., Marks, I., Ramm, L., & Stern, R. (1981). Guided mourning for morbid grief: A controlled study. *British Journal of Psychiatry, 138,* 185–193.

McAndrew, I. (1976). Children with a handicap and their families. *Child: Care, Health, and Development, 2,* 213–237.

McCandlish, B. M. (1987). Against all odds: Lesbian mother family dynamics. In F. W. Bozett (Ed.), *Gay and Lesbian Parents* (pp. 23–36). New York: Praeger.

McChesney, K. Y. (1986a). Families: The new homeless. *Family Professional, 1*(1), 13–14.

McChesney, K. Y. (1986b). New findings on homeless families. *Family Professional, 1*(2), 12-15.

McChesney, K. Y. (1987). Paths to family homelessness. In M. J. Robertson & M. Greenblatt (Eds.), *Homelessness: The National Perspective.* New York: Plenum Press.

McClowry, S. G., Davies, E. B., May, K. A., Kulenkamp, E. J., & Martinson, I. M. (1987). The empty space phenomenon: The process of grief in the bereaved family. *Death Studies, 11,* 361-374.

McCubbin, M. A. (1989). Family stress and family strengths: A comparison of single- and two-parent families with handicapped children. *Research in Nursing & Health, 12,* 101-110.

McGonigel, M. (1988). *Families Meeting on Pediatric AIDS.* Washington, DC: Association for the Care of Children's Health.

McKeever, P. (1983). Siblings of chronically ill children: A literature review with implications for research and practice. *American Journal of Orthopsychiatry, 53,* 281-289.

McLanahan, S., & Adams, J. (1987). Parenthood and psychological well-being. *Annual Review of Immunology, 5,* 237-257.

McLanahan, S., & Booth, K. (1989). Mother-only families: Problems, prospects, and politics. *Journal of Marriage and the Family, 51,* 557-580.

McLanahan, S. S., Wedemeyer, N. V., & Adelberg, T. (1981). Network structure, social support, and psychological well-being in the single-parent family. *Journal of Marriage and The Family, 43,* 601-612.

Mechanic, D. (1974). Social structure and personal adaptation: Some neglected dimensions. In G. V. Coelho, D. A. Hamburg, & J. E. Adams (Eds.), *Coping and Adaptation* (pp. 32-44). New York: Basic Books.

Melton, G. B. (1989). Ethical and legal issues in research and intervention. *Journal of Adolescent Health Care, 10*(3, Suppl.), 365-445.

Meltzoff, A. N., & Moore, M. K. (1983). Newborn infants imitate adult facial gestures. *Child Development, 54,* 702-709.

Menninger, K. A. (1954a). Psychological aspects of the organism under stress. Part I, the homeostatic regulatory function of the ego. *Journal of the American Psychoanalytic Association, 2,* 67-106.

Menninger, K. A. (1954b). Psychological aspects of the organism under stress, part II. Regulatory devices of the ego under major stress. *Journal of the American Psychoanalytic Association, 2,* 280-310.

Mercer, R. T. (1973). *Responses of Five Multigravidae to the Event of the Birth of an Infant with a Defect.* Unpublished dissertation, University of Pittsburgh.

Mercer, R. T. (1974). Mothers' responses to their infants with defects. *Nursing Research, 23,* 133-137.

Mercer, R. T. (1975). Responses of mothers to the birth of an infant with a defect. In *ANA Clinical Sessions 1974, San Francisco* (pp. 340-349). New York: Appleton-Century-Crofts.

Mercer, R. T. (1977a). *Nursing Care For Parents at Risk.* Thorofare, NJ: C. B. Slack, Inc.

Mercer, R. T. (1977b). Postpartum: Illness and the acquaintance-attachment process. *American Journal of Nursing, 77,* 1174-1178.

Mercer, R. T. (1979). *Perspectives on Adolescent Health Care.* Philadelphia: J. B. Lippincott.

Mercer, R. T. (1980). Teenage motherhood: The first year. *Journal of Obstetric, Gynecologic, and Neonatal Nursing, 9,* 16–27.

Mercer, R. T. (1981a). A theoretical framework for studying factors that impact on the maternal role. *Nursing Research, 30,* 73–77.

Mercer, R. T. (1981b). The nurse and maternal tasks of early postpartum. *MCN, The American Journal of Maternal Child Nursing, 6,* 341–345.

Mercer, R. T. (1983). Parent-infant attachment. In L. J. Sonstegard, K. M. Kowalski, & B. Jennings (Eds.) *Women's Health, vol. II. Childbearing* (pp. 17–42). New York: Grune & Stratton.

Mercer, R. T. (1984). Health of the children of adolescents. In E. R. McAnarney (Ed.), *The Adolescent Family* (pp. 60–71). Columbus, OH: Ross Laboratories.

Mercer, R. T. (1985a). The process of maternal role attainment over the first year. *Nursing Research, 34,* 198–204.

Mercer, R. T. (1985b). The relationship of the birth experience to later mothering behavior. *Journal of Nurse Midwifery, 30,* 204–211.

Mercer, R. T. (1985c). The relationship of age and other variables to gratification in mothering. *Health Care for Women International, 6,* 295–308.

Mercer, R. T. (1986a). *First-Time Motherhood: Experiences From Teens to Forties.* New York: Springer Publishing Co.

Mercer, R. T. (1986b). The relationship of developmental variables to maternal behavior. *Research in Nursing & Health, 9,* 25–33.

Mercer, R. T. (1986c). Predictors of maternal role attainment at one year postbith. *Western Journal of Nursing Research, 8*(1), 9–32.

Mercer, R. T., & Ferketich, S. L. (1988). Stress and social support as predictors of anxiety and depression during pregnancy. *Advances in Nursing Science, 10*(2), 26–39.

Mercer, R. T., & Ferketich, S. L. (1990a). Predictors of parental attachment during early parenthood. *Journal of Advanced Nursing, 15,* 268–280.

Mercer, R. T., & Ferketich, S. L. (1990b). Predictors of family functioning eight months following birth. *Nursing Research, 39,* 76–82.

Mercer, R. T., & Ferketich, S. L., DeJoseph, J., May, K. A., & Sollid, D. (1988). Effect of stress on family functioning during pregnancy. *Nursing Research, 37,* 268–275.

Mercer, R. T., & Ferketich, S. L., May, K. A., DeJoseph, J., & Sollid, D. (1987). *Antepartum Stress: Effect on Family Health and Functioning.* Final Report of Project Supported by Grant Number R01 NR 01064, Center for Nursing Research, National Institutes of Health. San Francisco: Dept. of Family Health Care Nursing, University of California, San Franciso.

Mercer, R. T., & Ferketich, S. L., May, K., DeJoseph, J., & Sollid, D. (1988). Further exploration of maternal and paternal fetal attachment. *Research in Nursing & Health, 11,* 83–95.

Mercer, R. T., Hackley, K. C., & Bostrom, A. (1982). *Factors Having an Impact on Maternal Role Attainment the First Year of Motherhood.* Final report of project supported by grant number MC-R-060435, Maternal and Child Health

(Social Security Act, Title V). San Francisco: Department of Family Health Care Nursing, University of California, San Francisco.

Mercer, R. T., Hackley, K. C., & Bostrom, A. (1983). Relationship of psychosocial and perinatal variables to perception of childbirth. *Nursing Research, 32,* 202–207.

Mercer, R. T., Hackley, K. C., & Bostrom, A. (1984a). Adolescent motherhood comparison of outcome with older mothers. *Journal of Adolescent Health Care, 5,* 7–13.

Mercer, R. T., Hackley, K. C., & Bostrom, A. (1984b). Social support of teenage mothers. *March of Dimes Birth Defects Foundation Birth Defects: Original Article Series, 20*(5), 245–279.

Mercer, R. T., May, K. A., Ferketich, S., & DeJoseph, J. (1986). Theoretical models for studying the effect of antepartum stress on the family. *Nursing Research, 35,* 339–346.

Mercer, R. T., Nichols, E. G., & Doyle, G. C. (1989). *Transitions in a Woman's Life: Major Life Events in Developmental Context.* New York: Springer Publishing Co.

Meyer, D. (1986). Fathers of handicapped children. In R. Fewell & P. Vadasy (Eds.), *Families of Handicapped Children* (pp. 35–73). Austin, TX: Pro-Ed.

Miller, B. C., & Sollie, D. L. (1980). Normal stresses during the transition to parenthood. *Family Relations, 29,* 459–465.

Millor, G. K. (1981). A theoretical framework for nursing research in child abuse and neglect. *Nursing Research, 30,* 78–83.

Minde, K. K., Marton, P., Manning, D., & Hines, B. (1980). Some determinants of mother-infant interaction in the premature nursery. *Journal of the American Academy of Child Psychiatry, 19,* 1–21.

Minde, K., Perrotta, M., & Marton, P. (1985). Maternal caretaking and play with full-term and premature infants. *Journal of Child Psychology & Psychiatry, 26,* 231–244.

Mishel, M. H. (1988). Uncertainty in illness. *Image: Journal of Nursing Scholarship, 20,* 225–232.

Mishel, M. H., & Braden, C. J. (1987). Uncertainty: A mediator between support and adjustment. *Western Journal of Nursing Research, 9*(1), 43–57.

Mishel, M. H., & Braden, C. J. (1988). Finding meaning: Antecedents of uncertainty in illness. *Nursing Research, 37,* 98–103.

Mitchell, J. J. (1976). Adolescent intimacy. *Adolescence, 11*(42), 275–280.

Mitchell, J. (1989, September). *The Natural History of AIDS in Women and in Pregnancy.* Paper presented at the Fifth Annual National Pediatric AIDS Conference, Los Angeles, CA.

Moise, R., Reed, B., & Connell, C. (1981). Women in drug abuse treatment programs: Factors that influence retention at very early and late stages in two treatment modalities. *International Journal of the Addictions, 16,* 1295–1300.

Molnar, J., & Klein, T. (1988). *Home is Where the Heart is: The Crisis of Homeless Children and Families in New York City.* New York: Bank Street College of Education.

Mondonaro, J. (1977). Women: Pregnancy, children, and addiction. *Journal of Psychedelic Drugs, 9,* 56–67.

Monsen, R. (1986). Phases in the caring relationship: From adversary to ally to coordinator. *MCN, The American Journal of Maternal Child Nursing, 11,* 316–318.

Moreno, C. A. (1989). Utilization of medical services by single-parent and two-parent families. *Journal of Family Practice, 28,* 194–199.

Morgan, B. S., & Barden, M. E. (1985). Unwed and pregnant: Nurses' attitudes toward unmarried mothers. *MCN, The American Journal of Maternal Child Nursing, 10,* 114–117.

Morrison, C. (1987). Establishing a therapeutic environment: Institutional resources. In J. Durham & F. Cohen (Eds.), *The Person with AIDS; Nursing Perspectives* (pp. 110–125). New York: Springer Publishing Co.

Moynihan, D. P. (1986). *Nation and family.* San Diego: Harcourt, Brace, Jovanovich.

Murphy, A., & Pueschel, S. M. (1975). Early intervention with families of newborns with Down's syndrome. *Maternal-Child Nursing Journal, 4*(1), 1–7.

Murphy, L. B. (1962). *The Widening World of Childhood.* New York: Basic Books.

Murphy, M. A. (1982). The family with a handicapped child: A review of the literature. *Developmental and Behavioral Pediatrics, 3*(2), 73–82.

Nathanson, M., Baird, A., & Jemail, J. (1986). Family functioning and the adolescent mother: A systems approach. *Adolescence, 21*(84), 827–841.

National Center for Health Statistics. (1988). Births, marriages, divorces, and deaths for 1987. *NCHS Monthly Vital Statistics Report, 36*(12), 1.

National Center for Health Statistics. (July, 1988). Advance report of final natality statistics, 1986. *NCHS Monthly Vital Statistics Report, 37*(3, Suppl.), 7.

National Center for Health Statistics. (June, 1989). Advance report of final natality statistics, 1987. *Monthly Vital Statistics Report, 38*(3, Suppl.), 1–8.

National Committee for Prevention of Child Abuse. (March, 1989). *Child Abuse Fatalities Continue to Rise: The Results of the 1988 Annual Fifty State Survey.* Chicago: National Committee for Prevention of Child Abuse Publications.

Newman, B. M. (1979). Coping and adaptation in adolescence. *Human Development, 22,* 255–262.

Newman, L. F. (1980). Parents' perceptions of their low birth weight infants. *Paediatrician, 9,* 182–190.

Newton, L. R. (1983). Helping parents cope with infant crying. *Journal of Obstetric, Gynecologic, and Neonatal Nursing, 12,* 199–204.

Norbeck, J. S. (1981). Social support: A model for clinical research and application. *Advances in Nursing Science, 3*(4), 43–59.

Norbeck, J. S., & Sheiner, M. (1982). Sources of social support related to single-parent functioning. *Research in Nursing & Health, 5,* 3–12.

Norbeck, J. S., & Tilden, V. P. (1983). Life stress, social support, and emotional disequilibrium in complications of pregnancy: A prospective, multivariate study. *Journal of Health and Social Behavior, 24,* 30–46.

Novello, A. (1989). *Women's Issues and HIV Infection.* Paper presented at the Fifth Annual National Pediatric AIDS Conference, September, Los Angeles, CA.

Nuckolls, K. B., Cassel, J., & Kaplan, B. H. (1972). Psychosocial assets, life crisis and the prognosis of pregnancy. *Journal of Epidemiology, 95,* 431–441.

Nurcombe, B., Howell, D. C., Rauh, V. A., Teti, D. M., Ruoff, P., & Brennan, J. (1984). An intervention program for mothers of low-birthweight infants: Preliminary results. *Journal of the American Academy of Child Psychiatry, 23*, 319-325.

Nurius, P. S. (1989). The self-concept: A social-cognitive update. *Social Casework: The Journal of Contemporary Social Work*, May, 285-294.

Olds, D. L., Henderson, C. R., Jr., Tatelbaum, R., & Chamberlin, R. (1986a). Improving the delivery of prenatal care and outcomes of pregnancy: a randomized trial of nurse home visitation. *Pediatrics, 77*, 16-28.

Olds, D. L., Henderson, C. R., Jr., Chamberlin, R., & Tatelbaum, R. (1986b). Preventing child abuse and neglect: a randomized trial of nurse home visitation. *Pediatrics, 78*, 65-78.

Olds, D. L., Henderson, C. R., Jr., Tatelbaum, R., & Chamberlin, R. (1988). Improving the life-course development of socially disadvantaged mothers: A randomized trial of nurse home visitation. *American Journal of Public Health, 78*, 1436-1445.

Oleske, J. (1987). Natural history of HIV infection II. *Report of the Surgeon General's Workshop on Children with HIV Infection and Their Families* (DHHS Publication No. HRS-D-MC 87-1). Washington, DC: Department of Health and Human Services.

Oleske, J. (1989, September). *Medical Management of Child with AIDS.* Paper presented at the Fifth Annual National Pediatric AIDS Conference, Los Angeles, CA.

Orlosky, J. L. (1976). Intimacy status: Relationship to interpersonal perception. *Journal of Youth and Adolescence, 5*, 73-88.

Orlofsky, J. L., Marcia, J. E., & Lesser, I. M. (1973). Ego identity status and the intimacy versus isolation crisis of young adulthood. *Journal of Personality and Social Psychology, 27*, 211-219.

Olshansky, S. (1962). Chronic sorrow: A response to having a mentally defective child. *Social Casework, 43*, 190-193.

Padawer, J. A., Fagan, C., Janoff-Bulman, R. N., & Strickland, B. R. (1988). Women's psychological adjustment following emergency cesarean versus vaginal delivery. *Psychology of Women Quarterly, 12*, 25-34.

Palfrey, J. S., Walker, D. K., Butler, J. A., & Singer, J. D. (1989). Patterns of response in families of chronically disabled children: An assessment in five metropolitan school districts. *American Journal of Orthopsychiatry, 59*, 94-104.

Palkovitz, R. (1985). Father's birth attendance, early contact, and extended contact with their newborns: A critical review. *Child Development, 56*, 392-406.

Palkovitz, R. (1988). Sources of father-infant bonding beliefs: Implications for childbirth educators. *Maternal-Child Nursing Journal, 17*, 101-113.

Parkes, C. M. (1970). The first year of bereavement. *Psychiatry, 33*, 444-467.

Parkes, C. M. (1972). *Bereavement: Studies of Grief in Adult Life.* New York: International Universities Press.

Patterson, J. M., & McCubbin, H. I. (1983). Chronic illness: Family stress and coping. In C. R. Figley & H. I. McCubbin (Eds.), *Stress and the Family: vol. II. Coping with Catastrophe* (pp. 21-36). New York: Brunner/Mazel.

Pearlin, L. I., & Schooler, C. (1978). The structure of coping. *Journal of Health and Social Behavior, 19*, 2–21.

Pearlin, L. I., Lieberman, M. A., Menaghan, E. G., & Mullan, J. T. (1981). The stress process. *Journal of Health and Social Behavior, 22*, 337–356.

Pederson, D. R., Bento, S., Chance, G. W., Evans, B., & Fox, A. M. (1987). Maternal emotional responses to preterm birth. *American Journal of Orthopsychiatry, 57*, 15–21.

Pennington, S. B. (1987). Children of lesbian mothers. In F. W. Bozett (Ed.), *Gay and Lesbian Parents* (pp. 58–74). New York: Praeger.

Penticuff, J. H. (1988). Neonatal intensive care: Parental prerogatives. *Journal of Perinatal and Neonatal Nursing, 1*(3), 77–86.

Perez, R. (1980). Care for parents. *American Journal of Nursing, 80*, 1343.

Pernoll, M. L., Benda, G. I., Babson, G. I., & Simpson, K. (1986). *Diagnosis and Management of the Fetus and Neonate At Risk* (5th ed.). St. Louis: C. V. Mosby.

Perry, S. E., Parer, J. T., & Inturrisi, M. (1986). Intrauterine transfusion for severe isoimmunization. *MCN, The American Journal of Maternal Child Nursing, 11*, 182–189.

Person, P., Retka, R., & Woodward, J. (1977). *A Method for Estimating Heroin Use Prevalence*. Rockville, MD: National Institute of Drug Abuse.

Phillip, C. (1983). Parental perceptions of children who were hospitalized in neonatal intensive care units. *Child Psychiatry and Human Development, 14*, 76–86.

Phillips, K. (1986). Neonatal drug addicts. *Nursing Times, 43*, 36–38.

Pianta, R. C., Sroufe, L. A., & Egeland, B. (1989). Continuity and discontinuity in maternal sensitivity at 6, 24, and 42 months in a high-risk sample. *Child Development, 60*, 481–487.

Pies, C. (1985). *Considering parenthood: A workbook for lesbians*. San Francisco: Spinster's Ink.

Pittman, K., & Adams, G. (1988, January/March). *Teenage Pregnancy: An Advocate's Guide to the Numbers*. Washington, DC: Children's Defense Fund.

Plunkett, J. W., Meisels, S. J., Stiefel, G. S., Pasick, P. L., & Roloff, D. W. (1986). Patterns of attachment among preterm infants of varying biological risk. *Journal of the American Academy of Child Psychiatry, 25*, 794–800.

Poole, C. J., & Hoffman, M. (1981). Mothers of adolescent mothers: How do they cope. *Pediatric Nursing, 7*, 28–31.

Porter, R. H., Cernoch, J. M., & Perry, S. (1983). The importance of odors in mother-infant interactions. *Maternal-Child Nursing Journal, 12*, 147–154.

Presser, H. B. (1989). Some economic complexities of child care provided by grandmothers. *Journal of Marriage and the Family, 51*, 581–591.

Pridham, K. F. (1981). Infant feeding and anticipatory care: Supporting the adaptation of parents to their new babies. *Maternal-Child Nursing Journal, 10*, 111–126.

Protinsky, H., Sporakowski, M., & Atkins, P. (1982). Identity formation: Pregnant and non-pregnant adolescents. *Adolescence, 17*(65), 73–80.

Provence, S., & Lipton, R. C. (1962). *Infants in Institutions*. New York: International Universities Press.

Radloff, L. (1977). The CES-D scale: A self-report depression scale for research in the general population. *Journal of Applied Psychological Measurement, 1*, 385–401.

Raff, B. S. (1986). Introduction: Nursing care of high-risk infants and their families. *Journal of Obstetric, Gynecologic, and Neonatal Nursing, 15*, 141.

Ramey, C. T., Sparling, J. J., Bryant, D. M., & Waski, B. H. (1982). Primary prevention of developmental retardation during infancy. *Prevention in Human Services, 1*(4), 61–83.

Ramsey, C. N., Jr., Abell, T. D., & Baker, L. C. (1986). The relationship between family functioning, life events, family structure, and the outcome of pregnancy. *Journal of Family Practice, 22*, 521–527.

Randell, B. P. (1988). *Older Primiparous Women: The Evolution of Maternal Self Perception Within the Context or Mother-Daughter and Spousal Relationships.* Unpublished dissertation, University of California, San Francisco.

Randolph, E. M., & Dye, C. A. (1981). The peter pan profile: Development of a scale to measure reluctance to grow up. *Adolescence, 16*(64), 841–850.

Rankin, E. A. D., Campbell, N. D., & Soeken, K. L. (1985). Adaptation to parenthood: Differing expectations of social supports for mothers versus fathers. *Journal of Primary Prevention, 5*, 145–153.

Rapoport, L. (1965). The state of crisis: Some theoretical considerations. In H. J. Parad (Ed.), *Crisis Intervention: Selected Readings* (pp. 22–31). New York: Family Service Association of America.

Rich, O. J. (1973). Temporal and spatial experience as reflected in the verbalizations of multiparous women during labor. *Maternal-Child Nursing Journal, 2*, 239–325.

Rich, O. J. (1978). The sociogram: A tool for depicting support in pregnancy. *Maternal-Child Nursing Journal, 7*(1), 1–9.

Richardson, P. (1987a). Women's important relationships during pregnancy and the preterm labor event. *Western Journal of Nursing Research, 9*(2), 203–222.

Richardson, P. (1987b). Psychosocial factors signaling risk for preterm labor: An emerging model. *Search Improved Nursing Care Through Research, 11*(2), 4–5.

Riddle, I. (1973). Caring for children and their families. In E. Anderson et al., (Eds.), *Current Concepts in Clinical Nursing*, vol. 4 (pp. 85–94). St. Louis: C. V. Mosby.

Rivara, F. P., Sweeney, P. J., & Henderson, B. F. (1986). Black teenage fathers: What happens when the child is born? *Pediatrics, 78*, 151–158.

Rivera, R. R. (1987). Legal issues in gay and lesbian parenting. In F. W. Bozett (Ed.), *Gay and Lesbian Parenting* (pp. 199–227). New York: Praeger.

Robinson, B. E. (1988). Teenage pregnancy from the father's perspective. *American Journal of Orthopsychiatry, 58*, 46–51.

Robson, K. S., & Moss, H. A. (1970). Patterns and determinants of maternal attachment. *Journal of Pediatrics, 77*, 967–985.

Rodgers, R. H. (1964). Toward a theory of family development. *Journal of Marriage and the Family, 26*, 262–270.

Roelofse, R., & Middleton, M. R. (1985). The family functioning in adolescence questionnaire: A measure of psychosocial family health during adolescence. *Journal of Adolescence, 8*, 33–45.

Rogers, M. (1989, September). *Epidemiology and Transmission of HIV in Women and*

Children. Paper presented at the Fifth Annual National Pediatric AIDS Conference, Los Angeles, CA.

Rose, M. H., & Thomas, R. B. (1987). *Children With Chronic Conditions*. New York: Grune & Stratton.

Rosen, E. L. (1975). Concerns of an obstetric patient experiencing long-term hospitalization. *JOGN Nursing, 4*(2), 15–19.

Rosenbaum, M. (1979). Difficulty in taking care of business: Women addicts as mothers. *American Journal of Drug and Alcohol Abuse, 6,* 431–446.

Rosenberg, M. (1965). *Society and the Adolescent Self Image.* Princeton, NJ: Princeton University Press.

Rosenthal, D. A., Gurney, R. M., & Moore, S. M. (1981). From trust to intimacy: A new inventory for examining Erikson's stages of psychosocial development. *Journal of Youth and Adolescence, 10,* 525–537.

Rosenthal, M. K. (1973). Attachment and mother-infant interaction: Some research impasse and a suggested change in orientation. *Journal of Child Psychology and Psychiatry, 14,* 201–207.

Ross, A. O. (1964). *The Exceptional Child in the Family.* New York: Grune & Stratton.

Rowe, I., & Marcia, J. E. (1980). Ego identity status, formal operations, and moral development. *Journal of Youth and Adolescence, 9,* 87–99.

Rozansky, G. I., & Linde, L. M. (1971). Psychiatric study of parents of children with cyanotic congenital heart disease. *Pediatrics, 48,* 450–451.

Rubin, R. (1963). Maternal touch. *Nursing Outlook, 11,* 828–831.

Rubin, R. (1964). Behavioral definitions in nursing therapy. *Conference on Maternal and Child Nursing: Current Concepts in Nursing Care.* Columbus, OH: Ross Laboratories.

Rubin, R. (1967). Attainment of the maternal role: Part I. Processes. *Nursing Research, 16,* 237–245.

Rubin, R. (1975). Maternal tasks in pregnancy. *Maternal-Child Nursing Journal, 4,* 143–153.

Rubin, R. (1977). Binding-in in the postpartum period. *Maternal-Child Nursing Journal, 6,* 65–75.

Rubin, R. (1984). *Maternal Identity and the Maternal Experience.* New York: Springer Publishing Co.

Ruggles, P., & Marton, W. P. (1986). *Measuring the Size of Characteristics of the Underclass: How Much Do We Know?* Washington, DC: Urban Institute.

Russell, C. S. (1974). Transition to parenthood: Problems and gratifications. *Journal of Marriage and the Family, 36,* 294–301.

Sabbeth, B. F., & Leventhal, J. M. (1984). Marital adjustment to chronic childhood illness: A critique of the literature. *Pediatrics, 73,* 762–768.

Sameroff, A. J., Seifer, R., & Elias, P. K. (1982). Sociocultural variability in infant temperament ratings. *Child Development, 53,* 164–173.

Sandelowski, M., & Bustamante, R. (1986). Cesarean birth outside the natural childbirth culture. *Research in Nursing & Health, 9,* 81–88.

Sander, L. W. (1962). Issues in early mother-child interaction. *Journal of the American Academy of Child Psychiatry, 1,* 141–166.

Sandler, I. N. (1980). Social support resources, stress, and maladjustment of poor children. *American Journal of Community Psychology, 8*, 41–52.

Sandler, I. N., & Lakey, B. (1982). Locus of control as a stress moderator: The role of control perceptions and social support. *American Journal of Community Psychology, 10*, 65–80.

Sarason, I. G., & Sarason, B. R. (1985). Social support—insights from assessment and experimentation. In I. G. Sarason & B. R. Sarason (Eds.), *Social Support: Theory, Research, and Applications* (pp. 39–50). Boston: Martinus Nijhoff.

Schilder, P. (1950). *The Image and Appearance of the Human Body.* New York: International Universities Press.

Schinke, S. P., Gilchrist, L. D., & Small, R. W. (1979). Preventing unwanted teenage pregnancy: A cognitive-behavioral approach. *American Journal of Orthopsychiatry, 49*, 81–88.

Schorr, L. B. (1988). *Within Our Reach: Breaking the Cycle of Disadvantage.* New York: Doubleday.

Schraeder, B. D. (1980). Attachment and parenting despite lengthy intensive care. *MCN, The American Journal of Maternal Child Nursing, 5*, 37–41.

Schultz, J. R. (1984). Psychological aspects of birth defects involving the genitals. *Feelings & Their Medical Significance, 26*(1), 1–4.

Selye, H. (1982). History and present status of the stress concept. In L. Goldberger & S. Breznitz (Eds.), *Handbook of Stress* (pp. 7–17). New York: Free Press.

Septimus, A. (1989). Psycho-social aspects of caring for families of infants infected with human immunodeficiency virus. *Seminars in Perinatology, 13*, 49–54.

Setoguchi, Y. (1968). The team approach to the limb-deficient child. *Clinical Proceedings of Children's Hospital, Washington, D.C., 24*, 127–141.

Shapiro, J. (1989). Stress, depression, and support group participation in mothers of developmentally delayed children. *Family Relations, 38*, 169–173.

Shelton, T. L., Jeppson, E. S., & Johnson, B. H. (1987). *Family-Centered Care for Children With Special Health Care Needs.* Washington, DC: Association for the Care of Children's Health.

Shereshefsky, P. M., & Yarrow, L. J. (1973). *Psychological Aspects of a First Pregnancy and Early Postnatal Adaptation.* New York: Raven Press.

Sherwen, L. N. (1987). *Psychosocial Dimensions of the Pregnant Family.* New York: Springer Publishing Co.

Sigman, M., Cohen, S. E., Beckwith, L., & Parmelee, A. H. (1981). Social and familial influences on the development of preterm infants. *Journal of Pediatric Psychology, 6*, 1–13.

Silverman, P. R. (1982). Transitions and models of intervention. *Annals of the American Academy of Political and Social Science, 464*, 174–187.

Simonds, M. P., & Simonds, J. F. (1981). Relationship of maternal parenting behaviors to preschool children's temperament. *Child Psychiatry and Human Development, 12*, 19–31.

Slesinger, D. P. (1981). *Mothercraft and Infant Health.* Lexington, MA: Lexington Books, D. C. Heath.

Smilkstein, G., Helsper-Lucas, A., Ashworth, C., Montano, D., & Pagel, M. (1984). Prediction of pregnancy complications: An application of the biopsychosocial model. *Social Science Medicine, 18*, 315–321.

Smith, L. (1983). A conceptual model of families incorporating an adolescent mother and child into the household. *Advances in Nursing Science, 6*(1), 45–60.

Smith, L., & Hagen, V. (1984). Relationship between the home environment and sensorimotor development of down syndrome and nonretarded infants. *American Journal of Mental Deficiency, 89*, 124–132.

Smith, R. (1979). The fetal alcohol syndrome. *Hospital Practice, 5*(6), 121–128.

Smoller, J., & Ooms, T. (1987). *Young Unwed Fathers: Research Review, Policy Dilemmas and Options.* Rockville, MD: Shared Resource Center.

Snyder, D. J. (1988). Peer group support for high-risk mothers. *MCN, The American Journal of Maternal Child Nursing, 13*, 114–117.

Sokol, R. J., Rosen, M. G., Stojkov, J., & Chik, L. (1977). Clinical application of high-risk scoring on an obstetric service. *American Journal of Obstetrics and Gynecology, 28*, 652–661.

Spielberger, C., Gorsuch, R., Lushene, R., Vagg, P. R., & Jacobs, G. A. (1983). *The State-Trait Anxiety Inventory.* Palo Alto, CA: Consulting Psychologists Press.

Speraw, S. (1987). Adolescents' perceptions of pregnancy: A cross-cultural perspective. *Western Journal of Nursing Research, 9*(2), 180–202.

Spietz, A. (1986, June). Teenage moms. *NCAST (Nursing Child Assessment Satellite Training) National News, 2*(3), 5–6.

Spohr, H., & Steinhausen, H. (1984). Clinical psychopathological and developmental aspects in children with the fetal alcohol syndrome: A four year follow-up study. In *CIBA Foundation Symposium 105, Mechanisms of Alcohol Damage in Utero* (pp. 197–217). London: Pitman Press.

Sroufe, L. A., & Waters, E. (1977). Attachment as an organizational construct. *Child Development, 48*, 118–199.

Stainton, M. C. (1985a). The fetus: A growing member of the family. *Family Relations, 34*, 321–326.

Stainton, M. C. (1985b). *Origin of Attachment: Culture and Cue Sensitivity.* Unpublished doctoral dissertation, University of California, San Francisco.

Stemp, P. S., Turner, R. J., & Noh, S. (1986). Psychological distress in the postpartum period: The significance of social support. *Journal of Marriage and the Family, 48*, 271–277.

Stevens, P. E., & Hall, J. M. (1988). Stigma, health beliefs, and experiences with health care in lesbian women. *Image, Journal of Nursing Scholarship, 20*, 69–73.

Stullenbarger, B., Norris, J., Edgil, A. E., & Prosser, M. J. (1987). Family adaptation to cystic fibrosis. *Pediatric Nursing, 13*, 29–31.

Szajnberg, N., Ward, M. J., Krauss, A., & Kessler, D. B. (1987). Low birthweight prematures: Preventive intervention and maternal attitude. *Child Psychiatry and Human Development, 17*, 152–165.

Taylor, S. E. (1983). Adjustment to threatening events. *American Psychologist, 38*, 1161–1173.

Termine, N. T., & Izard, C. E. (1988). Infants' responses to their mothers' expressions of joy and sadness. *Developmental Psychology, 24*, 223–229.

Thompson, M. S. (1986). The influence of supportive relations on the psychological well-being of teenage mothers. *Social Forces, 64,* 1006–1024.

Thompson, M. S., & Ensminger, M. E. (1989). Psychological well-being among mothers with school age children: Evolving family structures. *Social Forces, 67,* 715–730.

Thornton, A. (1989). Changing attitudes toward family issues in the United States. *Journal of Marriage and the Family, 51,* 873–893.

Thornton, R., & Nardi, P. M. (1975). The dynamics of role acquisition. *American Journal of Sociology, 80,* 870–885.

Tilden, V. P. (1983). Perceptions of single vs. partnered adult gravidas in the midtrimester. *Journal of Obstetric, Gynecologic, and Neonatal Nursing, 12,* 40–48.

Tilden, V. P. (1983). The relation of life stress and social support to emotional disequilibrium during pregnancy. *Research in Nursing and Health, 6,* 167–174.

Tilden, V. P. (1984). The relation of selected psychosocial variables to single status of adult women during pregnancy. *Nursing Research, 33,* 102–107.

Tilden, V. P., & Lipson, J. G. (1981). Ceasarean childbirth: Variables affecting psychological impact. *Western Journal of Nursing Research, 3*(2), 127–141.

Toffler, A. (1970). *Future Shock.* New York: Random House.

Tomlinson, P. S. (1987a). Spousal differences in marital satisfaction during transition to parenthood. *Nursing Research, 36,* 239–243.

Tomlinson, P. S. (1987b). Father involvement with first-born infants: Interpersonal and situational factors. *Pediatric Nursing, 13,* 101–105.

Trause, M. A., & Kramer, L. I. (1983). The effects of premature birth on parents and their relationship. *Developmental Medicine & Child Neurology, 25,* 459–465.

Trickett, P. K., & Susman, E. J. (1988). Parental perceptions of childrearing practices in physically abusive and nonabusive families. *Developmental Psychology, 24,* 270–276.

Trowell, J. (1982). Possible effects of emergency caesarian section on the mother-child relationship. *Early Human Development, 7,* 41–51.

Unger, D. G., & Wandersman, L. P. (1985). Social support and adolescent mothers: Action research contributions to theory and application. *Journal of Social Issues, 41,* 29–45.

Unger, D. G., & Wandersman, L. P. (1988). The relation of family and partner support to the adjustment of adolescent mothers. *Child Development, 59,* 1056–1060.

United States Conference of Mayors. (1987). *A Status Report on Homeless Families in America's Cities: A 29-City Survey.* Washington, DC: United States Conference of Mayors.

U.S. Bureau of the Census (1988). Household and family characteristics, 1987. *Current Population Reports,* Series P-20, No. 423. Washington, DC: Government Printing Office.

U.S. Congress, House of Representatives, Committee on Ways and Means. (1985). *Children in Poverty.* Washington, DC: U.S. Government Printing Office.

U.S. Congress, House of Representatives Select Committee on Children, Youth, and Families. (1987a). *The Crisis in Homelessness: Effects on Children and Families.* Washington, DC: U.S. Government Printing Office.

U.S. Congress, House of Representatives, Select Committee on Children, Youth, and Families. (1987b). *U.S. Children and Their Families: Current Conditions and Recent Trends.* Washington, DC: U.S. Government Printing Office.

Vadasy, P. F., Fewell, R. R., Meyer, D. J., & Schell, G. (1984). Siblings of handicapped children: A developmental perspective on family interactions. *Family Relations, 33,* 155–167.

Valliant, C. E. (1977). *Adaptation to Life.* Boston: Little, Brown, & Co.

Van Meter, M. J. S., & Agronow, S. J. (1982). The stress of multiple roles: The case for role strain among married college women. *Family Relations, 31,* 131–138.

Ventura, J. N. (1982). Parent coping behaviors, parent functioning, and infant temperament characteristics. *Nursing Research, 31,* 269–273.

Vukelich, C., & Kliman, D. S. (1985). Mature and teenage mothers' infant growth expectations and use of child development information sources. *Family Relations, 34,* 189–196.

Wachsman, L., Schultz, S., Chan, L., & Wingert, L. (1989). What happens to babies exposed to PCP in utero. *American Journal of Drug and Alcohol Abuse, 15,* 31–39.

Waechter, E. H. (1970). The birth of an exceptional child. *Nursing Forum, 9*(2), 202–216.

Walker, L. O. (1989). Stress process among mothers of infants: Preliminary model testing. *Nursing Research, 38,* 10–16.

Walker, L. O., Crain, H., & Thompson, E. (1986a). Maternal role attainment and identity in the postpartum period: Stability and change. *Nursing Research, 35,* 68–71.

Walker, L. O., Crain, H., & Thompson, E. (1986b). Mothering behavior and maternal role attainment during the postpartum period. *Nursing Research, 35,* 352–355.

Waller, D. A., Todres, I. D., Cassem, N. H., & Anderten, A. (1979). Coping with poor prognosis in the pediatric intensive care unit. *American Journal of Diseases in Children, 133,* 1121–1125.

Wandersman, L., Wandersman, A., & Kahn, S. (1980). Social support in the transition to parenthood. *Journal of Community Psychology, 8,* 332–342.

Wandersman, L. P. (1980). The adjustment of fathers to their first baby: The roles of parenting groups and marital relationship. *Birth and Family Journal, 7,* 155–161.

Weaver, R. H., & Cranley, M. S. (1983). An exploration of paternal-fetal attachment behavior. *Nursing Research, 32,* 68–72.

Weibley, T. T. (1989). Inside the incubator. *MCN, The American Journal of Maternal Child Nursing, 14,* 96–100.

Weiner, L., & Morse, B. (1988). F. A. S.: Clinical perspectives and prevention. In I. J. Chassnoff (Ed.), *Drugs, Alcohol, Pregnancy, and Parenting* (pp. 127–148). United Kingdom: Kluwer Academic Publishers.

Weinraub, M., & Wolf, B. M. (1983). Effects of stress and social supports on mother-child interactions in single- and two-parent families. *Child Development, 54,* 1297–1311.

Weitzman, J., & Cook, R. E. (1986). Attachment theory and clinical implications for at-risk children. *Child Psychiatry and Human Development, 17*, 95–103.

Wellisch, E., & Steinberg, M. (1980). Parenting attitudes of addict mothers. *The International Journal of the Addictions, 15*, 808–819.

Werner, H. (1967). The concept of development from a comparative and organismic point of view. In D. B. Harris (Ed.), *The Concept of Development* (pp. 125–148). Minneapolis, MN: University of Minnesota Press.

Westney, O. E., Cole, O. J., & Munford, T. L. (1986). Adolescent unwed prospective fathers: Readiness for fatherhood and behaviors toward the mother and the expected infant. *Adolescence, 21*(84), 901–911.

Wetzel, J. R. (1987). *American Youth: A Statistical Snapshot.* Washington, DC: The William T. Grant Foundation.

White, M., & Ritchie, J. (1984). Psychological stressors in antepartum hospitalization: Reports from pregnant women. *Maternal-Child Nursing Journal, 13,* 47–56.

White, R. W. (1974). Strategies of adaptation: An attempt at systematic description. In G. V. Coelho, D. A. Hamburg, and J. E. Adams (Eds.) *Coping and Adaptation* (pp. 47–68). New York: Basic Books.

White-Traut, R. C., & Nelson, M. N. (1988). Maternally administered tactile, auditory, visual, and vestibular stimulation: Relationship to later interactions between mothers and premature infants. *Research in Nursing & Health, 11,* 31–39.

Whitfield, C. (1987). *Healing the Child Within.* Deerfield Beach, FL: Health Communications, Inc.

Whitley, N. (1979). A comparison of prepared childbirth couples and conventional prenatal class couples. *Journal of Obstetric, Gynecologic, and Neonatal Nursing, 8,* 109–111.

Whitman, D., & Thornton, J. (1986). A nation apart. *U.S. News & World Report, 17,* 18–21.

Wiggins, K. M. (1983). *The Origins of Attachment: An Exploratory Study of Prenatal Maternal Attachment.* Unpublished dissertation, Syracuse University.

Wilcox, B. L., & Vernberg, E. M. (1985). Conceptual and theoretical dilemmas facing social support research. In I. G. Sarason & B. R. Sarason (Eds.), *Social Support: Theory, Research, and Applications* (pp. 3–19). Boston: Martinus Nijhoff.

Williams, M. L. (1986). Long-term hospitalization of women with high-risk pregnancies. *Journal of Obstetric, Gynecologic, and Neonatal Nursing, 15,* 17–21.

Williams, T. M., Joy, L. A., Travis, L., Gotowiec, A., Blum-Steele, M., Aiken, L. S., Painter, S. L., & Davidson, S. M. (1987). Transition to motherhood: A longitudinal study. *Infant Mental Health Journal, 8,* 251–265.

Wilson, G., McCreary, R., Kean, J., & Baxter, J. (1979). The development of children of heroin-addicted mothers: A controlled study. *Pediatrics, 63,* 135–141.

Wilson, W. J. (1987). *The Truly Disadvantaged: The Inner City, the Underclass and Public Policy.* Chicago: University of Chicago Press.

Wilson, W. J., & Neckerman, K. M. (1986). Poverty and family structure: The widening gap between evidence and public policy issues. In S. H. Danziger & D. H. Weinberg (Eds.), *Fighting Poverty* (pp. 232–259). Cambridge, MA: Harvard University Press.

Wilton, J. (1988). Breastfeeding by the chemically dependent woman. In I. J. Chasnoff (Ed.), *Drugs, Alcohol, Pregnancy, and Parenting* (pp. 149–159). United Kingdom: Kluwer Academic Publishers.

Wismont, J. M., & Reame, N. E. (1989). The lesbian childbearing experience: Assessing developmental tasks. *Image: Journal of Nursing Scholarship, 21,* 137–141.

Wolfensberger, W., & Kurtz, R. A. (1971). Measurement of parents' perceptions of their children's development. *Genetic Psychology Monographs, 83,* 3–92.

Wright, J. D. (1989). *Address Unknown: The Homeless in America.* New York: Aldine de Gruyer.

Wylie, R. C. (1974). *The Self-Concept,* vol. 1, (rev. ed.). Lincoln, NE: University of Nebraska Press.

Zahr, L. (1987). Lebanese mother and infant temperaments as determinants of mother-infant interaction. *Journal of Pediatric Nursing, 2,* 418–427.

Zaslow, M. J., Pedersen, F. A., Cain, R. L., Suwalsky, J. T. D., & Kramer, E. L. (1985). Depressed mood in new fathers: Associations with parent-infant interaction. *Genetic, Social, and General Psychology Monographs, 111*(2), 133–150.

Zuckerman, B., Amaro, H., Bauchner, H., & Cabral, H. (1989). Depressive symptoms during pregnancy: Relationship to poor health behaviors. *American Journal of Obstetrics and Gynecology, 160,* 1107–1111.

Zuckerman, B., Frank, D., Hingson, R., Amaro, H., Levenson, S., Herbert, K., Parker, S., Vince, R., Aboagye, K., Fried, L., Cabral, H., Timperi, R., & Bauchner, H. (1989). The effects of maternal marijuana and cocaine use on fetal growth. *New England Journal of Medicine, 320,* 762–768.

Zuk, G. H. (1962). The cultural dilemma and spiritual crisis of the family with a handicapped child. *Exceptional Children, 28,* 405–408.

Index

DATE DUE